Austin Clarke
A STUDY OF HIS WRITINGS

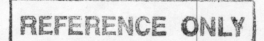

Austin Clarke
A STUDY OF HIS WRITINGS

G. CRAIG TAPPING

THE ACADEMY PRESS · DUBLIN

ACKNOWLEDGEMENTS

I would like to thank my parents, the Canada Council and the Academy Press for encouraging and supporting my research and urging the publication of this study. Nora Clarke deserves more than my gratitude, as do Richard Weber and Fergus Foley. I would also like to thank Liam Miller of the Dolmen Press for permission to quote from Austin Clarke's works.

First published 1981
Copyright © 1981 G. Craig Tapping

ISBN 0 906187 33 3

Typeset in the Republic of Ireland by M.A. O'Brien
Printed in Great Britain by Blackwell Press

The Academy Press
124 Ranelagh, Dublin 6, Ireland

CONTENTS

NOTES ON CITATION AND SPELLING

References to Clarke's works are explained as they occur. For convenience, four major books are abbreviated and references to them are made in parentheses, with abbreviated title and page number. These books are:

> *Collected Poems* abbreviated as *Poems*;
> *Collected Plays* abbreviated as *Plays*;
> *A Penny in the Clouds* abbreviated as *Penny*; and
> *Twice Round the Black Church* abbreviated as *Black Church*.

Thus, a poem from the *Collected Poems* which appears on page 309 will be cited as: (*Poems*, 309). Please note that an earlier collection of Clarke's poems was made in 1936. These were incorporated into the later *Collected Poems*. They will be referred to as the *Collected Poems* of 1936 to avoid confusion where it is necessary to cite the earlier collection.

The following uncollected plays will be cited in parentheses with page numbers from the editions listed in the bibliography of Clarke's works:

> *Two Interludes* adapted from Cervantes,
> *The Impuritans*,
> *The Third Kiss* and
> *Liberty Lane*.

The *Irish University Review: Austin Clarke Special Issue* is frequently cited in this book. For convenience it will be abbreviated after the first citation as *IUR:Austin Clarke Special Issue* without volume number or date. Another frequently cited work is the anthology, *A Tribute to Austin Clarke on his Seventieth Birthday*. Contributions to this work are untitled. After the first citation, therefore, it will be referred to with the contributor's name and the abbreviated title, *A Tribute*.

Clarke was by no means consistent in his spellings of Irish names. Though he usually consistent within a given work, his spelling of names often differs from one work to another. Thus we encounter the name *Aengus* in *As the Crow Flies*, while the same name is spelt *Aongus* in *The Sun Dances at Easter*. Please note also the variants Fionn/Finn, Grainne/Grania, Patric/Patrick and Eithne/Ethna.

BIBLIOGRAPHY OF THE PUBLISHED WORKS OF AUSTIN CLARKE, as referred to in the text, and in chronological order.

Poetry

The Vengeance of Fionn. Maunsel and Company Ltd., Dublin and London, 1917.

The Fires of Baal. Maunsel and Roberts Ltd., Dublin and London, 1921.

The Sword of the West. Maunsel and Roberts Ltd., Dublin and London, 1921.

The Cattledrive in Connaught and Other Poems. George Allen and Unwin Ltd., London, 1925.

Pilgrimage and Other Poems. George Allen and Unwin Ltd., London, 1929.

The Collected Poems, with an introduction by Padraic Colum. Poems and Verse Plays. George Allen and Unwin Ltd., London, 1936.

Night and Morning, being Number One of the Tower Press Booklets, Third Series. The Orwell Press, Dublin, 1938.

Ancient Lights, Poems and Satires: First Series, Bridge Press, Dublin, 1955.

Too Great A Vine, Poems and Satires: Second Series. Bridge Press, Dublin, 1957.

The Horse Eaters, Poems and Satires: Third Series. Bridge Press, Dublin, 1960.

Later Poems. Dolmen Press, Dublin, 1961.

Flight to Africa and Other Poems. Dolmen Press, Dublin, 1963.

Mnemosyne Lay in Dust. Dolmen Editions III, Dolmen Press, Dublin, 1966.

Old-Fashioned Pilgrimage and Other Poems. Dolmen Press, Dublin, 1967.

The Echo at Coole and Other Poems. Dolmen Press, Dublin, 1968.

A Sermon on Swift and Other Poems. Printed at Dolmen for Bridge Press, Dublin, 1968.

Orphide and Other Poems. Printed at Dorset Press for Bridge Press, Dublin, 1970.

Tiresias, a poem. Printed at Dorset Press for Bridge Press, Dublin, 1971.

Collected Poems. Dolmen Press, Dublin, 1974.

Plays

Collected Plays. Dolmen Press, Dublin, 1963.

Two Interludes, adapted from Cervantes: *The Student from Salamanca* and *The Silent Lover.* The New Dolmen Chapbooks 7, Dolmen Press, Dublin, 1968.

The Impuritans, a play in one act freely adapted from the story 'Goodman Brown' by Nathaniel Hawthorne. Dolmen Editions XVIII, Dolmen Press, Dublin, 1973.

The Third Kiss, A Comedy in One Act. Dolmen Editions XXIV, Dolmen Press, Dublin, 1976

Liberty Lane, a Ballad Play of Dublin in Two Acts with a Prologue. Dolmen Editions XXVII, 1978.

Novels

The Bright Temptation, a romance. George Allen and Unwin Ltd., London, 1932.
— Second edition, Dolmen Press, Dublin, 1965.
The Singing Men at Cashel. George Allen and Unwin Ltd., London, 1936.
The Sun Dances at Easter, a romance. Andrew Melrose, London, 1952.

Memoirs

First Visit to England and Other Memories. The Bridge Press, Dublin, 1945.
Twice Round the Black Church: Early Memories of Ireland and England. Routledge and Kegan Paul, London, 1952.
A Penny in the Clouds: More Memories of Ireland and England. Routledge and Kegan Paul, London, 1968.

Essays and Criticism

'Verse-speaking and Verse Drama'. *Dublin Magazine*, vol. xii (new series), no. 4 (October-December, 1937) pp. 9-17.
'W.B. Yeats'. *Dublin Magazine*, vol. xiv (new series), no. 2, (April-June, 1939) pp. 6-10.
Poetry in Modern Ireland. Published for the Cultural Relations Committee of Ireland at the Sign of the Three Candles, Dublin, 1951.
— Second, revised edition, 1962.
'Foreword' to *The Poems of Joseph Campbell*, edited by Clarke. An Chomairle Ealaion Series of Irish Authors, number one. Allen Figgis, Dublin, 1963.
'The Poetry of Swift', chapter vi in *Jonathan Swift, 1667-1967: A Dublin Tercentenary Tribute*, edited by Roger McHugh and Philip Edwards. Dolmen Press, Dublin, 1967.
Introduction to *The Plays of George Fitzmaurice: Dramatic Fantasies*, pp. vii-xv. Dolmen Press, Dublin, 1967.
The Celtic Twilight and the Nineties. Tower Series of Anglo-Irish Studies 1, Dolmen Press, Dublin, 1969.
'Anglo-Irish Poetry', in *Literature in Celtic Countries*: Taliesin Congress Lectures, edited by J.E. Caerwyn Williams. University of Wales Press, Cardiff, 1971.
'Gaelic Ireland Rediscovered: The Early Period', in *Irish Poets in English*, The Thomas Davis Lectures in Anglo-Irish Poetry, edited by Sean Lucy. Cork and Dublin. 1972.

Recording

Beyond the Pale: Austin Clarke reads his own poetry. Claddagh Records Ltd., no. CCT 2, Dublin, 1964.

There is a listing of Clarke's journalistic essays and reviews in the Appendix.

Introduction

Austin Clarke was born in Dublin in 1896 and died there in 1974. His life spans a cataclysmic period in Irish political and cultural history: the exciting years of Yeats' Anglo-Irish literary renaissance and the growth of nationalist fervour that led to the 1916 Easter Rebellion, the subsequent Anglo-Irish War and the bitter civil war, the emergence in the form of the Free State of an independent Irish nation, the depressions and poverty of the thirties, the dark ages of censorship and puritanical Catholicism up to the end of the fifties and then the gradual emergence of an Ireland developing economically and coming to terms with its political and cultural identity.

In a somewhat uncertain way critics of Anglo-Irish literature have felt Austin Clarke to be the most important of the crop of Irish poets (including Patrick Kavanagh and Louis MacNeice) that came after Yeats. Clarke's career was marked by two long periods of poetic silence from *Pilgrimage* (1929) to *Night and Morning* (1938) and then to *Ancient Lights* (1955). During these intervals he wrote three prose romances (all of which were banned in Ireland) and twelve verse dramas, but by the 1950s his poetic career seemed in the words of Thomas Kinsella 'curiously unfulfilled'. Then, from his fifty-ninth year in 1955 to his death in 1974, Clarke produced an outpouring of great poetry that was astonishingly new, albeit developing from and building on the elements of his earlier literary career both poetic and otherwise. The critical uncertainty is therefore scarcely surprising. Clarke's career was already being pigeon-holed before his later great poetry was published. Furthermore, the late poetry did not correspond to received poetic moulds and was not always fully appreciated. There were accusations of obscurity and parochialism, of eccentricity and fragmentation.

Now, however, the true scope of Clarke's poetry and
indeed of his literary output in general is beginning to be
appreciated. Clarke is a great writer, one who, in escaping
from the overpowering influence of Yeats, has forged for
himself one of the most significant literary careers of the
twentieth century, remoulding the Anglo-Irish literary
tradition and giving to English literature a radically new
dimension. He is indeed the other 'great Irish poet', his
imagination as resourceful as it is ultimately profound, his
poetry varied and developing over a long career, relying on
verbal and metrical effects of striking originality and often
subtle beauty and involving in the final analysis a poetic craft
learned and practised to the level of ease.

Richard Loftus begins a review of twentieth century poetry
in Ireland with the story of Sweeney, a mad seventh century
king. The story is deeply significant for this study of Austin
Clarke:

> 'For God's sake,' said the hag, 'leap for us now one of
> the leaps you used to leap when you were mad.' With
> these words the mill-hag of Loingseachan taunts Suibhne,
> son of Colman Cuar, who, cursed by a holy man, had
> fled insane from the battle of MagRath and then for
> seven years wandered restlessly over Ireland until at last
> his sense and memory returned to him. But the mill-hag
> taunts Suibhne and he leaps back into his madness and
> the hag leaps after him; and, matching his prowess leap
> for leap, she pursues Suibhne through all of Erin and he
> cannot escape her. Such is the story of *The Frenzy of
> Suibhne*, one of the most unusual tales to have come
> down to us from ancient Ireland — with its riddling
> dialogue, its catalogues of sacred animals and trees, its
> curious mingling of pagan and Christian lore. Many
> elements of the story are strikingly relevant to the
> course of poetry in modern Ireland — the intense love
> of the countryside, the element of bitter political strife,
> the ideological conflict between druidic and Christian
> belief, and especially the episode of Suibhne driven to
> frenzy by the relentless pursuit of the hag. At the close
> of the nineteenth century the poets of the Irish cultural
> revival chose to personify their country as Cathleen Ni

Houlihan, the romantic heroine of an eighteenth-century love ballad. In the years that followed, though, the choice must have often seemed a poor one; for modern Ireland, the Ireland to which all poets had dedicated their art, at times more closely approximated Suibhne's mill-hag than the oppressed yet queenly heroine . . . The men who helped to shape the Irish cultural revival in the eighteen-nineties . . . dedicated themselves to the regeneration of their race and nation. They sought to ennoble the Irishman's soul and by doing so to make him worthy of his ancient heritage. Inevitably, however, they were to be disappointed.[1]

Austin Clarke was one of the writers who were heirs to that disappointment. Clarke grew up in those earlier, more heroic days of Irish literature and his early 'juvenile' poetry is typical of Celtic Twilight romanticism. However, the account which follows of his poetry, drama and novels chronicles his development of new modes of Irish writing capable of responding to the unheroic, frequently harsh, realities of the post-independence state.

Clarke published his first book of poetry in 1917 when he was twenty-one. *The Vengeance of Fionn* is a fine example of Celtic Twilight romanticism. Clarke attempts to retell legend and myth in a semi-fantastical style. The book is the first of five such grandiose and immature attempts. By 1925 the fascination with Ireland's prehistoric past was over and Clarke began writing experimentally about the historical Celto-Romanesque period from the coming of Christianity to the Middle Ages. Not only did he change his style and subject matter, but he actually destroyed unpublished fragments of further attempts at epic fantasy.

In 1921 Clarke left Ireland and lived in England with his wife and children until 1937. With the publication of *Pilgrimage and Other Poems* in 1929 and *The Collected Poems* of 1936, his poetry began to assume its unique voice, perceptions and craftsmanship. The style is still overtly romantic, but the poet experiments with putting Gaelic prosody and metrical discipline into English verse. The poetry is remarkable for its fresh sensitivity to the Irish landscape and its concern with the historical period of early Christian Ireland. What is really striking, however, is the originality of theme, diction and metrical device and the sense that we are reading poetry that is disciplined, subtle and powerful. But there are hints too of what is to come, and the subdued criticisms of Christianity in particular foreshadow the later, more aggressive poetry. This poetry is the first stage of an experiment in craft which was to reach its full development only after a silence of thirty years.

Night and Morning in 1938 (the year after his return from England) was the only book of poems which Clarke published between 1936 and 1955. The poetry is confessional and it represents a major development in his work. The poems reflect a personal loss of faith and crisis of identity and the poet's involvement is, on occasion, painfully clear. The style is a further development in the experiment with Celto-Romanesque poetry. Gaelic intricacy is woven into modern English. There are anagrammatic patterns, ironic puns and a denser language than Clarke had used before.

In those sixteen years he spent in England and during the seventeen years from 1938 until his next book of poems was published, Clarke's writing career changed. In England he had begun another career as a journalist and critic. Working for various newspapers and critical journals, including the *Times Literary Supplement*, he was to write several hundred reviews and articles over the next fifty years. Some of them are only occasional and irrelevant to any understanding of his more important work. Some of this day-to-day writing, however, is important and, together with the more substantial articles he wrote for journals such as *The Dublin Magazine* and his radio broadcasts, it can be used to illuminate his literary career.

As already mentioned, three novels (or prose romances) were published when no poetry was: in 1932 *The Bright Temptation*, in 1936 *The Singing Men at Cashel* and in 1952 *The Sun Dances at Easter*. All three are romances in the technical sense that the narratives are loosely structured and digressive, the characters become involved in many far-fetched adventures, the narrator intrudes his opinions and happy endings are provided. Clarke concentrates his technical experiments in the area of creating a strong sense of historical authenticity that provides a realistic surface from which to satirise both the historical Ireland in which the works are set and its present-day counterpart. At one level the satirical attack is directed at the Catholic church's sexually repressive attitudes; at a deeper level the whole religious and moral fabric of Christianity is juxtaposed with the natural religion and morality of life. This develops the subdued criticisms observed in *Pilgrimage and Other Poems* and the theme was to be a central one throughout Clarke's work. The romances, it must be added, are full of excellent writing and at times they are whimsical and very humorous. Their lyrical descriptions of the Irish countryside represent the continuation of the romantic element in Clarke's writing.

In 1927 Clarke published the first of many verse plays, *The Son of Learning*. Twelve plays in all appeared between 1927 and 1953. These were republished in 1963 as *The Collected Plays*. They include a marvellous experiment in writing for the radio, *As The Crow Flies*, 1943. With the exception of three somewhat quieter pieces, all the plays are exuberant, comic and teeming with characters.

Until his death in 1974, Clarke continued to write for the stage. He enlarged the tradition of Yeatsian verse drama and founded a theatre company to foster this neglected art. Ironically, he began writing his first plays in reaction to the grand style of Yeats' theatre. Yet he emerges as champion of that tradition. Clarke's plays are less austere than Yeats'. They explore conflicts of individual conscience and will set against the sometimes overpowering dogma of the community. These plays are not well known; nor have they been widely performed. There is a human depth in Clarke's drama which is more satisfying than the symbolism of Yeats' theatre. There is a more varied and articulate use of poetry in the dialogue, which is at times ironic, comic, tragic and despairing. Clarke's plays all hinge on the central theme of Catholic authoritarianism. His heroes and heroines are all victims of religious dogma and social repression. Those who survive excommunication or ostracism escape by means of their wits. They develop a healthy sense of the absurd. Their comedy is central to Clarke's vision. The history of Irish theatre can only be partially written or understood while Clarke's contribution to it is ignored.

It is in the plays and novels that we must find whatever clues there are to explain the dramatic change in Clarke's poetry that took place from 1955 onwards. Until 1938 the poetry manifests much of the inherited trappings of Irish romanticism. Clarke himself was apparently aware of the dangers that the Celtic Twilight traditions represented for his poetry and he attempted, albeit gradually, to strip them away. When *Ancient Lights*, the first of the three books of satirical poetry appears in 1955, we are reading a different poet. In the poetry which followed rapidly after 1955, Clarke fused his earlier technical achievements with a harsh, uncompromisingly modern vision. There are two more satirical collections: *Too Great A Vine* in 1957 and *The Horse Eaters* in 1960. In 1961 Dolmen Press collected the poems from 1929-1960 as *Later Poems*. These and the four volumes which Dolmen published during the 1960s (*Flight to Africa* in 1963, *Mnemosyne Lay in Dust* in 1966, *Old-Fashioned Pilgrimage* in 1967 and *The Echo at Coole* in 1968), are referred to by some critics as Clarke's 'late flowering'. I have continued this usage and treat this poetry written between 1955 and 1968 as the 'later' poetry.

This poetry offers a direct challenge to the cultural convictions and assumptions that underly the work of earlier Anglo-Irish poets. It is significant in this respect, that Clarke in the last years of his life saw his role in Anglo-Irish literature as being related to that of Swift whose 'savage indignation' can scarcely be read as an accretion of Celtic romanticism.

From 1968 until his death, Clarke, as he had done earlier, wrote and published his work at The Bridge Press in Templeogue, Dublin, where he lived. This had been a small, private venture begun by him and his wife, Nora, in the late 1930s. In the late 1960s and early 1970s there emerged from this press some of the greatest poetry written in Ireland this century. These truly 'late' poems (*A Sermon on Swift* in 1968, *Orphide* in 1970 and *Tiresias* in 1971) are Clarke's masterworks.

In these last poems he turned to Irish myth and Latin legend for his sources. The poetry is ornately sensuous and bawdily obscene. Like other great poetry in this century, Clarke's last poems celebrate a liberation. Yeats' last poems are a meditation on art and tragic beauty which he uses in an attempt to transcend the failures of the flesh and death itself. Eliot in his last poems contemplates and seeks a spiritual realm beyond all endeavour. Pound's final Cantos, like Williams' 'Paterson', are a tribute to the creative imagination. Clarke's final poems are about sexual passion, love and the

human body. In these last outbursts against repression,
Clarke's poetry achieves a grandeur which, while celebrating
life itself, merges the animal and the miraculous in humankind.

What had seemed idiosyncratic and fragmented in Clarke's
poetic development is now consolidated into a line that is
classically disciplined and yet free of any apparent technical
burdens. Thematically these last poems reach out across a
writing career of fifty-seven years and link Clarke's final
ribaldries with those first immature romantic gestures. The
revolt against that inherited romanticism is finally explained
and justified. These last poems also forge the link between
what Clarke had sought to establish as an autonomous Irish
tradition in English literature and that which he had earlier
railed against, the Anglo-Irish tradition of Swift and Yeats.

Clarke's realistic attention to social and geographical detail
in his poetry combined with his radically original development
of themes and poetic techniques drawn from Gaelic literature
compel a complete reassessment of the nature of the influence
of the Gaelic cultural tradition on Anglo-Irish literature. The
critical categories used to analyse and label the work of
earlier Anglo-Irish writers are quite inadequate to soften the
rigour of what is some of the greatest of modern poetry.

There are, incidentally, several intrusions of the Sweeney
story in these last works, with his attendant mill-hag. At the
end of a long writing career, Clarke turns back to an image
from the 1936 poem 'Wandering Men':

> shapes no priest can see,
> The Centaur at a house of prayer.
> (*Poems*, 177)

Indeed, a subtitle for this study could well be 'Sweeney and
the Centaur'.

During his lifetime, Clarke published two major volumes of
autobiographical reminiscences, *Twice Round the Black
Church* in 1962 and *A Penny in the Clouds* in 1968. They
provide an invaluable reference to the life and explain many
of the poetry's larger preoccupations.

In 1971 Clarke began the last critical work of his life,
editing and collecting his own eighteen books of poetry and
various fragments into one volume. When he died in 1974,
that work was taken over and completed by Liam Miller of

the Dolmen Press, who published *Collected Poems* in the
same year.

(ii)

In their structures, themes and concerns, Clarke's writings
constitute an ideal introduction to contemporary Irish
literature. The early romantic treatments of the heroic sagas
were discarded in favour of poetry that was still romantic but
dealt with the Irish countryside and early Christian Ireland in
a diction and metre that are taut and imaginatively original.
This in turn gave way to the drama and novels, which investigate the transition from the idealised world of the Celtic
revivalists to the real world of post-independence Ireland. On
his return to poetry in 1955 Clarke scrutinised the complex
amalgam of modern Irish life, which to an outsider may
frequently seem illogical and disjointed. His investigation of
this Irish, English-speaking, Catholic world enlarges his
readers' consciousness. To read his poetry is to become
involved in an exercise of intelligence which transcends mere
literary debate; it is to begin questioning the conditioning
and learning processes which have moulded individual ethics,
identity and morality in the twentieth century.

   Much has been said in comparing Clarke with Joyce and
Yeats, and indeed there was an early danger that he would be
remembered only as a minor character in their more illustrious
lives. The comparison with Yeats is perhaps inescapable;
Clarke is the other great Irish poet of the period. His achievements, though different, are no less remarkable. The difference
in their poetic achievements can be seen most strikingly in
the opposing uses the two writers make of the Gaelic past
— Yeats' idealised romantic readings of what he took to be
an heroic age as opposed to Clarke's immersion in the actual
literary techniques and cultural traditions of Gaelic Ireland.
Clarke sought that past in order to define the present, which he
minutely scrutinised, politically, religiously and emotionally.
The result is that Clarke's poetry published in the 1950s and
1960s, apparently in sections and fragments, transforms the
reader's conception of Ireland.

   I have mentioned that Clarke's work cannot be properly
assessed within the critical categories traditionally applied to
Anglo-Irish literature. The term Anglo-Irish literature refers

to literature written in the English language by Irish people. However, English is of course an adopted language in Ireland and for many centuries was used only by the English colonial establishment. Until the nineteenth century, Gaelic, the native language of the Irish, was spoken by the majority of the people. The Gaelic literary tradition itself consists of many periods and facets. It includes the *prehistoric* cycles of saga literature that provided the raw material for Yeats' attempt to create a national literature — an Irish national mythology in the English language. The Gaelic tradition that Austin Clarke turned to, however, was that of what may broadly be termed the bardic poets from *historical*, early Christian Ireland. The bardic poets, who continued to practice until the eighteenth century, were highly trained professional poets representing a 'classical' tradition in Gaelic literature. In the early Christian period the art of poetry was practised by monk and layman alike and in Latin as well as Gaelic.

The interaction between the Gaelic and the English cultural and literary traditions is central to the development of Anglo-Irish literature. Yeats, like most of the Anglo-Irish writers before him, was of colonial ascendancy stock and was a Protestant. As such, he came to the Gaelic tradition from the outside. Austin Clarke, however, like James Joyce and most of the writers of this century, was of native Irish stock and Catholic. Educated like Joyce in Belvedere College and University College Dublin — the earlier writers went to Trinity College — Clarke assimilated the Gaelic tradition from the inside. He studied Gaelic literature at University College Dublin and it was this that enabled him to turn to the Gaelic poets as models when he began to reject Celtic Twilight romanticism. Gaelic prosody is radically different from that of English. The daring experiment that Clarke undertook was to attempt to write English poetry with prosody borrowed from Gaelic.

The best bardic poetry is intricate and highly crafted. The function of the bardic poet in society is also quite different from that assumed by the romantic poet. The romantic poet envisages himself as the seer in whose individual imagination is to be conceived the elements of poetic truth. The bardic poet adopted no such pretence; his voice was from within society. Its function was to record, satirise, explain, even to entertain. Its method was its craft, learned by the poet, and in turn developed by him.

Aside from his knowledge and use of the Gaelic tradition, Clarke is most obviously distinguishable from Yeats in that he was, like Joyce, a Catholic. Yeats regarded Catholicism, as observed in the Irish peasantry, as superstitious, primitive and almost magical. Clarke saw it in a very different light, as making demands on his intellect and moral sense which he could not eschew. It is significant that Clarke claimed that Joyce's *A Portrait of an Artist as a Young Man* was his story too. It is also significant that in their respective literary careers both rejected their early romantic outlooks. In the work of both writers the theme of Irish Catholicism was never too far removed.

There are other points of comparison between Clarke and Joyce. When he emigrated to England in 1921, Clarke saw himself as, like Joyce, going into exile. He had already survived the confusion of a failed marriage, a thirteen-month stay in St Patrick's Hospital because of a nervous breakdown and the loss of a teaching job at University College, Dublin. The teaching job was presumed to have been lost because his marriage had taken place in a registry office, and not a church. He spent sixteen years in exile before returning to Dublin with his second wife and family, determined to re-integrate himself into Irish life.

Back in Ireland Clarke became president of the Irish section of the international organisation P.E.N. (Poets, Essayists and Novelists). He founded the Verse-Speaking Society which became the Lyric Theatre Company and continued his journalism. He entered and resigned from the Irish Academy of Letters. With his wife, Clarke published his own work in small, private editions at the Bridge Press.

The work which came off the presses in Templeogue is the conscious effort by Clarke to examine those nets from which Joyce (through the character of Stephen Daedalus) had attempted to escape: language, religion and the politics of nationalism. The writer and his writing became enmeshed in the daily grit of Irish life. The measured austerity and control in Clarke's later poetry transcend its parochial concerns. The poems record the modern consciousness struggling to maintain and support individual freedom against great odds.

Austin Clarke's Tradition
A DEFINITION OF MODERN CLASSICISM

(i)

In the generation of Anglo-Irish writers which followed Yeats, many turned away from the mythologies of his early poetry to create new artistic models. Louis MacNeice's explanation of this revolt is typical: 'Yeats' own view of Ireland was not consistent throughout his life and was itself, it must be admitted, sometimes distorted by abstractions, by wishful thinking, by sentimentality, by partisanship. In his early days, he tried to equate Ireland with a Celtic Utopia — a land of beautiful dreams.'[1] Yeats was not alone in this romanticism. Frank Kermode has argued that this tendency permeates the poetry of those other masters of early twentieth century poetry, Eliot and Pound. The 'theory of dissociation of sensibility', Kermode contends, has to be understood before one can appreciate the beauties in the poetry of these last Romantics. The theory is

> the most successful version of a Symbolist attempt to explain why the modern world resists works of art that testify to the poet's special anti-intellectual way of knowing truth. And this attempt obviously involves the hypothesis of an age which was different . . . some golden age when the prevalent mode of knowing was not positivist and anti-imaginative . . . when art was not on the defensive against mechanical and systematic modes of enquiry. Since the order of reality postulated as the proper study of the poet tends, in one way or another, to be granted supernatural attributes, the ideal epoch is usually a religious one.[2]

Ireland, for political, geographic and economic reasons, fulfils this prescription aptly. Celtic romanticism proclaims the higher realm of its art, evading the full human realities of history. On the edge of Europe, oppressed through political subjugation, famine and poverty, the native Irish clung to a dying language and to a religion which Yeats, a Protestant, saw as magical and superstitious. Folktales he read or heard in English had an added dimension of quaintness because their translation into Hiberno-English often reflected the syntax and occasionally the idiom of their Gaelic originals. A great proportion of the Gaelic tradition, however, because it was foreign to the *fin de siecle* aesthetic of the Celtic Twilight remained untranslated.

Yeats stands as the towering literary figure of the Irish cultural and political movement that took shape in the 1880s and was the central influence on Irish history from that time until the achievement of independence in 1922. Yeats did not start the cultural revival, not even its literary side, but he did take it upon himself to mould it and give it direction and to make it literary in a truly artistic sense. Cultural nationalism in Ireland as elsewhere was romantic, based on racial myths and subject to excesses of chauvinism and indeed of racialism. Yeats' excepted, much of the poetry of this Celtic Twilight period is indeed soft-centred, sentimental and romantic in the worst sense.

As part of the nationalist movement generally it can be argued that Celtic Twilight poetry offered, in place of the real Ireland, a potent myth. The myth created by the nationalist movement was so powerful that until recently there was a common enough belief that the Celtic race was endowed with special artistic sensibilities and its people possessed of suffering, magnificent souls. Ireland, denied a larger place in the world and hungry for self-importance, was a fertile ground for the growth of this myth of its own greatness. Poverty and other social problems were largely ignored by the writers as well as the politicians. Rational enquiry was sublimated. Irish romanticism celebrated the spiritual values of a mythic people and fostered a cult of the Gael which contrasted

> the ideal Celt who embodied all the spiritual qualities implicit in the concept of the 'noble savage', and the brutal materialism of contemporary civilisation. . . .
> Celts are a shy, sensitive and imaginative race pushed

back to the outermost fringes of western Europe where,
lost to the world, they cling tenaciously to their unique
institutions, language, and traditions, asking only to be
left alone. Their society is bound together by kinship,
and they have always been thrust back upon themselves,
and they are given to defending lost causes. Fatalistic
and resigned, their obsession with the past is seen in their
cult of the dead, and in the sadness of their poetry and
music.[3]

The pervasive lack of irony in this nineteenth century fantasy
allowed artists to patronise these 'noble savages' and to
portray only those Irish traits which seemed suitable for
poetic treatment. The myth created a peasantry not starving
but dreaming, and an aristocracy entertaining themselves
across enormous social barriers.

In his autobiographical memoir, *A Penny in the Clouds*,
Austin Clarke comments on the language and literary image
of the Abbey playwrights and points to the artistic dangers
inherent in them.

The playwrights of the Abbey Theatre have a copious
idiomatic speech of city and country upon which they
can draw. But the ease with which they have been able
to cram their notebooks with dialect and humorous
sayings has not been without danger. They have advanced
very little since the comicalities of rustic and slum
speech were re-discovered. . . . This vivacious dialect,
which in real life is used often as not to conceal rather
than to reveal thought, interposes itself between them
and the characters which they wish to analyse. As a
result, their characterization is too often a form of
patronage.

(Penny, 65)

(ii)

In 1929 Clarke voiced the critical attitude which was to re-
define Irish poetry and expose another view of Ireland. In
the notes to his *Pilgrimage and Other Poems*, he remarks that
Gaelic poetry would seem very strange with its formal and
thematic precisions to the poets of the Celtic Revival. He

repeated and enlarged this idea with the 1961 re-publication
of the book as part of the *Later Poems*, when he suggested
that these earlier writers had been unaware of the currents of
Irish life and thought: 'The drama of racial conscience was as
strange to the previous Celtic School as Gaelic art.'[4]

In *Pilgrimage and Other Poems* Clarke begins an illuminating
exploration of those 'unique institutions, language and
traditions' about which there was much to learn. A subtle
distinction, between learning and dreaming, is the key
to understanding the aesthetic differences between Celtic
romanticism and Clarke's understanding of tradition. Mythology, dream and fiction are carefully scrutinised in the light
of discoverable fact. Clarke wrote his poetry with a studied
perfection that earlier Anglo-Irish poetry had not known.
The new direction found in his writings sprang from a fundamentally altered aesthetic. In his poetry, drama, novels
and criticism there emerges a 'classical' concept of the artist
and his society.

To admit alternatives to a view of Ireland with her glories
intact, however, was to court public disapproval. It was never
a popular task, as AE found with his economic writings, or
Joyce and O'Casey with their literary endeavours. To describe,
as Clarke does, 'the Hag of Dingle . . . clamant with piety'
(*Poems*, 293), is to incur the censure of the more devout
followers of Cathleen Ni Houlihan. To question the place of
religion in a fiercely Christian country, to expose the implicit
racialism of its nationalist ideas and to question the morality
of a self-righteous people are difficult, unenviable tasks. It is
also (and this is an essential consideration in understanding
the present argument) to forego the personal satisfaction and
beauty of an 'artistic', synthesised whole. As one reads
Clarke's work, series of cross-references become discernible;
but to write about and attempt to root out the fallacies of
that other Ireland means that Clarke must deal in fragments.
It also meant that during his lifetime Clarke had to fight
official censure and its attendant bureaucracy. Until his death,
he kept a wry watch on public debates, church rulings and
the like:

The National temper worsened when Senator MacCarthy,
the Irish-American lawyer, started his campaign in the
United States. As it was quite evident that Ireland was

safe from Communistic influence, attention was gradually diverted to Irish poets and novelists. Urged by its most vehement member, James Joyce, an elderly citizen, who had a fanatical dislike of his great namesake, the Censorship Board became as ferocious as that in Spain or Russia. Books by George Moore, Sean O'Casey, Liam O'Flaherty, Con O'Leary, Sean O'Faolain, Frank O'Connor, myself and others were banned. *The Green Lion,* an autobiographical novel of Kilkenny, by Francis Hackett, was placed on the prohibited list for its 'obscenity' because of a single, outspoken paragraph. Ecclesiastical pressure increased, when the late Fr. Joseph Deery, parish priest of Mount Merrion, was appointed Chairman of the Board. Stricture reached a point that seemed scarcely sane. Kate O'Brien's fine novel *Land of Spices* was banned for a single sentence . . .

Soon after the Second Ecumenical Council came to an inconclusive end, the Catholic Archbishop of Dublin consoled his bewildered flock in a special message: 'You may have been worried by much talk of changes to come. Allow me to reassure you no change will worry the tranquility of your Christian lives.' But the spirit of toleration is already spreading. Catholic Doctors, laymen and women, discuss now in the correspondence columns of the *Irish Times* such subjects as contraception, divorce, the *Ne Temere* decree, and courageously allow their names and addresses to be printed. Ignorance still watches from its smoky cell.

(Penny, 62-4)

Clarke recognises the sad Irish legacy of dreams and politics gone sour (he christened Ireland 'the Ill-fare State') as he describes the boat journey to England. (Compare this with the romantic view of the Celtic character):

Only too well did I get to know that crossing of the Irish Sea. Usually I travelled by night and, in the steerage, watched our people emigrating or coming back to see their relatives. Most of them were from remote glens and backward places, shabby and rough, subdued or numbed by the strangeness of their surroundings. Their ill-fitting clothes, their little brown-paper parcels and

cheap battered cases stirred vague feelings in my mind.
Despite myself, I shrank from their uncouthness and felt
ashamed of them, yet raged at the historic circumstances
which forced them into exile at a time when our new
Free State had been established. The wild drinking of
the fellows who had never learned to hold their liquor
like their betters filled me with pity, though I knew that
in less than an hour most of them would be reeling and
spewing all over the place. Here, indeed, was the floating
ark of my kindred . . . Symbolised by that ship's rope was
the separation between the well-to-do and the poor which
has been increasing every year in our small republic.

(*Black Church*, 77)

Others have written of the poverty and distress of the Irish.
Emigration was, until very recently, an unavoidable fact of
life. Here, the striking note is the simplicity of a language
which is compassionate, free of platitude and suffused with a
personal honesty. Clarke movingly and powerfully demonstrates the difference between the *ideals* of the new Free
State and the shabby, tired reality. His view leaves no room
for romanticism.

Unfortunately, Clarke's work has not to date received the
critical attention it deserves. Scholarly research and critical
investigation have concentrated on Anglo-Irish literature of
the earlier part of the century. The shadows of Ireland's
'great' writers obscure more contemporary and often less
romantic writers.

Clarke's view of modern Ireland will be discussed more
fully in later sections of this book. Our main concern now is
to define the critical terms in which his work will be assessed.
As Clarke's work develops and his position in the Anglo-Irish
canon emerges, the most evident characteristic of his work is
that he takes great care to relate his writing to daily Irish life.
He does so in a distinctively unromantic manner. Lilian
Furst, in her critical work *Romanticism*, has written:

... it can be argued that much of the writing of the
twentieth century is in the wake of Romanticism; its
anarchic individualism, ebullient imaginativeness and
emotional vehemence were certainly implicit in the
more extreme manifestations of the Romantic move-

ment which offers precedents also for the search for new forms and symbols, the experimentation with time and place, the preference for an organic structure dependent on an associative fabric of recurrent images, the re-interpretation of myths, all considered characteristic of our century.[5]

T.E. Hulme attacked romanticism in twentieth century literature because he saw it as 'split religion'.[6] Because of a specialised concept of man, and particularly the poet or artist, as the infinite reservoir of possibilities, the self-preoccupations and mythopoetic yearnings of romanticism are still characteristic of much contemporary writing. Hulme believed the 'classical' approach was more than a response to such pretension and sought to free the term from any associations with a specific historical period. He saw the tenets of classicism as rational, its subject matter necessarily social man: 'In the classic it is always the light of ordinary day, never the light that was never on land or sea. It is always perfectly human and never exaggerated: man is always man and never a god.'[7] In a radio broadcast (part of the Thomas Davis lecture series) made towards the end of his life, Austin Clarke made this very point when explaining the roots of his own poetry: 'Throughout the centuries the English poets have borrowed their mythology . . . but our poets experienced an emotion which was unknown to the English poets, an emotion which gives their work its poetic intensity . . . our poets went out of doors.'[8]

It is remarkable (but understandable during an age in which so many people question and doubt the Christian interpretation of life) that an artist should invest his work with the miraculous, seeking to elevate the individual imagination to the status of the divine. The rational complaint against this retreat into fantasy is that an artist who labours under the consequent illusions about the power, truth and import of his own creativity is inevitably disappointed (and, perhaps, more than faintly ridiculous). Intense emotions and imaginative leaps of intellect cannot transform social reality. Recent history amply demonstrates this truism and also shows the crippling isolation of much modern art. If an aesthetic is to bear any relation to the society in which a writer lives, then a reasoned morality must be part of that aesthetic. Extreme romanticism demands that art transcend mundane concerns.

The romantic attempt to re-define the world through individual vision and myth enabled writers to preserve philosophical and religious ideas of the soul and of transcendence and to guard generous, humane ideals during a crucial period in history. By the end of the nineteenth century, however, the Romantic Movement in England developed an almost private poetic to which many potential readers were denied access because they were often left uninformed of the movements, such as symbolism and imagism, which influenced the style of early modern poetry. In contrast, Clarke began writing in a very romantic style and evolved gradually into a classicist who believed in the social relevance of his poetry and frequently tried to explain its preoccupations to a wider public. But because of the popular predilection for romanticism, his later, more socially relevant poetry is widely unknown. Shelley claimed that poets are unacknowledged legislators. The problem is that, because of inherent romanticism, many, particularly less articulate, people have been left in ignorance of their more relevant laws and have therefore come to distrust them as legislators.

Writing that is socially relevant and immersed in daily life and common pursuits requires a keener, more directly shared language than does the chronicle of exiled imagination or the record of private meditation and experience. As Clarke's writing developed during the late 1920s and onwards, his language eschewed the personal and subjective. It is a 'classical' language which we find in his later poetry: a language bound by logical forms and syntactical structures. With this new language, he tries to reach and to communicate with his public. Even when writing 'confessional' poetry (that is poetry based on explanations of his own life or personal journeys towards sane maturity), Clarke's language and imagery are conventional, not stylised or subjective. In the later poetry 'style' gradually becomes unobtrusive and the rhymes, though they become more intricately patterned, are nonetheless employed with such ultimate craftsmanship that one enjoys the play of language and sound without immediately recognising the skill. Clarke cannot afford snobbery because his main intention is to influence his readers' opinions and to challenge their moral assumptions. A large part of his poetry is consequently satirical, but there are also many individual poems in which Clarke betrays an enjoyment of the structures of everyday language and of the various levels of meaning in everyday conversation.

Donald Davie, a contemporary critic and poet, has written that 'what is common to all modern poetry is the assertion or the assumption . . . that syntax in poetry is totally different from syntax as understood by logicians or grammarians'.[9] Accordingly, the image and not the sentence is the basis of truly modern poetry. Poetic language, as opposed to normal discourse, is evocative. Discursive poetry (its meanings carried by syntactical structures and cognitive rather than evocative metaphors) is anti-modern.[10] Clarke's poetry challenges these assumptions. In his mature writing Clarke is not caught up with either symbol or image. He avoids this private language. He dismisses any claim to a unique status as artist. The tolerance and reason which pervade his entire work also call into question the norms of modern (usually romantically-biased) poetry.

Yeats' late poetry grew out of a disenchantment with nineteenth century romanticism. Whereas Yeats reshaped and disciplined the aesthetic and rhetoric of symbolism into a commanding poetry, structured according to concepts of artifice and personae, Clarke's poetry developed as he learned to reject the tradition outright.[11] 'Rhetoric' and 'aesthetic' can be objective critical terms to define the manner, personal voice, language and content of a poet's writing. For Yeats, rhetoric was something to distrust, the language of the politician and the reporter. Clarke's 'rhetoric' is a classical usage: the discipline, syntax and vocabulary of a poet's language. Rhetoric is a study which informs technique. Yeats' poetry is deeply concerned with 'artifice', the building of another reality through art. Clarke is more concerned in his writing with artefact, the building of a specific poem or play, novel or article. That concern with artefact underlies Clarke's various experiments with different genres; each will demand different techniques. Clarke's mature work is deeply concerned with the structures of language and the architecture of specific pieces through which meanings are conveyed directly and implicitly. Both poets use personae. Yeats' characters and voices are often masks for the poet, who is ultimately a mask himself behind which is art, eternal truth or nothing. Clarke's characters are real people, individuals whose stories he tells. Sometimes he will intrude personal opinions or judg-

ments, but the poet is, for Clarke, an imitator, not a shaper
of reality.

Augustan literature is generally understood as the embodiment in English of classical standards. It was 'socially committed in a way no other body of English literature has ever
been'.[12] Genius to the Augustans meant talent or skill in
using language to communicate universal truths. Because of
the continuing romantic disapproval of the intellect (poetry
was inspired, often at the expense of technique), Augustan
literature is currently in critical disfavour. In Clarke's poetry
one discovers an Augustan command of and delight in language. His work contains social involvement and a passionate
democratic instinct. There is acute satire in the work, too.
All these characteristics are anachronistic in this more self-
conscious age. The formalism of Clarke's work is dictated by
a humble yet fierce commitment to daily life, and it is the
embodiment of his own rationalism. A sceptical irony and
self-effacing humanism prevent Clarke from making greater
claims through his art. All of these factors combine with the
poet's trascendent, celebrant wit to make it clear that Clarke's
later writings must be acknowledged as classical.

(iii)

Let us now turn to a consideration of Clarke's authorities
and models, the 'classics' which inform his writing. Clarke's
primary inspiration did not come from English poetry nor
from the Celtic Twilight school which exerted its influence
on the Anglo-Irish Literary Revival during his youth. Like
Joyce, with whom he shares a common background and
schooling, Clarke stands almost an outsider to the literary
tradition Yeats struggled to found. Celtic myth, of course,
has affected his work, but the direction and guidance that
Clarke sought came from the upsurge in Gaelic scholarship
which had begun prior to the Literary Revival. Clarke's
'authorities' are his teachers and the scholars who unearthed
manuscripts, translated the old stories and studied Gaelic
literature.

Hyde, Sigerson and MacDonagh opened the world of Gaelic
literature to Clarke. In *Twice Round the Black Church*
Clarke recalled the impression made on him by his first
introduction to Ireland's literary traditions:

As an undergraduate I escaped at one step from the
snobbery of school life and discovered the Love Songs
of Connaught, those poems and translations which had
started our Literary Revival. Their poet-translator was
on the rostrum, and, though I could not always follow
the swift rush of Dr Hyde's western Irish, I knew from
his gestures that he was speaking a living language. . . .
On the morning of our first term, he spoke of the aims
and ideals of the language revival: we were all equal, all
united in the Gaelic movement. There was no vulgar
competition, no showing-off, no twopence-halfpenny
looking down on twopence. Those plain words changed
me in a few seconds. The hands of our lost centuries
were laid on me.
To meet Dr Sigerson, the last of the great pioneers, was
to become aware of a distant Victorian period when our
literary traditions were saved from extinction by a few
idealists. From him I learned about the subtle art of our
formal poetry. Then, to complete so much good fortune,
there was Stephen MacKenna — moody, eloquent, a
man consumed by some inner flame. He would turn
from Rabelais to roll out some passionate protest of Ua
Bruadair, forget Plotinus to denounce those who belittled
the elegance of Carolan and failed to appreciate his
rhythmic improvisations.

(Black Church, 169)

Douglas Hyde's *A Literary History of Ireland* exerted a
tremendous influence on Clarke's early work, delineating as it
does the themes, styles and importance of Gaelic literature
from druidic times to the close of the eighteenth century.
Perhaps over-presumptuous in its claims, Hyde's enthusiasm
nevertheless supplied Clarke with incident, anecdote and
direction throughout his career.

   Clarke mentions that George Sigerson taught him the
formalities of Irish poetry; he used 'double rhyme and jingling
internal rhyme' in his own poetry (*Penny*, 42). In his introduction to *Bards of the Gael and Gall*, Sigerson states that
Bardic poetry was an intensely disciplined art. He says of the
Irish:

Their artistic skill, which enabled them to produce such

admirable effects in gold, silver, and bronze work, and later illuminations, exquisite in form and colour, was most fully displayed in the art of versification. . . . They made it the most refined and delicate instrument of artistic structure which the ingenuity of human intelligence could invent to charm, without fatiguing the ear, by the modulation of sound. They avoided in Gaelic the tinkle of repeated words regularly recurring at the ends of lines. They had echoes and half-echoes of broad and slight vowels, and of consonants, differentiated into classes so that it was not necessary to repeat even the same letter, and these echoing sounds, now full, now slender . . . came at varied intervals, not merely at the close, but within and between the lines.[13]

Sigerson distinguished between the generally accepted idea of what Irish poetry is and his understanding of Gaelic style:

No translator can hope to reproduce, in English, the finer traits of this art, because these demand a language of open vowels, and other aids. . . . Those who are wont to associate Irish poetry with effusiveness of thought and luxuriance of language will be surprised to find that bardic poetry was characterised by classic reserve in thought, form, and expression.[14]

It was not, however, until he had been writing for ten years that Clarke began to explore the possibilities of using the English language in the Gaelic manner described by Sigerson. Sigerson's words and insights are the direct inspiration for Clarke's experiments with assonantal rhyme in *Pilgrimage and Other Poems* (1929).

Thomas MacDonagh, a lecturer in English literature, later executed after the 1916 Rising (Clarke succeeded to the lectureship after his death), propounded a theory of the 'Irish mode in literature'. Although more nationalistic than critical, MacDonagh's *Literature in Ireland* laments the loss of assonance, a device he thought to be largely responsible for the beauty of Irish poetry. Clarke admitted, however, that he was somewhat confused by MacDonagh's theories, which he found 'as elusive as the long and short syllables, heavy and light stresses, which tormented my ear' (*Penny*, 23-5).

George Russell (AE) introduced Clarke to an essay by William Larminie, who first suggested that English poetry could be enriched by the use of Gaelic poetic devices. Larminie's own poetry is prosaic and stumbles along, labouring to demonstrate the theories about assonance advanced in his essay, 'The Development of English Metres'. [15]

Osborn Bergin and Kuno Meyer were two early twentieth century scholars who devoted their research to Irish literary traditions. A collection of Bergin's lectures and papers were reissued under the title *Irish Bardic Poetry*. Meyer's *Selections from Ancient Irish Poetry* was a landmark in this cross-cultural investigation. Meyer's later translations were an important influence on Clarke's own versions of Irish poems and plays. Especially important was Meyer's translation and valuable introductory essay about goliards (or wandering minstrels), the *Aislinge Meic Conglinne*. The golliard, Anier MacConglinne, appears as an important character in some of Clarke's work.

Austin Clarke is a modern classicist. His poetic, while rejecting the predominant conventions of poetry in English, did not arise in a vacuum. He learned a great deal from the early pioneers in the study of Gaelic literature. They are his classical authorities. Significantly, Clarke never wrote in the Gaelic language despite his passionate commitment to the Gaelic literary tradition throughout his life. Conscious of the possibly terminal nature of Gaelic as a living language (and therefore assuming the literature doomed), Clarke has reached back in a consciously salvaging gesture. He does not translate, but rather 'imitates' in an eighteenth century manner, preserving where possible that which is redeemable from a culture all but lost to the modern consciousness. Imitation suggests the derivative and secondhand to our post-Romantic ears. Until the nineteenth century, imitation was used to describe a process by which a writer sought with his modern skills to achieve the excellence he discovered in the classics. Imitation is both a discipline whereby apprentices may learn some craft and an art form which preserves standards and models of perfection. (Robert Lowell, for example, published an entire collection of *Imitations*). Clarke's entire collection of poetry is a 'sustained act of translation . . . a lifetime effort to connect the English language into which he was born, with an Irish past towards which he feels a deep imaginative sympathy'. [16]

T.S. Eliot wrote that such gestures were necessary to creative literature:

> ... the classics have, during the latter part of the nineteenth century and up to the present moment, lost their place as a pillar of the social and political system. ... If they are to survive, to justify themselves as literature, as an element in the European mind, as the foundation for the literature we hope to create, they are badly in need of persons capable of propounding them.[17]

The problem is intensified in the smaller arena of Ireland. A government-sponsored system of compulsory Irish in schools has actually discouraged interest in the Irish language. Clarke struggled for Irish poetry against a tide of apathy. He wrote to save what he could in a form faithful to the original and yet accessible to the contemporary reader. He has not retold his Irish tales in such a way as to create personal myth but has rather forged a style he can claim as the 'imitation' of an advanced Gaelic mode of poetry.

Sigerson's comments on Gaelic poetry are strikingly applicable to Clarke's work. If Sigerson and his colleagues were wrong in their analyses, Clarke's classical stance would also be wrong — a creative misreading of history. There is, however, a wealth of more contemporary critical discussion about Gaelic poetry to test the evidence.

In the introduction to his *Early Irish Literature*, James Carney sounds a familiar warning:

> The study of this literature is too often bedevilled by an eighteenth/nineteenth century Romanticism that idealizes the 'primitive' and likes to look upon the early Irish writer as almost a passive traditor of ancient thoughts and ideas of which he himself had no fully conscious understanding. ... We must ... be more humble in our approach. ... They were, at times, as sophisticated as the scholars who in modern times have undertaken the edition and translation of their works. ... A feature of their verse is their academic delight in learned riddle, paradox, contrast, and elaborate metaphor.[18]

And for Myles Dillon the task of translating Gaelic poetry

into English is 'an almost hopeless undertaking' because of its 'ornament of alliteration, assonance, consonance, and rhyme'. It is a poetry marked by 'the abandonment of rhythm for rhyme alone' and characterised by an internal maze of echoes and half-echoing vowel patterns.[19]

In *Irish Classical Poetry*, Eleanor Knott explains that 'the poet, amongst other obligations had to maintain a high standard in his compositions; to avoid slovenliness of in- accuracy (*sic*) in prosody or in diction'. The form and not the idea of the poem is of major importance. The poem

> is, with the possible exception of certain didactic com- positions, composed for the ear, and at all periods of its history has been associated with music, the word-music of its own characteristic form and the music of an accompanying instrument. . . . This delight in the music of words is what gives to Irish Poetry its especial aesthetic character. The balance between delight for the ear and satisfaction for the mind may in many official com- positions appear to be unevenly held, but . . . aural enjoyment was, though not the whole, an integral part of every poem. Each stanza is an aural design . . . a complex mosaic of sound.[20]

Much of what has been said about the verbal ingenuities and wit of Bardic poetry, about its assonance and formal architecture, will relate directly to the poems of Clarke, and can be used (with only minor alterations) as a critical framework within which to view his work.

In view of the universally acknowledged difficulties of translation from Gaelic into English, Clarke cannot be dis- missed as a mere copyist. When he does 'imitate' particular originals in Gaelic his poetry transcends the literal. With the knowledge he gleaned from Gaelic poetry, Clarke struggled with the English language and its poetic conventions. From that struggle he moulded a unique poetic language and style which are forceful but not forced, intellectually satisfying but not academically dry. At its heart Clarke's work carries forward the essence of the Irish literary tradition, enlarging that of Anglo-Irish poetry. Irish poetry written in English has been altered by Clarke's example. A younger Irish poet, John Montague, has written:

In one aspect of his work Austin Clarke is the fulfilment
of MacDonagh's dream of a separate Irish mode; the first
completely Irish poet to write in English. . . . He has
opened up the Gaelic tradition. . . . He has helped us to
learn how to write English poetry, with an Irish accent.[21]

From Romanticism to Celto-Romanesque

(i)

In his autobiographical memoir, *Twice Round The Black Church*, Clarke humorously deflates his earlier Romantic pretensions as a poet. An anecdote about a favourite hat offers a witty insight into those peculiar, flawed, early poems:

I am used to being mistaken for a priest and so I am no longer embarrassed by the respect paid to my cloth. As a provincial youth, ignorant of new literary ways, I believed that a poet must wear a wide-brimmed black hat and grave suit. Sometimes as I cycled along country roads, I was saluted by carter or stone-breaker, so I consulted a clerical student, who was an intimate friend of mine. He told me what to do in order to spare the feelings of passers-by who might salute me. For a year or so after his ordination, a young priest always raises his hat, gradually he learns only to touch it; then he moves his hand only as far as his shoulder — and at last a mere showing of his right palm suffices. With the increasing ruralizing of Dublin and the spread of religious action since the Civil War, my hand is kept busy. . . . Sometimes I am tempted to take vicarious advantage of my old-fashioned poetic garb. When I draw my black muffler closer to hide my lack of celluloid collar, I am offered a seat immediately in an over-crowded bus, receive attention in tea-shops, quicker sherries in the larger hotels — and I need never wait more than a few seconds outside a telephone booth.

(*Black Church*, 32)

The Vengeance of Fionn (1917), *The Fires of Baal* (1921)

and *The Sword of the West* (1912) do not, however, escape
so light-heartedly from their 'old-fashioned poetic garb'.
Ventures in epic style, these early poems are marred by the
young poet's idealism, his preconceptions of what an artist
must write and in what manner. They are filled with pompous
and unfulfilled ambitions and, at times, are completely
obscured by vague poeticism and misty allusion. Clarke
criticised these poems himself and altered them first in 1936
and again in 1974 (in the two volumes of his collected poems).

Although Clarke's teachers had attempted to communicate
their enthusiasms for Gaelic literary traditions, the young
poet first turned to Anglo-Irish literature for formal inspiration. When *The Vengeance of Fionn* was published in 1917,
its theme and style conflicted with contemporary events.
Because of his youth, idealism and view of poetry, Clarke
could not grasp the civil and political turmoils which were
around him. His commitment to literature contrasted with
the commitment of his contemporaries to rebellion. Clarke
turned to Yeats and AE as his models, and these two poets
determined the direction and intent of his early poetry.
Under this influence Clarke wrote of an ancient, mythically
compelling past and did not relate his poetry to modern
Ireland at all.

AE — poet, mystic, pamphleteeer, tireless worker in the
agricultural co-operative movement and idealistic socialist —
had the more immediate and enduring effect on Clarke.
Surprisingly, for a writer who is generally regarded as a
dreamer and impractical mystic, AE clearly was involved
deeply with the people of rural Ireland, and he wrote affect-
ingly about the wrongs visited on the countryside and its
people by the disorganised, money-grabbing growth of
technology and its complementary bureaucracy. AE keenly
understood the stigma attaching to communism in the Irish
public's mind and the consequent elimination of any con-
structive discussion connected with it. He chose instead to
propound the ideal of rural co-operatives and was for a time
secretary of Sir Horace Plunkett's co-operative movement.
His most immediate influence on Clarke was, however, poetic.
In *A Penny in the Clouds* Clarke explains that AE was responsible for the publishing of his first book of poetry *The
Vengeance of Fionn* and that AE's humanism checked the
young poet's blinder and more naive nationalism.

AE appears in Clarke's autobiography as the great liberator. Unfortunately, this is hard for us to understand today. AE's poetry, on the whole, indulges in a pantheistic exploration of man's destiny and of man's soul in relationship to the earth and its mythological history. An apostate theosophist, AE believed that the actual mystical experiences of being were incommunicable and infinitely more important than his poetry which seeks to awaken awareness of the eternal. The poems are filled with the sincerest of vagaries.

But AE was unstinting in his efforts to aid younger, aspiring poets. According to Monk Gibbon he was 'allergic to the trends of the early thirties' and disliked the poetry of Eliot but reacted to Irish poets in a different way: 'He scents them out, fosters their talent, tries to protect them from themselves.'[1] It is to AE's passionate idealism that Clarke pays tribute in the 1936 *Collected Poems*: 'To AE Who sustained the cause of Irish poetry, giving imaginative courage and hope to all of us, I dedicate this Collection in sadness and memory'. Indeed, a line from what is arguably one of AE's finest poems 'On Behalf of some Irishmen not Followers of Tradition' could stand as a fitting title to Clarke's satires of the 1950s and '60s: 'The golden heresy of truth'.

Yeats was more awesome to the younger poets and held more aloof than did AE. Clarke believed Yeats was not merely aloof but that he 'regarded the younger generation with disfavour after AE had gathered their poems in a small anthology' (*Penny*, 73). Clarke mentions Yeats' grand, solemn manner — an aristocratic pose discussed by several critics of the older poet. The figure of Yeats looms, however, behind all of Clarke's earliest writings and it is therefore not inappropriate to quote a more recent poem by Clarke which explains the philosophical distance between the two:

> A.E., taking the pipe from his mouth again, like
> A stout Faun or rather bib-bearded Pan,
> Remarked as he pondered in his chair:
> > 'The old man
> Is talking to himself.'
> > I saw behind him,
> Gold-leafed, with their dark blue or olive bindings,
> The *Collected Poems* of William Butler Yeats,
> Macmillan'd in a row.

> I wondered were they
> A Purgatory the poet had ghosted from hatred,
> Incessant, inner circles, of repetition
> Systematised by metaphysics, late
> Excuse for fantasies, that never let him
> Be still when he became a man of letters,
> Discovered in old age the physical.
> 'His lyrics are Saturnian rings illumined
> By colder fire.'
>
>   'What of our common ill?
> Do they explain it?'
>
>   'If rhetoric can last,
> Then all that lonely, premeditated art must.'
>
>   (*Poems*, 402)

The younger poet turned away from Yeats because he disapproved of Yeats' rhetorical flourishes and because he sensed a grand disdain for contemporary Ireland in the master's poetry. Yeats omitted Clarke from his anthology, *The Oxford Book of Modern Verse*, in 1936 but included other, less significant and now forgotten Irish poets. It was many years before Clarke could write about Yeats' enmity towards him. In the poem above Clarke rather typically portrays AE as the gentle go-between who tactfully ignores the younger poet's question.

In a recent appraisal of Clarke, discussing his relation to Yeats and to the various traditions of Irish literature, Eavan Boland has pinpointed the aesthetic conflict involved:

> An excellent argument exists – I believe – for maintaining that the servants of the Celtic twilight all but destroyed the culture they were noisily rescuing. This they did by their obvious sentimentality, nostalgia. Above all, they failed to serve it by turning it into a platitudinous axis, the twin poles of which were simplicity and sadness. . . . The decadence of one culture was infecting the revival of another. Clarke, in some way or other, recognised this. His poetry bears witness to the fact that for him Irish culture was a vigorous, disparate thing, rather more invested in the black wit of their (sic) satirical poets than the wails of their new discoverers.[2]

Clarke's first four attempted epics are marred by a naive enthusiasm which led him to attempt to correct Yeats' reading of the legendary past. Of course, Clarke had the advantage of Yeats in one respect; he knew the Cuchullin cycle at first hand, while Yeats knew the stories only from fragmentary translations. Thomas Kinsella, introducing his own more recent version of the Ulster epic, *The Tain*, points out certain faulty misrepresentations in Lady Gregory's *Cuchulain of Muirthemne* which was Yeats' source: 'Even as a paraphrase, (it) seemed lacking in some important ways, refining away the coarse elements and rationalising the monstrous and gigantesque.'[3] In reading Clarke's stories about Cuchullin, it is always necessary, however, to refer to his source, Hyde's scholarly interpretations of the legend in *A Literary History of Ireland*. Yeats' highly refined plays which centre on Cuchulain may be far removed from the primal quality of the Ulster epic; but they are great literature. Clarke's early imitations — though important for the light they throw on his national idealism — fail because of his preoccupation with Victorian decoration: affected elegance of language and poetic style, music, vague rhythms, unclear development and an imagery which, while attempting the particular, fails because of its abstractions. By 1936 Clarke admitted this failure and changed his direction; he has altered some of these poems, deleted others, and turned away from unwieldy, pretentious poems about Ireland's mythic and legendary past.

The story of Diarmuid and Grainne, as told in *The Vengeance of Fionn*, is exceptional among the early poems and remains one of Clarke's finest pastorals. It is an idyllic yet surprisingly dramatic narrative about love, the Irish countryside and the transience of youth. In this attempt at epic Clarke affects the technique of associational stream of memory. It begins on the lovers' last day together, with Diarmuid leaving Grainne for the hunt with Fionn, and ends with Grainne alone at nightfall, aware of Fionn's druidic cunning and his treacherous part in Diarmuid's death. There is a memorable evocation of the land across which they had fled years before and of the bonds uniting the young lovers. The youthful vitality and love of Diarmuid and Grainne is characterised in passages like this:

He looked — across the silver shining lake
And islets thick with grassgreen trees asleep
Like their long olive shadows in the deep —
Upon the mountain forests, waterfalls
Unravelling white sunlight from the crags
Above, furze yellow slopes and far away
Blue misted summits.
                              'Yonder, bounding stags
Antler the wind unstalked, the squirrels play
Beneath the red-stemmed pines in thrushy glens
And streamlets trickle through cool moss.'
                                            'O sweet
The fluty blackbirds, Diarmuid, and the wrens
Flutter and warble here.'
                              'Sweeter, from the heat
To lie i' green-dimmed woodlands thou and I,
Or, the last summit gained, under the sea-blue sky
We two, beyond pursuit, forever free, our feet
Eagle-high!'

                                            (*Poems*, 31)

A similar passage describes how, on that last lonely day,
Diarmuid remembers their earlier time together, especially
one nightfall when he returned from a hunt to search for
Grainne:

Through the flitting pines he hurried
Calling 'Grainne, come to me
Night is here and woodlands darken
Come, O Grainne, come to me.'
Out to a blue twilight
He wandered and the grim
Purple shadowed mountains
Sprang up and beckoned him.
In a glen of elms
As he sped
Ancient noises slowly stirred and wakened
And like aged birds heavily fled.
Soon through the starlight forest
Pale fragrances
Of blossomy elder
Floated around him.

'O Grainne, Grainne'
He called and in a happy glade
Of bluebells and sleep
Under dim green clouds of elm
He heard a woman weep.
She slowly rose and came with night to him.
Strangely they paused, gazing, they two alone
'Diarmuid'
       'O Grainne'
             — and their voices were one.
                (*Poems*, 38-9)

Clarke's descriptions of the hillside at dawn and the forest at night, with their pre-Raphaelite imagery and drowsy rhythms, tend to get in the way of his story. It is in the active lyric, in the conversations and in the dramatic movement and meeting of his characters that the poet is able to create the legend anew. His subtle understanding of character compensates for the sometimes intrusive descriptions, and his suggestion that the two lovers have perhaps lost some of their passion with the approach of old age strikes a movingly elegiac note. The imagery used to describe Diarmuid and Grainne's feelings is much more effective than the imagery he uses to evoke the natural environment. Those 'ancient noises' moving like heavy, 'aged birds' magnificently evoke Diarmuid's fear.

Diarmuid and Fionn argue. It is the contrast between Diarmuid's now fleeting youth and Fionn's old age which will destroy them both. They are both doomed to lose Grainne. There are moves towards a reconciliation, but neither believes the truth of such words. Both are warriors and both face old age. Stark images of remembered youth and heroic abilities intrude on the two men's attempts to delude one another. Grainne will be the ultimate loser. Diarmuid will die and she will have to face the guile of an already decrepit Fionn. Her sorrow inspires one of the most heightened sections of the poem:

           I will be quiet though it is old
Though all these days are old, these quiet days
That flowing seemed one summer's day
Undarkened nor disturbed by night and sleep.
But even as shining waters calmed in deep

Pools, — and all the peaceful household hours ...
— and the prattled words
Of children and of waters at the fords.
Never on the hilltops shall I see again
Diarmuid and the antler-burdened men
Darkly speared against the saffron west
Homecoming ...
Yet I could almost weep that all these days
Are gone forever. Night from its flooded weir
Is rushing blackly on me and I must gaze
Into its gloom and I am full of fear.

(Poems, 14)

The entire poem is a sustained lyric, saved from Clarke's youthful excesses by his sense of the dramatic and his adept shifting of time sequences. The men laugh at and taunt each other, daring each other on to death — the alternative to death is old age, a less than honourable end for a hero. Only Grainne will suffer. Clarke emphasises the fullness of Fionn's revenge and Grainne's defeat by introducing two anonymous young lovers. The cycle repeats itself and the legendary characters are forgotten; youth carelessly ignores the example of its elders. 'And I saw poor Grainne in the sunlight,' the girl tells her lover, 'Wrinkled and ugly' (*Poems*, 40).

The Fires of Baal is a complete departure. Forced imagery and syntax characterise this story about Moses and the exodus to the promised land. One is tempted to interpret Palestine — with its sheep and musical shepherds — as an allegory of Ireland. Clarke's end notes reinforce this idea. But the comparison is not explicit enough to be meaningful. Suck lack of explicitness is rare in Clarke's poetry. The confusion of the leaderless Israelites could easily represent Ireland's confusion in 1921, but the comparison is awkwardly made. Clarke seems to spend his words and ideas in an almost incomprehensible rush. The poem opens with a first 'sentence' which appropriately illustrates this fault:

After the fierce-sunned tribes of Israel,
For generations wandering the desert
Clouded and pillared by the fire of God,
Had marched from Hazeroth, the hill of palms,
And barren lands of brass and wool, they saw

Across the wide unwatered plains of Moab,
The fabled mountains of the Promised Land
Against the skies; and aged fighting-men
Carried bedridden from the sheepskin tents
Gazed blindly, muttering of the mountain-gods
Beyond the cateracts when they were slaves
Mill-turning in the wheaten land of Nile,
Around them the sons of their second seed,
As lions whelped amid the burning sands,
There grown to lion-like manhood, by their wives
And suckling children, grimly stared at a dream
Until, out of the dazzle came twelve spies
Among the clamorous crowd, with sun-struck limbs
Dripping, the luscious boughs of pomegranate
And grape-bunch, oozing coolness through the air,
On their bruised shoulders and with slobbering
     breath
Half-eaten honeycombs and of a rabble
Squabbling for a flung sword beneath four towers
And sun-doors, plated with a scorching bronze,
Chaldean concubines, their childless teats
Cupped with barbaric gold, who lay at noon
Beside the fountain trees on cold-veined marble
Among their tousled robes, a city's spoil,
Timbrelled by laughter.

                                                   (*Poems*, 41-2)

Here is, perhaps, the easiest gauge by which to measure
Clarke's later poetry. His periodic, almost Miltonic, constructions do lend some momentum; but the syntax is all
awry. A profusion of exotic details describing the women and
the riches of the land creates a somewhat overwhelming
sensuousness. Overcrowded with adjectives and poetically
strained, this fragment is typical of the poem. Clarke's conception of the poem is not at fault; the weakness of the poem
lies in Clarke's inability to mould his materials. Nowhere else
in his writing does Clarke so manifestly indulge his early
romanticism. *The Fires of Baal*, cluttered with poetic effects
which are derivatively Georgian or late Victorian, stands in
sharp contrast to his directly 'political' later poems. It also
appears insubstantial beside the controlled language of other
poems of the same period in his career.

The Sword of the West, which was dropped from the 1936 *Collected Poems* but reinstated and printed with its events in the proper chronological sequence in 1974, is an equally flawed poem but with some saving lyrical effects. It is an ambitious consolidation of two poems which explain the rise and fall of the Gaelic pantheon, the prehistoric cycles of civilisation in Ireland, Cuchullin's birth, the curse on the men of Ulster, the legend of Deirdre, the battle for the bull of Cooley and Maeve's druidical revenge on Cuchullin after her defeat. Clarke assumes that the reader will know many of the details of his subject matter already. Using techniques explored to their limits in *The Vengeance of Fionn,* he further complicates his themes by intertwining the various narratives with an account of a Bardic congress. Hyde's book explains the details of the cycle at length, but Clarke was content to preface the 1921 edition of the work with the cryptic and somewhat forced statement: 'It is well that the mythological world should remain clouded and that the fords are deep.' The poem is indeed clouded and lacks any obvious key, illustrating the absence of the depths, alleged in the preface. The surfeit of facts, images and mythological speculations seems to hide a basic lack of content. The narrative is often static. The first section, 'Concobar', contains some fine poetic effects, all of them dependent, however, on complicated periodic constructions of the sort used in *The Fires of Baal.* To introduce Concobar's kingdom in a climactic sequence of events and then to describe the land in parallel sequences adds formal strength. Inversions of normal syntax intensify the evocation of an ancient grandeur:

> Fertile the land
> of Concobar.
> His power was furrowed in the soil
> At dawn, and he had grasslands swept by rains
> Of forest, pasture of the shadowed hawk.
> In every field lambs tugged the slapdash dug
> And milch cows lowed at noon. In summer time
> Heather-brown honey dripped on mountain trees,
> Sky-blue in tangled cords the giant salmon
> Would drag the boathead down; the harvest came
> With blackbirds to the wild-red-appled glens,
> The breezes pushed knee-deep through barley,

> droves
> Of swine trampled in acorn-fattened oakwoods,
> And the shake of a nut-clustered hazel filled
> Pattering vats.
> > Fruitful his reign.
> > > (*Poems*, 59-60)

Although the style is strikingly similar to that of *The Fires of Baal*, there is a strength here not found in the earlier poem about Israel: a power gained by the concentration of peculiarly Irish details. The catalogue, however, lapses into wordiness and sound effects. Clarke has not yet discovered the province of his own art and throughout this book continues to experiment with another generation's aesthetic paraphernalia.

In a shorter lyrical poem Clarke recounts Cuchillin's last dream before his death. This poem was reprinted by itself in the 1936 *Collected Poems*. 'O Love There is no Beauty' is a remarkable example of the lyrical power and aptness of imagery which Clarke often obscures in the longer, epical poems:

> O Love there is no beauty,
> No sorrowful beauty, but I have seen;
> There is no island that has gathered sound
> Into dim stone from many reeded waters
> But we have known,
> > Heart of my sorrowful heart,
> Beauty fades out from sleepy pool to pool
> And there is a crying of wings about me
> And a crying in me lest I lose you. Glimmer
> Around me; sound, O weir, within my heart;
> Bring calm on many waters, for I will be hearing
> The salmon shatter the air into silver when
> The chill grass ends their leaping . . .
> > (*Poems*, 115)

The poem displays Clarke's expected preoccupation with atmosphere and sound effects, but there is a new emotional depth. Passion and sorrow are powerfully conveyed by the mannered idiom and elegant imagery. The images of the salmon-weir, the tapes of life, and of the woman whose love is stronger than bonds of the clan are woven in a manner which suggests the smoking incense that opens the section. This smoke ties the metaphysical ('westward praise of god') to the basic earthly images of bread, salt, fire and water. This intensity is heightened in the last six lines quoted here which have a deliberate vigour and sparseness. Clarke has already attempted similar verbal ambiguities, but here the power of such language is new.

Another section of the poem was altered and printed by itself in 1936 as 'The Music Healers'. In the 1974 *Collected Poems* it is reprinted as part of *The Sword of the West* (*Poems*, 83-110). It is important not for its story of his wife's attempt to heal Cuchullin's mind and guard him from the druidic enchantments of the mad dancers, nor for the example it gives of the technical formalities of assonance. (These early experiments are discussed in the next section). 'The Music Healers' is the first, almost casual, account Clarke gives us in his poetry of mental illness. It is an early, flawed prelude to his last great poems which are concerned with the curing of sick minds.

Clarke recognised his poetic confusion and had some obvious misgivings about his early work. In his notes to the 1936 *Collected Poems* he dismissed the entire third volume with the admission that 'it seemed wisest to forget as a whole, and not reprint'. By 1974 Clarke had pruned his more obvious excesses and yet, unlike Yeats, humbly allowed his apprentice-work (admittedly re-ordered but almost unrevised) to stand. There was other work that Clarke destroyed before it could be published:

When I had published my third book A.E. remarked quietly that my technique was going to pieces. Coming from so kindly a critic that remark had implications from which I could not escape. I tried to withdraw the book eventually, burned a long poem called 'The Intoxication of the Ulstermen', and started out to learn again.[4]

(ii)

Before reaching such a conclusion, Clarke tried once again to come to terms with the Ulster epic. It is significant that *The*

Cattledrive in Connaught (*Poems*, 117-52) is his first book
not solely composed of one major poem. The many small
poems mark another departure for Clarke as well — the
beginning of his interest in Gaelic assonance and prosody.
'The Fair at Windgap' and 'The Itinerary of Ua Clerigh' (the
Irish form of his surname) are some of his first experiments
with contemporary Irish themes. 'The Frenzy of Suibhne' is
a translation of the medieval saga of mad Sweeney, a character
who appears obsessively in all of Clarke's work. This story is
remarkable in that much of the same material is worked into
one of Clarke's novels and then, thirty-six years later, into
one of his last poems. This new period in Clarke's development is ushered in by the poem, 'Induction', in which Clarke
declares himself to be inspired by Mannanaun MacLir, the
Celtic sea-god, Ireland's Proteus. Mannanaun is joker, jester
and poet; his story proves to be a more fruitful source of
inspiration than the stories of the Cuchullin cycle. This volume
contains only the poems about the Ulster epic, the fragmentary 'The Circuit of Cuchullin' and the title-poem itself.

Queen Maeve of Connaught, the most prominent character
of these early works, appears in 'The Cattledrive in Connaught',
the comic title-poem. No longer attempting to construct
immense patterns inside his poems, Clarke now describes the
'Pillow Talk' at the opening of the Tain epic — the mundane
raillery of man and wife, arguing in bed over their comparative
wealth and power. Ailill's strong-willed wife will not concede
her point:

> Queen Maeve sat up in bed and shook once more
> Her snoring husband:
>   'And I cannot sleep
> An inch now for my head is full of words
> That spoiled the chessboard, held the drinking cups
> Half drained and climbed the more as candlelight
> Ran low and is there any doubt that I
> Had greater wealth when we were wed than you
> Had bargained with my hand — have I not filled
> The west with lowing herds, have I not fleeced
> The hills, have I not brought the middlemen
> From grassing plains to lift a wondering head
> From seaward clouds and count a rout of horses
> Graze beyond swimming where a few island women

Gallop them, bareback, to the little seas
Of Connaught? Have I now or have I not?
Tell me, have I not hung this draughty house
From family looms and put a golden bit
Upon the winter, silence on the floor . . .'

                                             (*Poems*, 135)

It is readily apparent that the style of this poem is developed
from the three earlier books. But it is a comic version of 'The
Pillow Talk', an actual section of The Tain epic. In this case,
Clarke is in control of his imagery, catalogues and syntax, all
of which combine to capture the character of queen and
matriarch, headstrong and vital. The bedroom farce continues
until Ailill is forced to admit the strength of her arguments.
He concedes with a sarcastic dig that she brought more wealth
to the marriage than he:

             'Aye, but you brought it all
    Upon your back'.
                        (*Poems*, 136)

The break with Clarke's former poetic niceties is striking.
The Anglo-Irish rhetorical trappings are discarded and his
characters emerge as convincing personalities in a way that
would have been impossible in his earlier poems. Clarke concentrates on the comic aspects of Maeve's domestic squabble,
ignoring the importance of this episode to the entire epic
cycle. He has abandoned epic for parody.

The language of the other characters also demonstrates
how far Clarke has moved from the florid style of his other
epics. In his previous epics warriors delivered their speeches
in a heightened, oratorical language. In *The Cattledrive*,
however, the characters speak in a rough, unadorned language
that contains hints of the Ulster dialect:

                    'The Bull!
    The Bull,
             They wull na' take the Bull.'
                        (*Poems*, 151)

Clarke has finished with his epic material. This treatment
of the Ulster cycle deflates his earlier efforts and marks a

turning point in his work. Brendan Kennelly remarks: 'Ironically, just when he appears to be on the point of writing a
good epic poem, he turns away from heroic saga.'[5] The real
irony lies not, however, in his abandonment of the ancient,
grand and heroic style, but rather in the fact that such
affectations should have so long obscured Clarke's true genius.
Here he has shed the 'old-fashioned poetic garb' which
hampers the early poetry and, with a harder rhetoric and a
flair for the dramatic, is ready to turn a new eye on his
country:

> The thousand tales of Ireland sink: I leave
> Unfinished what I had begun nor count
> As gain the youthful frenzy of those years;
> For I remember my own passing breath,
> Man's violence and the despair of brain
> That wind and river took in Glenasmole.
> (*Poems*, 179)

Clarke's apprentice-work was finished in 1936 with the
publication of the *Collected Poems*; his new work was visibly
reshaped. With these poems Clarke moved toward the poetic
drama. The collection also included poems taken from
Clarke's two novels. The four 'epic' volumes of poetry are no
longer the major body of his work. In Clarke's notes and in
Padraic Colum's introduction to the collection, both are sure
of the poet's new power and the skill with which he has
shifted his focus on Ireland. Clarke begins in these notes his
lifelong discussion of traditions, folk customs, natural events
and literary conventions in Ireland. Colum describes this new
element in Clarke's work as a move from the primeval heroic
world 'into the medieval ... the mid-Irish world, the Ireland
between the legends and the present-day folk-songs'. He has
found himself and his tradition. 'Clarke, through some strange
process, has been able to identify himself with the Gaelic
poets of the seventeenth and eighteenth centuries, times
which in Ireland were an extension of the medieval period.'[6]

(iii)

Pilgrimage and Other Poems was first published in 1929 and
then again in the *Later Poems* of 1961. It is central to an

aesthetic and social understanding of Clarke's superior
later poetry. *Pilgrimage and Other Poems* (*Poems*, 153-75) is
his escape from a vague past, his bridge into contemporary
Ireland. Into the Celto-Romanesque Ireland portrayed in
these poems Clarke subtly introduces the problems and
concerns of modern Ireland and evokes the lost or betrayed
ideals never achieved in the intervening period. By a technically dazzling manipulation of English poetry, he is able to
bring forward the heritage of ideas and skills bequeathed to
his generation by those Irish scholars whose work had inspired
him during his university career.

As in the satires of the 1950s, Clarke is not blind to the
conflicts and imposed restraints that hinder what may be
called his 'liberation'. Within the developing and strangely
harmonious society of a nearer-than-misty past, Clarke cham-
pions the country, the society and the individual. His heroes
are unhindered by dogma; they are healthy and self-sufficient.
The questions of free will and public and private conscience
(which later preoccupied him) are posed here in that 'forgotten
medieval Ireland when we almost had a religion of our own'
(*Black Church*, 142). G.T. Stokes, in his collection, *Ireland
and the Celtic Church*, is particularly illuminating about this
period in Irish history, between the establishment of an
independent church under Patrick and Columcille and the
Norman conquest in 1172, when Armagh, the religious centre
of Ireland, submitted to Rome.[7]

Pilgrimage and Other Poems is Clarke's exploration of this
past, a wandering quest in search of roots. A journey of discovery, anguish and final solace governs the book's shape.
This pattern is repeated in the later volumes, *Flight to
Africa*, *Old-Fashioned Pilgrimage*, and *Mnemosyne Lay in
Dust*. Indeed, Clarke's entire work can be seen as one long
pilgrimage away from the romantic illusions of his youth,
through the awesome realities of personal responsibility in
a contemporary world to the final benign visions of exuberant
freedom which fill his later works.

Here, Clarke has just begun. Having shaken off his sagaic
pomposities, he solemnly enters the Celto-Romanesque world,
described in the title poem, where:

> . . . by dim wells the women tied
> A wish on thorn, while rainfall

Was quiet as the turning of books
In the holy schools at dawn.

Grey holdings of rain
Had grown less with the fields,
As we came to that blessed place
Where hail and honey meet.
(*Poems*, 153)

Clarke has come in search of the beauty and inspiration which
Ireland can afford him. He finds them not in a mythological
past, but in the forgotten traditions of a real, historical
Ireland. The time and the land are grace-filled, hushed and
holy but by no means soft. Life in this region 'Where hail
and honey meet' is integrated, as the rest of the poem reveals.
The verse, its 'music as lovely as it is unfamiliar',[8] is a
departure as well. In his notes to the 1929 edition of these
poems, Clarke explained his attempt to capture the lost
cadences of Gaelic verse and, through assonance, to refashion
English poetry:

Assonance, more elaborate in Gaelic then in Spanish
poetry, takes the clapper from the bell of rhyme . . . .
The natural lack of double rhymes in English leads to
an avoidance of words of more than one syllable at the
end of the lyric line, except in blank alliteration with
rhyme. A movement constant in Continental languages
is absent. But by cross-rhyming or vowel-rhyming,
separately, one or more of the syllables of longer words,
on or off accent, the difficulty may be turned: lovely
and neglected words are advanced to the tonic place and
divide their echoes.

In the opening lines of 'Pilgrimage', quoted above, there
are alliterations, half-rhymes and consonance, all of which
cross the lines and join the stanzas. Words like 'wells' /
'women' / 'wish' / 'while' / 'was' alliteratively strengthen the
atmosphere of quiet in the 'showery breeze' and the holy
work of scholars. 'Tied' assonates with 'while' in the next
line and then 'quiet' in the following provide a good example
of the complex which Clarke attempts to build. 'Wish' not
only alliterates but also has assonance with 'women'. He has

pushed the rhyme back into the vowels, away from the end of the line (where one would normally expect to find it). This creates a structure of assonantal rhyme which is not confined to individual stanzas but is present throughout the poem. Notice, for example, the assonance of 'holy' and 'holdings'. Clarke justifies his method in the notes to the 1936 *Collected Poems*:

> Assonance . . . is not the enemy of rhyme. It helps us to respect rhyme which has been spoiled by mechanical use. By means of assonance we can gradually approach, lead up to rhyme, bring it out so clearly, so truly as the mood needs.

This technique has a musical effect. The subtle rhymes of 'rainfall' and 'dawn' ('rainfall' consonating in one syllable and assonating in the other with 'dawn'), 'rain' and 'place', 'fields' and 'meet', show Clarke's mastery of sound patterns. In the last two lines quoted above, the harmonies of 'came', 'place', and 'hail' effect a balance by leonine rhyme and assonance.

Some explanation of the various kinds of rhyme may be helpful at this point in my argument. True rhyme, as we are taught to recognise and expect it in most English poetry, is infrequent, and generally avoided in the technique adopted by Clarke. One finds instead the close repetition of consonant sounds and patterns (referred to hereafter as consonance) as well as the recurring patterns of vowel sounds which is, of course, assonance. Clarke's use of assonantal rhyming varies again from what one might call 'usual' practice in that syllables that rhyme in this manner are not always rhythmically stressed. Assonance is also called half-rhyme and sometimes unmet rhyme (that is, when a true rhyme is inferred but one meets instead with an assonantal rhyme). The following variations (defined in *A Reader's Guide to Literary Terms*) are also common in Clarke's poetry:

> *near, slant, oblique, approximate, half or imperfect rhyme*, all of which could be considered synonymous with assonantal rhyme;
> *analysed rhyme*, which is a 'complex arrangement of near rhymes in the four lines of a quatrain end-

ing, for example, thus: *pass, relief, laugh, peace*. Rhymes 1-4 and 2-3 exhibit consonance while rhymes 1-3 and 2-4 exhibit assonance';

apocopated rhyme, 'in which the rhyme word extends over two lines', similar to broken rhyme, in which only 'one of the rhyme words extends over two lines';

identical rhyme, which is 'the recurrence of two words which have exactly the same sound but are spelled differently and carry different meanings'. (This is also called 'rime riche' and is used extensively by Clarke in poems such as *Mnemosyne Lay in Dust*);

linked rhyme, which is found in Welsh and Irish poetry, is 'formed by joining a final syllable in one line to the first sound of the following line' and

leonine rhyme, 'in which the word before the caesura rhymes with the concluding word'.[9]

Returning to the poem 'Pilgrimage', the poet has arrived at Clonmacnoise, the holy school which represents Ireland's golden monastic age. The phrase 'crossed with light' evokes both the ruins as they appear today beside the bright Shannon waters and, more importantly, the monastery's ancient tradition of sanctity and learning. Clarke constructs an imaginably alive heritage, augmenting his belief in a vital and harmonious, yet forgotten, tradition. His new inspiration, the craft and technical skill of Bardic poetry, is caught magnificently in his rendering of the Celto-Romanesque integration of art, life, religion and craftsmanship:

> . . . those cloistered scholars,
> Whose knowledge of the gospel
> Is cast as metal in pure voices,
> Were all rejoicing daily,
>
> And cunning hands with cold and jewels
> Brought chalices to flame.
>
> . . . And in stained glass the holy day
> Was sainted as we passed
> Beyond that chancel where the dragons
> Are carved upon the arch.

Treasured with chasuble,
Sun-braided, rich-cloak'd wine-cup,
We saw, there, iron handbells,
Great annals in the shrine
A high-king bore to battle:
Where, from the branch of Adam,
The noble forms of language —
Brighter than green or blue enamels
Burned in white bronze — embodied
The wings and fiery animals
Which veil the chair of God.
                        (*Poems*, 153-4)

The architecture of these lines, subtle and complicated,
mirrors the art of the period. In these strange harmonies,
intertwined assonances and syntactic balances, Clarke formally
and imagistically celebrates the object of his praise. Christopher
Ricks praises Clarke's verbal dexterity, noting the puns on
words like 'sainted' and 'stained' (an assonantally-rhymed
anagram) or on 'praised' and 'Paradise'. Ricks says: 'the eye,
without halting for a crossword, can take in the effect of
such stealthy modellings'.[10] The paralleled structures at the
opening of the last stanza quoted above, the objects clustered
around the verb, is an obvious development from the awkward
technique of *The Fires of Baal*; but here the effect is steadier.
Clarke shows greater control over image and language. The
interpenetrating and fluid unity achieved here by grammatical
devices is mirrored in the rhyme-scheme.

It is in his images, however, that Clarke realises medieval
Ireland and its vitality. The rainfall is as 'quiet as the turning
of books in the holy schools at dawn'; the scholars have a
knowledge 'cast as metals in pure voices', and 'cunning hands'
have 'brought chalices to flame'. The holy inspiration that
guides these men is 'brighter than green or blue enamels
burned in white bronze', and the men are allowed to see,
awe-struck, 'the chancel where the dragons are carved upon
the arch', 'the wings and fiery animals which veil the chair of
God'. This Ireland is a land of scholars, saints and inspired,
proficient craftsmen: men able, in the organic society which
supports and is fostered by them, to come near to God and
to the spirit of their land. As a poet and idealist, Clarke has
set his goal by this religious example of a way of life wherein

'the noble forms of language' can embody such enthusiasm
and command such reverence. This is a different version of
romanticised Ireland from that which Clarke offered us in his
ealiest poems, but it is still unrealistic. This is the idealised
society against which he will gradually contrast the real
behaviour of his people in the novels and earliest satiric
poems. Now, however, he is still caught in a non-classical
world view.

Art, craft, culture, language and Godhead are held in
bright, holy union. This inter-dependence is conveyed by an
interpenetrating structure of images and grammar, and by a
continually shifting balance of sounds. An examination of
the last stanza above will show what a remarkable effect
Clarke's concept of Irish assonances and prosody has on
English poetry. Sounds and groups of sounds repeat themselves. 'Chalice' and 'chancel' are echoed in 'chasuble' which
is tied to 'treasured'; 'chasuble' is then linked to the larger
rhyme of 'handbells' which itself slides into 'annals' and
'animals'. Words agglutinate as in 'sun-braided, rich-cloak'd
wine-cup'. The long vowel sounds tie the sections into the
whole. Clarke's interlacing of sounds and words is as intricate
as the interlaced patterns so popular in Romanesque art. He
claimed as inspiration for some of the shorter lyrics in *The
Cattledrive in Connaught* the intertwinings of the Book of
Kells, with its fabulously intricate zoomorphics. The poem
itself is an example of the very art which the poet praises.

Clarke does not become preoccupied with the monastic
world of 'Pilgrimage'. The world he creates in this poem
represents a transition in his work. This is evident in the
poem itself as the ship moves out over the sea, past:

        . . . a barren isle
    Where Paradise is praised
    At daycome, smaller than the sea-gulls
    We heard white Culdees pray
    Until our hollow ship was kneeling
    Over the longer waves.

The waves and the hushed prayers of exiled hermits re-
emphasise the quiet grace which pervades this Ireland. The
lure of this naturally ordered, attractive land is contained in
images which unite past with present: the 'grey beaded

plains', the 'grey holdings of rain' and the settlements, now
ruins, still revered as places of worship. Cashel, Clonmacnoise, Croagh Patrick remain as witnesses to a remarkable
past history, and Clarke's natural descriptions of them evoke
an eternally beautiful landscape. John Montague, a younger
poet, has lauded Clarke for this evocation of the countryside:

> There are certain things I particularly admire in Austin
> Clarke. The first is the way, like the painter, Patrick
> Collins, he has made the Irish landscape the background
> of his work: those changing veils of rain and mist could
> not be anywhere else; yet they are not painted to attract
> visitors, but because they are part of the permanent
> furniture of our lives, like the rocks and thorns beneath.
> . . . Yeats began this, but his sense of colour owed more
> to the English lyric tradition, from Spenser to Tennyson,
> than to the impressionistic, almost Japanese details of
> Gaelic nature poetry. [11]

The clergy, a target of ridicule in other poems, are portrayed
as a beneficent force in Celto-Romanesque Ireland. There is
no rigid dogma though there is an implied sexual segregation.
Notice how Celtic Christianity tolerates the pagan practice of
the 'wish on thorn'. Tolerance is the rule in this poem.
Spiritual leaders are not a class of oppressors in this world but
a natural feature of a culturally rich society. The 'white
clergy', the 'fasting crowd at prayer' and the 'black congregation' are all important to the total picture. There is none
of the anger at Christianity which informs some of the later
poems. This pre-Norman Ireland has a religion of its own — a
happy combination of Christian ideal and pagan vitality.
Clarke's 'Pilgrimage' takes him to an Ireland only beginning
to grow. Its people are as yet independent and their lives
free-flowering. The men are scholars and craftsmen, priests
and artisans.

This is an Ireland in which the claims of faith and experience
are equally respected, a land whose people live full and vital
lives and where rituals deserve the reverence given them. The
respect with which Clarke describes this ideal conditions all
the writings that follow. On this first 'Pilgrimage' the poet
has found the standard by which all else will be judged,
praised or rebuked. The values of this forgotten Ireland, this

lost ideal, motivate his later parody and invective.

'Celibacy', the poem which follows, is an exploration of asceticism. It deals with a hermit's continuing struggle against sexual temptation:

>   . . . I sank
> In torment of her side;
> But still that woman stayed,
> For eye obeys the mind.
>
> Bedraggled in the briar
> And grey fire of the nettle,
> Three nights, I fell, I groaned
> On the flagstone of help
> To pluck her from my body;
> For servant ribbed with hunger
> May climb his rungs to God.
>   (*Poems*, 155)

This poem — more typical of Clarke's opinions about religion — describes the oppressiveness of Christianity. The hermit's attempts, vividly conveyed in the brutal images of nettle and briar, to subjugate his senses and to impose a rigid self-discipline betray his sheer unnatural effort of will. He pushes his body, hoping his soul can follow, into another world because 'eye obeys the mind', and hunger leads to heaven. The perversity of self-inflicted pain is starkly depicted. The idyllic world of the other poems in the collection is transformed into a personal hell. Normal responses and common situations are distorted. In his frenzy of asceticism, much that might be beautiful is lost. Human instincts open the way to devilry for this poor man:

> Eyelid stood back in sleep,
> I saw what seemed an angel:
> Dews dripped from those bright feet.
> But, O, I knew the stranger
> By her deceit and, tired
> All night by tempting flesh,
> I wrestled her in hair-shirt.

The distortion of reality results from the man's self-imposed

exile and from the denial of his natural desires. His very
hunger invites and creates of itself hallucinations instead of
the desired gift of atonement.

The poem is not as complex in its structure or cadence as
'Pilgrimage' (an intended comment, perhaps, on its pro-
tagonist's narrow doctrine of redemption) and it yet contains
an interesting scheme of syllabic rhyme. 'Hunger' is echoed in
the middle of the next line by 'rungs' in the stanza already
discussed, and the final syllable is left hanging. There is a chain
of assonances in the sequence 'sleep' — 'seemed' — 'feet'; a
similar pattern intrudes from the beginning of lines as in
'dews' — 'knew'.

Clarke casts final doubt not only on the actual presence of
the demon-woman but on the hermit's idea of God:

> . . . when I fought
> The arrow-headed airs
> That darken on the water.

Is all an illusion; has the eye only seen what the mind has
imagined? How is one to choose reality?

Clarke is on surer ground in his handling of the sensual
details of the hermit's temptation. Clarke's feet are firmly on
the ground, his heart and mind freely moved to celebrate
earthly delights.

In his notes to the next poem, 'The Confession of Queen
Gormlai', Clarke suggests that this woman's pathetic end
'may symbolise a conscience wounded by others'. Gormlai,
who has shared three beds and known the pleasures and
pain of human love, cannot be consoled by a chaste monk:

> Monk, do not lift the hood
> From black to hearing white;
> The shadows of the schoolmen
> That drift from fire to ice
> Stoop, and my mind is stirred,
> Remembering the books
> I closed, for I am Gormlai
> And she was beautiful.
>
> *(Poems,* 156)

What follows is Gormlai's impassioned, desperate account

of her ill-fated marriage to Cormac who chose celibacy and a
bishopric in preference to his wife:

> But I laughed with grave Cormac
> Above the candle-rows
> And heard the string leap back
> To men and women dancing.

It is other men and women who dance in Gormlai's reveries.
Her abandonment destroys her and this tragedy is the centre
of Clarke's poem:

> All night he turned to God
> Because the body dies;
> But had it been immodest
> For him to rest beside me?

Gormlai assumes symbolic importance for Clarke. As a
woman and as a poet whose pleasure and delight are bound
to earthly knowledge and sensual awareness, she exists at the
centre of his creative vision of life. A personality like hers
will always suffer under the regime of inhuman and strict
ideals which men call God's truth. Oppressed by religion,
bowed down with age, she is alone at the last, debating her
mortal share of life:

> I had not read in book
> That goodness can insult
> The mind, that meeting looks
> Are bright adultery.
> Though I have lain in three beds
> And many have blamed me,
> No man has seen me naked,
> Partaken in my shame.

Shame, and desolation, are the doubter's lot. Clarke's long-
enduring enmity to the sexual repression inculcated by the
Church, and his affirmation of mortal beauties and human
joys begins in this poem. He restrains his bitterness against
the Church, however, and concentrates compassionately on
Gormlai, 'murmuring of the sins / Whose hunger is the mind'.
This hunger Clarke fashions into Gormlai's last confession:

> Monk, if in matrimony
> The pair that has been blessed
> May please the lower limbs —
> My third bed was not less.
> I grieve our vessels shake
> The soul and though I grovel
> As Cormac in true shame,
> I am impure with love.

The human and the divine are irreconcilable, save by an act of denying will.

'The Scholar' and 'The Cardplayer' are both taken from *The Son of Learning*, a play central to Clarke's satiric development, which is discussed in the next chapter. 'The Scholar' again proves the poet's dexterity in creating sound-patterns and 'The Cardplayer' cavalierly restates Clarke's belief in love and human instinct in preference to Christian dogma. Both relieve the tension created by other poems in the volume.

'The Scholar' is a supreme example of Clarke's imitation, Gaelic verse turned into nimble-sounding English. Clarke avoids calling his lyric a translation. It is 'a free paraphrase of an anonymous poem', he notes. The poem captures the pleasant delights and indulgences of a vagrant student. It displays an intricate assonantal pattern:

> Summer delights the scholar
> With knowledge and reason.
> Who is happy in hedgerow
> Or meadow as he is?
>   (*Poems*, 162)

The words rhyme not at the ends of lines but at tonically stressed positions. 'Scholar' plays against 'knowledge', the last syllable of which carries the harmony into 'hedgerow' and then 'meadow'. The vowel sounds of 'and reason' are echoed by 'happy in' and repeated by the final 'as he is'. This proficient and subtle beauty turns the poem in on itself and back out again in a rich complex which one critic has compared with the 'characteristic embroidery of Irish music'.[12] The remaining stanzas are equally well formed. In the last stanza Clarke portrays Ireland's medieval grandeur:

But in winter by the big fires,
The ignorant hear his fiddle,
And he battles on the chessboard,
As the land lords bid him.

When one reads Frank O'Connor's 'The Student', a translation based on the same anonymous Gaelic lyric, it is clear
how ably Clarke handles such material. O'Connor's effort is
prosaic by any standard; its first stanza demonstrates the
irony in O'Connor's admission that 'the Irish is execrable but
the sentiment is of great distinction':

The student's life is pleasant
    And pleasant is his labour
Search all Ireland over
    You'll find not better neighbour.[13]

Robert Welch has clearly defined Clarke's attitude to Gaelic
poetry:

Generally speaking, these can hardly be called translations in any strict sense, since they perform a descant
on the themes and patterns of the Irish original, yet
they do have a reference to an actual poem in another
language. They are what Dryden would call 'imitations
. . . extraordinarily vivid representations of the imaginative impression the original made on Clarke, so that the
Irish poem out of which they grew reverberates or
shimmers through them. Translation here . . . becomes
an intense kind of literary criticism, so that the reader's
sense of the original and its context is enriched through
Clarke's treatment of it.[14]

'The Young Woman of Beare' takes up Gormlai's unresolved
questions about body and soul, shame and joy. The poem
also illustrates a new, more whimsical approach to his chosen
literary tradition. It is neither an attempt to translate nor to
imitate but extends Clarke's range by resetting an Irish classic,
'The Old Woman of Beare'. It tells the woman's story before
she was immortalised. Clarke's ironic aside about the 'un-
Gaelicness' of the Literary Revival writers, which appeared in
the notes to this poem in 1936, makes his intention explicit.

Clarke seeks to continue, enlarge, and redirect an Irish school of writing.

The heroine of this poem, though not old enough to share Gormlai's anguish, knows well enough her own power to excite men. She also knows how the Church views her life and judges the consequences. Her capacity for pleasure, like her youth, is doomed:

> Half clad in silken piles
> I lie upon a hot cheek.
> Half in dreams I lie there
> Until bad thoughts have bloomed
> In flushes of desire,
> Drowsy with indulgence,
> I please a secret eye
> That opens at the Judgment.
>
> (*Poems*, 164)

Her way of life and her emotions are an affront to the professed gentility and absolute morality of priest and upright citizen both. An outcast from society, she confronts polite society with a damning candour:

> The women at green stall
> And doorstep on a weekday,
> Who have been chinned with scorn
> Of me, could never sleep
> So well, could they but know
> Their husbands turn at midnight,
> And covet in a dream
> The touching of my flesh.

This is no queen, no ideal woman, but rather a real, physically present woman who is made by Clarke to represent Irish womanhood. The conflict has moved from the royal households of Gormlai into the towns and countryside of a more universal Ireland. The same morality and narrow faith remain, however, to condemn her. 'The episodes of this allegory are fanciful', but the implications are real. There is a wide gap between natural instinct and desire on the one side, and rational will and public morality on the other. Words alone cannot control the power of libidinous urges. In the

young woman's own words, 'I triumph in a dream.' With the
strength of her newly released emotions, she challenges the
conventional morality of marriage, a sacred issue in Ireland:

> Together in the dark —
> Sin-fast — we can enjoy
> What is allowed in marriage.
> The jingle of that coin
> Is still the same, though stolen.

Inciting passion in her men and, at turns, warning younger
women to avoid her ways (perhaps ironically?), she has had
to move from place to place across Ireland to avoid condemnation. She begins by addressing 'Young girls' in parody of
those 'virile pastorals (and laws) Parliament passes . . . against
temptations, the pleasures of dancing and courting' (notes to
Collected Poems of 1936, p. 313). The parody is made more
powerful by hints of her loneliness and fear:

> . . . keep from the dance-hall
> And dark side of the road;
> My common ways began
> In idle thought and courting.
> I strayed the mountain fields
> And got a bad name down
> In Beare. Yes, I became
> So careless of my placket,
> That after I was blamed,
> I went out to the islands.

She is another unfulfilled and now condemned wanderer
(a character who reappears in different guises throughout
Clarke's work). Her travels cover all of Ireland where men are
craftsmen and tradesmen, husbands, priests, monks and
culdees. She wanders by Lough Corrib where, in the earlier
poem, 'Celibacy', the hermit had struggled with his idea of
her. 'All those,' she admits, 'I have corrupted'. The humanity
and strength of her desire is brought out in the images of
'a conscience lost in flame' and she is moved to consider:
'Small wonder that men kneel the longer at confession'.
The sensuality of her proud flesh is matched in skilled,
precise rhyme:

Hidden as words in mouth,
My fingers can entice
Until the sight is dim
And conscience lost in flame.
Then, to a sound of bracelets
I look down and my locks
Are curtailed on a nape
That leads men into wrong.

In these lines of sexual fantasy we find again the patterns that
Clarke has perfected: the vowel rhymes crossing in and out of
the ends and middles of lines ('entice' — 'sight'); the rhymed
caesurae ('sound' — 'down'); and the syllabically shifted
assonance which helps to carry the poem forward to its
cadence ('flame' — 'bracelets' — 'curtailed' — 'nape').

Sound patterns reinforce the theme of the poem but they
cannot carry the whole message. Her words express the real
depth of her tragedy. The woman cannot return from exile
to live within the pale of Church order. The islands are always
there as an avenue of escape, but to live on the islands she
must give up human company and civilisation. Why must her
lovers be 'corrupted'? Why is she to blame? Why is her womanhood suppressed by the clergy? Unable to answer these
questions, she counsels caution:

Woman, obey the mission —
Be modest in your clothes.
Each manly look and wish
Is punished but the more.

Though she cautions other women not to court disaster, she
also senses that in one way she has triumphed over the Church;
she cannot be put down:

I am the bright temptation
In talk, in wine, in sleep.
Although the clergy pray,
I triumph in a dream.

The cost of her triumph, however, is great. She feels the
weight of church authority. Her individual conscience cannot
stand against the awesome power of 'lords of diocese . . .

coped / With gold'. As she sees her problem:

> I am the dark temptation
> Men know — and shining orders
> Of clergy have condemned me.

Clarke eventually moves away from the Celto-Romanesque world of the poems in this volume and focuses on contemporary Ireland. As he shifts his focus, his fear of the Church becomes anger, invective and ridicule. The desire for escape to the islands is replaced by the earnest demand to remain and live unhampered within the Pale. He knew that his hopes might be thwarted but he was motivated by an unsuppressable vitality (which can be seen in this poem) and he learned to live without fear of the Church.

Between 'The Young Woman of Beare' and the book's fine ending in 'Wandering Men' are some smaller poems which enhance the quality of the whole collection. 'South Westerly Gale' (*Poems*, 170), despite its title, is the quietest poem in the collection. While men struggle to land their ship in the midst of a blistering storm, Irish life goes on inside the safer mainland homes. A priest talks of eternal damnation while men play backgammon near the fire. Both are significant Irish pastimes. The comfortable Irish are oblivious of the foreigners' struggle with the outside world. 'The Marriage Night' (*Poems*, 171) is an allegory of Ireland whose present times contrast sharply with the

> ... morning she rode down
> Where topsails, that had brought
> A blessing from the Pope,
> Were scrolled in early water:
> Such light was on her cheekbone
> And chin — who would not praise
> In holy courts of Europe
> The wonder of our day?

The poem demonstrates Clarke's ability to deal with Irish life in a metaphorical mode, the deft ambiguities prelude the superb renderings of the 'aisling' (or vision poem) which follows. Avoiding bitterness and the danger of mere topicality, Clarke evinces a profound commitment to his country:

> But in deceit of smoke
> And fire, the spoilers came:
> Tower and unmortar'd wall broke
> Rich flight to street and gate.
> O she has curbed her bright head
> Upon the chancel rail
> With shame, and by her side
> Those heretics have lain.

Clarke uses images of delight and grace, sensuality and desire, to speak of his country. It is as a man and not as a dreamer that he loves Ireland. His idealism is emphatic acceptance and willed surrender to mistress and country. When both fail his imagination's demands, a disillusioned faith remains. The man is hurt, the artist angered and the critic moved to eloquence. This relationship made vital through sexual imagery to the countryside and its traditions shapes Clarke's attitudes. Here (as in the invectives of the 1950s) the woman and the country are understood as one being. Those who mistreat or abuse her trust are 'heretics'. She is forgiven and pleaded with; the spoilers who shame her are rebuked. Clarke's emotional ties to Ireland are those of the lover (though not always so gallant in their diction). The beauty of the land and the knowledge awaiting discovery therein enchant the poet. It is the compromise of politics and the intrusion of man-made rules and dictates which confront Clarke.

This affinity to the land allows Clarke in the poem which follows, 'The Planter's Daughter' (*Poems*, 173) to use an idiom akin to the 'Anglo-Irish folk verse of the bilingual period' in which 'assonantal patterns were sometimes used instinctively' (notes to 1936 *Collected Poems*, p. 309). A transplanted Ulsterwoman wins the Gael to her side; traditional enmity is overcome because 'her beauty was music in the mouth'. Grievances are forgotten and a community is held together by the force of her personality:

> Men that had seen her
> Drank deep and were silent,
> The women were speaking
> Wherever she went —
> As a bell that is rung
> Or a wonder told shyly,

And O she was the Sunday
In every week.

It is a nice touch to add that the women talk wherever she is
and do not wait until she is gone to talk behind her back.

'Aisling' (*Poems*, 173) is Clarke's most serious consideration
of Irish tradition as he understands it in the collection. It is
an elaborate, conventionalised vision-poem, and its stylisation
demands allegorical subtlety and an ability to concentrate
poetic effects. Daniel Corkery, in his study of the Gaelic
tradition, *The Hidden Ireland*, explains the art form involved:
as the literary tradition grew, it

> called for richer and richer music, and this it was given,
> lavishly, sumptuously, yet without vulgarity.... The
> word 'Aisling' means vision; and the vision the poet
> always sees is the spirit of Ireland as a majestic and
> radiant maiden.... Ireland is in all the 'aisling' poems;
> and the only lines in them that strike fire from us are
> those of her sorrows. [15]

Corkery places the 'aisling' in the tradition of Jacobite poetry,
a product of the bilingual period which Clarke has dealt with
imaginatively in the two preceding poems. Clarke uses this
classic form deftly. The beautiful woman, an allegory of
Ireland, is seen through finely erotic details and this vision of
her arouses an understandable yet ennobled desire:

> Coil of her hair, in cluster and ringlet,
> Had brightened round her forehead and those
>   curls —
> Closer than she could bind them on a finger —
> Were changing gleam and glitter. O she turned
> So gracefully aside, I thought her clothes
> Were flame and shadow while she slowly walked,
> Or that each breast was proud because it rode
> The cold air as the wave stayed by the stream.

The 'aisling' genre seems well fitted to Clarke's delight in
form and sensuality. His rapture in Ireland's past and present
glories culminates in this symbol and the poet is awe-struck.
Clarke, following convention, asks who she is because her

beauty seems so foreign.

The usual slightly veiled political message is absent from this 'aisling'. The unanswered and fragile ambiguities create instead a new vision of Ireland and her poetry. The inconclusive finale leaves Clarke scope to pursue his understanding of this strangely beautiful woman:

'Black and fair strangers leave upon the oar
And there is peace,' she answered. 'Companies
Are gathered in the house that I have known;
Claret is on the board and they are pleased
By storytelling. When the turf is redder
And airy packs of wonder have been told,
My women dance to bright steel that is wed,
Starlike, upon the anvil with one stroke'.

'Shall I, too, find at dark of rain,' I cried,
'Neighbours around a fire cast up by the ocean
And in that shining mansion hear the rise
Of companies, or bide among my own —
Pleasing a noble ear? O must I wander
Without praise, without wine, in rich strange lands?'
But with a smile the secret woman left me.
At morning in the coldness of Mount Brandon.

The 'aisling' convention demands that the poet assume a bewildered loneliness, but Clarke is exuberant and anticipatory. The way is open; the fabled woman is gone, but the optimism is significant.

'Wandering Men' (*Poems*, 177), one of Clarke's best poems, is a fitting conclusion to this book. Its assertion that the way to God is through the world grows in intensity with images of the man's loneliness and the visionary Brigid's solace, culminating in the final return to a sunlit forest. The poem is filled with a bold optimism and a compassionate plea for his own harmlessness. He has begun another pilgrimage filled with hope and devotion:

When sudden night had trapped the wood
We stumbled by dark earthing
To find a path we never knew
Though we went down on bare knee.

After confused wanderings in the forest, they find the path
that leads them to Brigid:

> Among her women on the threshold
> Great Brigid gave us welcome.
> She had concealed in colder veil
> Too soon the flaming of her forehead
> That drew our eyelids in the wood.

Jessie Weston, in *From Ritual to Romance*, states: 'Christianity
did no more than take over, and adapt to its own uses, a
symbolism already endowed with a deeply rooted prestige
and importance'.[16] Great Brigid's gradual Catholicisation is
matter, in Clarke's notes, for wry comment and, in Hyde's
larger work, for much speculation.[17] In the ambiguities of her
sainthood Brigid is an ultimate example of the Christian-
Celtic union: earth-mother and artist, solace and sustenance,
goddess of all arts (especially poetry); Brigid is 'Mary of the
Gael'.[18] Clarke intermingles imagery of saint and goddess,
the colder veil and companion nuns, the flaming forehead
and her mystical power of attraction. The combined symbols
lend power to this portrait. To divide and to categorise would
weaken her presence. She is beyond pagan or saint, the com-
forter of lost men. Brigid transcends the pagan and Christian
views of the world. Her compassion and tender care embody
a pervasive feminine principle. The visionary nature of this
poem links it to 'Pilgrimage', to the young woman in Beare
and to the Ireland of 'Marriage Night' and 'Aisling'. 'Wandering Men', in its warmth and emotion, offers a sharp contrast
to the stark, perverse visions of 'Celibacy'.

 The poem presents an ideal of life that is creatively and
imaginatively full. After a symbolic banquet the narrator sees
a vision of an Ireland so fertile that neither pagan nor Christian
philosophy can adequately contain it:

> I think it was the food of Eden
> We shared, for that new ale,
> Though brighter than the serpent-reed,
> Was not indeed of summer's brew,
> And drowsily we heard the calling
> Of voices from an instrument —
> Soft as the music that King Saul
> Had feared beyond the tent.

And all that night I was aware
Of shapes no priest can see,
The centaur at a house of prayer,
The sceptred strangers from the East.
Confined in dreams we saw again
How Brigid, while her women slept
Around her, templed by the flame,
Sat in a carven chair.

The visions in this poem of Ireland are also an image for Clarke's celebration of life. The inspiration is human rather than divine nature. The optimism of this vision and its imaginative freedom resurface in his last works.

The 'shapes no priest can see, / The centaur at a house of prayer' define Clarke's aesthetic realm. In this image Clarke fuses the ideals of spirituality and sexuality, denying the traditional Christian separation of flesh and spirit. Sensuality is elevated to the realm of the sacred, and natural instinct is seen both as a source of moral behaviour and a true guide to divine redemption.

Clarke may seem to cerebrate his way through involved poetic exercises and exhaust his language in intricate puns. Yet the conjunction in his writings of an impressively rigorous intellect with stylistic agility is that of a poet who celebrates above all else human life and its creative expression. The very agility with which Clarke writes can be seen as an expression of this creative principle. His complexities and their satisfying resolutions are those of a mind deeply committed to exploring the fullness of human potential. Clarke uses words in unexpected ways, just as he also contrives unexpected rhymes. By jolting his language and jostling that language's meanings and sounds, Clarke challenges cliché. He challenges convention through an attitude to language and a use of words which he was later to regard as parallel, if not equal, to the sexual or pro-creative urge. He seeks to explore human experience in all its manifestations. Clarke's vision of Ireland, his poetry, must be large enough to encompass a lifetime's experience of action, urge and thought. This world, a vale of tears for some, is for Clarke a source of joy, as can be readily seen in his descriptions of nature in 'The Wandering Men':

We wakened with the early blackbird

Before the oaks had drawn
An old sun-circle in the grass:
Sightly house was gone.

Nature surrounds the welcome men. The images describe an
archetypally holy environment: oaks and sun-circles, druid
priests and the memory of a woman who is perhaps a saint,
but also the mother of the earth, the keeper of the flame,
the inspiration for all lost men. Clarke returns again and
again to this forest shrine:

Yet we gave praise to that sky-woman
For wayfare and a vision shown
At night to harmless men who have
No parish of their own.

Clarke has come to grips with the issues that will dominate
his poetry. His themes and techniques render an Irish past in
imagery and language comprehensible in modern terms. As
man and poet, he gives 'praise to that sky-woman'. Brigid is
goddess of poetry; Clarke praises her with a studied appreciation and handling of Irish poetic traditions. He is at heart
one of those 'harmless men who have / No parish of their
own'. His work is not aimed at destroying the Ireland in
which he lives but is filled with human ideals of better days
and better ways to recognise the past and to shape a freer
present. His guiding belief is the beautiful ideal of this poem,
and the disparities are handled with a commanding integrity.
    The choice which 'Pilgrimage' forced on Clarke is met in
the collection; he continues his journey as a wandering man.
He will search the land around him to discover its traditions,
beliefs and realities.
    Thomas Kinsella, describing Clarke's poetic career, has
written:

As might be expected, the poetry written after the break
differs greatly from that before it. It is more forthright
and partisan in its concerns; it operates more intensely
on a narrower front; it is sharper in tone and diction,
bristling with particularities of time and place. Perhaps
because of the break, it is also highly idiosyncratic. For
a full appreciation of many of the later poems, it is useful

to have a great deal of specific local knowledge, but the
lack of it is not often a real obstacle to understanding. . . .
As the poems accumulated, in tiny private editions, it
became evident that a perfectly integral world was under
investigation, in which — despite the unusually minute
scale — the proportions of reality were more or less
preserved. [19]

Pilgrimage and Other Poems presents this reality intact. It is
thus a major book in Clarke's development and is fundamental
to an understanding of his writings.

The book, as part of *Later Poems* (1961), displays a
unity of theme and style with the later, more bitter poems
(the satiric poems of the 1950s). It manifests the stylistic
identification of a skilled writer with his medium, and
from this point Clarke's writings develop organically. The
fecundity and interwoven relationships of Celtic art and
Celto-Romanesque life, of man and nature, of body and soul,
so vividly depicted, create a tension from which Clarke's craft
and vision originate. The subtle music and sly persuasion in
these poems foreshadow his later, explicit clash with authority.
The 'very *vox caelestis*' which Clarke sought is found in this
collection (notes to *Collected Poems* of 1936, p. 309). From
this high point of artistic idealism, his poetry descends powerfully to deal with the mundane — often sad — realities of
Ireland. He abandons the idealistic manner of *Pilgrimage and
Other Poems*. It is the last romanticised version of Ireland he
will offer in his poetry. Yet the ideal he achieves in these
poems lies behind even the starkest of his later poetry. The
compassionate and generous vision of a harmonious way of
life which fills this volume ultimately informs all his work.
Pilgrimage and Other Poems refutes the critical accusations
that Clarke is too bitter in his later work, or that he is vulgar
and senile. This volume marks the break in his poetic development from the fussy, florid, romantic style of his earliest
poetry to the spare, stronger, more realistic style of his later
poetry.

The Poetic Drama

(i)

Enter Anier MacConglinne, laughing, full of visions, poetry and humour. He was so 'great at both eulogy and satire, that he was called "Anera" (the negative of 'era', 'denial') because there was no denial of his requests'.[1] The character of this young, apostate scholar, Anier MacConglinne, hero of a medieval wonder-tale, 'one of the highest points ever attained by the Irish comic genius',[2] seems perfectly fitted to Clarke's interpretation of the 'Irish tradition'. In his dreaming and his parodies, MacConglinne is central to Clarke's work during his middle period. Between the publication in 1929 of *Pilgrimage and Other Poems* and that of his satires in the late 1950s, Clarke published only one book of poems. The verse plays and novels which he wrote instead during this period are memorable for their anecdotes of Irish life and legend and for their subtle readings of character. Anier MacConglinne, first met in the play, *The Son of Learning* (1927, published later in the *Collected Plays*), and then again in the novel, *The Singing Men at Cashel* (1936), is recognisably a second Austin Clarke. It is MacConglinne who gives shape and lends comic power to Clarke's exuberant work of this period.

In describing Anier, his pranks and his reception by other Irish men and women, Clarke reveals much of himself. Anier is the 'unsanctified bard' of Clarke's first novel, *The Bright Temptation*, who knew the rhetorical disciplines of Gaelic poetry, having attended a small college before defecting to wander the roads of Ireland. A little learning is not too dangerous for such a rogue, and Anier seems more than content to be able to impress his fellow travellers with poems, ballads and dreams, rather than to concentrate his life studying an esoteric linguistic discipline.

Like Clarke in *Pilgrimage*, Anier knows the beauties of the
syllable and its cadences. Both pay homage, thematic and
structural, to Bardic poetry. Anier's escape from the classroom
parallels Clarke's attempt not to fall into the trap of an overtly
mechanical, dazzlingly intellectual poetic style. In *The Singing
Men at Cashel*, Clarke depicts Anier's conflict and describes
his decision to leave his studies and earn his living with
poetry. It is worth quoting at length:

> The best poems are composed beside running water,
> and Anier was proud of the practical hints concerning
> the poetic craft which he had picked up, while eaves-
> dropping outside the small doors of the lay-colleges. . . .
> Truth to tell, Anier was a disgrace to our holy faith and
> he would have been a disgrace, also, to the poetic orders
> had he belonged rightly to them. . . . Anier had roamed
> the lesser kingdoms, counting all their sunny places, ever
> since that unblessed morning in Connaught when the
> thought of roving first came into his head. At that time
> he was a clerical student in the school founded by Saint
> Enda, having been enrolled there because of the piety
> and pride of his parents. Six of his brothers had been
> ordained already to the priesthood and his twenty-six
> cousins were in minor orders. Neither the holy rod nor
> the quadrivium itself, however, enabled the western
> masters to keep Anier in a state of grace. Nightly he was
> occupied by thoughts of young women and by snatches
> of songs which he had heard in his secular days. He
> made but little struggle to resist the impudent visions
> that visited his cell. In fact he took considerable pleasure
> in them, for he was of an airy and joyful nature.
> It is well known that the best conversions are sudden
> and that many who have lain down in sin have wakened
> as saints. But no conversions could have been as sudden
> as Anier's resolve to go to the devil. On the morning
> that he made his resolution, airs were hurrying together
> along the coasts so lightly that even the ascetics in their
> stone houses felt their souls stir in thanksgiving to
> Heaven. Anier, as he sat in class, was suddenly aware
> that all Ireland was before him, that among its hills and
> valleys were fair, bright-cheeked women moving about
> their daily tasks or dreaming of pleasure. As soon as he

thought of that, he put up his hand in the middle of a
lecture and under the pretence of an urgent natural call,
obtained permission to leave the room. When he got
round the corner, he dropped his slate, which was
covered with inaccurate notes on the *Moralia* of Saint
Gregory, tucked in the tail of his shirt more comfortably,
tightened his belt and set out upon his travels.

(11-12)

The obvious humour of this passage, Clarke's subtle understanding of his character's mind and its inclinations, his ironic
twists to well-worn metaphors, might obscure an important
point; Anier becomes Clarke's excuse for his own predilections.
Because he is no longer translating Gaelic verse into English,
it is no longer necessary for Clarke to complain of the complexity which is necessarily a part of the exercise. Clarke, like
Anier, is more concerned with the spirit and inner coherence
of the poems he imitates than with detailed structural similarities. Neither Clarke nor Anier abandon their craft alto-
gether, however. Both are obliged to reach a public with their
readings and stories of Irish life. It is Clarke, not Anier, who
impresses that audience with his intelligence, command of
language and ability to deflate even his own somewhat grandiose endeavours. Anier represents the right kind of foil. He
is an idealistic prankster who flouts authority, or those older
than himself or those unimpressed by his mere presence. This
straying student is a valuable persona for Clarke, allowing the
poet to overcome his timidity and affording a protective guise
which precludes the need for apology.

Clarke, alone among contemporary Irish poets, can be said
to have concerned himself primarily with the Bardic literary
heritage and the attempt to translate this tradition into a
viable, modern poetic idiom. It is not insignificant that, when
he first uses this tradition, Clarke should closely identify himself with Anier MacConglinne. Anier and the other characters
in the play, *The Son of Learning*, say a good deal about the
young poet's character, always reinforcing and elaborating
the identification of Clarke with Anier.

In her book, *The Wandering Scholars* (first published in
1927, the same year as Clarke's play), Helen Waddell explores
the development of the secular lyric in the Middle Ages and
traces the rise of the goliards, or wandering poets, as the first

rebels against authority.[3] It is a book rich in anecdote and
full of allusions to Ireland's arch-poet of that era, Anier
MacConglinne. Clarke's play and Waddell's scholarship form
a composite, imaginative re-creation of a flourishing literary
period and lifestyle. In the play we hear how Anier told the
first story, or *rann*:

It was Mac Conglinne
That made the rann.
                    He tied the knot upon
The tale.
          They say he was
In Tirnanogue.
               A vagabond,
A rogue.
         They say he was in Hell, boys.
He went down by the black mouth of the Red Lake
And cheated the devil himself at a burning game
Of cards.
          The people say he knows
All tricks and magic.
                      A wicked unbeliever,
A great deceiver.
                  And he can dry a cow
With seven rhymes.
                   Oh, anybody could
Make poetry if he were lazy enough.

                                            (*Plays*, 7-8)

The description is a combination of fear, respect, admiration
and contempt for the heretic poet in words paralleled by
Waddell who, illustrating the Church's condemnation of
versifiers, quotes a maxim:

How to be a beggar and a fool? Would you know it?
Let you read books and learn to be a poet.[4]

Waddell explains the stature in the Middle Ages of Ovid
and other pagan, Classical authorities, who were regarded as
having set the standards in style and composition though not
in theme. She further discusses the effects of an education
based on pagan texts but intended for more edifying purposes.

'The Church taught the good monsters language, and their profit on't was they knew how to swear and also to write verses.'[5] Pagan literature opened their eyes to beauty and love and their attendant sensual delights, all of which were proscribed by the Church. In Ireland this conflict between pagan and Christian values culminated with the Anglo-Norman invasion and the submission of the Celtic Church to Rome. Early medieval Gaelic verse had freely celebrated nature, its simple pleasures, and the country's traditions of pagan lore and legend. In Europe, Waddell writes:

> it is towards the end of the eleventh century that one recognises the beginning of the craze for verse, which is almost universal in the twelfth ... by the end of the twelfth century, the writing of rhyming verse was absolutely forbidden to the members of the Cistercian order: its associations were too dangerous.[6]

These dangerous associations were frequently blasphemous. Lovers of life became, of necessity, truants of religion, because

> the Latin poetry of the twelfth and thirteenth century scholars is pagan ... Something has unshackled it from gauging the whole of life by measuring right and wrong. It does not defy heaven and hell: it is unaware of them ... And though pagan, it is not corrupt; its altars are to Cupid and to his mother not Priapus.[7]

To illustrate the force of the reaction against secular verse, Waddell draws an interesting analogy: '... the Puritan attack on the stage in the seventeenth century is emasculate in comparison with the medieval onslaught on the jongleur and the mime: above all the goliard, the clerk who had abandoned his business of edifying for this degrading business of the amuseur.'[8]

Anier, like his many fellow travellers, had no option but to wander, indignant that his talents should be banished from the halls of learning. The way to God, proclaimed goliard and apprentice rhymester alike (at first with subtelety and then with a vengeance), was not the exclusive road of the ascetic or the disciples of stern Rome. Waddell discusses 'the indignant accent of the poor scholar that is to become so familiar in

the twelfth century, the half-resentful astonishment that one
cannot live by scholarship, and must yoke oneself to a
benefice . . .'.[9] One also recognises Anier's complaint to the
monks in the play:

> Good Monk,
> Good Monk, before your crook was jewelled,
> Columcille opened the heavy door of praise
> For us. My mind has broken fast in schools
> Beyond the Shannon where the saints live. I
> Have read so bright a book that kings
> Warred for the lettered dragons and the gold.
> Harper I am, now, a rogue for merriment,
> A ballad-maker, a juggler at the fair
> Of gaping, a wandering scholar in the glens,
> With rain and hunger stitching in my bones,
> But I'll not praise your Lenten bread nor drink
> The parish whey.
>
> (*Plays*, 21)

Summarising this 'renaissance' of paganism, Waddell
explains the character of these condemned heroes in words
that vividly illuminate Anier's appeal to lesser men and,
perhaps more vividly, underline Clarke's motivations in using
this play, *The Son of Learning*, to re-direct his literary output:

> Some are born wanderers; some have it thrust upon
> them; but the word *vagus* denotes often a mental quality,
> as well as the physical condition.[10]

> Primas, Archpoet, Golias, the name is given indifferently,
> the same mask, and the eyes looking out from it, alike
> at least in mockery and hope. Rebels against authority,
> greedy of experience, haunted by beauty, spendthrift
> and generous, fastidious and gross, the temperament
> abides.[11]

> Whatever his life was, the songs that were his repertoire
> would challenge most Elizabethan or seventeenth century
> anthologies either for melody, or for romantic passion,
> and for comedy, go far beyond them. Even at his
> wickedest, he is never *louche*: he is only *magnus trutannus*

et magnus truffator.[12]

Clarke claims the status and convention of the goliard for his Anier, who is announced in the stage directions as a rogue and introduced 'on the top step in the moonlight. His clothes, thinned by skies, would suggest those of the wandering, medieval students of Europe, the vagi scholares goliardi seu bufones, as they were named by Church Councils, but with a racial or bardic touch' (*Plays*, 12). 'The heady scholar' is described by the Abbot in the words which not only describe Anier and the wandering scholars, but which forecast with an ironic pun Clarke's own long battle with the contemporary Church in Ireland. Anier is

A vagabond whose grey bed is the wood,
An idle clerk that mocks the Church. I have
Condemned him.

(*Plays*, 27)

The harmless wandering man (the images recall the final poem in *Pilgrimage*) has become an outlaw.

But *The Son of Learning* is a parody which attacks both clerical and secular authority. 'Medieval parody is graceless, even blasphemous, delighting even more than the scorpion to sting the faces of men.'[13] The *Aislinge Meic Conglinne*, the Irish original for Clarke's play, is no exception to this rule. It is 'the extravagantly embroidered production of a minstrel genuis who had a special grudge against the Church'.[14] The Vision or 'Aisling' of MacConglinne was originally a 'rustic gourmandise'. The mixture of poetry and prose offered the poet the 'desired opportunity of inserting a tirade against tithes, abuse of the monks, and a parody on the passion of Christ'. The 'act of nutrition' at the close of Act II of *The Son of Learning* and the song that opens Act III ('Upon Lough Ale we sailed at rise o' day') are obviously literal borrowings. Surely the scholar's 'O Saviour of all saviours!' in Act II parodies the passion of Christ. Meyer's introduction stated that 'the intention of presenting the condition of the vagrant scholar as advantageously as possible, and of abusing the hated clergy, the hereditary enemy of gleemen, as much as possible, is specially clear'. This view agrees with the portrait of wandering scholars as Waddell described them and it partially explains Clarke's artistic purpose in using the figure of Anier MacConglinne to move the focus of his work away from Ireland's vague, romantic past towards the present.

In Meyer's translation MacConglinne is by turns a splendid scholar, a poor scholar, a bard, a famous scholar with abundant knowledge, a dreaded satirist to whom no one dare refuse anything. He is a sage, an instrument of divine power, whose importance the Church has tried to usurp. Anier preaches with great success, and the devil himself says that MacConglinne possesses the grace of God, an abundance of wisdom and acuteness of intellect. He appears to envy the scholar's powers. MacConglinne says himself that heaven is open for him and that the heavenly hosts are patiently awaiting his soul's entry into paradise. The vision of the food and the miraculous cure of the king's gluttony are mere occasions (in the original) for Anier's learned invectives. The full humour of his riposte is understood only in context of the bombastic character portrait of Anier offered in the translation:

> a youngster of deep lore, entertaining and delightful. And he must be well served; for he is melancholy, passionate, impetuous, violent, and impatient; and he is eager, fond of eating early; and he is voracious, niggardly, greedy; and yet he is mild and gentle . . . easily moved to laughter. And he is a man great in thanksgivings and in upbraidings. And no wonder; for he has wit both to censure and to praise the hearth of a well-appointed, gentle, fine, mirthful house with a mead-hall.[15]

Clarke's play is more humorous and poetic, and much less vicious than his source. It is an essentially dramatic work, filled with the sense of stage and action. A gentle mockery is achieved by the over-all fixation on food and comfort. The beggars' 'childlike sing-song' and the monks' careful preparation of the royal banquet complement each other and bring out, by carefully selected details (concerning the personal interests of the various minor characters) the comic potential of this scene. Conversation between the beggars about milk teeth, apples and the general pleasures of food is an excuse for punning, doggerel and indirect comment on the state of affairs in the country. As they beggar one another for an equal share of charity and food, these chorus-like mendicants set the scene for the play and allude to its major issues:

OLD BLIND MAN:
Ssh! Holy men are praying for the
King.
AMADAN:
Oh, oh, oh!
My little milk-tooth is spilled, is spilled. There is
A devil in the baker's heel.
ONE-LEGGED MAN:
Had I
The heady buck-tooth that I weaned at Michaelmas
In Cashel Fair when I was daring man
And bucking horse, I'd bite.
ONE-ARMED MAN:
A lucky bit.

BLIND MAN:
Ssh! Holy men are praying for the King.
BLACK BEGGAR:
Like buckets in
The well of knowledge, hierarchies go
Up and down.
ONE-ARMED MAN:
... I did:
I seen you ducking in an empty barrel,
A cockshot for the boys.
ONE-LEGGED MAN:
It was
A stand-up fight, a roaring battle, tooth
And toe-nail.
BLIND MAN:
Their lovely prayers will cure the King.
RED BEGGAR:
Oh, there was many a fine horsey fight
In the old days before the hunger came.
(the others sing)
OLD BLIND MAN:
My curse upon you all,
I cannot say my beads.
RED BEGGAR:
Those were the days

For cadging the red pence until the King
Took bad and ate the people out of pot
And pocket.
ONE-LEGGED MAN:
                    I've seen publicans that had
An ale-bush at the fair grow lean again
As their own shutters.
AMADAN:
(running from PILGRIM)
                              Oh, oh, oh!

OTHERS:
(to AMADAN)
Grey droppings of a goose upon you. Quit
The man.
(to PILGRIM)
                    Was it a mortal sin
Behind a hedge put heaven in your mind
Or thinking?

                                        (*Plays*, 3-5)

The images and topics in this conversation all contain a superficial association with food. The conversation ranges over
cynicism about authority and hierarchies, the better days
before hunger came (ironic in a supposedly 'golden age')
and the casual but profound insight into the humanity
of sin (dreams of heaven are caused by the more common
failures of the flesh, or by too much idle speculation). The
men continue chattering, their growling stomachs causing
more comment on women and poetry. As one overhears
snatches of hungry conversations, one is able to infer a larger
meaning. In the midst of this rambling talk and expostulation
the question of MacConglinne's power is first discussed. His
dramatic entrance is accompanied by their childish awe and
superstition.

The monks, fat brother and thin brother, utter equally
banal snippets of conversation, and reduce religious orthodoxy
to drollery, asceticism to childish simplicity:

                    O Brother Dove,
I love to hear all day of miracles,
Small children cured of ringworm, milk in cow
Again, devotions at the blind man's well

And every parish cross; for knees are feet
When a great pope is walking through the land
With bell and cope. They say that Bridget pegged
Her saintly linen on a beam of sun
To dry . . .

(Plays, 24-5)

Their bickering is over-concerned with food. Images of cooking parody the torments of hell:

FAT BROTHER:
                              Had you
To sweat, to toil before the blaze, to toast,
To roast, to boil, to broil, to baste, to braze,
To stew, to simmer, to grill to the very spill
O' the spit . . .
THIN BROTHER:
                        And have I not to peel, to scrape,
To mince, to grind, to pluck, to singe, to draw
The guts o' the fowl, to crumble, season, truss
And skewer?

(Plays, 23)

It is in the main characters however (Ligach, the queen disguised as a penitent; Cathal, the gluttonous king; the officious organiser who is abbot; and MacConglinne, the youthful apostate) that the play's power resides. Their inter-action creates the necessary tensions of the drama, providing climax and underlining the issues. Clarke's thematic concerns are brought to the fore in a language that, while poetic and similar to the language of his assonantal verse, is more natural in its rhythm and full of drama.

Ligach, as might be expected of a woman in a monastery, causes the most controversy among her fellow players. Her presence is an affront to the celibates, a wonder to the mendicants and a delight to MacConglinne. The startling revelation in Act I that the pilgrim is a woman and the ensuing arguments as to which man may claim her is the first climax in the play. Her presence inspires the Scholar to utter some of the finest poetry in the first act, and she restores a sense of normality in assessing his dreams:

SCHOLAR:
Back, fleas and rags. You'd rob me, poachers of wood
And river, red-handed pilferers, bagmen,
Would steal the phoenix of her fiery egg.
Back, or you shall pace by the cold seas
Of Tirnanogue this night.

                          O Fairywoman,
What hill untroubled by the day
Or meddled dance has blessed this house? Are you
Etain, who washes in a basin of gold
With carven birds or that horsewoman, Niav,
Taking the fences of the sea? Are you
The wife of the musician, Craftine,
Who was unhappy when the holeheaded flute
Began to play and so is lost for ever
In the grass and cannot find her lover? Tell me,
For I have heard such music to-night, I fear
The waters work in mind.
WOMAN:
                       Oh,
I am so hungry.
SCHOLAR:
                  I will call food
For you, the pure white bread and honeycomb
That drips the summer, dishes of rung silver,
A skin of wine the wearied sons of Tuireann
Drank in the south.
WOMAN:
                  You dream;
And what shall I do now in a hostel for
Men.
SCHOLAR:
          I dream of the large ruddy fires
In a fairy house and of the beaching noise
In waves that dance as jugglers when they fling
White knives, that we are playing at the chess,
With Bishop, Knave and King upon the board,
For you are more beautiful than Deirdre or
Than Maeve.
WOMAN:
          I think you praise a dream,
Or a woman that is dead.
                           (*Plays*, 16-17)

It is not incidental that hunger should break through the scholar's illusions and once again tie the play together.

The thematic parallel between Anier's visions and the hermit's from the earlier poem, 'Celibacy', is interesting. The woman — a victim of men's fancies, but a realist — correctly understands her position. 'These are but words,' she says. 'Want of food has made him dream' (*Plays*, 18). It is also remarkable that Ligach is able to influence MacConglinne who is believed by everyone else to be wily and supremely self-sufficient. He believes that she loves him because she taunts Cathal and thus aids MacConglinne's magic. Watching Ligach perform, earning praise from a poet, anger from a king, and respect at last from an abbot, we realise that she is in control of the situation at all times and is efficient in her subtle manipulations of the men. One understands not only something of what Clarke has to say about the attraction of women and their power over men; one also recognises how far Clarke has moved in his gallery of Irish womanhood, from the lusty, unmanageable Maeve to the quiet, persuasive queen of this play. And Ligach, like MacConglinne, wins rather than loses in the over-all parody of the Magnificat; woman and poet are elevated in respect and wealth at the expense of both abbot and king.

The abbot, predictably enough, is a major foil for Anier's art. Officious, proud and rude, his fortunes suffer the greatest setback. With the aid of a hungry king, MacConglinne supplants the abbot in his own house:

> KING:
> > Am I in Cashel again?
> You have a harper hidden in the house.
> Oh, I'll have music too.
> ABBOT:
> > High King, it is
> A vagabond whose grey bed is the wood,
> An idle clerk that mocks the Church. I have
> Condemned him.
> KING:
> > Bring him in, for I will salt
> My supper with his music.
> > > > (*Plays*, 27)

The combat between scholar and cleric is never equal. Once his foot crosses the threshold, MacConglinne silences the abbot with a less than subtle threat. All semblance of order is abandoned:

SCHOLAR:
(to KING)

                                 I can amuse
You — for no doubt you are about to sup —
With merry tales of how the Dagda ate
Too much or how the wanton women made
Cuchullin blush again.
ABBOT:
                           Secular stories
Are most unsuitable. The King is on
Retreat.
SCHOLAR:
                 I have more edifying tales,
How Maravaun called dinner down from Heaven
To entertain King Guaire, how Saint Cieran
Rebuked a wench.
ABBOT:
                     No doubt you have a poem
Upon the Deadly Sins.
SCHOLAR:
                     On Simony
And how an abbot fell by pride.
ABBOT:

                            Perhaps
An edifying vision.
KING:
                     Visions! I
Have had enough of them.
SCHOLAR:
                     I made a lesson
Upon the supper I have had.
KING:
                     On victuals?
Go on. I love the marrow of sweet words.
                        (*Plays*, 28)

This exchange demonstrates Clarke's able handling of dialogue and burlesque. There is even an element of slap-stick in the scene. The king and the beggars learn, because of Anier's efforts, what perhaps they had already guessed. The monastery is a veritable storehouse of food and drink, despite the monks' pretence of Lenten temperance. When the king discovers that there is not only a harper and a feast in the wings, but a woman as well, all the pious pretensions to which the abbot may have clung are destroyed. The feast is transformed into a beggars' banquet at which MacConglinne burlesques the Church in a mock-exorcism. The abbot and his monks are reduced to insignificance.

The abbot is deceived by Anier's guile, the king by his own gluttony. Anier manipulates a delightful mock-exorcism and exposes the shallowness of the king's authority and his claim to Ligach. Having coaxed the torc (or chain of office) from the king's neck and onto his own, Anier is able to command a meal and an evening's entertainment which far exceed his earlier fond hopes. The humour in this final scene rests once again on the confusion, in the King's language, of speech with eating. The scholar teasingly infuriates the gluttonous king with revelations and mocks the liturgy once again. 'And litany, O litany,' he exclaims, 'it fills my mouth with rhyme' (*Plays*, 34). The King is made to realise his own folly but is gallantly offered the excuse of magic influences to avoid acknowledging his utter humiliation.

The comedy of the last act depends on the ironic difference between Anier's view of the situation and his audience's misguided interpretation of the same situation. Having feasted and flirted, MacConglinne now turns his attention to the king's possession and surprises everyone by bluntly denying the presence of a demon. His rational intellect elevates Anier above his superstitious fellows. They in turn believe him to be the agent of whatever magic they suppose to be at work. Ligach, however, is not swayed by fancy or dreams from her purpose in coming to the monastery — to cure and wed the king. Anier surpasses the other characters because he understands that, to impress and control, one must perform. The king, Anier explains in a rational, though unorthodox, manner is not possessed:

> A passion is his demon
> And his imagination must release him,
> For prayer and fasting are desire again.

He fed on richer thought and he is full.
But since true argument attends the eye
And hearing, I must do a trick or three
The conjurers despise.

(*Plays*, 49)

When the lights come on again, the effect is tremendous:
Anier is gone in a (coincidental?) flash of lightning, the king
is sane and steady once again, Ligach has become queen at
last and is thus accepted as a guest, and the abbot and his
monks are pious once more in their denunciation of Satan's
bag of tricks. Anier is called the devil's accomplice by the
clerics. Yet he is paid, however illegally, in the king's gold for
his performance and freed once more to ramble.

The play's exuberant and frolicsome travesty of the
established social order is overwhelming and might lead one
to miss a few subtle but important lines of discussion, which
not only tie the drama into a single, cohesive structure but
which also allude to and link *The Son of Learning* with other
plays and writings by Clarke. For example, some of Clarke's
poems from other collections are included. They are recited
by Anier, thus lending further credence to Clarke's identification with his vagabond hero. 'Induction' from *The
Cattledrive in Connaught* (*Poems*, 117), 'The Scholar' and
'The Cardplayer' (*Poems*, 162-3) from *Pilgrimage* appear in
the play. Ligach's perception of the events and their true
outcome is another aspect of the play which should be noticed.
Another important motif is the cynicism of the beggars in
Act I, who explicitly criticise the Church and its doctrines in a
manner which, if developed further and more subtly, is like
Clarke's desperate, satirical impulse to expose false doctrine
in the later poetry. Anier, in his outburst at the abbot, alludes
to the independent Celtic Church, a theme nurtured by Clarke
in *Pilgrimage* and always close to his heart. Finally, the idiom
and rhythm of this play are less intricate than in the poetry
because the imagery and assonance have had to fit the speech
and reactions of many characters and to achieve the dramatic
tension necessary to the stage.

The complexities of Clarke's more personal and more
direct poetry are here diluted for the theatre. Indeed, one
reacts to the language of *The Son of Learning* more immediately and, perhaps as a result, more favourably, than to the

language in the poetry that precedes it. The humour, the drama and the inflected abandon of its speeches are structurally perfect and respond to the theatre's special demands in an assured manner. With this play, a seminal work in his long career, he achieves a new two-fold prominence in his literary development. He has mastered comedy and poetic drama.

(ii)

Poets as diverse as Yeats and Eliot, Auden and Stevens, and cummings and Williams have tried to resurrect a poetic theatre for the twentieth century. There is an implicit devaluation of their efforts, however, in any discussion of a play which centres on language and neglects stagecraft. An obvious and crucial impediment to the experimental re-introduction of poetry as the medium of drama is the implied assertion that verse-drama is more important or more artistic than the plethora of less stylised, often more approachable, plays written in prose. The language of a play in verse is bound to poetic laws. The play can therefore be determined by the written and not the spoken word.

Poetic drama is often idealistic. It seeks to capture moments of dramatic power and eloquence in a language lifted above mundane speech into a grandeur that poetry can more readily communicate than its prosaic descendant, stage-speech. Poetic drama claims for itself a formal structure and intrinsic cohesiveness more intellectually satisfying than those of a prose drama. One could be easily misled, through reading the manifestoes of the poet-dramatists themselves, into considering poetic drama to be an elitist concern. Prose on the stage may be of lesser moment than a poetic encapsulation of similar insight. Yet, poetic drama remains distinctively a minority interest.

The verse-dramatist believes that prose speech is too close to common reality to be significant on the stage. Others could rightly claim that theatrical speech is already formal. Should theatrical speech be made even less natural by the addition of verse rhythms and patterns?[16]

To argue the aesthetics of the language of a play might lead one to forget the dramatic. The Shakespearean critic, G. Wilson Knight, defines the most suitable approach to verse-drama: 'We should regard each play as a visionary whole, close-knit in personification, atmospheric suggestion, and direct poetic symbolism.' [17]

In this century two writers, Yeats and Eliot, have worked more than any others to affect a viable poetic theatre. They are the prime influences on poetic drama in this century, both having worked in different directions towards their individual concepts of theatre. Eliot spent his dramatic career changing the poetic line and rhythm into a new medium which he hoped could compete with prose drama. His is a poetry stripped of grandeur and dramatically inconsequent allusion. Yeats, on the other hand, envisaged a theatre of noble art and unworldly language, and it is with Yeats' influence on Clarke's drama that we must concern ourselves.

The plays of Yeats, which Clarke saw when he was a student, were Clarke's chief inspiration to write for the stage. An anomaly arises here. Clarke, who chose to part with the Yeatsian style of Irish verse, seems now to re-enter the fold. Yeats the playwright is never subjected to the same level of challenge as Clarke directs against Yeats the poet and self-styled grand man of letters. His judgment of Yeats' plays is curiously isolated from his judgment of Yeats' verse. Clarke commends and protects the theatrical writings of a man whose poetry he cannot whole-heartedly esteem. In fact, so moved was Clarke by Yeats' plays and ideas about poetry in the theatre that he founded in 1938, with Roibeárd Ó Faracháin, the Dublin Verse-Speaking Society which developed in 1944 into the Lyric Theatre Company, headed by Clarke himself. This company concerned itself solely with theatrical pro- ductions and performed and broadcast poetic drama in Ireland on the stage and over the radio until the early 1950s.[18]

Avoiding the theorising of a generation of American and European poets who wanted to write for the stage, Clarke was able to approach the matter with a clear-headed and practical intention; he wanted to maintain the tradition in Anglo-Irish theatre which Yeats had begun. In spite of the many pronouncements about what could and could not be allowed on the stage in the name of art and poetry, Clarke wrote his plays with a spontaneity and vitality that never allow his drama to flounder in poeticisms, stilted perfections or mere propaganda.

Yeats' plays moved Clarke profoundly. When he wrote his own poetic drama he tried to maintain an equally tense and forceful conception of action and poetry. Clarke's plays are not so pure or ritualistic as Yeats' verse-dramas, but for Clarke the theatre was to be a more widely communicative medium than it was for his master.

Yeats' plays are a highly wrought, beautifully artificed medium of dramatic expression. They are extremely different in style, movement and language from Clarke's verse plays. Whereas Yeats' poetic line became a specifically personal idiom — even further refined in the philosophical and mythological meditations of his plays — Clarke's language and personality, so obvious in the poetry, are not so evident in the plays. Clarke's plays are less intricate than the impassioned complexities of his poetry. Perhaps this truth underlies Clarke's championship of Yeats, the playwright. Yeats' poetic theatre is far from a sterile exercise in technique. It is an imaginatively vital, viable departure for the stage. His plays are highly emotive meditations on heroism, the individual and life's spiritual order. Yeats' drama is less concerned with his public image than is his poetry. His theatre does not shape or demand a social reality and does not, therefore, distort the poet's reading of Ireland to fit an aesthetic demand. Clarke, therefore, would have been more favourable to this side of Yeats' creativity.

Clarke's plays portray a comic, anti-heroic world, and his half-rhymes, his unrarefied, at times crude, idiom reinforce his world view. Anier MacConglinne is like no character in Yeats' plays, but Clarke nevertheless acknowledges kinship with Yeats. Both playwrights deserve critical acclaim because, in their separate ways, Yeats and Clarke maintained in Irish literature the tradition of a poetic theatre when that tradition was dying, if not already dead, on the stages of America and England.

One could engage in a lengthy dissertation about poetic drama and the aesthetics and intentions behind the crusade to revive a lost genre. The topic has engaged many critics of this century. In his autobiography, *A Penny in the Clouds*, Clarke recalls his direct experience of poetic drama in perhaps the only theatre ever administrated, directed and used by a poet to develop his own ideals:

the plays of Yeats were a deeply imaginative experience, and, as the poet put on his own plays as often as possible,

the experience was a constant one. On such occasions
the theatre was almost empty. . . . Perhaps the actors
spoke the lyric lines in tones that had become hollow-
sounding with time, borrowing the archaic voice which
is normally reserved for religious services. It seemed
right that the poetic mysteries should be celebrated
reverently and with decorum. . . . Scarcely had the
desultory clapping ceased, when Yeats would appear
outside the stage curtain, a dim figure against the foot-
lights. He swayed and waved rhythmically, telling humbly
of his 'little play', how he had rewritten it, and what he
had meant to convey in its lines. . . . I enjoyed the poet's
curtain-lecture, almost as if it were a special benefit
performance for myself. . . . I did not realize at the time
that poetic drama was slowly vanishing from the Abbey
Theatre. It seems to me now that, conspicuously or not,
the poet might have been making a last despairing gesture
to call attention, not to his own picturesque person, but
to the struggling cause of poetry on the stage.

(*Penny*, 4)

In an end-note to his own *Collected Plays* Clarke once
more harkens back to those 'semi-legendary years when a
poet had his own theatre in Dublin. The Abbey actors who
performed the plays of W.B. Yeats spoke the lines with great
reverence. Despite my awe, I longed for more boldness on the
stage' (*Plays*, 397-8).

(iii)

Clarke's plays are more gently comic than either the invective
of his later poetry or the satire of his novels would lead one
to believe possible. In writing for the stage Clarke learned to
refine his language and pare his perceptions down to what is
absolutely essential. He claimed, however, to write for a
'bolder stage' wherein 'the drama of racial conscience' could
be fully explored. Yet it is surprising to discover that much
of his verse-drama is irrelevant to his later work. Many of
Clarke's plays are poor excuses for drama and offer little
insight into the development of the controlled language we
witness in the work which followed them.

The Son of Learning was full of promise. Yet some of the

plays are so obscure that they can only be understood through supplementary reading. There are plays which are dramatically captivating or interesting in purely literary terms but there is also dross. Severe discrimination is necessary to preserve those plays worthy of presentation. For the good plays are surely good and represent, 'after Yeats' dramatic work, the most impressive body of verse-plays in Anglo-Irish literature'.[19] Some of the longer plays, however, *Black Fast*, *Sister Eucharia*, *The Plot is Ready*, *The Moment Next to Nothing*, and perhaps *The Plot Succeeds* are hardly memorable.

Black Fast (1941) is definitely a failed play which leaves one wondering if the subject matter deserved dramatic treatment. Subtitled by Clarke 'a poetic farce', it is nevertheless not funny. 'The seventh century controversy over the exact date of Easter' and the ensuing 'culinary complications' (Clarke's introductory note on the background of the play) is best seen not as theatre but as history.

Characterisation is weak or almost non-existent, most of the cast being distinguished by their costumes only. The play's major concern is not a spectacle or intrigue but a learned debate, a clerical argument culled from Bede, as Clarke admits in his own preamble. The subject is best left to historical discussion. There is magic in *Black Fast* and humour, but their slightness extends the already apparent void in dramatic tension. Some humour is provided by an abbot's astonished condemnation of feminine wiles and sin:

> foolish women
> Who dig up beauty from the very clay,
> Redden their lips, unbar the modest stitch
> At neck and ankle that eye may find
> A short-cut to false Edens.
>   (*Plays*, 125-6)

But the humour is largely irrelevant and burdened with the author's intention to expose the human frailty behind supposedly infallible dogma. *Black Fast* earns our interest with its ideas and not with its drama.

The play is intellectually interesting for the hypocrisy it exposes. *Black Fast* is apposite to most of Clarke's other writings because of its emphasis on the faults of the clergy, but if Clarke's writing can be described as an attempt to re-define the Irish tradition, then the author is vulnerable to the failings evident in this play. Documentation is always ready to overcome literature.

Sister Eucharia (1939) is also based on an argument. Unlike the cast in *Black Fast*, the nuns here emerge as individual characters who are caught up in a drama which none can resolve. There is dramatic form and tension. The sceptical old nun contrasts well with the younger, more credulous nuns. The mother superior assumes the middle ground in the argument about Eucharia's saintliness: a point of view close to true orthodoxy but unfortunately also reminiscent of Shaw's view, that a miracle is any event which can inspire faith, in *Saint Joan*. The parallel, however unintentional, points to the central weakness of *Sister Eucharia* as a play. The symmetry of the cast (old to young, novice to superior, char to saint), the control evident in the assonantally rhyming dialogue, and the domestic hustle and bustle of the convent all obscure the disquiet and unease caused by a masochistic woman bent on distinction from her company of equals. The priest surely fails in this light, too. A young woman unashamedly deforms herself, seeking sainthood in brutal self-destruction, yet no one in the cast questions very deeply this black parody of sanctity. As a result, *Sister Eucharia* is a well-structured play that says little, remaining slight in spite of its complex and potentially dramatic theme. The conflict central to *Sister Eucharia* was more succinctly stated by Clarke in *Twice Round the Black Church*: 'There are thousands of martyrs to rheumatism and horrible diseases; few can escape suffering, yet we marvel at the self-infliction of pain or discomfort' (*Black Church*, 102).

The Plot is Ready (1944) is a better play, displaying a finer handling of character and argument. It is saved from being tedious by the sexual tension at its centre and also by its vivid evocation of magic, a power beyond that of any monk or mortal in the play. It is, however, thematically derivative. *The Plot is Ready* unfortunately reminds one constantly of Yeats' masterly *The Only Jealousy of Emer* in which a hero also dies in the presence of wife and mistress. Yeats' magic is symbolic and transcendent, his hero mythic and his women real and supernatural. Clarke, in contrast, offers a snarling monarch, a bitchily determined wife, a very real mistress, interfering clergy and a trick that, as magic, is debatably humorous.

The Viscount of Blarney (1944) is somewhat of a departure,
set in recent times (of the longer plays, it is the only one
which moves away from history and the cloister) and written
for the stage or radio. The fact that it can be performed for
radio is an important consideration in defining its structure
and dialogue. Though the play is experimental, it must be
admitted that *The Viscount of Blarney* gains much of its
power from Clarke's structural finesse. A technical skill
covers dialogue that is at times over-written.

It is easily read as a parable of the young in Ireland, whose
fears, superstitions and inhibitions create a fearful reality
from which Cauth Morrissey escapes with the help of a kindly
schoolmaster. Her upbringing as an orphan in a charitable
institution distorts her perceptions and understanding of the
world around her. She is confronted with the Pooka, the
Devil, an old hag, and the terrors of damnation, of drowning
and of childbirth. (By a playful twist, the Pooka and the
Devil are seen as contradictory characters, whereas they are
usually identified with each other in Irish tradition.) As a
child, Cauth is frightened by adult fears translated into childish
and phantasmagoric terms. The dénouement, with her rescue
and the schoolmaster's explanation that the forbidden corner
of the barn held no evil — indeed nothing more frightful than
a brooding hen — should be cathartic. In a land where suppression is the password into paradise, Cauth Morrissey exemplifies the potential hysteric who is unable to command
saintly honour. She will either succumb to the primitive fears
and imaginings revealed in her simple conversations with the
demons, or, like the schoolmaster, learn the root of fear and
live a freer life.

The macabre elements in the play — hints of murdered
children, orphans in slavery and the enigmatic, foul secret of
Ireland (What is in the midwife's bag: miscarried child or
slaughtered baby?) — underscore Cauth's neuroses. Many of
the elements of her fantasies are more infantile, bound up
with toy horses, rides beyond the stars and eerily glowing red
fires. The Pooka, who emerges as a real character instead of a
fantastic apparition, reinforces this interpretation by his
continual befriending of children. Who but a child would
seek love and friendship, adventure and protection, from a
phantom? The Pooka answers a deep need in Cauth's being

for security and affection and he points clearly to the primary source of childish nightmares:

POOKA:
                    Why are you shaking?
CAUTH:
I saw it twice when I was smaller,
Rising from mud floor, sill and wall.
What was it, Pooka?
POOKA:
                    Noah's flood,
That's sent to castigate the young
At night. They huddle half asleep
Because their minds have grown too big
For them and keep on falling, falling
Into the pit their terror digs.
Then wide awake, all of a sudden,
They see that flood-gleam, hide their heads
Beneath the bedclothes, see that flood-gleam
And are so much afraid of it,
They cannot scream until the fit
Is over.

(*Plays*, 229)

The logic of dream-reality is ideally matched by the many-faceted changes in setting and atmosphere in this play. *The Viscount of Blarney* has a structure readily adaptable to dramatic and powerful radio performance. Yet this very adaptability points to a possible flaw in the play. This work is very close in feeling to the surrealistic creations of the dream-obsessed film director, Luis Bunuel. The Spaniard, Bunuel, is, like Clarke, aware of the squalid suppressions in a Catholic country with a populace still composed largely of small farmers. In *The Discreet Charm of the Bourgeoisie*, Bunuel explores the perpetual neuroses of his authoritarian and corrupt society. His medium and methods are infinitely more sophisticated and his manner more challenging than Clarke's, but the analogy is apt. Bunuel is a more cynical artist than Clarke and dismisses any optimistic dream of liberation. The film's assault on the bourgeois social complex of Spain is unremitting and it is far more complicated than Clarke's play.

Yet Clarke — writing for the radio — has mastered a method which allows an exploration of reality through psychological perception and association. A radio play must work on several levels at once, engaging one with an interesting story-line but forcing depth into every word because it depends almost entirely on dialogue for its effect. Here, the words are relatively simple, however, and are innocently buried in an ever-shifting atmosphere. One reads deeper meaning into them only later.

As a stage play, *The Viscount of Blarney* is technically difficult because of the constantly shifting and gloomily evocative scene-changes, and the sudden emergence from the many layered dream-sequences into reality. Phantoms and human beings cross the same stage without seeing one another. Yet they must convey the idea that they are talking to invisible characters at the same time, a situation which strains the abilities of any cast and director. One must admire Clarke's technical virtuosity. With few stage effects, a concentration on lighting and a skilful manipulation of sparse stage pro-perties, *The Viscount of Blarney* evokes an intense emotional territory. The play demonstrates Clarke's understanding of both stage and radio.

It is a valuable work of apprenticeship in that it raises the issues involved in Clarke's master radio-drama, *As The Crow Flies*. His exploration of dreams in *The Viscount of Blarney* is an artistic problem which Clarke will attack again. He may have been trying to achieve a mode of expression which would allow greater scope for his social commentary. That he later chooses not the dream-sequence but direct polemic is no dis-misssal of this play.

Clarke's play, *As The Crow Flies*, arguably his most tightly constructed and most strongly evocative dramatic work, is subtitled 'a lyric drama for the air'. A radio play is different from stage drama. It contains no spectacle or visual dis-tractions which, as we have already seen, Clarke handles sometimes at cost to his drama.

In a radio play all power resides in speech; the writer can only imply a visual setting for his work. W.H. Auden explained this more powerfully: 'The imagination of the listener is not spoiled by any collision with visual reality.'[20] Louis MacNeice, a radio dramatist worthy of study, declared that the 'first virtue of a radio script is construction'.[21] The radio offers unique opportunities to a poet who can choose his voices and

avoid the directorial subversion of text so common in contemporary theatre. Like a film, the radio play permits almost
instantaneous changes in location and time. The radio actor is
not obliged to use his whole body to achieve a convincing
characterisation. His characterisation is concentrated in his
voice. The audience of a radio play is more easily persuaded
to accept the incongruous or the fabulous. This is because the
radio play demands an active imagination of its listeners;
where one cannot see, one must imagine. In short, the poet is
given the chance to try his hand at drama without having to
adjust his love of words to meet theatrical convention. 'All
physical action and all mass behaviour has to take place, so
to speak, "offstage", as conventional noises.'[22] The writer of
a radio play, working solely with words and noises, can create
a very intense and haunting play.

In *As The Crow Flies* (1943), Clarke exploits these opportunities magnificently. It is a memorable and beautiful work.
Once again he confronts us with the supernatural in the form
of a storm that is metaphorically rich in poetry, terror and
grim humour.

The plot is simple enough. Three monks seek shelter in a
cave because a storm has made their trip down the Shannon
impossible. One of the monks, Aengus, who has found the
cave and believes it to be the sanctified, ancient dwelling of a
hermit is exposed to voices and presences from a pagan
mythological past. Those presences are animals rich in
allusive meaning and significance. There is an eagle and her
eaglets. The Crow of Achill lures the eagle from the nest so
that he can eat the young. The eagle, while away, consults
the Stag of Leiterlone, the Salmon of Assaroe and the Blackbird of Derrycairn, who all discuss the weather and life's
meaning, finally alerting the eagle that her duties as a mother
have been neglected. On her return to the nest, the eagle
discovers her young have been devoured and keens through
the wind for their loss. Brother Manus hears none of this, and
frets his time in the cave worrying about the next stage of the
journey down the river. Father Virgilius hears part of the
animals' discourse but is able to accommodate such pagan
reality within his Christian beliefs. Aengus, however, cannot
reconcile all that he hears (the natural, undoctrined world
most fully represented by the Blackbird of Derrycairn) with
his Christianity and is cast out from the religious community

at the play's end.

Father Virgilius' advice to the younger monk that one can channel one's perceptions and quest for understanding in a single direction is found to be inadequate. Vergilius' Christian Faith can encompass both Christian orthodoxy and pre-Christian myths. He senses no contradiction in his references to the magical, pagan world of Finn. There is a subtle irony in his assurances:

> VIRGILIUS:
> God bless us all. I must
> Have nodded again. My head was in the sun . . .
> My eyes are gilded by it.
> > Brother Manus
> The best of spirits came upon the journey
> With us to-day.
> MANUS:
> > Father, I am uneasy
> Now. We've been resting on our oars too long
> And Brother Aengus is still away.
> VIRGILIUS:
> > We've time
> Enough upon our hands. We can be back
> At Clonmacnoise before the midnight bell rings.
> MANUS:
> But you don't know the Shannon, Father. This
> > boat-load
> Of rushes will be heavier than our faults
> The more we pull against it. Brother Aengus
> Should never have gone into the forest
> Alone.
> VIRGILIUS:
> > God will protect him.
> MANUS:
> But why did you let him go?
> VIRGILIUS:
> > Because he is young.
> And the young see but the eye in every bolt
> That keeps them from the meaning of Creation.
> Yes, they want all that breathing space
> Before bird, beast or reptile had been named
> And pain started the first rib.

MANUS:

But, Father . . .
I know too well what you are going to say,
Manus. For twenty years you've chased the raindrops
From Clonmacnoise with crossbeam, patches, glue-
    pot.
Whenever we dare to sneeze, you give a nail
Another rap and heal us with your hammer;
And if our old bones creak too much in church,
You hurry up the rungs to mend a joint
Or clap a comfortable cap of stone
About our chilling pates.

MANUS:

That's true.
But why did Father Abbot send me out
To cut him rushes in the wilderness?

VIRGILIUS:
Perhaps he sent you here
To learn the mercy of the elements.

MANUS:
Well, maybe so.

VIRGILIUS:

Do take
Another look at those gigantic reeds.
Whoever saw green toppings half their size
On any roof? They might have been cut down
To floor the heel of Finn. The very Salmon
Of Knowledge mentioned by the storytellers
Could scarcely jump their height.

MANUS:

I do not like
The look of them. They are unlucky, Father.

VIRGILIUS:
Well, then, we'll bless them in the shed
And sacristan will dip a few for me
When he has fired our own fasciculi.
Good soul, he hates to see me annotating
A manuscript at night. But they will strengthen
My hand and dry my ageing eyes . . .

MANUS:

Pardon
Me, Father. I see big clouds upon the hob.

We should be gone.
VIRGILIUS:
                    Call Aengus. He is sure
To hear you from that rock there.
                              (*Plays*, 165-7)

In the cave only Virgilius can interpret the voices and the
chaos, and he, like the eagle and the stag, remembers other
storms. All creatures, it would seem, need a past frame of
reference to help them come to terms with and weaken
present fears. Virgilius is calm within his catechism:

                                        And yet
Aengus, you want to be a hermit.
                                        God
Has let us hear the voices of the fallen.
His pleasure is revealed by miracle.
Kneel down, kneel down. The three of us will pray
Together.
                              (*Plays*, 172)

The phantoms of this play are not mere figments of the
monks' superstitious imaginations. They are the legendary
animals of Irish tradition, visitors from a pagan other-world
who strike terror into human hearts. Even the neglected
Blackbird of Derrycairn has its rightful place in this scheme
of things.

The Blackbird of Derrycairn was brought to Ireland by
Finn after one of his adventures in Norway. The tradition of
Gaelic poetry was that while Finn and Patrick (or some
equally important Christian figure) debated the issues of
pagan belief and heavenly salvation, the bird sang from its
perch on Finn's shoulder. The song is a counterpoint to both
the Christian and the pagan interpretations of life. It is a
metaphor for nature itself, transcending human moral debate.
The song the blackbird sings parodies actual birdsong and is
a magnificent imitation of a Gaelic fragment:

Stop, stop and listen for the bough top
Is whistling and the sun is brighter
Than God's own shadow in the cup now!
Forget the hour-bell. Mournful matins

Will sound, Patric, as well at nightfall.

Faintly through mist of broken water
Fionn heard my melody in Norway.
He found the forest track, he brought back
This beak to gild the branch and tell, there,
Why men must welcome in the daylight.

He loved the breeze that warns the blackgrouse,
The shouts of gillies in the morning
When packs are counted and the swans cloud
Loch Erne, but more than all those voices
My throat rejoicing from the hawthorn.

In little cells behind a cashel,
Patric, no handbell gives a glad sound.
But knowledge is found among the branches.
Listen! The song that shakes my feathers
Will thong the leather of your satchels.

                                        (*Plays*, 178)

The poem appears in the *Collected Poems* (203). In his notes
to it Clarke explains that it is based 'on Lon Doire an Chairn,
one of the early Ossianic lays'. The bird delays the beginning
of the narrative with rhetorical flourishes until this lovely
poem becomes almost moronically repetitive. Its insistence
that 'knowledge is found among the branches' is anti-Christian
and very like that in the last great poems Clarke was to write,
especially 'The Trees of the Forest'.

Despite the humorous impatience of the other creatures,
the blackbird underlines the conflict in the play. Patrick's
Christian interpretations and teachings are negated by the
lessons of nature. The birdsong embodies a doctrine which no
theology, in its comparative simplicity, can approach.

Virgilius' resignation to the will of God and to the wonder
of His miracles is a safe and expedient human solution. The
Salmon of Knowledge cannot rest so easily, however. It is he
who explains the Crow of Achill, as the incarnation of evil,
the bird of ill omen and the scavenger of life:

            That was the Crow
Of Achill and well I know her ways.
Mummified fingers of the plaything
She gave her children with the great ring

Carbuncled by the jewellers
Of Egypt — that was the hand of Nuadha.
Aye, at Moytura, she despoiled
Many a hero. In his boyhood
Cuchullin was her friend. She croaked
Three times upon the pillarstone
Before he died. She was alone
With him in his last moment. Mist
Of blood had hid her from his fist.
She ripped the lashes from each lid
And blinded him.
                        Homeless with age,
Her food has changed but not her guile.
On stormy nights when she has crept
Upon her belly like a reptile
Into a nest and the frightened chicks
Cry out that some thing cold and wicked
Is sticking to their mother's wing,
She tells her story, makes excuses
(if they are very small and juicy)
To send their parent far away,
That she may overlay and kill them.
                        (*Plays*, 185-6)

And the salmon knows the price of knowledge. He becomes
an exile from reason and the accepted norms of understanding
in this world. Addressing the eagle, he includes all creation in
his lament:

                        How can you guess,
Poor bird, dressing your carrion meat
With highflown feet, that every creature
We know is eaten by disease
Or violent blow! We are unseasoned,
Unsensed, unearthed, riddle-diddled
By what is hidden to the reason.
How can the forethought of defilement
Be reconciled with any faith
That teaches mortals to be mild?
A thousand years, I waited, prayed
And all my fears were only answered
By agony of ignorance.

How must reality be named
If carnal being is so shamed?
From this humiliating body
And brutal brain, these loathsome scales
Itching with lice that no salt water
Can purify, I cry to God
To pity my madness.

                                                    (*Plays*, 183)

His God is not Virgilius' God. The sheer brutality of this
other co-existent, incongruous world is seen by the youngest
monk, Aengus, and tragically understood. Aengus loses the
reason of faith which Virgilius upholds when, leaving the cave
after the storm, the monks see the crazed, keening eagle and
the two worlds of the play suddenly and startlingly overlap:

AENGUS:
              Look . . . Look . . . that speck within
The sky.
VIRGILIUS:
                    Where?
AENGUS:
                              Coming swiftly from the north.
VIRGILIUS:
I cannot see it.
AENGUS:
                                   Now a cloud
Has hidden it.
              There, there it is again.
It is the eagle.
MANUS:
                              Aengus is right. It is
An eagle. Never have I seen so fast
A goer.
VIRGILIUS:
                    I can see her now above
Us.
MANUS:
         She is turning.
                              She is striking from
The air.
AENGUS:

          No she is swooping to the cliff
Above the cave-mouth.
VIRGILIUS:
                          This is very strange.
But why is she hovering so heavily?
Why does she dash her wings against the rock
Like that?
MANUS:
                  She must be wounded in the breast.
AENGUS:
I know, I know.
VIRGILIUS:
                          What are you saying, Aengus?
AENGUS:
I've known it all the time.
                                  She is too late.
Her little ones are dead.
VIRGILIUS:
                          What do you mean,
My son? Why is your habit shivering?
Why are you frightened?
AENGUS:
                          Father, Father, I know
The ancient thought that men endure at night.
What wall or cave can hide us from that knowledge?
                                  (*Plays*, 187-8)

The awesome power of this play is achieved by Clarke's
amalgamating his early botched attempts to deal with the
legends of Ireland's *pre-history*, the fragmentary legends
that abound in *historical* medieval manuscripts, and the
ever-present Irish countryside. He has used this material to
explore in an impersonal way his spiritual doubts, which are
elsewhere handled in a more self-conscious, confessional
style. The knowledge that the salmon imparts to Aengus is
all the more unsettling because the structure of the play
with its flawless meld of whimsy, legend, fear and shock
resists easy interpretation. The workings of the universe are
shown to be irrational, anarchic and sometimes horrifying.
This is Clarke's answer to the enigma of existence. This is the
truth that Aengus comes to accept, and it is also behind
Father Virgilius' statement that one must learn 'the mercy of

the elements'. Clarke's play is a powerful evocation of impersonal nature.

The Plot Succeeds (1950) is very different from the earlier *The Plot is Ready*. Indeed, the earlier work was one of Clarke's most tedious, derivative and unexceptional plays; the contrast between the two lies in the excitement of the later play. If nothing else, *The Plot Succeeds* is a spectacular entertainment, fitly subtitled 'a poetic pantomime'. It is a lighthearted play which revolves only fitfully around religious ideas, political history and major events. Its high spirits remind us of Anier MacConglinne (without the satire). Manannaun MacLir provides jests and devilry. Clarke's last collection of epic poetry, *The Cattledrive in Connaught*, was dedicated to Manannaun MacLir, the sea god. His 'Prologue' to this play is the poem, 'The Son of Lir' from that collection (*Poems*, 117). Mongan's farcical attempts to regain his wife — he lost her in a card game — provide the conflict of the play. Bedroom intrigue, mistaken identities, magic spells and much spoofing bind the work together. Before he wrote *The Moment Next to Nothing*, *The Plot Succeeds* was the longest play in his repertoire, which is surprising for such a light-hearted work.

In 1953, Clarke published his last major play, *The Moment Next to Nothing*. Clarke's novel, *The Sun Dances at Easter*, was banned in Ireland. Because there was no theatrical censorship in Ireland (except the self-imposed and usually self-righteous managerial and directorial censorship), the play is a theatrical translation of the banned book.

Unfortunately, it palls when compared with the superior novel. The compressed, tightly-knit novel in which the story of Eithne and Ceasan is but one element, is here spun out into Clarke's longest play, and dramatic invention cannot save this long-winded, extra-dramatic endeavour. *The Moment Next to Nothing* once again challenges Christian doctrine. The daughter of a pagan God is found and indoctrinated by a Christian hermit who cannot, despite his growing love for her, save her from the otherworld. His love is depicted subtly in its growth from physical attraction to zeal for her soul and his final renunciation of both. The monk is thus forced to acknowledge the existence of a natural realm which St Patrick's doctrines ignored. Because the story dealt with forbidden subjects, Clarke lost much popularity with the Irish public.

His dramatisation of the novel was a sorry exercise in any event. *The Moment Next to Nothing* is tediously simple. Articles of faith are explained at great length and puzzled over at even greater length. One dreads to think that there is a possible, but surely dreary, ironic deflation intended. It seems as if Clarke, angered by the censors, has chosen to annoy his audience as well. When one reads the endnote ('the story may have been a myth of the struggle of two gods for a goddess'), there is an unmistakable sense of loss and missed opportunity. How different this play is from its possible complement, *As The Crow Flies*!

The first play Clarke wrote after *The Son of Learning* also challenged Christian obedience. *The Flame* (1930) — though hardly as complex as the three or four recognisably good plays by Clarke — is nonetheless a fine play. The story is developed rather quietly. It concerns a novice's rebellion and the effect of her rebellion on a community of nuns in Kildare. Nothing is so startling as Attracta's possession and her chanted insubordination as she flashes her head of curls before the shrine of Brigid. This is the ancient, now conventualised, flame of Brigid, that same figure of Celto-Romanesque controversy who exercised a deep influence on Clarke's imagination in 'Wandering Men'. The process by which Attracta loses her selfhood and the resolution of her panic into submissive prayer are deftly handled.

Much of the play's impact is derived from an imaginative handling of stage properties. The stage is sparsely decorated, according to the directions, so that attention focuses on the eternal enigma of the fire. With a subtle manipulation of lighting at climactic moments, carefully controlled by the author's stage directions throughout, much dramatic intensity is gained.

The Flame is a subdued masterpiece. It stands beside *The Son of Learning, The Viscount of Blarney*, and *As The Crow Flies* as equal testament to Clarke's belief in and ability to write for an Irish poetic theatre. One must dismiss a large number of Clarke's plays as derivative or tedious, but this is a necessary step in defining the particular dramatic voice Clarke achieved, a voice which is strong, controlled and challenging. The anger and polemic of the late poetry is conveyed in the plays through the more diffuse vehicle of verse-drama, and appears less direct, less extreme. The stamp of Clarke's personality, however, is no less evident in these plays, on which his reputation must stand: *The Son of Learning, The Flame, The Viscount of Blarney,* and *As The Crow Flies.* These four plays share none of the mediocrities of his other dramatic works, and justify unequivocally the assertion that he is dramatist as much as master-poet.

(iv)

Clarke wrote other plays which fall into a distinct group; they are short, unassuming, light, amusing, even bawdily hilarious. There are seven such plays: *The Kiss, The Second Kiss, The Silent Lover, The Student from Salamanca, The Impuritans, The Third Kiss* and *Liberty Lane.* They share a delightful concern with words and an equally flippant unconcern with 'real' action. In this they resemble the masques of an earlier time, intellectual titbits with no intention except that of poetic entertainment. No romantic or tragedian could have written any of these plays, which are the repertoire of an artist concerned not only with public theatre but also with the elegance and consciousness of his art. And Clarke's 'Classicism' is everywhere evident in these dramatic diversions.

The Kiss (1944) and *The Second Kiss* (1946) are two short, idyllic pieces written in elegant couplets and telling the delicate story of Pierrot, an ingenuous and love-struck young man. In the first the gallant and honourable young man kisses a hag and she is transformed into the girl of his dreams:

> PIERROT:
> All property is sacred in this land.
> When patriots can pick the public purse
> But not the private pocket, what is worse
> Than petty larceny? To rob more pence
> And not a bank increases the offence.
> If company directors are promoted
> For fraudulence and deputies have voted
> Large pensions for possession of a rifle,
> It is indictable to steal a trifle.
> Your takings are too modest, Madam ... Miss ...
> UIRGEAL:
> In that case, I will give you back your kiss.
>
> *(Plays, 152)*

The social satire is light, and the pair continue to debate the problems of love and their responsibilities to society:

UIRGEAL:
          But, Pierrot, you forget
One thing.
PIERROT:
          What is it? Let me know the worst.
UIRGEAL:
Morality. We must be married first,
If I am to be yours.
PIERROT:
          Then be my wife.
UIRGEAL:
You really mean it?
PIERROT:
          Darling, share my life.
UIRGEAL:
That would be very charming, Pierrot.
PIERROT:
          I would
Purchase a caravan of painted plywood,
All weather white, with cupboard, pantry, shelves,
A tiny sitting-room just for ourselves.
With innocent amusements we would pass
The summer, chaining daisies in the grass.
          (*Plays*, 155)

Uirgeal, masked and seen by Pierrot only as Columbine, the girl of his dreams, leaves him. The shock and pain are gleefully transmuted. As the play ends, Pierrot carves her real name on a tree.

Columbine appears again in *The Second Kiss*, a more obvious play with which Clarke has much fun. The play opens with a kiss which, according to the author's directions at the outset, 'should exceed by three seconds the emotional duration allowed by the Film Censor, for there is no Irish stage censorship yet' (*Plays*, 249). We watch Pierrot, now married to Pierrette, chafe under the mundane role of husband:

PIERROT:
          Let's misbehave!

Do something shocking!
PIERRETTE:

                             Quite impossible!
We're married now.

                    Come home to bed.
PIERROT:

                                     Who fell
Asleep at nine last night?
PIERRETTE:

                          I did.

PIERROT:

                              Then stay
Up late to-night . . .

              and we'll perform a play.
                          (*Plays*, 250)

This level of artifice is maintained throughout the play. Pierrot, upset by the tempter Harlequin and confronted with his dream of Columbine, tries desperately to regain his balance by reading the script:

    'A Comedy' . . . this light is much too dim . . .
    'By Austin Clarke' . . . I never heard of him.
                         (*Plays*, 256)

Connubial bliss restored, Pierrot and Pierrette leave the stage and retire to bed. Neither play demands very much from its audience beyond a leisurely indulgence of the playwright. Clarke seems to enjoy the ironic tension between illusion and reality which co-exist on the stage. If this dreaming is how life might be lived, the audience is made continually aware that reality is very much more complicated. Perhaps their dreamlike existence, so strangely simple except for the beautiful but unreal speech-patterns of Pierrot and wife, is cause in itself for humour.

Clarke's 1968 publication of *Two Interludes Adapted From Cervantes* illustrates the link between his short plays and the masque.[23] An interlude is, in its manner and presentation, the predecessor of the more regal masque:

It is not certain that the genre (interlude) was originally intended to be part of a banquet, but a tradition has grown up that it was. . . . Quite often the plays would have about one thousand lines, which suggests that they would not be the sole reason for assembling the audience, and one looks for other reasons which might provide the chief motive, a feast perhaps, or other items of display, agility, or music. The brevity of many interludes meant that the dramatic content must be simple, so that the great cosmic sweep of the mystery cycle and the morality play had to be cut down. . . . Nevertheless the action was often sufficiently complex to allow a mixture of comic and serious. The comedy might only be the mockery of a foolish or misguided hero, but there is a persistent concern to make the audience laugh, which suggests two things: an attempt to work out the serious effects of comedy; and the insistent demand that the audience be entertained.[24]

Clarke mentions in his introduction to these interludes that the original interlude would have been performed between morality plays during the later Middle Ages and early Renaissance. Considering the bawdiness of his offerings to the genre, this might seem an ironic comment on literary history. The interlude, however, descended from the platitudinous heights of the morality to comedy and social drama:

> Whereas the comic episodes in the moralities often signified moral depravity, they are much more complex in the interludes. The comic roles are expanded, and in some cases . . . the comedy becomes a matter of verbal ingenuity rather than crude farce. . . . Nevertheless farce remained a mainstay of the interlude, and the lack of decorum which the fooling entailed was the cause of much critical distaste at the end of the sixteenth century.[25]

Clarke's borrowings from Cervantes are ribald and remind the reader of the coarser comedies of Ben Jonson, whose own light and often grotesque interludes were equally bawdy and earned the generic title, anti-masque.[26]

Both *The Student from Salamanca* and *The Silent Lover* are farces about cuckoldry, elaborate exercises in sly, sexual innuendo. Neither plot is very complex and, although the

story of the wife and her accomplice who outwit a doting,
boring husband is an old story, common to farce and medieval
fabliau, Clarke offers a few wittily eloquent variations. In the
first play we watch Leonarda weep and wail, manipulating
her husband's departure. The dialogue is full of puns and
other richly suggestive, risqué language:

> LEONARDA:
> Good-bye to that foolery.
> The front and back o' my farthingale to you!
> Christina, he's never done, taking me out of
> My flounces, my petticoats, my nothings-on. Fancy,
> He wants to suck my cream and pink, as though
> I were a sweet to roll around on his tongue,
> Touch everywhere at once, impossible
> In matrimony, melt my sugar'd plums
> Between his gums. What wife could be contented
> With similes?
> CRISTINA:
> I thought your hugs, bye-bying,
> Would fetch his slippers, and spoil our goings-on
> To-night.
> LEONARDA:
> You mean our takings off! I wonder
> Whether our guests will really come.
>
>   (9)

The double-edged reveries of the women about their lovers,
a sacristan and a barber, display Clarke's verbal agility and
bawdy humour at their best:

> LEONARDA:
> All thanks to my sacristan — as generous
> As ever. When he spits, rubs, polishes
> His candlesticks, I am pure wax, wick-end
> Ready for spark. When he unchains and lifts up
> The thurible, I burn, all frankincense
> And fragrance. But O when he pulls the bell-rope, I
> Go up, go down — up, down — and cannot stop
> Myself until the clapper hangs again.
> And I am always late for evening devotions.
> CRISTINA:

And what about my Nicholas? My barber,
My basin holder and apothecary?
He manicures, he pedicures me, pounds
An opening physic when I need it, Madam.
He tilts the swivel chair when I am soapy
And shaves me where he shouldn't with long smooth
    strokes,
As though I were a Moorish dancing girl,
And, as you know, shampoos and sprays my person,
Turns on the nozzle of perfume until I kick
Up heels in my delight.

                                                    (10)

Before the first act is over, the sacristan himself displays an
equally obscene turn of phrase, using ecclesiastical borrowings
and erudition to avoid the crude or inelegant expletives he
has in mind:

REPONCE:
                                            Good evening,
Good evening, lovely ladies, here's a flask
To brim your cantharus, the serpent brew,
Red peppercorns, fiery cantharides,
Let us inebriate, then bifurcate
Gladly until our rude probosities
Conglutinate your vascularities
And share their calefaction.
LEONARDA:
                                    Why will you patter
In Latin like Erasmus? How can I pull down
The meaning if it dangles beyond the round hole
In the ringing loft?
NICHOLAS:
                                The words that I can read
And spell out with my fingers have four letters,
One syllable. But when I oil my strap,
I clean the lather from the razor blade
Before I hone it.

                                                    (12-13)

The dénouement, complicated by the introduction of a lusty
clerical student who begs a night's food and lodging, is

accomplished with song and fraudulent magic.

The Silent Lover treats the same theme with slight variations; this time the husband is quite old and impotent, but
very jealous. The wife explains to her maid when asked if he
keeps the house-keys on his person:

> I've felt him
> All over when he was full of snores, found nothing
> That could be of any use to me.
>
> (25)

Having fully exploited tonsorial and clerical vocabulary for
his risqué dialogue, Clarke now uses imagery culled from the
kitchen as, once more, the woman outsmarts an ignorant,
uncomprehending mate:

LORENZA:

> ... my gallant is here.
> He's at the very centrepiece about to cut
> My wedding cake for the first time, huge slice,
> Raisins and plums, cloves, cinnamon, spice.
> Warm icing melts my marzipan. I feel
> All in a crumble, dear. He wants to peel
> My little tangerines, unpip them, candy
> The pair. He's setting fire now to my brandy.
> How can I stop him porting my ampulla
> And butterflying my angelica?
> He dips his sop in wine until my trifle
> Is sherried, sugared brown. How can I trifle?
> All's in my sponge cake now. My mouth is bliss.

CRISTINA:

> She's pink confectionery like a kiss.
> What is he doing now, dear Auntie, tell me?

LORENZA:

> Why not? He's teaching me the facts of life.
> He's plucking my maidenhair fern, Love-lies-a-
>   bleeding.
> He pollens his arum lily, lightly roams
> Around my rosebuds, unwaxes my honeycombs.
> He jasmines me: magnolias meet:
> Our bushes mingle. He takes me with his sweet,
> Night-scented stock.

CRISTINA:

She's in the Garden

Of Eden now.
HUSBAND:

She's deflowering

The holy language of Teresa with
Her mad vocabulary.

(32-3)

The great anarch who lurks within all Clarke's writings makes
himself well-known in this passage. Even the most innocent
and the most unlikely words can take on sexual overtones in
this play. Clarke proclaims the yearning, awakened sexuality
of all words and human activity. *The Silent Lover* ends in
high spirits, amusement and song. It is not only conventional
for the genre, but supremely fitting.

Both of these adaptations from Cervantes and the 1970
play, *The Impuritans*, should really be discussed in relation to
Clarke's work of the late 1960s and early 1970s in which the
'holy madness' of sexuality is celebrated. The Interludes,
however, are also relevant to many of the conflicts in the
other plays. By 1968, when he published them, Clarke was
freer from repressive censorship and banning, but Irish law
had had its effect. He was accepted as an important Irish poet,
but school curriculums in the Republic of Ireland anthologised
early, safe, unrepresentative poems such as 'The Planter's
Daughter', 'The Lost Heifer' or 'The Fair at Windgap' — not
the stuff to fire student enthusiasm. The theatre-going public
remained largely unaware of his valuable contributions to the
Irish theatrical tradition. And his novels, if not still banned,
were not reprinted. The goal was won in personal and literary
terms, but no one among the public seemed to heed the
struggle anymore.

The Novels

But no mind ever grew fat on a diet of novels.
The pleasure which they occasionally offer is far
too heavily paid for: they undermine the finest
characters. They teach us to think ourselves into
other men's places. Thus we acquire a taste for
change. The personality becomes dissolved in
pleasing figments of imagination. The reader learns
to understand every point of view. Willingly, he
yields himself to the pursuit of other people's
goals and loses sight of his own. Novels are so
many wedges which the novelist, an actor with his
pen, inserts into the closed personality of the reader.
The better he calculates the size of the wedge and
the strength of the resistance, so much more completely does he crack open the personality of his
victim. Novels should be prohibited by the State.

Elias Canetti, *Auto da fé**

(i)

Clarke's three novels are central to an understanding of
his poetry. *The Bright Temptation* (1932), *The Singing
Men at Cashel* (1936) and *The Sun Dances at Easter* (1952)
provide the link which connects his early romantic poetry, the
political satires and invectives of the 1950s and the final great
poems concerned with nature and human sexuality.

The heroes of Clarke's dramas are victims of power, convention and tradition. They manage only occasionally to
achieve a hazardous individual freedom. This desperate
achievement underlies the poetry of the 1950s and early

* Elias Canetti, *Auto da fé*. Penguin, Harmondsworth, 1965, p. 47.

116

1960s which is filled with an explicit crankiness and what may seem senility. These poems are an onslaught against the rules and orders that subvert the individual expression of personality.

Fragments in the poetry (the vignettes of Martha Blake in Rathgar, nuns in Africa, American politicians visiting Ireland, destroyed men in the asylums of Dublin and celebates debating the issues of canonisation and contraception) merge into a larger pattern throughout Clarke's work only when we study and appreciate the full development of the novels.

The sudden shift in Clarke's final poetry towards mythology and natural miracles is explicable most clearly in the transition from the sermonic style of *The Bright Temptation* to the fabulous and intricate pattern of *The Sun Dances at Easter*. In summarising Clarke's career Denis Donoghue states:

> The poet who has emerged to our rueful delight in the past ten years is the prose man, and this is perhaps one way of naming his achievement; that in the years since *Ancient Lights* (1955) Mr Clarke has devised a singing line which moves with the vigour of his own best prose.[1]

The prose which Donoghue praises, however, was banned each time Clarke published a novel. *The Bright Temptation* was republished by the Dolmen Press in 1973. The other two novels were never reprinted and are now very difficult to find.

There evolves in the three novels not only the subtle language of revolt but a new, enlarged definition of life, different from that which informed *Pilgrimage and Other Poems*, a view of the individual and society in which all existence and human experience is a form of political action. In the fullest sense of the word 'political', everything that a character in Clarke's novels may witness, perceive or think about, and anything that he may do, is an action possible only by virtue of, and yet limited by, his social awareness and conditioning. Ultimately women, whose oppression and repression he studies in the novels, represent the human condition. Their behaviour and reception in society shows the essential oppression of the individual in society. A sad image of womankind gives Clarke's first novel its name:

Little wonder that Aidan was scared, for he had seen
Cile-na-gCich.

He had never heard, in fact, of the obscene female
image which was carven on the outside wall of certain
chapels at that time. Gazing in spiritual disgust on this
image, which revealed the true repulsiveness of womankind, the clergy shrank from the impurity of sin, they
snatched their souls from the danger of eternal damnation. True comment of the Celtic-Romanesque age
upon the nature of woman, the crumbling image of
Cil-na-gCich still lingers on ancient ruins, half hidden
by nettles, by thistles, so that the simple are affrighted
by its evil eye. On Lustymore Island, in Kilnaboy, on
that forsaken oratory by the waters of Lough Erne, on
the very pillar of Adamnan at Tara, she dwells in loneliness. But at dark, poets say that Sheila of the Paps still
goes by misty short-cut, by dark wood, hastening, like
the spirit of offended Irish womanhood, to the pillows
of the tonsured. In that midnight hour of temptation
the good clergy hear around them the horrid whispers
of the confession-box.[2]

It is important to remember the passage from an earlier
poem, 'The Young Woman of Beare', which gives the novel
its name:

> I am the bright temptation
> In talk, in wine, in sleep.
> Although the clergy pray,
> I triumph in a dream . . .
> I am the dark temptation
> Men know — and shining orders
> Of clergy have condemned me.
>   (*Poems*, 164-70)

In Clarke's novels it is this spiritual refinement and celibate
horror of feminism and sexuality which concern him. Taboo,
represented by Sheila of the Paps, prevents nothing and can
only pervert the natural innocence which Clarke holds sacred.
From fear comes repression which creates in its turn smug
obscenities. Clarke's concern with the emotional and psychological liberation of his female characters, has as its primary

aim a healthy society. He preaches the doctrine of an un-inhibited, instinctive vitality for men and women. Self-awareness and experience question and overturn the basic assumptions of the social environment in which the novels are set, which, of course, is Ireland past and present. Free-dom in sexuality is a metaphor for social freedom and self-determination. This is the most important theme in Clarke's writing. It underlies and connects the otherwise disparate corpus of his works.

The three novels are also romantic fantasies, which is significant. If Clarke's novels were as subversive as the censor obviously thought, then fantasy can be, in some circumstances, a more powerful — though apparently more subtle — vehicle for polemic than realistic fiction. Fantasy allows the author to impose his idiosyncratic reality upon the story, to trans-cend material experience where necessary and to build an unyielding scaffold of his own invention. Using fantasy, Clarke deftly slips into his stories' controversial ideas in a way that a more realistic narrative would not tolerate. Accept the character or follow his initial actions, and the rest, how-ever contrived, unpredictable or irrational, has its own logical reality. The inner monologues of Clarke's characters are convincing because those characters are explaining their mythic, fantastic existences to the reader. All of Clarke's characters are adept at posing questions which, when answered, alter the reader's ideas about the 'real' world outside the story.

Thomas Kilroy wrote that 'the centre of Irish fiction is the anecdote' and analysed modern Irish writing in terms of story-telling.[3] Clarke's three novels are rooted in this traditional form. What is unique is Clarke's delight and energy in playing with the forms of his stories. The novels move from the sermonic delivery of *The Bright Temptation*, in which the writer, like an old teller of tales, interrupts his narrative to comment upon it and life in general, to the supreme artifice of *The Sun Dances at Easter*, in which story overlays story and the reader must follow several strands of interlaced nar-rative, much in the manner of Celto-Romanesque illumination.

In a delightful sophistry in *The Singing Men at Cashel*, Clarke exposes the methods he employs in his own fictions. Ceallachan is an eleventh century monk whose task is to transcribe historical documents concerning an earlier queen and her husbands. Their story is a paraphrase of the novel we

are reading about Gormlai. The monk finds a fictionalised
love-story about the famous woman and begins to read it:

> It would take him some time to accustom himself to
> the secular manner of language. Absent was the severity
> which he liked and the monastic discipline of phrase,
> the brief logical sentence. Here was the rich many-
> sounding style of oral tradition which, after centuries of
> use and embellishment, had degenerated into flowing
> sentences almost entirely composed of adjectives that
> aired themselves, needlessly, in alliterative order and
> were graded at the same time according to subtle vari-
> ations of meaning, designed to defeat the attention of
> the listeners even while flattering their ears. . . . Moral
> adventures had replaced the old themes of physical
> danger and heroic feats, but in their pretended concern
> for the soul's salvation, the poets concealed their love of
> excited life . . . despite the exaggeration of the unknown
> narrator he could not deny that the praise was merited.
> He was aware that a literary and poetic revival was taking
> place throughout Ireland. . . . once more the pagan
> imagination of the past was astir in the minds of men,
> that the poets in their dark cells were conjuring up
> deceitful visions of immortal beings.
>
> (313-15)

The monk knows his literary history, too, and is able to
comment critically on the love-story:

> It was clear that the storyteller had taken the old
> Elopement Tales for his model, interweaving his own
> fancies with the plain facts. . . . Engrossed in the story
> despite himself, Ceallachan almost seemed to hear the
> sharp splashing of water, the eager cries, the unseemly
> laughter of the pagan women. He heard them so vividly
> indeed that it was some time before he realised that the
> sounds were coming towards his cell. He closed his eyes
> and grasped the desk in superstitious fear, but when he
> looked up, the past had vanished. He was still in the
> eleventh century.
>
> (316-17)

The decadent, flowery style which the monk criticises is the subtle prose Clarke has written, flattering the ears and managing to win the reader's sympathy for Gormlai while distracting the reader from any external frame of reference. Clarke is identified with these lay chroniclers of an earlier era, an identification which is reiterated in the pun that ends the novel. The reader is ingenuously told: 'So far, then, the love-story of Nial and Gormlai, set down by a poor *clerk* to keep body and soul together.' (382, my italics).

(ii)

The Bright Temptation is a carefully subversive fantasy. The picturesque, adventure-filled flight of the young boy and girl across Ireland wins them admiration and sympathy. The misfortunes they endure, the security they win against many odds and the places through which they flee are all depicted with a keen emotional empathy. The countryside itself is a character in the novel, offering by turns danger and solace. Clarke describes a land recognisable in its traditions, inhabitants and natural beauty as Ireland. This pastoral charm is created by merging the particular with the fanciful in a natural and convincing manner:

Aidan was only half-way down the slope. He had stopped a little breathlessly to look around him when Ethna had come to the frets of the pines below. The heather was dark against the bright skies and its shadows were browner than its own honey that comes so late. But the spotlike clusters of the whortleberries were quivering in the breeze here and there: they might have been pale-green steps that led down from every side to the tiny glen.

'How pleasant it is!' cried Ethna as they stood together, looking up at the amber-stemmed pines, lofty and clear-branched above the rocks. A stream was hurrying past them from pool to pool.

'See how the sun and shade, like dear soul-friends, share alike and are at peace.'

'These must be the last trees, for they have forgotten the great woods. They live all by themselves and are happy.'

The air between those dark-depthed branches was crystal as the pools below. The light that rested on stalk and grass-blade was gentle as though it were winged. Even the stream had a tune of its own, the music which is only heard in pure cold waters that are near the skies. Ethna was as quiet as Aidan, for she too had felt that they had come to a place where the sunlight was known by the small flowers, where they might forget all but their own wonder. Her step was more delicate, her glance was as timid as a bird's in a strange wood.

(101-2)

In this atmosphere, the love of Aidan and Ethna is unquestionably innocent. The reader is drawn into their adventures with the bogeyman and the madmen and shares their secret joy in the freedom of the wilderness. Ethna, telling the story of Diarmuid and Grania, makes the most explicit statement about the novel's method:

'And have you never heard of Diarmuid and Grania?' she exclaimed. 'I thought that a scholar knew everything. . . . Then I must tell you all about them as we go along, for there is no better way of shortening the path than by a story. . . . But you must not be uneasy, for all this was long ago, and even if we were pursued we could do what Diarmuid and Grania did in the western wood . . .'

(92-3)

The motif of a story within a story is found in many of Clarke's other 'pilgrimages'. (It is also interesting that the first poem Clarke ever published was the story of Diarmuid and Grania.) The many parts of his career coalesce gradually and discreetly.

All is well until Aidan strays, is lost and then found by a monk-hermit. The boy had been a clerical student and the evangelist reminds him of his vocation and of the place of women in that scheme of things. The monk's testimony of his own importance is hyperbolic in the grand style of *The Son of Learning*, with an interesting result. Here, the speaker's grandiose delusions recoil upon him. The saints he praises are seen to be adventurous, greedy, ambitious and ridiculous:

> 'All good laymen rejoice in giving their best acres to the clergy — who are the servants of God — for the sake of their souls. But this bad-tempered king actually tried to push me off my own land . . . but I raised my staff, I ordered my monks to ring their handbells. I pronounced a great curse on him.'

He rose to his feet and his eyes were dark with memory.

> 'You have heard of the curse which Saint Patric would have pronounced on the Decies, when the bishops tried to oppose him, had not Saint Declan implored him to spare his people? You have heard, too, of the curse uttered by Saint Ruadan among his clergy against the secular power of Tara? . . . No doubt, as a scholar, you know the curse which Columbanus made against the wicked Queen Brunehaut, when she was encouraged by the Frankish clergy . . . And the curse of Saint Moling against the Hy-Nial race? . . . The curses of Maelisa, Munchin, Mochuda, Dagan and many other holy men? . . . Mine was as powerful in its effect. The sky darkened, the streams roughened, the solitary fled. The king dropped his sword, he ran with a howl into the woods, seeking those glades where the mad congregate under the full moon. He became feathered from head to foot, so powerful was my word, and his abode was in the tree-tops that have been twigged by the herons. I have heard from a pilgrim that he went at last over sea to converse in other forests with the madmen of Britain.'
> (227-8)

The monk is telling the story of Sweeney, the crazed king who lives among the birds of the wood: a theme which recurs in Clarke's work. Sweeney is always treated sympathetically by Clarke. The not too subtle moral of his story is that theologians drive men mad. The monk in this story has therefore unknowingly condemned himself.

The monk forces the confessional upon the boy, explaining that:

> 'To yield even in thought to the desire of a woman is a

mortal sin, a sin that is punished by everlasting torture unless we repent. The filthy pleasures of fornication are unmanly: they destroy both body and soul; they are punished in this life by scandal or disease; in the next life by lasting torture. Avoid, my son, the cunning of women who have given themselves up to the promptings of lust. . . . Did you sin with her in that cave, either by look or touch? Did you do anything that you would be ashamed of telling to your own parents or to me?'

'I love her, Father! I love her!'

'You have not answered my question.'

'But everything was changed when I fell in love with her. I cannot explain, but she is beautiful, she is good . . . I have not explained. It was I who was wicked. It was I who led Ethna astray. She is good, I cannot tell you how good she is. If you had heard her speak you would know. It was, indeed, all my fault.'

'And do you mean to tell me,' cried the other angrily, 'that any pure girl would dream of wandering along among the hills with a young man, much less of lying at night beside him? My son, do not harden your heart against grace, or be deceived by the vanities of sight. Remember the pious examples of all those virgins who have given every moment of their lives to Heaven. . . . I myself have aided girls who were about to be married and saved them from that inferior state. They have kept the flower of their virginity for Heaven. They have entered convents, taken vows and dedicated body and soul to the King of Pain.'

(230-3)

That last obsessional 'King of Pain' strengthens this admittedly extreme reading of doctrine. The rigid philosophy of the monk stands in total contrast to the pagan exuberance and natural harmony which has filled the novel up to this point. According to the monk's doctrine, Ethna has led Aidan astray; actually she has led him towards reality.

Fortunately, in compliance with the best traditions of romantic fantasy, Aidan escapes. Cile-na-gCich and the Viking invasion offer the trauma through which Aidan recovers his natural aversion to priestly misogyny, finds Ethna and lives happily ever after. The reader is allowed the vicarious pleasures of revolt and heresy.

This, of course, is the subversion at the heart of Clarke's work, but *The Bright Temptation* is also the continuation of Clarke's comic re-writing of history which began in *The Son of Learning*. There the satire was explicit and more idealistic. Church and state were ridiculed with magic and high spirits. In this first novel Clarke's satire intrudes like a sermon and could easily overshadow the comedy of the story. Following the example of a previous generation of poets, Clarke venerated Ireland as a nearly human, goddess-like figure of inspiration: hence, the awe-inspired wonder and intensity of those poems, especially in *Pilgrimage*, which achieve Clarke's 'holy' vision of an integrated Irish culture. In complete contrast to this traditionally poetic treatment of ancient Ireland, *The Bright Temptation* opens in a manner which betrays a new and far from enervating love of things Irish:

Torbach was the chief illuminator of Ireland. In his daily work he was given special dispensation and privileges. The inner skin of yearling or lamb was stretched for him; it was sunned; it was brightened with fine sand, for he would only put pen to the finest vellum. Herbs and minerals were got for his inks and dyes, rare colours from Europe and the purple that is picked among the Connemara sea-rocks. He had a serving-lad to look after his pens of light and heavy feather, another to mind the ink-horns which were arrayed on his desk when he had not stuck them all for readiness in his belt.

Even on a Sunday Torbach was still engrossed in the diminutive and intricate patterns of his art, so that his eye was nearer than his hand to the holy page that he was illuminating. He turned the minute circles, the quatrefoils and interlacing lines around themselves, tracing through remarkable convolutions those fantastic birds and beasts whose claws are no less entangled than their many-times-twisted necks and legs, contracting those richly coloured creatures of imagination until their lengthened tongues were trumpeted around their tails and they had been lettered to their last extremities.

But the day before this night the sudden cry of the ink-lad, who had cut himself with a quill knife, caused the great illuminator to start up in alarm. Crossing himself because of the unholy exclamation which had escaped from his lips, Torbach dropped the pen from his sanctified first finger and thumb. He lost sight of the dragon's tail that he was winding through the last intricacies of its own coils into the spirals of a glorious capital which was to be his masterpiece and the commencement of a new Gospel. . . . Pushing aside his pens, his inks, his marking instruments, his polished rollers, Torbach began to search for the place at which he had left off. For hours he sought patiently and with increasing prayer among those multitudes of interwoven lines for the tip of the dragon's tail, but such was the intricacy and minuteness of his own work that he could not find it. At dark he invoked the aid of Columcille, who copied the fourfold Testament in a miraculous light that was fairer than the page beneath his pen; but the candle was smaller when Torbach started again to follow up each curve to its source, to unfasten every knot and unwind every spiral; and his toil was vain, for with aching eye he found that he was going round and coming back like the bewildered Children of Solomon in the pentagon and magical circles of their craft, so that at the end of his search he was no farther than he had been at the beginning.

While he slept, Torbach pursued his search, and in dreams he was lost in a strange world of fantastic birds that swallowed themselves as soon as he grabbed them, of scriptural animals that escaped from him by turning themselves inside out or mocked his clutching fingers by whirling their hides around their spines.

(1-3)

Torbach awakens and the story of Aidan's adventures begins and the famed illuminator is never again mentioned. This loving anecdote, full of respect for the craftsman, avoids the cloying homage of poetic worship and establishes a fine balance. Torbach is a monk and an artisan and his foibles are human. When Clarke introduces that other monk, the contrast could not be stronger. Yet both extremes are acceptable in the novel's scheme because just such minor characters as this Torbach live and achieve a deep credibility, easily and immediately.

(iii)

The Singing Men at Cashel also explores the misogyny of a masculine world. It is a grim story of fear and repression, lightened once in a while by human joy and incidental anecdote. Anier MacConglinne is used once more by Clarke to lessen the burden of his message with jest and ridiculous antics. Anier's character is consistent with what we know of him from the earlier play. He is still wandering the countryside, dreaming of women, beer and dishes of food as 'steamy as those which tempt the saints who live on stirabout' (16). As Anier wanders across Ireland in search of Gormlai, Clarke lovingly describes the countryside, so that once again the land itself assumes the importance of a character. It is through Anier's eyes that the reader first sees Gormlai and is moved to admire her beauty and innocence:

The noise of the crowd left Anier's hearing, the changing sights went from his eye, as he saw her for the first time. Clearly, as in a little space of quiet, he saw the daughter of Flann. Her face was pale, her dark hair bound across her brow by a thin circlet of gold. She seemed alone, unreached by the turmoil, as if indeed the fair sacrament of that morning guarded her spirit with its grace. He almost imagined, as he saw that dreamful face, that she was in the fair light of a poetic college, listening to the equal music of verse, and that he was looking through a chink forgetting awhile the cold earth-shelters and hills he knew too well. The chastity, the loveliness of that face filled him with hatred of himself. He had neglected his studies; he was too idle to master even the four principal metres of poetry.

(28)

To any reader of Clarke's earlier poetry, this is familiar ground. Throughout the novel Anier recites poems which Clarke has published elsewhere. Among the poems he recites in The Singing Men at Cashel are 'Wandering Men' and 'Repentance'. Chapter twelve of the novel is a parody of bardic conventions and signals Clarke's ultimate escape from the intellectual complications of Gaelic literature. 'The Blackbird of Derrycairn' is part of Gormlai's reverie and meditation in another part of the book. She dreams of her future at one point in lines from the previously mentioned poem, 'The Confession of Queen Gormlai'. These intertwined references to his own work strengthen the pun on 'poor clerk' with which Clarke ends the book.

It is essential that Gormlai should be seen in a sympathetic light. The reader can understand her, pity her and identify with her as a normal, sanely balanced and morally responsible young woman. The story portrays innocence brutalised by conventional morality and public insensibility. The irony of Anier's observation that 'the fair sacrament of that morning guarded her spirit' is only gradually revealed. The reader experiences the pain of her marriage to Cormac, the celibate bishop-king of Cashel, from Gormlai's point of view. Their marriage is to be a virtuous union of souls. But Clarke suggests there can be no virtue if Gormlai's normal desires and emotional needs are denied and Cormac's masochistically repressed. Cormac's virtue is, to Clarke, perverse. Gormlai's emotions and forebodings on her marriage night are revealing:

What was all her knowledge of poetry and story to her? There were secret Latin books which the clergy possessed in their schools, but no lay person would be permitted to read them, much less a woman. She must be instructed by her husband — and at the thought a mood of rebellion rose in her mind. . . . She shrank back for a natural refinement, a delicacy of spirit had guarded always the innocence of her young mind. With a pang of despair she remembered those holy virgins who were the glory of Ireland, for even as a child she had wanted to follow the example of their dedicated lives. . . . She thought of all those virgins of her own age, who shrank from the stain of life, and retired to lonely cells, untouched, unseen. Why should Heaven have deserted her and why should she be forced to this? Perhaps she had not attended her religious duties enough. She had become interested in poetry and in the fair world it revealed, yet she had never offended against that instinctive chastity. She had always remembered the practice of Saint Brigid, who had never washed even her feet in the presence of man. . . . Tonight that modesty which she had guarded must be cast aside. Always she had guarded

her limbs even from her own glance and touch, being
dainty in every act. She had known intuitively the
loveliness of her body, but it was as remote to her as the
sun along the hills or the moonlight on her counterpane.
Fair yet forbidden to sight or contemplation, her body
was pure and legendary to her so that she had guarded it
from her own soul with a fierce secret jealousy.

(56-7)

The understanding and shared sensitivity she seeks are never
found. Cormac willingly negates the physical side of their
marriage. The religion of her husband and his theologians is
divorced from real life, and the constraint of her unnatural
marriage nearly destroys Gormlai. The books she reads in
Cormac's library further confuse the issues Gormlai has tried
to understand:

Sentences which she could scarcely understand confronted her, horrible words that she knew instinctively
referred to some terrible evil at the very root of life.
Woman was denounced by the Early Fathers, arraigned
as the temptress, the bringer of spiritual evil and disease.
She read with growing indignation and horror. But she
must not yield to the emotion of revolt. She must read
calmly, coldly, submitting all to her intelligence. The
sacrament of matrimony was not what she had thought
of it in her innocence, it was not what the uneducated
laity thought of it. Cormac had been correct though
she doubted his word. It was an inferior spiritual state, a
refuge from concupiscence, and as some schoolmen and
theologians held, a state that was no more than tolerable.
She read of the widespread reign of lust in ancient cities,
the multiplying sins of the flesh. Those who were married
did not always escape from horrible sins that blotched
both body and soul. The very intimacy of the married
state brought with it the occasion of unnatural sins, and
a slow demoralization could be brought on by the
uxoriousness of that state.

The more she read, the more her mind was bewildered. Fornication, adultery, concupiscence, uncleanli-
ness of thought and act — the ominous words leaped
loudly from the pages as from a pulpit, but their meaning

was as vague to her as it was alarming. There was some
shame in womanhood and its periods, some mysterious
corruption due to the Fall which she could not ascertain.

(162-3)

Gormlai has understood for the first time the essential anti-
feminism of traditional Christian doctrine.

Eva Figes, in her study *Patriarchal Attitudes*, summarises
the theological masters whose works Gormlai has been studying; her argument is apposite:

Woman, presented with an image in a mirror, has danced
to that image in a hypnotic trance, and because she
thought the image was herself, it became just that. . . .
Man's vision of woman is not objective, but an uneasy
combination of what he wishes her to be and what he
fears her to be, and it is to this mirror image that
woman has had to comply. . . . Furthermore, it is not
only one glass, but the whole hall of mirrors which is
male-created. We are born into a world where the great
discoverers, philosophers, artists, and scientists have
almost all been male. Male law-makers, male conquerors,
even the God perpetuated in tradition, who still somehow
haunts the early days of childhood, is male. . . . one
might say that for the great majority of women the
obvious course of events is to subside meekly or gracefully into the traditional role assigned to them, whilst
for the really determined woman, for whom that role is
inadequate, unsatisfactory or simply unavailable, there
is an uphill struggle to compete in a game where all the
rules have been laid down by the other party without
her having been consulted, and where all the vital moves
were probably made before she arrived on the scene.[4]

Gormlai, and Ethna in *The Bright Temptation*, are both caught
in this predicament. Figes goes on to assert the religious
nature of western anti-feminism:

The voice of God is the voice of man. Religion does not
only embody human belief, it embodies the attitudes,
the moral and social codes of the human beings who
celebrate that religion, of the priests and scribes who

give it body and reality. The voice of the lawmaker is more likely to inspire unquestioning obedience if it can thunder out from behind a terrifying mask, or reveal its wishes from above. The male Jehovah is a stern Hebrew patriarch who leaves us in no doubt about the position of woman. Far from being the mother of all the races of men, the natural order has been reversed, and woman is born out of man, no more than a single male rib. . . . Had Mary not been a Virgin the lineage of the Son of God would have been in doubt. However, just in case woman should get ideas above her station by the high honour of giving birth to such great males . . . the full responsibility for the Fall is heaped upon her shoulders.

This interpretation of the origin of undesirable things was to prove very useful for a long time to come, and it served a double purpose. On the one hand it allowed man to assert his domination that much more forcibly, he literally had the whip hand and could go on punishing woman for what she was supposed to have done . . . and on the other hand it allowed him to externalize all flaws and weaknesses in himself and make woman the embodiment of them, leaving himself strong and intact and morally superior. And since sexuality is always the Achilles heel in this arrangement not only do the strongest taboos surround sex, but it is woman's sexuality that he most loathes and fears.[5]

It is a formidable argument of which Clarke's women, and especially Gormlai, are the embodiment. Gormlai's dreams become nightmares and her terror increases as her personality, through Cormac's careful guidance, disintegrates.

On a pilgrimage with Cormac, she visits a community of monks and unconsciously recognises the implicit phallicism of Ireland's round towers. A man she cannot recognise, the religious hermit of the monastery, appears, half-naked, before Gormlai:

He was motionless but for the terrible eyes glittering through the heavy glib that hid his forehead. Never had she seen so wild and ragged a creature. His head-hair came down to his shoulders mingling with his moustaches and knotted beard. His arms were heavy with muscles and among their reddish bristles were bruises and scars. The thorn-patched rags and twisted pelts that clad him were scarcely distinguishable from his matted chest but for the ugly paps bared by their rents. The next moment in utter horror she realized that he was human only to the waist. Often on sculptured cross and stone she had seen those serpents which the talkend banished long ago and so she recognized the snake-sign. She could not see the coils but among the tatters that hung around the stranger's waist, a snake had raised its head, as if about to strike.

Her sight reeled and she felt that she was about to collapse on the rock. She was confronted by evil, she was in the presence of a phantom. The Devil was standing there, in semi-human shape, watching her — watching her without a movement. . . . Rage seized him, his eyes lit with hatred, he raised his big hand.

'Deviless! Deviless!'

(108-12)

Gormlai misunderstands what should be obvious. Her mind, which before marriage had been independent, curious and creative, does not question her sense of guilt or ponder her sense of security while she is away from her husband's house in the open countryside. Gormlai's conditioning is so complete that she feels guilty for being normal, until that last night when, unknown to her, Cormac has seen her regain a knowledge of her body and its sexuality. Cormac's self-mutilation before the altar of God on their last night together is seared on Gormlai's memory.

Annulment of the marriage promises relief. The Church's dogmatic insistence that marriage is low on the spiritual scale of values is rejected, and Gormlai begins to hope for some kind of happiness.

Her second husband is no better, however. Gormlai is rushed into another political match and again brutalised. Carrol's violence is as damaging to her spirit as Cormac's over-sensitivity. Rebellion offers little hope and confessional guidance less. Her confessor's guidance is coloured with emotional and moral blackmail. The priest tells her that 'Marriage is a pure and virtuous state', which is appallingly ironic. He continues in an even more paternalistic manner:

'Men are constituted differently,' he explained, 'and the physical needs of some are greater than the needs of others. It is your duty, therefore, to obey your husband, provided that he acts with due respect and within reason. That is to say, he must avoid the promptings of that lust which corrupts those who are outside the married state. But do not deceive yourself, do not hide from yourself, the sin which you are committing by disobedience, the greater sin you may be preparing by that very unwillingness. Remember that it is your primal duty to keep your husband from concupiscence. By your present conduct, you may drive him into sin. Your neglect may cause him to commit fornication and in that way you, alone, will be responsible for the loss of his soul, you, alone, will hurl him into the eternal flames.'

(291)

Clarke's case for Gormlai's liberation is complete. When Carrol beats her, one of the three insults to womanhood in Old Irish tradition, there are grounds for divorce, but it is really his death that frees Gormlai to marry the man of her choice and to live scandalously but happily at last. Part of the bardic clerk's literary equipment was a collection of sometimes enigmatic sayings, usually connecting events or objects in groups of three (like the three insults to womanhood mentioned above). These 'triads', at their simplest, are an obvious aid to a reciter, who may use one of them to delay his narrative, thus digressing from and ornamenting his version of the story, while he tries to remember the next episode. Clarke uses this technique in his novel to lend an impression of authenticity.[6]

The Singing Men at Cashel is no light fantasy; it is the logical development of *The Bright Temptation*'s image of Cile-na-gCich. Its gloom is not exactly dispelled, but somewhat alleviated by the youthful adventures and high spirits of Anier MacConglinne, whose story runs parallel to and eventually overlaps with Gormlai's history. He appears all over Ireland in many different mishaps, joyfully refuting Church and social convention. Anier's story is the perfect contrast for the larger, more serious story. His one aim in life, after food, song and drink, is to 'perform the oldest and best known of Irish jigs, heel and toe, together in the dark' (154). In an otherwise tortuous exploration of repression, Anier vindicates human joy. Only heretics like Anier enjoy themselves.

It is interesting to realise how Clarke's style has altered from that in *The Bright Temptation*. In that first novel Clarke borrowed from tradition the framework of the love-epic, a form which was traditionally composed for recitation. Hence, the narrator's explanatory and didactic asides which seem to destroy the story's continuity can be justified as integral to the author's purpose and effect. One reads *The Bright Temptation* fully aware of its storyteller's prejudices. Paradoxically, those biases merge with the story and reveal one of its more subtle aspects.

Each marriage ceremonial is a repetition of the others. The phrases and repeated images of church grandeur and ceremony parody the rite and satirise its significance. Repetition is a technique Clarke borrows from the style of oral narrative. It lends to the novel a certain historicity. Another level of artifice is added when the eleventh century copyist intrudes to comment on the story. But the real complications set in with Anier MacConglinne, whose adventures Clarke invents and enumerates. By enlarging Anier's story to include adventures very much in keeping with other medieval tales of Ireland, Clarke is credibly enlarging history, and practising what I have called a modern form of classical imitation. Anier chats with country girls, conjures up visions to excite an old man's flagging pretence of virility, challenges the poets of Leinster and Ulster and emerges victoriously unrepentant. Anier's comic adventures not only rescue the otherwise grim story of Gormlai, but also create the impression that one is reading a genuine history. This false authenticity is, of course, a classic motif of the medieval romance. The author of the romance creates an imaginary, often fantastic, world for which he nevertheless claims historical or classical authority as his source, and the reader willingly accepts this pretence of authenticity. Clarke uses this literary device to challenge the conventions of the real world. As part of the 'historical' world of his story he introduces motifs and concerns which are patently modern. For the novels are, like so much in Clarke's writing, satires directed at modern Ireland.

Anier performs another important function in the novel. His journey to the cave, which is the mouth of Purgatory, is

fraught with terror and psychological horrors as real as any
that beset Gormlai. Trapped by his own guile, Anier must
endure a visit to the lonely Cave of Hell. His fear and breakdown in the darkness of the cave from which he cannot
escape are the analogue to Gormlai's sufferings:

> If he did not resist sleep with all his strength of will,
> cling desperately to his conscious self, that other self,
> which no man knows but by deceptive symbols, would
> be drawn from his body and he would have to go with
> it. He would pass into the world of ghosts, alone, unpro-
> tected by those senses which guard life when it is obscured
> from all past knowledge of itself. . . . He had been
> blinded by fear, by a life of sin and it was that sinfulness
> which made his soul so horrible that he shrank from it.
> That was why it stirred when he stirred, why it waited
> so slyly, brooding to itself. It had not entirely freed itself
> from his body. He could feel its roots below his mind.
> All his lies and acts of trickery had made it cunning and
> it knew that he was not its master. It would grow angered
> if he delayed much longer, if he continued to resist its
> impulse to destroy itself for ever.
>
> (367-8)

Anier emerges from his suicidal brooding in the cave, full of
his usual fancy and convinces the world that he is himself
miraculous. His ability to awe and outwit the simple-minded
clerics places religious doctrine on the level of childish wonder
and naive superstition. Anier is the self-possessed, victorious
individual who realises what is perhaps the most optimistic
interpretation of human life in the novel:

> He was perfect now as Adam, who wakened suddenly
> into life, with adult mind and new senses unspoiled by
> the twilight years and errors of childhood. He knew at
> last that the common sunlight is indeed the radiance
> which, temperate yet glorious, shines through the circular
> courts of Heaven, that even when we are at our daily
> tasks we move in that celestial light.
>
> (375)

Significantly, it is at this point that Anier once more meets

Gormlai, when she is happily married at last, and the novel ends.

The Singing Men at Cashel is peopled with characters who live in a recognisable, real world. The novel has its own coherent logic. Crowded with detailed personal histories and psychologies, it gains an atmosphere of authenticity by the inclusion of many relevant vignettes of Irish history and custom. It represents an integration in Clarke's work of the disparate strands of his sermonic intention, his historical models and his necessarily inventive subject matter.

(iv)

Anier MacConglinne, whose genius for debate, satire and practical joke has been shown to underlie much of Clarke's transitional work, is replaced in *The Sun Dances at Easter* by Aongus (Clarke's spelling), lord of Tir Na Nogue and (according to that other modern Irish novel in which he is a major character, *The Crock of Gold*) god of song, love, imagination and happiness. In Stephens' novel Angus (Stephens' spelling) is the head of the Irish pantheon and depicted as a tragic hero, beautiful but saddened at the state of the world:

> The god was slender and as swift as a wind. His hair swung about his face like golden blossoms. His eyes were mild and dancing and his lips smiled with quiet sweetness. About his head there flew perpetually a ring of singing birds, and when he spoke his voice came sweetly from a centre of sweetness.
>
> 'Health to you, daughter of Murrachu,' said he, and he sat down.
>
> 'I do not know you, sir,' the terrified girl whispered.
>
> 'I cannot be known until I make myself known,' he replied. 'I am called Infinite Joy, O daughter of Murrachu, and I am called Love.'[7]

Stephens creates this stylised god in character with the Celtic and theosophical themes of his novel. His romantic Angus could not be more different from Clarke's portrait of the same god. Another quotation from *The Crock of Gold* will suffice to make this distinction clear:

Then Angus Og put upon his bride glorious raiment, and they went out to the sunlight. It was the early morning, the sun had just risen and the dew was sparkling on the heather and the grass. There was a keen stir in the air that stung the blood to joy, so that Caitilin danced in uncontrollable gaiety, and Angus, with a merry voice, chanted to the sky and danced also. About his shining head the birds were flying; for every kiss he gave to Caitilin became a bird, the messengers of love and wisdom, and they also burst into triumphant melody, so that the quiet place rang with their glee. Constantly from the circling birds one would go flying with great speed to all quarters of space. These were his messengers flying to every fort and dun, every rath and glen and valley of Eire to raise the Sluaige Shee (the Fairy Host). They were birds of love that flew, for this a hosting of happiness, and, therefore, the Shee would not bring weapons with them.[8]

Thematically confused and caught in the mists of the Celtic Twilight, this story is very different from that which Clarke tells in *The Sun Dances at Easter*. Indeed, Clarke's entire work has studiously evolved away from the linguistic affectation that was common to Stephens and many of the earlier generation of writers. Stephens' language is more akin to that of Clarke's early verse. Clarke's portrait of Aongus introduces a very different style of writing:

He was cloistered beyond all charity in his own findings: scraps of frieze, loom-droppings, patches of fur, pelts that a ragpicker would have thrown away; and these treasures of his were tied and twisted with *sugaun*, pinned to their quadragesimal knots with huge thorns, skewered and pothooked from shoulder to muddied hem. He was out at the knees and in at the elbows. He was so enormously fat that the entire collection clung to him or clambered about him in fleshly bulges and bursts of frightened modesty. He was a standing humiliation and a holy show. But as he chuckled and clucked to himself, some of the tattings, the taggles, shook with little jokes of their own, despite their insecurity, and bobbed the hundreds of withered burrs which they had

caught in last year's woods. His chesty beard wagged
beneath the goatskin hood which almost hid his red
face. His paunch rumbled with such mirth beneath an
enormous hairy hand-grasp that at one moment his
robes were all holes, at the next moment all mendings,
and the moment after that the seams had changed places
again and the uncountable rips went into little stitches
of laughter.

Even in her confusion, Orla could not help seeing
the ramshackle brogues on his feet. They were too large
for his toes, and too small for his bunions, and were so
cobbled to the buckle, clouted, lasted and broken again
by iron and stone, that for all her alarm she could not
keep from smiling.

(14-15)

The language here is purged of musical melancholy; without his Celtic sadness and ritualised language, Aongus becomes
the god of comedy. This god is approachable. Robust, frolicsome, the god of love, youth and merriment, Aongus is the
central focus and genius of the novel. *The Sun Dances at
Easter* offers a vision concerned with the fertility of life and
the creativity of the imagination.

The plot is based on a pilgrimage to a holy well undertaken
by Orla, the wife of Flann, who is apparently a petty chief-
tain. Orla has been married for two years but has remained
childless and is advised by a hermit whom she considers to be
a saint (but who eventually turns out to be Aongus) to make
a pilgrimage to the well of St Naal at which the prayers of
women in Orla's predicament are said to be answered. Orla
sets out on her journey accompanied by her maid Blanaid,
having first convinced her husband of the powers of the well
and its saint by giving him an account of the saint and his
well told to her by the local scribe, who is 'very old and a
little stupid'. Although she is reluctant to tell her mistress,
Blanaid is much more aware of the true powers of the well,
being from that locality and also being a more earthy person
than Orla. The two women make their journey through the
uplands of west Connaught. Along the way they fall in with a
student monk, Enda, who is experiencing a crisis of religious
uncertainty. Orla, a sweet and innocent creature, takes pity
on Enda who is about her age and seems to have a mysterious

attraction for her. Enda enthralls her with his conversation as they pass along the way while Blanaid engages in other, unexplained pursuits. It soon becomes apparent that the relationship between Orla and Enda is more than an accident of common itinerary. Enda reminds her of her husband, although he is much more handsome and bears a love mark reminiscent of that of Diarmuid in the story of 'Diarmuid and Grainne'.

On the first night of the pilgrimage Orla and Enda separate, Orla and Blanaid spending the night in a convent, and Enda in a monastery. Orla's experience in the convent is less than satisfactory and includes an unexplained vision, of angels or the Sidhe — she is not sure which. When she rejoins Enda to continue the journey, he tells her the first of two long and intensely powerful tales within the tale; the story of 'The House of the Two Golden Methers'. Orla's reaction to this taut mythological story is that it is a very sad story and capable of many interpretations.

Shortly after the completion of the first tale, Orla and Enda come to the vicinity of the well and Enda departs on his way to the local monastery while Blanaid goes to visit her people, leaving Orla to participate in the preparation for the Saint's festival the next day. At this stage it begins to be apparent to Orla that the ceremonies associated with the well are somewhat different from what she had expected. She is offered some 'uisce beatha' by one of the many women who have come for the blessing of the saint, and before long she is in the midst of a mad dance of fertility and carnival. The well of St Naal (supposedly a corruption of St Natalis) is in fact a survival from the pagan past. As it turns out both Blanaid and Enda were aware of this, and just when Orla is succumbing to the pagan ritual she is rescued by Enda. There follows a sequence of dream and magic in which Enda and Orla are whisked behind the 'fead fiad', the boundary between this world and that of Aongus. Enda then tells the second tale within the tale, 'The One Jealousy of Congal More'. This is a 'comic' story in contrast to the first which was a 'religious' story. Again the moving power of the story is Aongus and the story concerns the turning (in dream or in reality, we are not sure) of Congal the Ard Rí into a goat. As a goat, Congal learns more about reality than he has ever learned as a man. The ostensible reason for the telling of the second

story is that Enda and Orla may pass the time in each other's
company without moral danger. However, Clarke has now
succeeded in bringing the symbolic and mythological power
of Enda's two tales to bear on the relationship between Enda
and Orla and it is therefore consummated (again whether in
dream or reality, we are not really sure). Aongus has brought
his scheme to completion. The purpose of Orla's pilgrimage
has been fulfilled. She will have a child and it will look like
its father. Reluctantly, Orla returns to the well for the
Saint's festival. She ties the wish cloth on a thorn at the well
in accordance with the superstition, is rejoined by Blanaid
and then is met by her husband Flann who has come to take
her home.

At a superficial level *The Sun Dances at Easter* is a fable of
happy fulfilment. Orla, the 'lady' full of natural innocence
and simple openness and charm, has her wish of having a
child fulfilled. Were it not for its relationship to the two tales
within the story, the manner of this fulfilment might be read
at most as a cleverly drawn satire directed against the narrow-
ness and repressiveness of Christian morality, especially the
Irish Catholic version of it. But it is by welding the story of
Orla and Enda with the two myths that Clarke enlarges the
scope of the book so that it comes to be a fable of imaginative
discovery into the depths of human experience. Much of the
two tales has the quality of an intense, nightmarish dream
world. Ceasan's futile struggle with the swollen waters of the
Boyne ford in order to escape from the horrors of his relapse
into paganism to the refuge of his meeting with Patric is a
case in point. Ceasan's horrors are more internal than external
though. In the other story Congal wakes up in his own bed,
after intensely comic and sometimes nightmarish experiences
as a goat. In this case, however, a definite doubt is left as to
whether Congal's experiences were real (magical) or in
dream. Congal's doctor, presumably a man of real (or magical)
knowledge compared to the Lord Abbot Macuad, is quite
aware that the distinction between real and imaginary is of
little consequence; it is in the power of the imagination that
the intensity of Congal's experience is ultimately grounded.
In this sphere real merges with imaginary and the magical
itself has a powerful existence.

Clarke again begins this book on a solid and realistic basis.
The starting point of the novel is once more the question of a

woman's self-awareness. Orla is more knowledgeable than either Gormlai or Ethna, and her unfulfilled wishes more practical and immediate. The style with which Clarke conveys Orla's view of herself and at the same time intimates the parameters of the book is most striking:

Month after month she had lived between disappointed hopes and joyful starts, spying on herself in the dark lest her happiness might come to her unawares. She had wakened in the greyness of dawn, when the snores of the household were more foolish, and sat up blushing, only to find that she had been mocked by a confusing dream. . . . Summer would come and still there would be no news beneath her heart, although she had prayed and fasted regularly. What had she done to deserve all this unhappiness? . . . Why should she be different from other women, when she only wanted to be the same as them? Even as a small girl, she was always playing with her babog, dressing it up in red and blue bits of cloth, crooning over it like a mother at dusk when the stars could still be counted. Long before she knew where babies come from, she used to look for one under a fairy thorn near her home, while the other children were picking luck-flowers. Then, one day, she met a ragged little girl driving a cow along a ridge near the thorn-tree. The waif had asked her what she was looking for, and when she told her, blabbed the truth and showed her the soul's button beneath her bib. Orla did not tell her big secret to anyone for she was frightened, but soon she was very proud of her mysterious knowledge. After that, she tripped along with her curly head in air and she never looked under a bush again.

As Orla thought with a smile of her childhood, a new fear came into her mind. Suppose the years went by and nothing ever happened — what would she do? She stared beyond the hill-ridges with their thin streaks of tillage and their wood-edges, beyond the mountains themselves, into the sky, as if she were trying in desperation to see the courts of Heaven.

(11-13)

Orla's reverie is innocent, simple and human. Her morés

may be conditioned by superstition or religion, but her instincts are inviolate. Her wonder at fertility is conveyed in compassionate, natural imagery:

> Why indeed should she be ashamed of the wish which was nearest her heart? The three most beautiful things in the world, according to the triad, were: a wood under fruit, a boat in sail, and a woman great with child. She only wanted to be as great as other women and to please her husband.
>
> (2)

Sympathetic imagery pervades the descriptions of Orla's mind; nevertheless a sense of irony and even satire always underlies the language:

> . . . as she gazed at that sow, too gross to stagger up and run away with blind flaps, grunting and squealing from the hoofs, she was contrite, and when she thought of all its mighty mothering, she felt pity for the dirtiest of God's creatures.
>
> She began to think, afterwards, of the patience of all such fat ugly creatures everywhere, basking in the sunshiny dust, waiting until their time had come. Even the fierce wolves and other wild creatures that hid in the higher places and rarely came down because of their fear of man, crouched in cave or earthing, waiting painfully for their litter. She was sad when she remembered how in Eden long ago there was no fierceness or unhappiness among the animals and birds. The bigger animals did not kill and eat the smaller ones, the hawk did not drop down with terrible claws, even the tinier birds never gobbled up insect and worm. All creatures, following the example of man, chose the green herb as their meat. She was wondering to herself why some animals remained gentle after the Fall, while others became savage, when Blanaid caught her arm.
>
> (32-3)

The simple directness with which Orla's question arises from her experience of natural phenomena exemplifies an aspect of Clarke's way of reading life. Before she decides to visit Saint Naal's well, Orla, ingenuously, has tried all else:

> For a long time she had lain close to the wall in order
> that Flann and she might be as far from each other as
> possible. During the seven weeks of Lent she had kept
> to her own half, in order that Heaven might be favourable
> at last to her husband and herself. But Flann had been
> vexed by her vow of abstinence, and many a night they
> had quarrelled with each other, bolstering their argu-
> ments and nagging with the same niggardly words so
> often that their heads seemed all tongue and ears. . . .
> She knew indeed that she had been unfair to Flann, but
> it was not wholly her fault. She had been unkind only
> because she wanted to offer up their acts of self-denial
> to Heaven. He had refused to see it in that way and
> blamed her for her selfishness. But her intentions were
> holy and she knew that she was not being selfish. It
> was her duty as a good wife to obey him, she knew that
> only too well. . . . Men were really ridiculous, all gobbles
> and grabs one minute, and the minute after that nothing
> but contented snores. . . . But in two years of married
> life Orla had learned things before her husband's back
> was turned, and she knew that for modest wives a half
> stolen pleasure is the sweetest. She smiled in the dark-
> ness, for she was aware of a new confidence and guile in
> herself. . . . When a man is in bed he is a poor creature,
> with little will of his own and entirely at a woman's
> mercy.
>
> (19)

The couple's ignorance of how children are conceived shows
how little they know of the natural order. On the other hand,
the assumption that conception is associated with sexual
repression motivated by Christian asceticism suggests that
Christianity has somehow overturned the natural order. There
is more than a suggestion that Flann's crude sexual advances
are not up to defeating Orla's 'modesty'. She finely weighs
the degree of her fault while commenting on the ridiculousness of men. Clarke's irony is pervasive. The humour is directed
principally against Christianity. Orla's ignorance is innocent,
however, and she will escape; her vow has not destroyed her
natural instincts. Enda, when she meets him, will challenge

her ignorance but the challenge will remain implicit and subtle. Because, unlike Gormlai, she has retained her natural innocence, she is not repelled by her discovery of the natural order. Her pilgrimage is a woman's journey back to her instinctive and natural fulfilment. It is only right that images of birth, and childhood, should proliferate along her road. Enda quickly upsets any hope of explaining away the incongruities in life. He is ingenuous in his enthusiasms. Clarke allows the reader to infer the doubts raised about Christian discipline for himself as Enda indulges in hyperbolic hagiography. Enda too is on a quest:

'Then one fine day, doubt came suddenly into my mind, as I was standing outside the refectory. I was pushing a pebble with my sandal, when a thought struck me as if it had jumped up from the ground. We were all living in the past rather than the present. We were dreaming of centuries which were gone . . . in no place could I find anyone who had ever seen a miracle with his own eyes. I questioned men in the fields, and at night by the fire I talked with the old people. But they spoke of the Sidhe-mounds and repeated old stories, word by word, slowly as if they dared not change them.'

(50-1)

Enda's only religious experience has been a vision during which he encountered bird-droppings instead of the dews of Heaven, and he has acquired a doubting and questioning spirit from the satirists. Likeable and easygoing, he is eager to tell the legends, myths and histories he has learned. His joining Orla and Blanaid enlarges the metaphor of the pilgrimage, giving it a Chaucerian form. Indeed, the ironic overview which is casually yet carefully offered the reader is also Chaucerian. The tension generated along the route is not due to miracles or angels. The overt Christian motives of the quest are overwhelmed by the natural world through which the pilgrims travel.

When Orla first saw Enda she imagined that 'the hermit (Aongus) was stooping over her shoulder to bless them both'. Aongus is the spiritual director of the pilgrimage and its purpose is to discover the natural happiness and love he represents. This discovery is not intended by the pilgrims, and the well is only incidental to Aongus' master-plan.

Orla makes a definite advance in discovery of her true self when she and Blanaid leave Enda to stay overnight in a convent's hostelry. As a woman growing in her awareness of her natural instincts, she is out of place in the presence of nuns. Even the conversation is stilted and uncertain.

> '. . . she asked me to thank you for the generous gift
> which you have brought to us and to say that we will
> pray for your special intention.'
> 'An intention which my husband shares with me,'
> said Orla piously, looking down at her plate.
> 'We hope indeed that your special intention will
> be granted,' replied the nun, carefully ignoring Orla's
> correction . . .
> 'There's something strange about it, Blanaid,' said
> Orla thoughtfully. 'It's as if they had some secret they
> were trying to conceal from strangers. I could hardly get
> a word out of either of them the whole time.'
>
> (59-60)

The secret the nuns wish to conceal may be the barrenness of their repressed ascetic lives. By contrast, in a beautifully described moonlight scene in the convent, Orla discovered a new sense of her body:

> Before she knew how it had happened, she was standing
> in the middle of the ray with nothing on her. But she
> was delighted, for her finger-nails were polished as she
> spread her hands in that lovely light, and when she
> looked down at herself she was lost in admiration — for
> everything she saw and should not see was aureate and
> glossy.
>
> (62)

But the nuns are seen to have a more tangible secret in the vision which Orla has of beautiful young men engaging in a middle-of-the-night building operation in the convent. The identity of the young men — angels or Sidhe — is never fully revealed in the book, but the reader is on familiar ground here, for Clarke has already used such fantasy dream sequences as a means of underscoring the sense of libidinous urges and their repression.

Orla leaves quickly, to rejoin her travelling companion and Enda's telling of the first story follows: ' "Since this is a pilgrimage," he smiled, "it will have to be a pious one!" "I love religious stories" ' (73). The story is indeed religious but not perhaps in the sense that Orla had intended. Enda's story is about Ceasan and Eithne, the subject of Clarke's longest play, *The Moment Next to Nothing*. Myles Dillon, in his book *Early Irish Literature*, discusses the source-tale for this incident, 'The Nurture of the House of the Two Milk-Vessels'. [9] The telling of this tale was supposed to impart to the audience 'safety on a journey, good hunting, happiness, and fertility in marriage'. These motifs are integral to Clarke's novel; Clarke himself describes the legend in his notes to *The Moment Next to Nothing* (*Plays*, 402) as 'a myth of the struggle of two gods for a goddess'. The story, as Clarke renders it, is set at the time of the introduction of Christianity in Ireland. Eithne, who has long since lost her druidic soul, enters the human world and learns of the new God. In Dillon's explanation of the original, she comes to be converted and the gods who watch her wait to see Patrick themselves before reclaiming Eithne. Naturally, in the Christian version, Eithne is baptised, dies and enters Heaven. Clarke's version of the story combines the sense of awe engendered by the theme with a language full of subtle irony and revealing symbolism. Ceasan, himself in some doubt about the basis of his Christian faith and sent by Patric (Clarke's spelling) to pray and contemplate as a hermit, takes upon himself the conversion of Eithne the beautiful, pagan goddess. The language captures the naivete of the aspiring cleric who can hardly be blamed for not understanding that his growing devotion to the conversion of Eithne has a motive other than his zeal and Christian ardour for the salvation of her soul:

As she stood there by the low stone-wall in the twilight he told her how the mystery of human existence, which distracted pagan philosophers for so many centuries, was revealed in a holy book brought from the East. Simply as he could, he explained the doctrine of the Trinity, the nature of the soul, the dangers which surround us during our earthly trial. Countless were the ranks of the angels, but despite their state of bliss, many among those light-bearers had rebelled. After the Great War in Heaven, the material world was created and since then all thoughts and conditions had their opposites. The vacant thrones left by the defeated angels would be filled by good men and women, the elect of this earthly life. Were it not for the Fall of Man, the earth would be as fair as Heaven, fruitful in every season and as brightly watered. He heard her gentle sighs when he spoke of the pain and misery which the Ri of Heaven had endured on earth, the humiliations of the human form, the mockery of the fallen angels who tempt in waste places. She followed his words with such attention and trust that he was moved to deeper holiness, for he felt that he was saving a soul from mortal error. She would be his first convert and he experienced in all its intensity the spiritual joy of guiding another mind to grace, sharing with another soul the far-come truths of religion.

(80)

In his excitement Ceasan has forgotten social conventions. Only later does he ask her name and personal history, after remembering the not-so-edifying tales of sudden death upon conversion, the shock of 'grace' being too much for some souls. The simple awe with which Ceasan recalls Patric's dead converts convinces Ceasan that to save Eithne, he must proceed more calmly: 'The difficulties of faith were many and he must guard himself against his own eagerness and rash words. He would unfold all to her by quiet precept and parable, choosing the examples which he had learned in class as a beginner' (91). This, in fact, is what Clarke is doing in the novel. The larger moral of the intertwined tales unfolds slowly 'by quiet precept and parable'. Orla will say that such parables 'have many meanings', and Clarke is keen to impress on the reader that life, like the novel itself, is too various for a single, narrow interpretation.

Ceasan's zeal is not censured directly, and the language conveys his love of the forest in which he lives in harmony with the other inhabitants (including once again the ever-present blackbird). Ceasan's hermitage is more a natural paradise than a penance:

His own faith was on trial and that was why Patric had

sent him to live alone and ignorantly in the woods. He
would implore grace in order that he might outwit the
fallen spirits who were trying to craze his mind. Why
was he afraid, at this very moment, to go to the hollow
tree, afraid to look into the basket which he had put
back on his way back this morning? He did not fear the
dark tricksters any more, he would walk with a firm
step. But as he came towards the tree he began to
tremble because of the sweetness that met him. Already
the seasons were mingling once more, the sloe blossom
had come back, under low branches the shadowy nooks
were bluebelling and around him was the fragrance of
autumn.

(108-9)

Clarke's appreciation of nature once again underlies the
mythological and romantic.

Ceasan's mind is constantly changing, unsure how to
interpret what he sees because he feels obliged to classify
his perceptions according to his concepts of Heaven, Hell
and fallen world. Clarke convincingly portrays the naive
optimism and fears of an illusioned man.

When the trauma occurs which exiles Ceasan from faith
it is symbolically powerful but not unexpected. Clarke has
built up the tension through the sense of dream, hallucination
and pagan mystery and the repetition of motifs such as the
Salmon of Knowledge, the delicate food left by Aongus, the
lovely body of Eithne half covered by the fleece (related to
the perfection of the risen body in Christian dogma). In his
role as Eithne's teacher Ceasan's mind began its precipitous
leaps, as he tried to reason out his beliefs. We are 'lost each
one alone, in a strange world', he explained, except for the
solace of Christianity (86). His vision of Tir Na Nogue is
deftly manipulated to suit his blind needs:

He turned and became aware of what she saw beyond
the water. Paradise was there and the very air that hid
it from his own sight was hushed with awe. That everlasting happiness was within reach of body and soul.
He closed his eyes as if he were conscious of all the
human race moving through the wretchedness and misery
of time towards that glory of being. . . . Suddenly the

suspicions which stirred in his mind late at night among
the woods were clear to him in the sunlight. The Tuatha
De Danaan were there beyond the water; they were
behind the Faed Fiad: but Eithne could see them,
could hear those voices calling them. . . . He had tried
not to believe in them, had tried to forget the earliest
fears of his childhood, but reason was failing him and
ancient superstitions were beating through his veins.
He could struggle no longer, yet Eithne was resisting
their power, and her body was rigid with suffering. He
knew, then, that she was sustained by the holy doctrines he had taught her. . . .

(105-6)

The recognition of other gods undermines Christianity,
and the collapse of Ceasan's belief, once this gap in his faith
opens, is rapid:

'Aongus Oge is there and all his companies. Tell him, tell
him that the hazels are cut down, the wells desecrated,
the fire-rings trampled out. Tell him that few worship
the Tuathe De Danaan now and the folly of their sacred
places will soon be forgotten. . . . What of those momen-
tary love-beds then — the devilish flux that doubles joy
— when none pray to Aongus, none read their own
destiny in the flight of his birds. No . . . No . . . my wits
are straying, I did not mean what I said, my lips have
belied me. Tell him to show himself among the Ever-
young to me, for I cannot endure the torment of
ignorance, the riddles which have too many answers, tell
him that I am half mad for that unending happiness,
for that knowledge which is its cause. Let me but see
him for an instant, let my own eyes unblind me.

(112-13)

Aongus meets the monk's challenge in the main story of *The
Sun Dances at Easter*.
This version of the legend of Ceasan is very different in
style from the pervasive tedium of the same story in *The
Moment Next to Nothing*. For intensity and power, this tale
within a tale can be compared in excellence to *As The Crow
Flies*. Ceasan is cut off from normal life and happiness by his

attempt to baptise Eithne. In the actual attempt at baptism,
Christian and pagan ritual become powerfully confused. The
primeval symbols of fire and water themselves challenge the
straight Christian interpretation. Ceasan loses both Eithne
and his peace of mind:

> He saw her shiver a little from mortal cold but no com-
> plaint escaped her lips and, as he bent down to her, he
> forgot all but the greatness of what he was about to do.
> Both as symbol and element, water represents by its
> cleanly act the purification of body and soul, joined
> here and hereafter, when the centuries are gone. With
> mercy, his own sins would be expiated in the next world
> by the symbol and element of fire, beyond the ardency
> of pain, he would meet Eithne again in Paradise. He laid
> his hand gently on the crown of her head and the light
> of her coming grace suddenly shone around her so that
> she did not seem mortal. Her flesh was glorified, her
> smile was so joyful that he closed his eyes from such a
> wonder and began to pronounce the words of the ancient
> rite. But scarcely had he uttered a syllable when the
> chill of horror held him. His fingers touched nothing
> and he knew that he was alone. He sprang back and
> stared at the spot where Eithne had been, stared at the
> rushing waters, and, then, from the cliff-wood, came, in
> echo, his own cry of disbelief.
>
> (131)

This legend, titled by Clarke 'The House of the Two Golden
Methers', is central to *The Sun Dances at Easter*. It deals with
the same themes that occupy the main story of the novel.
Enda's telling of this story is a challenge to Christian morality
and theology. Orla tells Enda that she has seen 'a saint' and
he realises that her journey will fulfil his quest too; miracles
still occur, she assuringly says. The legend has another role
in the novel. It postulates the co-existence of Eithne's erotic
god of love and Ceasan's pure god of spirit. Aongus' role is to
transform Orla's sexuality from its repressed, Christian existence to its natural fullness, symbolised by Moymell (the plain
of honey). This contrasts, of course, with the crazed, orgiastic
revels which she first encounters at the well. Enda's stories,
though full of sexual symbolism, do not appal Orla. They are

moving and beautiful, never crude.

There is no crudity either in the superbly comic story of
Congal's metamorphosis from jealous husband into goat
(with its descriptions of how it feels to chew the cud for the
first time and to have horns, and of Congal's indignation
when handled by goat-breeders). The aim of this story is no
longer instructive but persuasive and the narrative is embellished with marvellously lyrical and evocative passages of
writing always pervaded by irony and parody:

> Long ago when the second order of holiness spread
> throughout Ireland and discipline was stronger, the
> blessed who lived alone in the woods or green deserts
> spent much time in teaching wild creatures, big and
> small, to behave themselves. The stag, the wolf, the
> missel-thrush, the beetle and the houseless fly, learned
> obedience and came to foot or hand. Our saints under-
> took this task so that the good might walk even in remote
> places without offence to eye or immodesty of thought,
> and their patience is not to be wondered at when we
> consider the care with which even lay men and women
> train their domestic pets to respect the fourth, sixth,
> seventh, and ninth commandments. Some memory of
> that instruction still lingered in the woods long after the
> lesser saints had gone into glory, for often, at the mere
> sound of a human step, there would be a flutter of
> wings from a dusty patch of ground, a shaken twig, a
> flutter of eight little paws through the grass. As a mongrel
> slinks away with his tail between his legs or a cat leaps
> down from a dish on the table, so the wild creatures
> fled, conscience-stricken, from their courtship and open
> air sports.

(171)

It is a curious interpretation of innocence. But then the story
is ostensibly a means of filling time and avoiding the sexual
tension between the eager yet unwilling Enda and Orla.
Ironically, the end of Congal's experiences as a goat is his
acceptance sexually as a member of a herd of wild goats.

Enda tells how 'the reverend Macuad was the most renowned
moralist in Ireland, and wherever he went he was both feared
and respected' (172). The Lord Abbot-bishop's sermon is a

parody of the zealously haranguing style of Clarke's contemporary, John Charles MacQuaid, Archbishop of Dublin.
Macuad's moralistic purge is interrupted by 'a fat monk with
a red foolish face' who was:

> whispering merrily to those around him. His listeners
> were nudging each other as if he were telling them a
> dirty story they had never heard before, and they grabbed
> at their bigger lip to keep in the bursts of laughter.
> Macuad believed what he saw to be an illusion of the
> Adversary, for he was often distracted by the foul one,
> but his voice was narrow, terrible, when he raised it
> again:
>   'There are evil-doers who mock openly at religion
> and authority, misguided men and women who have lost
> all self-respect and do not fear the laws of Heaven. But
> I warn them now . . .'
>   (174)

Congal's story progresses to the goat-king's final moral:
'Celibates could never leave well enough alone' (230). This
judgment, however, is only of secondary importance. The
story's effect is certainly more direct. Orla recognises her saint
as the monk who interrupts Macuad. Enda explains:

> Aongus has taken as many shapes as his Greek cousin,
> according to the poets, for love itself is like that, a
> solemn play in which there must be two comic parts,
> grave when it is gayest, gross and yet most delicate,
> when all that is beyond meaning has been grasped.
>   (235)

The complexities are explained; they are under Aongus'
protection, behind the 'faed fiad', in the house of the two
golden methers and free, in this enchantment, from Ireland's
curious eyes. The symbols of the Salmon of Knowledge and
Aongus' special food recur, but 'the milk of the doe' has
been replaced by nectar. The ending of the Ceasan/Eithne
tale was tragic; baptism did not bring them to Moymell. For
Orla and Enda, however, Aongus has brought *them* (despite
Orla's scruples) 'together, their lips touching for the first
time'. Orla has a lover; Enda, his vision of angels:

Her wish was granted and in due course she presented
her husband with a fine bouncing boy. Little Flann had
one red-gold curl, and whenever his mother suckled him
she looked down at it, knowing that he would soon have
as many of them as his daddy.

(255)

This is comedy of a far wider significance than Anier
MacConglinne's satire and ridicule. Clarke has moved from
his concern with sermons in his first novel and with psychological repression in his second to psychological liberation in
his third. When she set out on her pilgrimage, Orla had a
curious experience. She met some children and danced with
them in a circle. The effect is surprising:

Round and round all of them went, keeping time with
their voices, faster and faster, so that Orla was dizzy
with the sweet sounds of bird-flocking and the tuning of
harp trebles.
     But suddenly she was disappearing, head and
shoulders, into memories of her own childhood, while
all that happiness raced below her hips. She was whirling
from the warm sun-flashes into the twilight around the
fairy thorn near her home. She was groping through the
dim troubles of the past, enduring the furtive curiosity
and fears, the bad words repeated by older children,
the miserable wettings, the slaps and all the wretched
wrongs. But she was no longer dancing under the fairy
thorn, she was being dragged around that other tree in
the cold shadowy Garden of Eden where no children
ever played. She was unbaptizing herself, searching into
the false horrors of the soul. Suddenly there was a howl,
and she startled herself back into the sunlight.

(39-40)

The Sun Dances at Easter (the title comes from the survival
of a pagan superstition associated with Easter) is a celebration
of freedom in which myth and poetry unrestrainedly and
powerfully involve themselves with human life. The characters
discover the source of their creative vitality. The novel is a
romantic comedy which offers a sustaining vision of human
nature and the unending delight of life. That image of exor-

cism, of unbaptism, which affects Orla and Ceasan, binds the joy of this final novel to the other two. It is an image which we must now discuss in relation to Clarke's more recent poetry.

The Sun Dances at Easter, described by Vivian Mercier as 'the most charming comic-romantic fantasy by a modern Irishman',[10] is the goal at the end of Clarke's personal pilgrimage. It endorses the critical judgment that 'the function of romance in our time may well prove to have been not wish-fulfilment but exorcism'.[11] Yet this coherent and marvellously sustained blend of erotic and mythological themes is unknown, and unavilable to the public. Mercier attributes the novel's neglect to his own theory of Irish comedy, contrasting its style to the coyness of *The Crock of Gold*. Clarke's novel 'does not match the Anglo-Saxon stereotype of Irish humour and fantasy; it therefore passed almost unnoticed at its publication.'[12] The fact of the matter is that since its banning on its publication in October, 1952, the novel has never been publicly available.

The Sun Dances at Easter gives meaning to (and provides a standard by which to measure) the poetry of the 1950s and early 1960s which Clarke wrote from the unexorcised, dark side of his poetic spirit. It stands beside his final poems as an evocation of the fulfilment to be found in a truly liberated imagination.

Sweeney Maddened
THE POETRY FROM 1938 TO 1961

'I like Ireland as much as James Joyce liked it:
but I chose to live here.'   AUSTIN CLARKE

(i)

I have called this chapter 'Sweeney Maddened' in reference to
the myth summarised in the introduction: Sweeney, a local
king, stood against the Church, and was cursed with madness.
In the poems studied in this chapter — all of which were
collected together in 1961 as *Later Poems* — Clarke elucidates
the ancient king's madness in poems full of conflict and satire
about modern Ireland. It was this 1961 collection, which
included *Night and Morning* (1938) and the three volumes
of satires from 1955, 1957 and 1960, that brought Clarke
international attention as a poet.

From 1922 until 1937 Clarke lived in London and worked
for various newspapers and journals (such as *The New Statesman, The Nation* and *The Observer*).[1] During this time many
of his plays and the first two novels were written. In 1928
he won the Irish National Award for Poetry. His friend, F.R.
Higgins, brought the statuette to him at the train station
where Clarke was boarding to return to England. Clarke is
reported to have said, 'My grateful country offers me a
statuette, but I have to emigrate to earn my bread.'[2]

In 1937 Clarke returned with his family to live in Ireland.
His mother made an arrangement with a religious community
for Clarke and his dependents to live in Bridge House,
Templeogue, until his death, at which time the house became
the property of the community again. While this arrangement
eased his financial burden during the forties and fifties, he
was much later to write on the lack of long-term security for
his wife and children.

In 1945 Clarke, with his wife Nora's help, began to publish
his own work from Bridge House. Bridge Press editions were
small in number, limited to two hundred copies and put

together with great care. This independent venture allowed
Clarke to avoid editorial intrusion and possible censure. But
it was the 1961 publication by Dolmen Press of *Later Poems*,
with its international distribution, that established Clarke
more widely as a modern poet.

Writing unsentimentally about modern life is a more
difficult task than romanticising the past. In his approach to
the unwieldy mass of facts about the contemporary situation,
Clarke directly challenges a previous generation of poets and
their ideals of heroic art. He openly confronts the tradition
of Yeats in Anglo-Irish poetry. In recognising the vitality
of Clarke's aesthetic programme, one must eventually reconsider the defining qualities of Irish poetry.

Clarke was committed to what may be called the 'reality'
of Ireland. His drama of racial conscience is an art of social
comment, a poetry 'concerning itself analytically with the
mental and religious problems which have made us what we
are'.[3] Clarke had discarded the poetic niceties of late romanticism, where the poetic persona despairs or is ecstatic,
ponders the world, but is ultimately alone, an exile in aesthetic
perfection. The work of the masters of early modern poetry
is an elegantly articulated retreat from the chaos and dis-
unity of a disintegrating world. In this poetry the reader
finds a beguiling, passionate assertion of individual worth.
The essentially non-social nature of the poetry is obvious,
not only in Yeats' work but also in other poets of the same
era and inclinations — in Eliot and Pound especially. Pound's
idiosyncratic and paranoid insistence that the poet could
change the world, and his *Cantos*, monumental but largely
inaccessible, exemplify this kind of poetry in all its excesses.
Yet, Pound has been called 'the greatest literary influence
since Wordsworth'.[4]

Clarke has no such messianic pretences. Because of his
early disenchantment with this malaise, he set about his own
literary explorations with different, more local guidelines.
Had he clung to the Celto-Romanesque world of legend and
romantic farce — an important transitional stage in his
work — Clarke would be just one more poet lost in artifice,
clinging to destroyed myths while the real world clamoured
outside the mythical world of his creation. The outrage and
sincerity of his compassionate apologies for the victims of an
earlier time would, ultimately, be evasions. However, in

Night and Morning and Other Poems (1938), Clarke began his personal exploration of Ireland with unrelenting commitment. He treats the town and country in which he lives, the people of his local acquaintance and the real experiences which have influenced or inspired him. We are shown in the poetry written since 1955 an uncompromising version of contemporary life permeated with the strength of Clarke's personality. Clarke's view of the state of Ireland might seem to be parochial, but his ideas acquired more universal application. This fusion of the general with the local is convincing because Clarke did not try to weld the disparate fragments into a continuously sound work of art; in his poems the disparities and contradictions of modern Ireland are thrown into relief. Such particularity lends an impression of veracity and indeed integrity, to Clarke's work.

Clarke wrote a series of highly detailed, sometimes extremely complicated, and often arrestingly intricate fragments. These fragments or vignettes can nevertheless be viewed as part of a larger, coherent work with a consistent point of view:

He has lived in an Ireland intensely conscious of its nationalism, and also experienced the more international outlook of the time before the Rebellion and that of today. It may be that this has turned him, in so many of his later poems, towards the consideration of exactly what values are to be found in the country in which he lives. He has seen the country created, and, therefore, is less inclined to accept it blindly, and more inclined to question, satirize, and judge. It has been very difficult to make a selection of Mr. Clarke's later poems, for they should properly be read in bulk, each poem contributing towards a panoramic whole of extraordinary range and passion. [5]

As the poems accumulated, in tiny private editions, it became evident that a perfectly integral world was under investigation in which — despite the unusually minute scale — the proportions of reality were more or less preserved. [6]

Clarke's 'journalistic' tendencies allowed him little room for generalisations or sentimental gloss. His late poetry

conveys the rich, varied and often paradoxical fabric of
modern life. Journalism has undoubtedly strengthened a
poetic line and diction already technically proficient. Louis
MacNeice explained the relationship between poetry and
journalism: '... the normal poet includes the journalist –
but he must be subservient to him. The normal poet –
witness the Elizabethians – should not be afraid of touching
pitch. But the pitch is so thick on the world's thoroughfares
nowadays that a poet needs exceptional strength not to
stick in it.' [7]

* In his poetic maturity Clarke grasped the minutiae of
daily experience and realised common woes, common values.
This tendency reminds one of the poetry of William Carlos
Williams in America. Confronted and angered by the force
of Eliot's rejection of Whitman in particular and American
culture in general, Williams strove to achieve an American
diction, an American epic. *Paterson*, Williams' ultimate
success, is very like Clarke's later work: detailed, disparate,
and yet irrefutably an artistic whole. Its influence on younger
poets parallels the influence on younger Irish poets attributed
to Clarke's poetry. The analogy 'Yeats/Clarke: Eliot/Williams'
is not facile. Williams, like Clarke, wrote steadily in near
oblivion, until his public recognition as an important poet
in the late 1950s. [8]

(ii)

In *A Penny in the Clouds* Clarke remembers his early years
as a poet and comments significantly about contemporary
trends: 'It took me many years before I was able to write
about the present age, and when I did so, I found that other
poets had retired to the campus and quadrangle, having
rejected the belief that writers should be concerned with
social reform.' (*Penny*, 199) His first poems about the present,
in the volume *Night and Morning*, are strangely direct and
personal, even confessional. I use this term hesitantly because
of Clarke's avowed loathing of 'the insidious questioning of
the confessional' (*Black Church*, 89). Yet M.L. Rosenthal
says of modern poetry:

the private life of the poet himself, especially under
stress of psychological crisis, becomes a major theme.

Often it is felt at the same time as a symbolic embodiment of national and cultural crisis. Hence the
idiom can be at once private and public, lyrical and
rhetorical ... the continuing power of the Romantic
tradition is clear, the specifically modern turn being
the strongly confessional, literally self-exposing vulnera-
bility characteristic of the statement.[9]

As much as I object to the use of 'Romantic tradition'
in connection with Clarke's work, the term 'confessional'
nevertheless seems appropriate.

Rosenthal discusses not only the work of Lowell, Plath,
and Ginsberg in this light but also Clarke's *Mnemosyne Lay
in Dust*. Though the Americans tend to use their personal
neuroses as symbolic embodiments of larger concerns,
Clarke avoids this tendency. His attack on national and
cultural issues is explicit and clearly directed. Clarke's poetry
is not so morbidly self-analytical as that, for example, of
Lowell or Plath, but in Rosenthal's discussion of Lowell's
poetry, one more readily accepts the appelation 'confessional':

Because of the way Lowell brought his private humiliations, sufferings, and psychological problems into
the poems of *Life Studies*, the word 'confessional'
seemed appropriate enough. Sexual guilt, alcoholism,
repeated confinement in a mental hospital ... these
are explicit themes of a number of the poems, usually
developed in the first person and intended without
question to point to the author himself. [10]

Mnemosyne Lay in Dust, discussed in the next chapter,
admittedly bears such a reading, but Clarke decorously saves
himself from the American tendency to over-expostulate
his own victimisation. He also claims a more traditional
authority for his own confession-poems: 'The Confession
poem', he writes in his notes to the *Collected Poems* (1974),
'was a recognised literary form in Gaelic and lasted till the
eighteenth century' (p. 548). However, it is society, not his
crazed self, that is Clarke's major theme in the poems of this
period.

The poems of *Night and Morning* deal with Clarke's
spiritual crisis and subsequent battle with the Church in

complicated structures and weighty, ambiguous imagery.
Of course, this struggle seems a commonplace in Irish writing
this century, best exemplified in the novels of James Joyce.
A critic has written of Joyce that: 'the trouble is that the
Church fails to conform to his high ideal of what a church
should be . . . Not he, but the Church is insufficiently Catholic . . . Joyce remained obsessed with what he had rejected.
Religion and family joined nation among his literary preoccupations.'[11]

Clarke admitted his resemblance to Stephen Daedalus but,
unlike Joyce, did not remain obsessed with the Church
and its various forms of mystery and ritual. The Church
was for Clarke the final hindrance to his poetry. The language of humanity and commitment was denied Clarke by
the dogmas of eternal truth. Clarke lacked Joyce's pride but
was more deeply rebellious, striving for complete freedom.
Richard Ellmann, describing Joyce's decision to quit the
Church, aptly explains the situation: 'It was becoming
clearer to him that, of the two ways of leaving the Church
that were open to him, denial and transmutation, he would
choose the second. He would retain faith . . .'   The faith that
Joyce retained included much of the abstract fabric of
received dogma, abstracted, that is, from what he had rejected
in his Irish Catholic background, and transmuted into a
'Joyceanity' that in its formal structure, if not in its specific
tenets, was modelled on Christianity.

Clarke's rebellion was more thorough. In his imagination
Christian imagery is not an aesthetic amusement. It is in its
manifestations in human affairs terrifyingly powerful and
potentially dangerous. Clarke does not attempt to transmute
Christianity; he denies it. Nevertheless his poetry is frequently
centred on symbols and images derived from Christian
dogma or ritual. The intention, however, is always to satirise
and to destroy them as Christian images and to seek in their
place the secular, human images for which they may be
masquerading. Clarke's frequent juxtaposition of the image
of sexual love with images of the Eucharist is a case in point.

Sly and humorous, Clarke's memoir, *Twice Round the
Black Church*, offers a remarkable contrast to the self revealed
in what I will call his confessional poetry. It is a valuable
key to understanding the darker themes of that poetry.
Clarke describes his childhood in Dublin as if it were a con-

tinual, and delightful, challenge to outwit his spiritual mentors
and to discover a life of freedom beyond his catechism. He
alludes constantly in proverb, and with typical irony, to his
fundamental unpiety: ' "The nearer the Church, the farther
from God". So runs the proverb and, by an inscrutable set of
circumstances, I spent most of my early life within stone's
throw of some Church or another' (*Black Church*, 142).
Throughout the autobiography there is a constant admission
of heresy. The Church and its orthodoxy stand in Clarke's
way, and to gain his freedom, his integrity, Clarke gleefully
lashes out at 'our strange European teaching' (*Black Church*,
71). He aptly summarises his spiritual education in a single
sentence: 'I had been brought up in the belief that all mortal
activity was vain, and that nothing mattered but the pursuit
of eternal pleasure' (*Black Church*, 105). In another aside he
captures the essential conflict between this teaching and
humane ideals: '. . . it takes us many years to learn that the
passion for justice and the welfare of all, once it has been
aroused, is the deepest one in mortal life' (*Black Church*, 121).
This aroused passion leads Clarke, as he puts it, out of the
Counter-Reformation, which remains always just behind him
with its cassocked figures, and into the modern world.

The analogy with Joyce is clearly acknowledged by Clarke
when discussing his Paris meeting with the older writer.
Joyce attended the same school as Clarke, though earlier,
and it is Clarke who says:

The 'Portrait of the Artist' had long since become
confused with my own memories or had completed
them and, set up by his recollecting presence, I heard,
as in correspondence, the murmur of classes and chalk
squealing on the blackboard until teeth cringed, saw
the faces of boys that I had hated and Jesuits in black
soutanes, the brass of candlesticks . . . and, with heart
in shoes, I waited, having had, as I fancied, those thoughts
that are forbidden by the Sixth Commandment, for the
fatal sound of the sliding panel of the confession box,
until suddenly the tenuous voice of Dedalus broke the
silence like falling glass — and Jesuits, boys, candlesticks and sins against the Blessed Virgin and all the
abracadabra of childhood vanished down the trap-
doors of the mind to lie in wait for the next dream or

perilous temperature.

(Black Church, 26-7)

Daedalus' 'non serviam' is a serious inspiration, but unlike
Joyce, Clarke went to Paris to forget Ireland and its Catholicism. Clarke's alter-ego, Maurice Devane, who is the subject
of *Mnemosyne Lay in Dust*, also appears in the poem, 'A
Student in Paris' (which is fully discussed in Chapter Six).
One of Clarke's bawdiest poems, 'A Student in Paris' clearly
demonstrates how different were his preoccupations — when
he was abroad — from Joyce's.

The overall impression of *Twice Round the Black Church*
is one of liberated joy, capriciously underlined by its magnificent closing tribute to Milton:

Gradually the vision of the great Puritan poet eliminated
from my mind the last fears of the hell of Alighieri, in
which, cut up, boiled, roasted, our bits had shrieked
through the years of infancy and boyhood. Imaginatively
I ventured into the visible darkness, moved by the lakes
of burning marl, peered into pandemonium and admired
those majestic fallen angels, who, despite continual
pain, spoke so proudly and with such courage . . . The
speeches of revolt stirred my mind so that I forgot the
grovelling and insincerity of our medieval training . . .

Although I had been conditioned from a tender age,
I can remember little of the gradual process of indoctrination. There are, however, certain names and
words which I cannot hear without an involuntary
shudder: for instance, Henry VIII, Darwin, evolution.
Socialism, also, is a word which almost makes me
murmur a protective aspiration despite my interest in
Irish reform . . . I was even more surprised when I
realised for the first time that what I had supposed to
be plain facts were beliefs which had to be defended
by argument. Although I had no words for my thoughts,
I realised dimly that we, too, could exercise private
judgment on condition that we agreed with the arguments given to us (in the catechism lessons) . . . Soon I
became much more interested in the questions in the
book than in the answers, being secretly thrilled by the
audacity of them . . . Without guessing anything about

symbolism, I delighted in the first line and a half of
Paradise Lost, fervently rejecting the implied consequences. I watched frequently the Tree of Knowledge and — whether my eyes were closed or wide
open — its bark and all its boughs were glittering.
(*Black Church*, 172-4)

Clarke's poems about his religious revolt are very different;
they are searing, anguished and full of questioning. The goal
is always in sight: that humanism so hesitant on the young
catechist's tongue.

(iii)

There is one curiously sombre statement that stands clearly
apart from the rest of *Twice Round the Black Church*. It
is Clarke's definition of poetry:

Ibsen, in one of his lyrics, gives us a definition of
poetry which seems appropriate to our needs, more so
than many of those well-known definitions which we
borrow from the English critics to our confusion.
    Poetry — 'tis a Court
Of Judgment on the soul.
. . . Our preoccupations with the next world is surely
fit subject for our poetry. But we still need complex
forms which reflect the intellectual excitement of the
ages and our own earliest intimations.
(*Black Church*, 19-21)

Night and Morning and Other Poems (1938) uses complex
forms to reflect an intellectural excitement and an agonising,
personal intimation of the soul in eternity. This collection
represents Clarke's movement towards a poetry which
reflects contemporary Ireland. The density of the poems
is not like the density of the technical ingenuities and artifice of his Celto-Romanesque poems. Instead this density
underlines more complicated issues. 'I was matching my
wits against the centuries', Clarke wrote in *Twice Round
the Black Church* (138). These poems concern all the tortuous ambiguities of belief and despair. Dogma, standing
in the way of an instinctive humanism, is challenged with

technical skill and a new spiritual candour.

'The Straying Student' is perhaps the most accessible poem in the collection, relating to earlier poems of wayward students and knowledgeable, godless women:

> Long had she lived in Rome when Popes were bad,
> The wealth of every age she makes her own,
> Yet smiled on me in eager admiration,
> And for a summer taught me all I know,
> Banishing shame with her great laugh that rang
> As if a pillar caught it back alone.
>
> (*Poems*, 188)

The casual criticism of papal fallibility and the all-saving laughter are those of Anier MacConglinne and the young 'Woman of Beare', as is the hidden assonance. The use of the first person singular, however, is new. It dramatically reinforces the final brutal image of fear and despair:

> And yet I tremble lest she may deceive me
> And leave me in this land, where every woman's
>   son
> Must carry his own coffin and believe,
> In dread, all that the clergy teach the young.

There are similar poems in the collection. 'Her Voice Could not be Softer' (*Poems*, 189), for example, concerns deception and desertion. 'Repentance' (*Poems*, 186) describes Clarke's career. Yet even as he fondly remembers his early enthusiasms, the poet is caught by an image of Patrick and the memory of a bad confession. Driven by terror, he hopes for absolution:

> I count the sorrowful mysteries
> Of earth before the celebrant
> Has turned to wash his mouth in wine.
> The soul is confined to a holy vessel,
> And intellect less than desire.
> O I will stay to the last Gospel,
> Cupping my heart with prayer:
> Knuckle and knee are all we know
> When the mind is half-despairing.

Faith, in its compelling simplicities, is secure, and the poet, alone in his doubt, cannot yet abandon his soul's safety. (The image of the priest turning away, incidentally, recurs throughout the collection.) 'No Recompense' (*Poems*, 190) is also unsettling and challenges the ideal of fame, stating with its title and mournful conclusion that the world is nothing when a man's soul is at stake. 'Mortal Pride' (*Poems*, 182) completes this side of the collection, which is concerned with definitions of the soul, questioning its value and re-treating in despair at the first inkling of damnation. Its image of the defiled sacrament of marriage (the impossibility of finding a 'husband in the state of grace') links 'Mortal Pride' to Clarke's other poems of heretical sexuality. 'Mortal Pride' is a sombre poem. It seems to deny the possibility of innocence. Sin exists in thought as well as action and the mind naturally indulges fancies. All are doomed; the only difference is that some men are aware of their damnation:

> When thought of all our thought has crossed
> The mind in pain, God only knows
> What we must suffer to be lost,
> What soul is called our own.

There is an important point in these lines. The second objective clause challenges metaphysical reality: 'God only knows . . . What soul is called our own'. If 'God only knows', then it is impossible for churchmen to know the truth about redemption and salvation; the poet has stumbled onto a liberating insight.

'Penal Law' (*Poems*, 189), epigrammatic, stern and hinged on ambiguities that are by no means fortuitous, is alone in the collection in its determined independence and self-assurance. 'Burn Ovid with the rest', the poet pronounces and then lashes at authority with licentious and newly relevant puns from Irish history and tradition. 'Lovers will find a hedge-school' refers to Penal Times, when the Irish were denied their education and had to meet secretly behind the hedges to preserve their Catholic heritage. The tables are turned; the Church is now the tyrant that forbids natural education which young Irish men and women will learn behind their own hedges, defying the Church and yet perhaps still its victims. The final line is ambiguous, suggesting

both repentance and illicit love in its imagery: 'When hands are
joined and head bows in the dark'. The arrogance and forceful
challenge of this poem is at once strikingly dissimilar to any
other poem of this collection and close in tone to the voice of
Clarke one hears, only much later, in such rousing poems as 'A
Sermon on Swift'. This pride and power, with the allusion
to Ovid, are also significant in that Clarke's last, and certainly
his most ribald and licentious, poetry is derived from a
creative reading of Ovid's *Metamorphoses*, most obviously
in 'The Dilemma of Iphis' and *Tiresias*.

The most serious poems in this collection, however,
treat intellectual freedom rather than sexual permissiveness
and are, as a result, more complex in their anguish and more
embittered against orthodox opinions. 'The Lucky Coin'
(*Poems*, 187) points to the Joycean paradox of Irish freedom;
politically and morally, people may be careless in their
liberation and remain subservient to the tyranny of the
pulpit. 'Tenebrae' (*Poems*, 183) is a meditation on despair
and man's final reckoning. Clarke suggests that man is 'betrayed at every station of the cross'. Reason alone is perhaps
futile against the eternity of Christ's passion, which underlines our own existence. An image of protest, with Lutheran
overtones is central to the poem:

> I hammer on that common door,
> Too frantic in my superstition,
> Transfix with nails that I have broken,
> The angry notice of the mind.

The personal understanding of responsibility in the image
of 'nails that I have broken' plunges the poet into abject
gloom. 'Tenebrae' (which title implies the matins and lauds
at the end of Holy Week with Christ dead and the world
darkened) is an intense speculation about the cost of freedom
to man's soul. 'An open mind disturbs the soul', he writes. He
is also pre-occupied with images of Christ's suffering and of
human damnation in the 'Darkness that man must dread at
last'. The poet finds himself in a vicious circle; unable to
leap into faith, he is caught alone and undefended from the
terror of ultimate damnation.

'Night and Morning' which opens the volume and 'The
Jewels' which closes it are less personal in their manner

than the other poems in this collection. 'Night and Morning' opens with a weary confession of 'injured pride' and night time despair. At night the mind dwells on images from a past more secure in its beliefs and on images of present desires, summoned and released by the poet's dreams. Yet mornings in church do not resolve the questions and forebodings of the night:

> The very elements remain
> Appearances upon the altar.
> Adoring priest has turned his back
> Of gold upon the congregation.

Once more we encounter the image of the priest turning away from the congregation to the altar, suggesting a church absorbed in its own ritual, indifferent to the needs of real people. His punning, and his constant use of irony and conceit, work to Clarke's credit. The poetic diction is at once personal and 'Augustan', firmly refuting any suggestion of the romantic in Clarke's use of confessional poetry. The priest is transformed here into a part of the ritual, as though he were part of the gold altar furniture. The uncomprehending congregation is left behind, used and then ignored in what is ultimately a solipsistic act of worship. Clarke puns again without glee:

> All saints have had their day at last,
> But thought still lives in pain.

The idea of thought and of mankind's rational achievements summons the final image of regret. Men have forgotten their original freedom and have lost a valuable heritage of independent thought:

> How many councils and decrees
> Have perished in the simple prayer
> That gave obedience to the knee.

Clarke praises then the neglected suffering of braver men:

> Forgotten as the minds that bled
> For us, a miracle that raised
> A language from the dead.

This image of praiseworthy but forgotten martyrs who suffered mentally for 'us' is the most difficult in the whole collection. That 'it is the secular vision of the universe, authenticated by centuries of human achievement, which prevents him from submitting to the theological view' is a valuable, if somewhat simplified critical insight.[13] We must look to the final stanza of 'Night and Morning' for a more complex evocation of his secular vision:

> O when all Europe was astir
> With echo of learned controversy
> The voice of logic led the choir.
> Such quality was in all being,
> The forks of heaven and this earth
> Had met, town-walled, in mortal view
> And in the pride that we ignore,
> The holy rage of argument,
> God was made man once more.

The idea that man's godliness is his intellectual capacity is prominent in the entire collection. Clarke takes personal delight in and inspiration from 'the holy rage of argument'. This age of reason was a time to be alive; a faith that cannot embrace intelligence and debate is a faith to be discarded. Dogma stifles the inspiring vitality of rational inquiry. Faith and knowledge are now irreconcilable; the latter denies God, the former limits his creation, mankind.

'The Jewels' (*Poems*, 191) attempts to answer the questions raised in the opening poem and its successors:

> The crumbling centuries are thrust
> In hands that are too frail for them
> And we, who squabble with our dust
> Have learned in anguish to dissemble.

That 'thrust' is essential. Clarke admits that one cannot avoid the burden of Europe; one cannot ignore the soul and its intimations, cannot, like the priest, turn one's back on doctrines valid and necessary through so many centuries. To do so would be careless and irresponsible; one must submit or withdraw. Facing this dilemma, Clarke admirably acknowledges that

> ... taken in the darkest need
> Of mind, no faith makes me ashamed.
> Whether the breath is foul or sweet
> The truth is still the same.

And the truth that is still the same is a sad one: 'We are bred among stories that are older than ourselves and we disappear from sight, with the last aid of a little Latin, in the fond hope that all cannot be rot' (*Black Church*, 63). Alone, one can only use whatever symbols are at hand to comprehend such truth.

The Church will not admit such glossing of reality, maintaining its attempt to falsify the nature of existence as an eternal cycle of rebirth. As a belief it is replete with spiritual bounties, but it fails:

> The sanctuary lamp is lowered
> In witness of our ignorance;
> Greed of religion makes us old
> Before our time. We are undone
> Within the winking of an eyelid,
> The very heavens are assailed
> And there is nothing can be hidden:
> Love darts and thunders from the rail.

The poet abandons his suffering. To continue is to admit the rightness of a Church he can no longer respect. The only hope in a labyrinth of damnation and despair is rational inquiry and common sense. The intellect, he knows, has always striven against fear and the emotionalism of creed or superstition:

> The misery of common faith
> Was ours before the age of reason,
> Hurrying years cannot mistake
> The smile for the decaying teeth,
> The last confusion of our senses.

Rationalism is, unfortunately, a sad strength with which to face life. Gone are the wonder, the ingenuous childhood belief and delight in the mysteries of religion:

> But O to think, when I was younger
> and could not tell the difference,
> God lay upon this tongue.

With this nostalgic farewell to Christianity, Clarke has laid his ghosts and enters his poetic maturity.

(iv)

In 1938 when he published *Night and Morning and Other Poems*, Clarke was in the middle of another career as playwright, novelist and literary critic. Nine years had passed since he published *Pilgrimage and Other Poems*, and it would be seventeen before another volume of poetry appeared. For the full development of his continued argument with Christianity one must look to plays such as *The Son of Learning*, *The Viscount of Blarney*, and *As The Crow Flies* and to his three novels, in which dogmatic assertions about the nature of life conflict with an otherwise free and natural existence. The series of satires begun in 1955 are on the other side already. The Church is no longer of interest to Clarke as a power with which to argue the issues of morality and salvation. In as much as the Irish Catholic church is mentioned, it is as a menacing, passionless, political institution which is able to (and does) obstruct social progress. Socialism, and one must use this word after a reading of Clarke's 'political' poetry, preaches a well-being in the immediate or foreseeable future, and thus erodes the basis of the Church's authority. In any system of belief which promises non-earthly and more enduring rewards than man can envisage, the material condition and situation of its adherents are clearly of secondary importance. Clarke, however, looks around himself in outrage at the condition of the world; he is not to be taken in by the promise of happiness hereafter.

The Ireland of romantic fantasy was a land of dreams, love, and freedom, wherein an individual could outwit his superiors and die happily. Ireland, fifty years after the 1916 rebellion and independence, is, as Clarke saw it, the ill-fare state complete. One is reminded of O'Casey's bitter summing-up of the Irish situation: 'Things had changed, but not utterly; and no terrible beauty was to be born.'[14] Clarke's scrutiny of affairs, however, is more continuous and up-to-date. In *A Penny in the Clouds*, he states: 'Anger is good. I think discipline may be better' (16). The anger in these satires is always disciplined, though often fierce. His subject matter is frequently startling. Richard Loftus wrote:

> For the poet determined to dedicate his art to his native country — and Clarke has been just as determined to do this as were Yeats and Pearse and Colum — there remained little choice but to look at the reality and to comment upon it . . . The result is a sustained, bitter satire against the Irish Catholic Church and the ruling middle-class establishment . . . Stephen's satires are tempered by his humor, those of Yeats by his sense of aristocratic dignity and the rhetorical discipline of his art. Clarke's later poetry knows no such restraint. Gone are the backdrop of medieval Ireland, the neo-pagan ideals, the occasional burst of comic humor. What remains is a savage rage that Ireland has not known since Swift in the seventeenth century and the Gaelic bards of an earlier age. [15]

It is important to emphasise the thematic impact of these satires since it can sometimes be missed in an overly technical discussion of their style and method. Richard Loftus wrote: 'Both Swift's prose and Clarke's poems offend our sense of decorum. But no doubt that is precisely what each of them intended; for the purpose of such satire is not to please men but to castigate them.' [16]

In these poems Clarke satirises the reality of modern Irish life which cannot hide behind its convenient, facile myths of moral righteousness and national destiny. He refuses to allow these clichés to intrude on his poetry. 'But how can I make room for them,' he asks in one poem, 'In a mind too horrible with life?' (*Poems*, 201).

Throughout the first collection of satires, Clarke's humanity is evident. In poems like 'Emancipation', 'Return from England', and 'Ancient Lights', we are continually reminded of his own beliefs and doubts. 'Ancient Lights', which opens with a delightfully autobiographical sketch, recounts Clarke's conversion to humane ideals:

> When all of us wore smaller shoes
> And knew the next world better than
> The knots we broke, I used to hurry
> On missions of my own to Capel
> Street, Bolton Street and Granby Row
> To see what man has made.
>
> (*Poems*, 199)

This poem, like many others, is tied to Clarke's intimate knowledge of Dublin geography. Local news and incident and a sense of particular location bind this new poetry with a grim hardness unlike, for example, the Celto-Romanesque verse of 1929. There, a hermit fought his instincts on some island in the west of Ireland. Here, a labourer's wife dies in the Liberties of Dublin and a beggar stands, hand outstretched, on O'Connell Bridge. 'Ancient Lights' leaves the physical present for a moment's backward look and introspection, and begins to assume the kind of argument which underlies *Night and Morning and Other Poems*. The poem consists of a series of 'epiphanies' couched in dense and difficult language that chart the poet's progress to intellectual freedom:

> Nature read in a flutter
> An evening lesson above my head.
> Atwirl beyond the leadings, corbels,
> A cage-bird came among sparrows
> (The moral inescapable)
> Plucked, roof-mired, all in mad bits. O
> The pizzicato of its wires!

Clarke considers the inescapable moral, sees himself as the cage-bird, weakened and victimised by rigid thinking, orthodoxy and dogma. Freedom is to think and to liberate oneself from such a cage-like superstructure of belief. This didactic aside is, however, a backward glance for Clarke and misses the issues that now most interest him. Academic argument about individual will and intellectual freedom, argument with Church ruling, is argument in a void. The poet refuses the bait. If he argues with the Church, he will lose sight of his real subject and argue with the past. His intentions are clear:

> No, let me abandon
> Night's jakes. Self-persecuted of late
> Among the hatreds of rent Europe,
> Poetry burns at another stake.

The rude dismissal of self-analysis in terms of spiritual debate is strengthened by the inquisitional imagery of the final line. It hurls condemnation at early Christian indoctrination which can still mislead the poet and it emphasises the just epithet, 'Self-persecuted', which is applied to poetry. Wit informs the poet's anger. Poetry, like Clarke arguing with the Church, has become tortuously introverted, retreating from the larger concerns of the modern world. This poem, giving the collection its name, reveals Clarke's purposes. It is a poetic attempt to re-enter the world of social, political and moral conflicts. The poet cannot afford to indulge narcissistic, aloof solipsisms. The world exists independently of the individual who so seldom sees this reality because he is caught in personally significant but fundamentally irrelevant crises. The experience of his youth is important to Clarke because it was then that he gained his ability to look openly at the world:

> I had absolved myself:
> Feast-day effulgence, as though I had gained
> For life a plenary indulgence.

The events in this poem incidentally explain the significance of the recurrent image of the Black Church. Not only heretical, the Protestant church was also superstitiously forbidden to his childish wanderings. Clarke overcame his fears standing in its doorway and found a new meaning in life. The devil did not appear as promised in the childhood rhyme about going around the Black Church thrice. Clarke thus overcame a superstitious bigotry. 'Ancient Lights' refuses to become sidetracked on religious issues, however, and finishes with a vision of innocence and its strength against dogmatic moral guidance. Clarke describes the experience in concrete imagery that demonstrates his joy and sheer physical sense of the world in which he has discovered his relationship to life:

> The sun came out, new smoke flew up,

The gutters of the Black Church rang
With services. Waste water mocked
The ballcocks: down-pipes sparrowing,
And all around the spires of Dublin
Such swallowing in the air, such cowling
To keep high offices pure: I heard
From shore to shore, the iron gratings
Take half our heavens with a roar.

'Return from England' (*Poems*, 205) states Clarke's
dilemma clearly, revealing the attitudes he acquired while
working in England. Overcome with nostalgia for Ireland
and a general homesickness, he returned but was shaken by
conditions at home and people's attitudes to them:

But mind, pretending pity,
Unslaves me in like haste,
Only to take me closer
With some new tale of wrong here,
Holy retreat of tongue.

The attack is in the final line with its image of the pious
distancing themselves from a foul world. The paradox that
ends the poem is an ironic deflation of a traditional Irish
attitude. In England, though he was poor, Clarke could sleep
more soundly and untroubled than he could in Ireland:

When I had brought my wife
And children, wave over wave,
From exile, could I have known
That I would sleep in England
Still, lie awake at home?

'Emancipation' is a fuller explication of Ireland's lack of
social awareness and public conscience: 'pity is a kind of lust'
which is abundant. There is no public undertaking to aid the
poor. Beggars, depending on charitable cast-offs, roam the
streets in rags. For Clarke they are new symbols of Irish
'freedom':

That wretched girl still wakes me up
At night, for all she wore had been thrown

Away. I see her by O'Connell Bridge
And think: 'Yes, more than a century
Ago, religion went in such rags here.'
                    (*Poems*, 203)

There are fangs in that metaphorical parallel to the Church.
'Inscription for a Headstone' (*Poems*, 202) is a companion
poem to 'Emancipation'. Its hero, James Larkin, was an
emancipator, leader of hungry crowds, strike-organiser and
socialist. He has become the conversational pet-topic, Clarke
declares, of dilettantes, his message smothered by bourgeois
affectations. Church and State have worked to obscure the
issues of economic unrest.[17] Clarke complains in bitter
satire that the real reason why Larkin should be remembered
is forgotten:

His name endures on our holiest page,
Scrawled in rage by Dublin's poor.
                    (*Poems*, 202)

'Offerings', 'Bequests', 'An Early Start', 'Fashion', and
'The Envy of Poor Lovers' describe an Ireland for which the
Church no longer has meaning. Having dismissed its con-
gregations' material welfare as irrelevant to more eternal
reality, the Church nonetheless enriches itself with grander
churches, larger bells and more magnificent charities and
lottery pools. Clarke's purpose in these poems is to plead
for the people of Ireland against a system that fails to understand and ignores their human needs, divorced from them as
it is by its dogma and hypocrisy.

Ancient Lights, Poems and Satires begins with the poem,
'Celebrations', which satirically commemorates the Eucha-
ristic Congress of 1932 in Dublin:

open hearts are celebrating
Prosperity of church and state
In the shade of Dublin Castle.
                    (*Poems*, 195)

The religious imagery of the poem is aggressively yoked to
Clarke's declaration that Ireland's theocracy is corrupt and
self-seeking, adding a blasphemous intimation to the image

of 'open hearts'. The last stanza of 'Celebrations' attacks smug public piety:

> Let ageing politicians pray
> Again, hoardings recount our faith,
> The blindfold woman in a rage
> Condemn her own for treason:
> No steeple topped the scale that Monday,
> Rebel souls had lost their savings,
> And looters braved the street.

Among the politicians was, of course, de Valera, himself once a rebel leader. The sense of injustice prompts Clarke to an intricate poetic statement of destroyed ideals and lost glory. In *Twice Round the Black Church* he wrote:

> There is no doubt that a country in which an ever-increasing number of celibate orders continually exert influence must suffer from a hidden uneasiness. No theologian nowadays believes with Aquinas on succubation; no vow of chastity can prevent man or youth experiencing natural pleasure in what a merry hedge-schoolmaster of the Penal Age used to call 'somnium humidissimum'. Our hidden war against natural instinct was intensified as soon as we had gained our freedom and the British troopships sailed from our southern harbours. While Mr de Valera's republican army and the new regiments of Mr Cosgrave's Provisional Government were jeering one another in the streets of Dublin and the Civil War was imminent, the suppressors of vice were already active. Despatch riders patrolled the city laneways at night time in search of skirt-lifters. Led by a friar, devoted bands closed down the brothel district by means which were not strictly legal but had the secret approval of the new Government. In a few years there were several serious outbreaks of what used to be called unnatural vice.
>
> (*Black Church*, 164)

The 'looters' of 'Celebration' are the officials of Church and State. The real perversion was not 'unnatural vice' but unnatural 'justice'. Clarke's wrath against immoral perversions of justice has an outraged Swiftian intensity.

'Marriage', though less densely intricate, is no less powerful. It has, for example, a certain dramatic humour:

> Parents are sinful now, for they must whisper
> Too much in the dark. Aye, there's the rub!
>
> (*Poems*, 196)

The humour of these lines fades, however, when we recognise the realisation of the situation revealed in this poem.
The parents must whisper and the children cannot help
hearing; Clarke is describing Dublin's poor in their over-
crowded houses and flats.[18]He employs an epigrammatic
intensity to condemn an authoritarian church. Crushed
and confined by the narrow, authoritarian rulings of the
Church, parents are forced to

> . . . steal the crumbs
> From their own wedding breakfast, spare expense
> And keep in warmth the children they have
>   nourished.

Without reservations regarding the proper subject of poetry,
Clarke turns to discuss the methods of contraception favoured
by the Catholic Church:

> But shall the sweet promise of the sacrament
> Gladden the heart, if mortals calculate
> Their pleasures by the calendar? Night-school
> Of love where all, who learn to cheat, grow pale
> With guilty hope at every change of moon!

Here poetry has been moulded with compelling power for
the purposes of political and social debate. It must be said,
however, that there is no clear evidence as to the extent of
its influence on the pace of social reform in Ireland. State
legislation regulating the availability of contraceptives, for
example, came only in 1979, twenty-four years after the
publication of this poem, and then in a form which Clarke
might not have been entirely happy with.

'Mother and Child' (*Poems*, 202) is another politically
topical poem which gains much of its power from the ironic

interplay in the title and the last two lines between the
'mother and child' and the madonna. Dealing with the defeat
of a coalition government over its proposed legislation to offer
free medical care to all mothers and their newly born children
in Ireland, this poem shows the political causes of Clarke's
antagonism to the Church:

> Obedient keys rattled in locks,
> Bottles in old dispensaries
> Were shaken and the ballot boxes
> Hid politicians on their knees
> When pity showed us what we are.
> 'Why should we care,' votes cried, 'for child
> Or mother? Common help is harmful
> and state-control must starve the soul.'
> One doctor spoke out. Bishops mitred.

Politicians had bent to the will of the Irish hierarchy and
the bill was defeated. The 'one doctor' who 'spoke out' was
Noel Browne, then Minister for Health, who introduced the
controversial bill. His mistake, according to the received
view, was that the proposed law did not discriminate between
legitimate and illegitimate births and thus provoked the
Church's righteous indignation. For what is mercy towards
sinners but a crime against the community as a whole?
Recently, the situation has again been debated, prompting
Noel Browne to write to the newspapers explaining his part
in this affair:

> These are the facts. The 'Browne' Mother-and-Child
> Scheme included a free scheme for *all* mothers in
> motherhood, and *all* children up to the age of sixteen
> years; *all* medicines too, were to be free. There were to
> be no more doctors' or chemists' bill *and there was to
> be no means test*. My successor, Dr. Ryan's scheme . . .
> on the contrary, *introduced a means test*, a central issue
> in the whole controversy. This circumscribed the right
> of eligibility for the maternity part of the scheme. He
> also reduced the eligibility for children of 'eligible
> mothers', from sixteen years to *six weeks*. Drugs and
> medicines were to be paid for by the ineligible groups.
>   Under renewed pressure from the bishops once again

on their scheme, de Valera and Ryan bowed to the
episcopal diktat. I, too, was offered, and could have
restored 'amity between Church and State', on these
terms of unconditional surrender. Instead, I chose to
'accept their ruling', but declined to implement their
alterations, and resigned my Ministry.

It seems reasonable to me to claim that few parents
of families would share the apparent belief of the sheltered celibates in our religious communities that these
'alterations' were *insubstantial*. [19]

'Eligible mothers' were legally married mothers. Illegitimacy
was not to be supported. Clarke's poem satirises this clash
between Church and State by relating it to the new postage
stamp of the same year which bore a portrait of Mary and
Jesus. The uncomfortable blasphemy, the suggestion of
Christ's illegitimacy under Irish law, is fully intended.

'Three Poems About Children' (*Poems*, 196) are, I believe,
the most upsetting of Clarke's satires. They are exercises in
scholastic logic and false comfort. All three poems show by
their carefully logical, yet spurious arguments the Church's
equally spurious lack of normal human sympathy. Children
who die young, some at birth and unbaptised, unblessed, are
of little concern to the Church:

> flowers
> That wither in the heat
> Of benediction, one
> By one, are thrown away.

An orphanage that burned down, claiming the lives of all its
children is cruelly blessed:

> Has not a Bishop declared
> That flame-wrapped babes are spared
> Our life-time of temptation?
> Leap, mind, in consolation
> For heart can only lodge
> Itself, plucked out by logic.
> Those children, charred in Cavan,
> Passed straight through Hell to Heaven.

This is Clarke's satire at its savage best. The rhetoric is coiled,
controlled and logical, the language simple and direct, the
irony vehement — and the effect devastating.

(v)

The anecdote, concentrated with irony, is employed again
in Clarke's two later collections of satiric verse, *Too Great A
Vine* (1957) and *The Horse-Eaters* (1960). In his notes Clarke
justifies his satires on local events. Finding among his own
predecessors a colourful eccentric who was also a writer of satiric ballads, Clarke typically understates his own poetic aims:

> A great-grandfather of mine, who was a skinner, lived in
> the Liberties of Dublin and had a tannery in Watling
> Street, near Usher's Quay. In his later years he seems
> to have become eccentric for he wore wigs of different
> colour during the week. He amused himself by writing
> occasional verses of a satiric kind about his fellow-
> traders and got the ballad-singers from Thomas Street
> to recite these outside their shop-doors.
>
> As I have few personal interests left, I have con-
> centrated on local notions and concerns which are of
> more importance than we are, keep us employed and
> last long . . . In their notices of *Ancient Lights: Poems
> and Satires, First Series,* a few critics suggested that some
> of the pieces were too mild to be called satires. I hope
> that I have made amends.
>
> (*Poems*, 549)

The poems in both collections are different, however, from
those in *Ancient Lights.* The short poems, though as tight and
witty, are not so deeply unsettling as, for example, Clarke's
poems about children or his 'Mother and Child'. They are
more worldly and more vindictively rational.

'Pilgrimage' (*Collected Poems*, 218), for instance, attacks
popular credulity about Lourdes and modern miracles. Clarke
demolishes ingenuous speculation with his immediate and
truthful cry that 'No bed that walks is worth such pain'. He
describes the industry and materialism which surround the
modern Delphi, its commercialism, and exploitation of
human agony:

The many thousands are brought to pray
Because our wonder must have crowds
Purchasing trifles at stall and tray
To make a holiday of hope,
Then, stare at stretcher, limbs that grope.

The anger here is not Swiftian but more humane and compassionate.

Many of the poems cover ground similar to that of Clarke's
previous satires; these are 'Past and Present', 'Irish Mother',
'Intercessors', 'Christmas Eve', 'Marian Chimes', 'Wolfe Tone',
and 'The Trial of Robert Emmet'. 'Local Complainer' describes a public subscription to erect a statue of Mary in Cork
at the dockside, and deflates the pious intentions of such
action with an ironic use of religious language and sexual
innuendo:

> Our chequebooks
> Are opened gladly for their statue,
> Despite the Decalogue. So few can
> Refuse to give or pray for lost souls:
> The loyalist become Loyola,
> Each week another Fontenoy won.
> We scarcely know ourselves on Sunday.
> (*Poems*, 211)

In his notes to this poem Clarke vents further anger at this
pious erection of icon and monument:

> As the result of wide organising, religious statues have
> been erected in many towns and villages, by the road-
> side, on hilltops, outside factories, quarries and mines,
> and in the poorer districts of Dublin. Most of these are
> painted plaster casts, supplied by enterprising firms. They
> may prove our public piety, but certainly display our
> total lack of artistic taste.
> (*Poems*, 550)

'In The New Statesman Office' and 'Irish-American Dignitary' wryly comment on foreign influences on Irish life,
prefiguring the various concerns of Clarke's later poetry, as
in *Flight to Africa*. In the first he recalls an encounter with

Dr Marie Stopes and punningly considers her pioneering efforts
to legalise contraception:

> Though Ireland shook in my veins, denouncing
> The poor man's friend, I futured. Popes,
> Far-seen in total white and lace,
> Will pity our overbearing creed,
> Somehow prevent the loss of grace—
> And fewer orphanages need
> Those begging letters (Mercy's fount)
> Dispatched in plain envelopes.
>
> (Poems, 227)

Idealism and hope for reform is not a common note in
Clarke's satire. 'Irish-American Dignitary' (*Poems*, 221) is
more typical, expressing mock gratitude for a hurried, thought-
less, but politic visit to Ireland.

Some poems in these two collections look forward to later,
larger poems. 'Abbey Theatre Fire' (*Poems*, 207) relates
directly to the Yeats poems in *The Echo At Coole*. 'Miss
Marnell' (*Poems*, 210) is of a kind with, though slighter than,
the Martha Blake poems. Two of the poems, 'St Christopher'
(*Poems*, 219) and 'Knacker Rhymes' (*Poems*, 222), are important for the light they shed on more substantial poems in
the collections under discussion; they introduce what represents Clarke's major innovation in these final satires: a
prolonged consideration of politics and social necessity and
a meditation on his own understanding of humanity and art
and their relationship to life. It is to these more substantial
poems, 'Loss of Strength', 'The Flock At Dawn', and 'The
Hippophagi', that I will now turn.

'The Loss of Strength' (*Poems*, 212), written after severe
illness, is the *tour de force* of this period. Inspired by
Coleridge's 'Youth and Age', a major theme of Clarke's poem
is based on Coleridge's melancholic reveries, about youthful
enthusiasm and the problem of ageing (See *Poems*, 355).
Clarke's poem is not as vague as Coleridge's, and it is bound
to his particular realisation of approaching old age and the
changes which he has witnessed in Ireland during his lifetime.

'The Loss of Strength' is rooted thematically and symbolically in an image from nature and Clarke's exploration of its
moral. Material progress in the course of Clarke's lifetime

caused the spoiling of the countryside and the subsequent
loss of its pleasures:

> Farm-brooks that come down from Rathfarnham
> By grange-wall, tree-stop, from the hills,
> Might never have heard the rustle in barn dance,
> The sluicing, bolting of their flour-mills,
> Nor have been of use in the steady reel
> On step-boards of the iron wheel-rim,
> For Dublin crowds them in: they wheeze now
> Beneath new pavements, name old laneways,
> Discharge, excrete, their centuries,
> Man-trapped in concrete, deeper drainage.

It is remarkable how gracefully and with what apparent ease
Clarke is able to tie his half-rhymes and conglomerate words.
The lines move effortlessly with an assonance reminding one
of earlier poems. The rhyme helps to establish a subtle
rhythm: 'Rath*farnham*' — '*barn dance*', '*laneways*' — '*drainage*',
'*reel*' — '*wheel*-rim' — '*wheeze* now' — 'cent*uries*', 'B*eneath*'
— 'ex*crete*' — 'con*crete*' — '*deep*er'. The pun on 'reel', relating backwards to the barn dance, is felicitous. The full impact
of these lines is conveyed by the careful transposition of what
might have developed into a pathetic fallacy. It is not the
rivers themselves, discharging their past, who have never
known a calmer, pastoral existence. This is made clear with
the image of a sprawling town crowding the countryside,
trapping the clean, flowing waters, and polluting its own past.
Knowledge of small but important traditions like place-names
is forgotten as man continues to impoverish his own estate.
Clarke closes the stanza with his own surprised discovery of a
small stream, 'littling itself', and then depicts its unsullied,
neglected grandeur:

> No artificial fly or wet-hook
> Could stickel it. Summer was cressing
> Her mats, an inch from reeds. The brooklet
> Ran clearly under bramble. Dressed
> In the newest of feathers, black, trimmed
> With white, a pair of waterhens dimmed
> Away from me, with just a dot
> Of red. Three visitors, one soul

Among them or not. Know-all can tot it
Up. Lesser bits of life console us:
Nature at jest in light and shade,
Though somewhat afraid.

Clarke conveys a sense of small, delightful, unexpected victories, beautifully implicit throughout the poem with its
urgent appeal for calm and order. Clarke is writing of every-
man's individual structure of calm and achievement, of his
own instincts that certain bonds will hold against the chaos
and disaffections of life. His own bonds are found in nature's
consoling peace with mankind, an insight gained in his youth
when he cycled across Ireland. He is now older and painfully
yet tenderly aware of his own diminished powers:

I climb among the hills no more
To taste a last water, hide in cloud-mist
From sheep and goat. The days are downpour.
Cycle is gone, warm patch on trousers.
All, all, drive faster, stink without,
Spirit and spark within, no doubt.
When hope was active, I stood taller
Than my own sons. Beloved strength
Springs past me, three to one.

'But', Clarke writes and one can almost hear him expostulate,
'I knew the stone beds of Ireland':

Now only a wishing-cap could leave me
On the top of Slieve Mish.

The reference to his three sons, full of loving awareness of
his own limited mortality, and his own recounted adventures
lead Clarke to consider the moral education of young people:

The young must have a solitude
To feel the strength in mind, restore
Small world of liking. Saints have spewed
Too much.

Instinctively he knows the veracity of his statement. His own
untrammelled exploration of the countryside and its tradi-

tions gave him freedom and taught him about nature's bene-
volence. Significantly he uses the verb 'spewed' to describe
saints, linking them to the technological harnessers of Ireland's
rivers. The habitat of gods and mystery is now scientifically
demystified:

> Now engineering
> Machinery destroys the weirs,
> Directs, monk-like, our natural flow:
> Yet it was pleasant at Castleconnell
> To watch the salmon brighten their raincoats.
> The reeds wade out for what is gone:
> That mile of spray faraway on the rapids
> Is hidden in a tap.

Clarke's point, surely, is not that one should disown the modern century, even were this possible, but rather that this century has wrought its doom by failing to replace the myths and
culture it destroyed for the sake of progress. The machine is
impressively effective, but significantly hollow:

> Should man complain of plans that curb
> Torrent in turbine? Great disturbance:
> The hush of light. Why keep with Fintan
> The Falls of Assaroe, trample
> Of transmigration, void of man
> In shape of salmon? Those currents were ample.
> Voltage has turned them, riddle and all,
> To a piddle and blank wall.

This reflection with its allusion to the mythology he exploited in *As The Crow Flies* leads immediately to criticism
of the Church, an institution whose powerful mythology
Clarke understands and to which he is, paradoxically it might
seem, opposed. Did not Clarke's quest for a natural mythology
involve him to considerable extent in medieval Ireland and
its Celto-Romanesque Church? And yet, Clarke is the arch-
critic and poet-denouncer of this same, now larger, Church.
In a typical lunge, Clarke speaks against that mythological
power and recognises himself bound to its influence:

> Celibacy is our best rule still,

Restraint increasing its adherents.
Stuck-honey embitters. Though the schoolmen
Denounce our senses, what can fear add?
Let women masculate with hair-cuts,
Piety hates their very guts
But makes no comment on what shortens.
Refrain, poor sight, for much goes bare:
Walking temptations, visible mortal
Sins, churched by fashion. Fewer stare now.
Layman watches the theologian,
Both, us. A cogent clan.

This religion of embittered repression, whatever claim it may
have upon Clarke's soul, is not the affirmation of humanity
and instinctive calm which Clarke propounds at the poem's
beginning.

In an earlier image of machinery which destroys salmon
weirs and takes over nature, Clarke made the analogy between
technology and Catholicism. Engineering, he wrote, 'Directs,
monk-like, our natural flow'. This parallel perversion of the
natural countryside and human nature, with its attendant
imagery of hollowness and pollution, removes the paradox.
To underline his distinction, Clarke once again summarises
his rejection of the catechism and his return to Ireland:

Too long near London, I broke in exile
Another bread. The nightingales
Naturalised my own vexation:
Yet, dearer on Inish Caltra, one boat-hail
At dawn . . .
                    No friend of Alcuin's,
I saw God's light through ruins.

The God Clarke found in Celtic Ireland is not the Church's
God. God is the measure of man's striving soul, the inspiration
of possible achievement and its human memory, and the re-
minder of man's unsullied, naturally beautiful place in this
world. Clarke rails against the modern Church and State
because both institutions work against and manipulate human
nature. Both, with hand in fisted glove, mislead people and
empty their lives of true meaning. Both remove nature from
the realm of everyday life, denying its ability to interfere with

their powers.

Rather whimsically, Clarke proposes that scientific explanations can be found to account for religious miracles or, failing that, they could be dismissed as the exaggeration of zealous hagiographers. Nevertheless the Church thrives and Irish people continue to suffer:

> Too great a vine, they say, can sour
> The best of clay.

In his poem of the same collection, 'St Christopher' (*Poems*, 219), Clarke further elucidates the epigrammatic centre of 'The Loss of Strength' and, indeed, elucidates the significance of the entire collection. In 'St Christopher' the Church is the great vine carried on the back of an ill-faring but pious country. Religion is rooted in Irish life and sours the land, like technology, by sucking and draining its riches away. The freedom which the Irish sought is eroded by the very people who should benefit from it:

> Our Easter Rising—a scratch
> In empire, self-wounded by war and truce.

The Church's reconciliation with progress is seen as sinister and inevitable. The bitter symbol of the combined power to crush a people's spirit and kill a country is the aeroplane, named after saints, taking invalids in search of the miraculous cure to Lourdes:

> Hope that no specialist has smiled on
> Removes our corporal disorders.
> Above the clouds where all is white
> And blue, with nothing to alight on,
> Annual pilgrimages, sprinkled
> With blessings, go: flown hospitals . . .
> Through grottoes of cloud they come; few cured
> At Lourdes: all reassured.

Against such odds, his own mortal rage at the inhumanities of life in Ireland is impotent.

'The Loss of Strength' reverberates with meaning. Its various levels of identity and analogy, its associative yet logical construction of argument, and its insights into a modern soul, make it a masterpiece in modern poetry. The poem touches universal human concerns, and Clarke's use of particular locale, idiosyncratic place-names, and his own reading of history do not detract from the reader's grasp of the poem's content and significance. Too great a vine may kill the land; by the close of 'The Loss of Strength' Clarke seems very much aware that too great a rage may destroy his own humanity, or pollute his own spirit. The poem ends with the poet once more turning to nature, to the little stream, and saving at least his own soul:

> Loss but repeats the startling legend
> Of time. A poet wants no more
> To palliate his mind . . .
> May the Deuce
> Take all of them and thought get better
> While faith and country play a far hand!
> Plod on, tired rhyme. The streams that wetted
> Forgotten wheels push past Rathfarnham,
> Half underground: slime steps on stone.
> I count them—not my own.

The reliance on nature as a refuge and source of joy brings to mind the Sweeney myth. In *The Singing Men at Cashel*, Clarke set the pattern which he was to follow in his own rebellion. Gormlai who was, it will be remembered, tortuously repressed by public sanctity and morality sought refuge away from men. At one point she thinks of the legendary mad king and receives some comfort from his story:

> Despite herself, she began to think of Suibhne: often she had thought of the unhappy, royal poet, for he had wandered in wild glens to which even the hermits never came. He was excommunicated by Saint Ronan because he had refused to give him a site for a new church and had thrown the saint's psalter into a lake. The saint crazed his mind by the power of a curse, but Suibhne found healing at times in those brakes towards which his disturbed spirit drove him. Had he not found gentleness in all creatures? Had he not known the last peaks

even as the rains know them? She imagined him busy
about the edges of woods or attentive at dawn:

> The brambles know that I am ragged,
> But I have music far from men,
> The gentle clamour of the stag
> His voice above the glen.

She loved the poems of Suibhne because he had praised
what others despised . . . Knowledge came to him at
times when he was gathering cress for himself from the
streams or hiding his store of hazel nuts for the winter . . .
Suibhne was the unhappiest, the loneliest of the poets.
But when his end was near he came again to Saint
Ronan and after his repentance he received the Body
and Blood of Christ. She must not think of his last
hours, she would be unhappy for she had often wept
to think of them.

(77-8)

'The Loss of Strength' suggests that Clarke found knowledge in nature, just as did the mad poet, Sweeney.

'The Flock At Dawn' (*Poems*, 225) is a mischievous
piece based on an extended metaphor which links crows,
jackdaws, and starlings with Jesuits. One feels this 'satire'
is only a pretence, however, behind which Clarke indulges
an obvious fondness and delight in untried rhymes. It allows
an unexpected and unprecedented view of Clarke himself,
the elderly man of letters playing at being angry, finding
entertainment in his rapidly associative imagination. Half
awake, Clarke would have us believe, he is aware of the birds
around his house fancifully pursuing their antics. He is
immediately drawn into considering his near neighbours, a
Jesuit community:

> That hoarseness had come down the chimney pot.
> Hearing mistook the spot. No rhyme but the jack-
>   daw,
> Who glosses a neighbourly fir-branch with his beak
> And wants to be my tenant, left that caw.
> Already the starling, tall as his twitter and tweak,
> Was spangling himself, nearby, upon the gutter.
> I turned, sheeting my doubtful self, and drowsed
> While pinchbeck stims were inching past the shutter

> Edges; then suddenly thought of that mighty un-
>   housing
> A mile away, rooks elming in a flock
> Above Rathfarnham Castle, hunger in bits,
> Whirring, time-struck, its own alarum clock:
> Thousandfold call, not one, for Jesuits
> In elmy, shadowy bedrooms, their birettas,
> Soutanes off, spiritual weapons racked.

The assonance of these lines contributes to the onomato-
poeic conceit of the bustling, active birds and conveys
Clarke's joy in building a poem not only from his freely
wandering associations but also from his sensual appreciation
of sound impressions. It is Clarke's outrageous delight to
imagine resting, undressed Jesuits and to pun in such a way
as to remind the reader that these are the army of Christ.
Surely the facetious phrase, 'spiritual weapons racked', has an
inquisitional connotation which cuts across an otherwise
absurdly indulgent conjecture? Clarke then is able to recall
more of the ridiculous in recognising the Jesuitical pride of
spirit:

> — a portrait row of saints,
> So much alike, they make the varnish dull.

The tone of his rebuke is far from severe and belies any
apparent anger in the poem.
   Despite his criticism of his Christian neighbours, the poet's
comments on their regular morning habits are offered with
a grin:

> morning faith like the milk supplied
> In bottles comes to us now with clatter and jolt.

Clarke, considering his words and the world in general, is
relaxed and more carefree than usual:

> The English language
> Was loopholed here for centuries. But the night
> That Edmund jumped the wave-tops — faerie castle
> A torch — our rivers ran with Thames to spite us.
> We lost in that war of words. The syllables

Which measure all delight: mouth-exile. Scansion's
Our darling fondled over sea.
                                                Who cares?
Our monks reside in eighteenth-century mansions
Now. Hell-fire rakes have spirited these heirs.
Always in debt to banks, they plan more buildings,
Made reckless by the vow of poverty,
Pile up the sums that burning souls have willed
To them in clock-tower, high walls, such debris;
Teach alms to gamble, while agents share the kitty.
Communities ply from abroad, new planters
Lording our land once more.

The puns here on planters and landlords demonstrate how
subtly Clarke is able to expose the lie of Irish freedom
(the Jesuits being just one more set of symbolic tyrants
like the English before them in the figure of Edmund Spenser).
Clarke also dismisses the parochial arguments for a national
language as unrealistic and irrelevant, drawing his own
justification and tradition from the time of Spenser's unhappy stay in Ireland where some of *The Faerie Queene* was
written. Implicit in these lines is that thought that at least
those earlier tyrants left something of value in Ireland when
they left. Especially pointed, therefore, is the humorously
ironic deflation of the Jesuits' material aggrandisement, 'Made
reckless by the vow of poverty'. This is not a coherently
argued or logically structured poem. 'The Flock At Dawn' is
brought to its end by the repetition of one of the images of
the flock, 'Hunger in bits', after which the poet is lulled to
sleep again by an amusingly erotic catalogue of place-names.
Clarke sees the birds in flight and dozes happily, finding
much to entertain his mind in the world outside his window:

                                        Hunger in bits,
The flock is flying from the dawn to scantle
Among the dairy farms. Tired of complaint,
I dream of revellers unvaulted, place-names
In County Dublin left by the unsaintly,
When few that crossed themselves had buckle or lace,
Mount Venus, Cupidstown, the Feather Bed . . .

Sleep nodded to life's nothing. Emptihead.

'The Hippophagi' (*Poems* 229) is more serious and directly
related to 'The Loss of Strength'. It is an enlarged version of
'Knacker Rhymes' in the same collection. 'Knacker' is a
slang-word for the trade of collecting horse corpses and
using the hooves and other parts for making glue. It is only
truthful to admit, however, that this poem about the sacrilege
of eating horse-flesh covers much ground that is already
familiar (and not always ably or lucidly). Its power lies in
Clarke's ability to join his heretical religious beliefs and
political opinions with his sense of wrongdoing in the horse
trade. Throughout the poem Clarke develops his sociological
view that the Irish have discrete perceptions, allowing much
that would upset them to pass unnoticed. Thus, the sensuality of religion is 'asterisked' away, leaving only a bleak and
cold system of belief. Clarke's problems in this quarter began
when he 'mitched from miracles' (to mitch is to play truant)
and tried to discover the human world around him. The
horses of bygone days have been replaced by cars. The streets
are now more deadly, mechanical and uninteresting. In the
same way, ideals have been replaced by a deadly materialism.
Technology is now omnipotent and horses, which were
important in the past, are shipped on board boat and plane
to the tables of Europe: 'Old bets are soon betrayed.' The
horses are shipped alive because such a business is less obvious
and less offensive than slaughtering them in Ireland where the
public would be obliged to witness or, at least, to be aware of
the sacrilege.

Despite its tight imagery and compact ironies, its conceited
language and technical virtuosity, 'The Hippophagi' is anti-
climactic in Clarke's three books of satiric verse. Clarke
rounds off each assonantally rich stanza with identical
rhymes, but fails to tighten his arguments correspondingly,
or to direct his anger sufficiently clearly. Clarke's explanation
of his own technique is interesting:

Rime riche is the perfect rhyme, since two identical
words, with separate meaning, are in accord . . . In
English the second homonym seems at times to be
ironic in effect, and in composite self-rhyme may lead
back, perhaps, to the mood . . . in which the rhyme
becomes a running commentary.

(*Poems*, 555)

'The Hippophagi' abounds with identical rhymes, which
suggest another purpose as well, not unlike that of the
final couplet in a Shakespearean sonnet which summarily
concludes an extended discourse. A few examples should
suffice:

> Thought plays
> The devil, unsought. Should the Almighty
> Destroy it after All . . . might he?
>
> *(Poems,* 231)

> Loaders at the North Wall
> Hurrah for the Hippophagi,
> Tots echo: 'Let's hip off a gee.'
>
> *(Poems,* 233)

> Unsure in time, as moth
> Or behemoth, man steadies his wonders.
> Backache, wing-thundered on its ledge, ends.
> Fact stole, fell, goes beyond all legends.
>
> *(Poems,* 234)

The sheer complexity and compression of 'The Hippophagi'
raise questions as to the extent to which its ultimate implications are defined or integrated. In any case, it does have one
important merit in that it reads like an exercise or study
prefiguring Clarke's masterful *Forget Me Not.*

(vi)

In 1969 Clarke was commissioned by the Arts Council of
Great Britain to write, for the 'Poetry at the Mermaid'
Festival in London, a long poem. *Forget Me Not* is the
logical and unforgettable extension to his work in both
'The Hippophagi' and 'The Flock at Dawn'. Published singly
by the Dolmen Press in 1962, and then as part of the col-
lection, *Flight to Africa and Other Poems* in 1963, *Forget
Me Not* was printed separately in the 1974 *Collected Poems.*
Readings from history, Irish political questions, experiment
in rhythm, an 'ars poetica', and his own adventures with
'All the gentling, custom of mind/And instinct, close affection'
of horses are all combined with a truly finished grace. *Forget*

Me Not, if idiosyncratic, is startling and impressive. It is the autobiographical, summing up of Clarke's moral self-education and career, a fitting and enchanting epitaph for this period of his life.

A 'work-a-day, holiday jingle' which Clarke learned as a child riding in his Uncle John's trap holds the poem together, intruding on occasion only to inspire further comment and gentle reverie by the poet:

> Up the hill,
> Hurry me not;
> Down the hill,
> Worry me not;
> On the level,
> Spare me not,
> In the stable,
> Forget me not.
> (*Poems*, 237)

This childhood chant is used as an invocation from which Clarke launches immediately into the academic realm of classical literary definition, obviously enjoying the sounds of the terminology:

> Trochaic dimeter, amphimacer
> And choriamb, with hyper catalexis,
> Grammatical inversion, springing of double
> Rhyme. So we learned to scan all, analyse
> Lyric and ode, elegy, anonymous patter,
> For what is song itself but substitution?
> Let classical terms unroll, with a flourish, the scroll
> Of baccalaureate.

This opening is daring. The cadence of his catalogue gives Clarke full range for assonance and allows the equation between the more elegant genres of poetry and 'anonymous patter'. The childhood rhymes he remembers are not only justified, but elevated to a new dignity and mimicked in the final lines: Clarke's homage to the intellectual and necessary aural disciplines of poetry. The danger of the audience being distracted by the catalogue of technical terms is fully countered by Clarke's manipulation of the music and physical rhythms of the anachronistic poetical terms.

The tension between classical form and childhood wonder is maintained in the next stanza. Clarke associates intelligent criticism and an intellectual understanding of poetry with Coleridge, and finds in Coleridge's notebooks the explanation he seeks:

> Coleridge had picked
> That phrase for us — *vergiss-mein-nicht*, emblem
> Of love and friendship, delicate sentiments.
> Forget-me-nots, forget-me-nots:
> Blue, sunny-eyed young hopefuls! He left a nosegay,
> A keepsake for Kate Greenway.

Poetry, like a flower, is picked for its sentimental values (and with the sentimental poetry of Kate Greenaway and her brightly coloured storybooks, we are back in the country of Clarke's childhood). He reinforces the suggestion of child-hood with an echo of the horse-cart jingle.

In the next section of *Forget Me Not*, Clarke describes his early love of horses and his introduction to poetry. Riding in his uncle's trap, he discovered that

> Verse came like that, simple
> As join-hands, yet ambiguous, lesson
> Implied, a flower-puzzle in final verb
> And negative. All was personification
> As we drove on: invisibility
> Becoming audible. A kindness spoke.
> Assumed the god; consensus everywhere
> In County Dublin. Place-names, full of Sunday,
> Stepaside, Pass-if-you-can Lane, Hole in the Wall.
> Such foliage in the Dargle hid Lovers Leap,
> We scarcely heard the waters fall-at-all.
> Often the open road to Celbridge: we came back
> By Lucan Looks Lovely, pulled in at the Straw-
>   berry Beds,
> Walked up the steep of Knockmaroon. Only
> The darkness could complete our rounds. The pony
> Helped, took the bit. Coat-buttoned up, well-rugg'd
> I drowsed till the clatter of city sets, warning
> Of echoes around St Mary's Place, woke me.

Here is that same richness of life's simpler delights celebrated in 'The Flock at Dawn' and lamented in the 'The
Loss of Strength'. The city is seen in a negative light with its
pious street-names, discipline, rules and bigotry. Clarke
passes rapidly, however, beyond his religiously narrow upbringing and concentrates instead upon the freedom he
learned in the streets and the natural wonders he found
there. 'Ancient Lights' describes how he wandered these
same streets to 'see what man has made' and how in his
wanderings he turned away from Catholicism. Here, Clarke
displays that other life, and explains the lessons he learned,
the wonders he saw:

> 'Gee up,' 'whoa,' 'steady,' 'hike,'
> 'Hike ow'a that.' Rough street-words, cheerful, im-
>   patient:
> The hearers knew their own names as well. Horses,
> Men, going together to daily work; dairy
> Cart, baker's van, slow dray, quick grocery
> Deliveries. Street-words, the chaff in them.
> Suddenly in Mountjoy Street, at five o'clock
> Yes, five in the evening, work rhymed for a minute
>   with sport
> Church-echoing wheel-rim, roof-beat, tattle of harness
> Around the corner of St Mary's Place:
> Cabs, outside cars, the drivers unranked in race
> For tips; their horses eager to compete,
> With spark and hubbub, greet with their own heat
> Galway Express that puffed to Broadstone Station.

The elegant pace of this existence was doomed by more
than just 'the metamorphosis of steam'. Progress involved
not only the end of the horse-drawn carts but the advent
of Irish freedom and the coming domination of the Catholic
church in Irish life. For a brief moment, however, Clarke is
right to remember the glory of a time when 'Nature had
learned to share our worldliness'. That memory sums up the
alienation and frustration of the modern era which occasioned
'The Loss of Strength'.

   With the dawning of the age of petroleum and motor-
cars, horses — symbols of nature in co-operation and harmony
with man, and poetic images of Clarke's childhood — were

out of date:

>   Mechanised vehicles:
> Horse-power by handle-turn. My Uncle John
> Lost stable companions, drivers, all. Though poor,
> He kept his last mare out on grass. They aged
> Together. At twenty-one, I thought it right
> And Proper.

Before the advent of the motorcar the horse always con-
ferred a certain chivalric status on his owner. A team of
horses symbolised financial well-being. The horse was also
a work-mate, a companion. The trade in horse-meat reduced
the status of the horse from partner to inanimate scrap.
No wonder Clarke saw the new horse-trade as brutal and
traitorous. Clarke now develops the themes of 'The Hippophagi' in superlative fashion. 'What are they now,' he
demands, 'but hundredweights of meat?', condemning
the newly coarsened, material inspiration of farmer, butcher
and merchant alike:

> A double trade. Greed with a new gag of mercy
> Grants happy release in our whited abbatoirs.
> 'Gentlemen, businessmen, kill on the spot! O
> That,' exclaim the good, 'should be your motto.
> Combine in a single trade all profits, save
> Sensitive animals from channelling wave,
> Continental docking, knackering down.
> We dread bad weather, zig-zag, tap of Morse.'
> Well-meaning fools, who only pat the horse
> That looks so grand on our Irish half-crown.

The essay in vituperative rhetoric (notice that 'whited ab-
batoir' with its allusion to 'sepulchre') is checked with an
artful, conversational aside, 'I've more to say'. Clarke thus
cancels the deadening impact of his earlier variations on the
same theme. He continues with a reading from Classical
history. Greek, Latin, and Celtic legend all held the horse
in reverence. There were many things a man might do in dire
circumstances but he would never be allowed to abuse the
trust, affection and strength of his horse. Modern butchery,

by contrast, is exposed by Clarke's epigrammatic jibe: 'Men
pick the ribs of Rosinante/In restaurants now.' Cervantes,
like Coleridge, inspires the idealist in Clarke, who now
attacks this moral abasement with a profound image that
shows man as victim of his own self-mutilating progress:

>   I hear in the lateness of Empires,
> A neighing, man's cry in engines.

This prophetic insight (echoing Joyce's 'army charging upon
the land') would alone prove the power of *Forget Me Not*.

Turning again to the chivalric ideal, Clarke introduces
an Irish theme in an allusion which prefigures his final
acknowledgement of Yeats: 'Horseman, the pass-word'.
There follows an aisling-like stanza in which Clarke uses the
convention he first tried in 1929 but leaves the vision and
dreams behind to look at Ireland now:

>   Too much historied
> Land, wrong in policies, armings, hope in prelates
> At courts abroad! Rags were your retribution,
> Hedge schools, a visionary knowledge in verse
> That hid itself. The rain-drip cabin'd the dream
> Of foreign aid . . . Democracy at last.

The angry pity is genuine, but so is the snub in that final
statement. Clarke explains his full irony and disillusionment
with an historic, newly relevant, image:

>   A Gaelic poet,
> Pitch-capped in the Rebellion of '98,
> Called this Republic in an allegory
> The Slight Red Steed.

Ireland offers a poor compromise when thought of in terms
of the dreams and ideals that went into achievement of its
independence. In his penultimate image, Clarke disparages a
country founded now on lotteries and materialism, and con-
demns the neglect in a rhetorical flourish that concludes with
a barb of irony alluding to Ireland's first modern poet:

>   Word-loss is now our gain:

Put mare to stud. Is Ireland any worse
Than countries that fly-blow the map, rattle the sky,
Drop down from it? Tipsters respect our grand sires,
Thorough-breds, jumpers o' the best.
Our grass still makes a noble show, and the roar
Of money cheers us at the winning post.
So pack tradition in the meat-sack, Boys,
Write off the epitaph of Yeats.

The rage too has a literary source. In that first image of countries in the sky, dropping to earth, Clarke is echoing Swift's
equally vehement distaste for Irish ways: the image is Laputa.

The emblematic horse and sentimental flower have achieved
a profound significance in *Forget Me Not*. The neglected art
of poetry itself has been raised through these images to an
important status — a vehicle for the defence of morality,
virtue, and truth. To close his poem, Clarke turns back to the
rhyme which now speaks for himself, and his works as well:

Up the hill,
Hurry me not;
Down the hill,
Worry me not;
On the level,
Spare me not,
In the stable,
Forget me not.

Forget me not.

And so the poem ends, tied finally to that image and en-
blem

Of love and friendship, delicate sentiments.
Forget-me-nots, forget-me-nots:
Blue, sunny-eyed young hopefuls! He left a nosegay.

Satire in a New Mood
CLARKE'S POETRY IN THE 1960S

(i)

From 1963 to 1968 Clarke published five volumes of poetry which are remarkable for their assurance and range of theme and style. These volumes were *Flight to Africa* (1963), *Mnemosyne Lay in Dust* (1966), *Old-Fashioned Pilgrimage and Other Poems* (1967), *The Echo at Coole and Other Poems* (1968) and *A Sermon on Swift and Other Poems* (1968). This period of Clarke's literary career is characterised by the most systematic publication of his work that he was to enjoy.

The work dealt with here is ushered in by a poem (1963) written at Mount Parnassus which comments significantly on Clarke's development:

> . . . I must
> Learn, straight from the horse's mouth,
> To kick up my own dust.
> Here is the source. Here was our must.
> I see no flowers to grass us,
> Only the scale of Mount Parnassus:
> Simplicity of snow
> Above, the pillared drouth,
> The worn-out, below.
> I stray from American, German, tourists,
> Greek guide, feel in my two wrists
> Answer for which I have come,
> The Oracle, not yet dumb.
>
> (*Poems*, 245)

Here are ideas and styles he played with earlier — notably

the idiosyncratic identification with horses, the renewing use of cliché, and a disregard for more subtle rhyme forms in favour of deliberately identical, punning end-rhyme. The Oracle in his wrists is Clarke's vitality, a creativity bound not to god-like utterance but to the pulse of his existence. We are reminded once again of the centaur in the house of prayer.

In the poems we now consider, much will be familiar. More often, however, the reader recognises an advance, a gathering of insights and technical invention into a poetry by which Clarke's reputation must ultimately be judged. It is not always a gentle and 'poetic' art.

Clarke's earlier work in various poetic genres is extended. He consolidates disparate elements from previous experiments. Much is undeniably personal, while even the least autobiographical and directly social writing conveys the sense of the poet himself as a citizen in many worlds. His political pronouncements are less vitriolic and broader in focus than those of the earlier satires. Travel poems extend the metaphor of pilgrimage and involve the reader directly in the poet's life and observations. These observations range from reminiscences of past friendships and other poets to considerations of the past's achievements and comments on the present situation of man and poet in the world. The preacher who self-consciously modelled his aesthetic on the understanding of Gaelic prosody now makes room for the poet who enjoys experiments in metre and form, searching for patterns worthy of imitation. Innovation remains an act of preservation, an integral part of Clarke's continuing criticism of the negative aspects of modernism. What is new, however, is the delight in rediscovered music and the creative freedom rooted in the disciplines and forms of Gaelic poetry.

In numerous earlier works, Clarke employed various personae (like the wandering scholar, the liberated and the repressed women, the callous bard eager to employ his wit rather than come to terms with his horror at vicious inhumanities) to distance himself from his work while also casting a wicked but understanding grin at the reader. A fierce integrity informs the new poetry. The skill with which Clarke builds his poems and the honesty with which he describes his various concerns and interests command our respect. This allows the poet to reveal an idiosyncratic world which we accept:

> There begins a new dramatic, less occasional investigation of the significant scene, carried out ... in poems written in the key of reminiscence, of autobiographical summing up — a developing autobiography of ideas, feelings, significant scraps, the darts and twists of life. In Clarke's new poetic voice, certainly by the time he is writing the poems in *Flight to Africa*, nothing is unsayable.[1]

The mature voice we now encounter is that of a poet not morbidly self-analytical nor zealously egoistic (as is much poetry in the contemporary autobiographical manner) but personal in an old fashioned way. Clarke reveals himself in order to understand himself and thus to allow his reader to appreciate an individual view of the world. This cautious and detailed scrutiny of even banal circumstances bears its reward in the work:

> The later poems accumulate in this way; they establish relationships among themselves and help to illuminate each other. With detail after detail of personal history brooded upon, of local hypocrisy and meanness cursed or pitied, a microcosm of the whole human scene — with Templeogue as centre, and very little radius — is described. Raising a fundamental question of obscurity, these poems, by their authority and integrity, lay the question to rest.[2]

In this chapter the poems will be discussed not in strict chronological order but will focus on groups of poems having the same or analogous themes. We examine in section ii the Martha Blake poems and similar satires on the human condition, considering both the poetic qualities and the social implications of these finely drawn vignettes. This section will also discuss those satires that focus directly on the personal, human consequences of political or religious questions of the day such as the debate on birth control or the 'mother and child' controversy. Many of these poems are centred on the plight of inidividual characters, though with a power that gives them a universal significance. Section iii covers the satires concerned with more general political issues and public events such as emigration or the Taoiseach's visit to Africa.

In some of these poems Clarke moves away from Irish subjects to larger world issues: the EEC, the Viet Nam war, etc. Some poems from *A Sermon on Swift* (1968) are discussed in this section. The title poem on Swift, however, is discussed at the beginning of Chapter Seven. In 1967 Clarke visited the United States of America and wrote as a result a series of poems giving a diary of his experiences there. These poems, published in *Old-Fashioned Pilgrimage* (1967), and the attempts at literary criticism in verse from *The Echo at Coole* (1968) are dealt with in section iv. Some of this poetry, it will be seen, is not Clarke's best. Section v deals with his 'translations' from and imitations of Gaelic poets in the second half of his collection *Flight to Africa* (1963). The last section of this chapter is an analysis of Clarke's important, longer autobiographical poem, *Mnemosyne Lay in Dust* (1966).

(ii)

The style and tone of Clarke's satire in this period is altered. Clarke's outrage, which was earlier couched in a rhetoric of anger and abusive logic, is gradually replaced by a more wordly, and at times wry, compassion. Clarke is at once less parochial in his concern and more humane. His tone is that of a man rudely aware of much that is unnecessarily, and even anachronistically, painful. A diction once savage and correct is now passionate and secular. The poetry is remarkable for a new tenderness and an exacting concern with detail.

'Martha Blake' in 1938 and 'Miss Marnell' in 1957 would, of course, belie such an interpretation of Clarke's poetic development. The inclusion of both poems in earlier collections is odd. Surrounded by the agonised complaints of *Night and Morning*, 'Martha Blake' is strikingly different, while the slighter 'Miss Marnell' also differs from its companion pieces and is more correctly discussed with more recent poems.

The imagery of 'Martha Blake' illustrates my point. There are similarities between Martha's joy in hurrying through Dublin to Mass and Clarke's wondering evocation of medieval Cashel in the first 'Pilgrimage':

> she dares
> The silence of the street
> Until the double bells are thrown back
> For Mass and echoes bound
> In the chapel yard, O then her soul
> Makes bold in the arms of sound.
>
> (*Poems*, 184)

With another image also used in 'Pilgrimage' ('And in stained glass the holy day/Was sainted'), the second stanza is under-cut by the ironic use of Christian ritual:

> But in the shadow of the nave
> Her well-taught knees are humble,
> She does not see through any saint
> That stands in the sun
> With veins of lead, with painful crown;
> She waits that dreaded coming,
> When all the congregation bows
> And none may look up.

The conceit in the third to fifth lines is different, however, from anything in the earlier poem. There are several other effects (like Martha kneeling at the rail, 'Starching beneath her chin') which quietly explore the woman's uncomfortable propriety. The poem rests finally on diction and imagery, and on a technical effect used more effectively in an earlier poem. In the fourth stanza, for example, Martha receives Communion with a joy that 'is the glittering of candles/ and benediction sung'. This stylish diction is borrowed directly from the earlier 'Planter's Daughter' where it skillfully describes the girl's beauty as 'music in the mouth' and the girl herself as 'the Sunday in every week' (*Poems*, 173). Such linguistic affectation, however, is of limited durability.

What distinguishes 'Martha Blake' is the last stanza:

> So to begin the common day
> She needs a miracle,
> Knowing the safety of angels
> That see her home again,
> Yet ignorant of all the rest,

The hidden grace that people
Hurrying to business
Look after in the street.

The magnanimous juxtaposition of misguided 'holiness'
with the everyday, common 'grace' of the street is a characteristic of Clarke's poetry in the 1960s. Anier MacConglinne
mocked the singleminded religious view of life, and Clarke
wrote that his mind was 'too horrible with life'. Now the
overt controversy with the Church begins to be ignored.
Clarke's revulsion is overcome, and his poetry is free to concentrate on the 'music' of mundane experience.

'Miss Marnell' (*Poems*, 210) is another early poem that
presages this new direction in Clarke's work. This small
portrait of a pious spinster is neither vindictive nor harsh,
as are the satiric pieces which accompany it. Clarke's anger,
however, is implicit as he recalls the self-sacrifice of the
faded gentlewoman. His target is the aspiration that destroyed her:

    False teeth got little acid from her food:
    But scribble helped to keep much mortar wet
    For convent, college, higher institution,
    To build new churches or reduce their debt.
    The figure on her cross-cheque made restitution
    For many sins.

The conceited diction is of a piece with the concise, satirical verse Clarke wrote during the 1950s. 'Miss Marnell'
betrays a hesitant compassion, however, in its opening
gestures of hospitality and in its admitted incomprehension
of the woman's life:

        She had become a Catholic
    So long ago, we smiled, did good by stealth,
    Bade her good-day, invited her to tea
    With deep respect. Forgetting her loss of wealth,
    She took barmbrack and cake so hungrily,
    We pitied her, wondered about her past.
    But her poor mind had not been organized;
    She was taken away, fingering to the last
    Her ivory decades. Every room surprised:

Wardrobes of bombazine, silk dress, stank:
Cobwebby shrouds, pantries, cupboard, bone-bare.

'Miss Marnell' and 'Martha Blake' form a bridge between the
satires, with their harsh anger, and Clarke's more recent
poetry. Clarke distills from the lives of these women something of the universal condition of ordinary humanity, a
condition which the Church imposes while it exploits the
women's zeal with

pleas that made her madder
To comfort those who need for holy living
Their daily post: litterings, flyblown, miced
In corners, faded notes of thanksgiving,
All signed — 'Yours gratefully, In Jesus Christ.'

These early poems lead us directly to a consideration of
poems like 'Miss Rosanna Ford', 'The Vocation' and 'Martha
Blake at Fifty-One', extensions of Clarke's earliest concern
for 'the long martyrdom of women throughout the centuries'
(Black Church, 116). Shorn of its romantic dimensions and
epic pretensions, the poetry is now no longer concerned
with claims to freedom and moral superiority. Clarke explores a blighted area of contemporary life in these portraits
of common, often older women. As in his drama, victims
now occupy the stage.

'The Vocation' (Poems, 439) describes the innocence
of Angelica, who aspires to the conventual life. It is delicat-
ely handled as Clarke describes the girl's joyful haste to
help others:

On the grass near the old sluice-gate
She sat and watched the water slew
Below, excited, happy. 'I've
only a day left now. Indeed,
Scarce time', she smiled, 'for a good deed'.
She heard far down the quiet tinkle
Of a pool, and then, behind the ivied
Wall of the mill, a drunken tinker
And his trull squabbling, got up, ran
To plead with them, all little random
Words.

> Religion, cold, unfeeling
> Came nearer, darkening the fields.
> The man muttered, the woman wailed
> Into her shawl. Both shambled away.

Comic at first sight, Angelica's worldly incompetence is made tragic by the muted understatement of her failure to help. Carefully selecting image and incident (consider, for example, the implication of the word 'trull') Clarke is able to suggest the events of an entire life in only thirty lines of poetry. Understatement, new to Clarke's poetry, is central to the effect achieved in his description of Angelica's life:

> Angelica was not robust
> Enough to scrub the convent floors,
> That ritual of humble pride.
> An old nun handed her a duster
> Or pushed her a tin of polish, pried:
> And still her visions were sweetly floral
> As she drifted towards the altar scent.
> But in a year she was sent away.

In a final external image, the bleak and desolate hours that lay ahead for Angelica's shamed soul are clear:

> Sometimes I see her in a car,
> Ashamed to meet acquaintances,
> Unhappy, her prayers of no avail,
> Beyond the reach of her dear saints.
> No longer is her young soul carried
> To joy. The Mass bell will not ring
> For her. She must not see through the veil,
> Wear for the first time a marriage ring.

The fitful use of identical rhyme, the lack of an explicit emotion or comment, and the definite but unobtrusive presence of the poet at the fringe of Angelica's life, combine to lend this poem its quiet sense of desolation.

'Miss Rosanna Ford' depicting lonely poverty is another poem rich in implication (*Poems*, 436):

> Spinster of 37 Wexford Street,

> She lived alone, aloof at eighty-four,
> So indigent she seldom could afford
> Sufficient warmth or food for the cupboard shelf.

Ignored until it is too late, the woman is discovered

> Half dressed, almost deceased on the floor,
> Because she had no shilling for the gas,
> Blue-handed, freezing . . .

Her story is unknown. The furniture in her frozen room, which is already up for rent again, has been sold, 'auctioned, inarticulate'. The cruelty of winter and the callousness of the Christmas festivities are seen for a moment and then, like this forgotten woman, removed:

> Outside, the passing motor cars, the Ford vans,
> Were hushed by the funeral of the late snow.
> A church-bell, tongue in cheek, remarked the date
> And Christmas presents in fashionable stores,
> Dropping their pretty veils of crepe, vanished.

The indifference of the world is demonstrated by the careful juxtaposition of her incidental death and the sudden truth of the pun that describes the bell's mechanism.

The diction of these poems — so different from *The Echo at Coole* — is significant. Clarke's powerful invective has been overlaid with a more subtle and allusive manner. The language is more descriptive, less intellectually dazzling. Puns are used sparingly and the reader — no longer distracted by such rhetorical devices — can now see Clarke's characters as individuals and his vignettes as 'epiphanised' summaries of their lives. The adjective 'epiphanised' is used with some justification. One can describe Clarke's poetry in this Joycean mode or, indeed, as Chekhovian at times. Action or minor incident, situation, and dilemma are described in an apparently objective way with a compellingly allusive imagery. Robert F. Garratt, in his article, 'Austin Clarke in Transition', makes a similar comparison between the characters in Joyce's and Clarke's works:

Life in modern Dublin is presented as a routine existence, recalling the sense of paralysis and death in Joyce's *Dubliners*. The people in Clarke's poems exist in a world described by spiritual paralysis, death-in-life, robot patterns of behaviour. . . . Other characters from the city are presented, each a reflection of the living-death, the lonely frustration of Joycean emptiness. [3]

Clarke uses techniques similar to those of the short story writer, and the reader is made to enter a relationship with the various characters. Clarke's opinions are understated and his almost deadpan presentation of the circumstances in which his characters live determines one's response. A similar development occurred, of course, in the technique of his novels. He minimised the sermonic aside, concentrating instead on a strengthened and enriched ironic fabric to make his point.

Nowhere is this change more evident than in 'Martha Blake at Fifty-One' (*Poems*, 265). Gone are the conceits and paradoxical concentration of images which placed 'Martha Blake' beside Clarke's earlier confrontations with Christianity. In their place, the undistinguished details of Martha's life and dying (already evident in the earlier poem) fill the poem. The continuity between the poems is enhanced by the immediate allusion in 'Martha Blake at Fifty-One' to the final stanza in 'Martha Blake'. In the latter, Martha walked home after Mass, oblivious of the common miracle around her in the street and yet assured by the knowledge of 'angels that see her home again'. Now, the same woman is described as 'Angeling the road' on her way to church. This phrase which also demonstrates his fondness for inventing verbs shows that Clarke sometimes had imagistic tendencies. 'Angeling the road' goes beyond mere allusion to convey the dramatic but obsequious presence of Martha in this world.

There is another major difference in Clarke's tone here. 'Martha Blake' was dense with intellectual images and a conceited intensity that betrayed Clarke's own involvement with and despair at the seemingly hollow rituals of worship. 'Martha Blake at Fifty-One' is devoid of this personal intrusion. Clarke observes and records her actions, empathising with her aspirations but tightening his syntax to achieve a new ambiguity. Thomas Kinsella has remarked on the same change in Clarke's work:

> Particularity, minute precision, is an element of artis-
> tic strength, and as it developed in Clarke's work, it
> is one of the reasons he has become an imporant poet. It
> is everywhere, in varying manifestations, in the later
> poems; in the drab and painful Chamber-Gothic, for
> example, of 'Martha Blake at Fifty-One'. 4

Images and details of a typical morning in Martha's life are
mentioned but are not justified or explained:

> She knelt
> Illumined. In gold-hemmed alb,
> The priest intoned. Wax melted.
>
> Waiting for daily Communion, bowed head
> At rail, she hears a murmur.
> Latin is near. In a sweet cloud
> That cherub'd, all occurred.
> The voice went by.

These simple sentences lend to the poem a camera-like
intensity. Clarke's mastery of his own proud anguish is
masterfully displayed in a language at once bare and profound. The careful shift to the past tense implies the pathetic
isolation of Martha Blake which gradually overwhelms the
reader.

The details of her life are built up through mundane
images like the boiling of an egg, the buying of a chop,
until the shocking and private pain she endures is revealed:

> She suffered from dropped stomach, heartburn
> Scalding, water-brash
> And when she brought her wind up, turning
> Red with the weight of mashed
> Potato, mint could not relieve her.
> In vain her many belches,
> For all below was swelling, heaving
> Wamble, gurgle, squelch.
>
> She lay on the sofa with legs up,

> A decade on her lip,
> At four o'clock, taking a cup
> Of lukewarm water, sip
> By sip, but still her daily food
> Repeated and the bile
> Tormented her. In a blue hood,
> The Virgin sadly smiled.

Gross agony is momentarily left aside as Martha considers her saints, sublimating her pain in visions of simple piety. The pain is unrelieved and Martha surrenders:

> In ambush of night, an angel wounded
>   The Spaniard to the heart
> With iron tip on fire. Swooning
>   With pain and bliss as a dart
> Moved up and down within her bowels
>   Quicker, quicker, each cell
> Sweating as if rubbed with towels,
>   Her spirit rose and fell.

Clarke's imagery captures Martha's confusion and inability to withstand her private purgatory. Details of her disorientation and final grovelling before the very emblems from which she had sought consolation establish Martha's plight:

>   Heart palpitates
>   And terror in her stiffens.
> Heart misses one beat, two . . . flutters . . . stops.
>   For ears are full of sound.
> Half fainting, she stares at the grandfather clock
>   As if it were overwound.
>
> The fit had come. Ill-natured flesh
>   Despised her soul. No bending
> Could ease rib. Around her heart, pressure
>   Of wind grew worse. Again,
>
> Again, armchaired without relief,
>   She eructated, phlegm
> In mouth, forgot the woe, the grief,
>   Foretold at Bethlehem.

Martha's utter isolation is convincingly stated; she changes churches rather than visit a doctor.

Martha emerges as an endearingly pathetic and frail woman through the account of her life's small pleasures. The fact that her new church is near St Stephen's Green, for example, allows her to visit the duck pond. Her motive for going to the new church, too, is expressed in mundane, familiar terms; she is 'Tired of the same faces, side-altars'. The poem sympathetically realises the woman's life by placing her in exact localities and by relating her concerns (like the purchase in advance of a nice cemetery plot and her hopes of avoiding long purgatorial pain after death).

Martha has also dreamed of what will be the saddest irony in the poem, her retirement:

> Often she thought of a quiet sick-ward,
>   Nuns, with delicious ways,
> Consoling the miserable: quick
>   Tea, toast on trays.

'Kind neighbours' upset Martha's hopes and, 'wishing to rid themselves of her', send Martha to a different hospital where, unexamined and maltreated, she slowly dies. The contrast between Martha's ideal nuns and this hospital with its expedient rules and wilful mistreatment of her, speaks for itself:

> Mother Superior believed
>   That she was obstinate, self-willed.
> Sisters ignored her, hands-in-sleeves,
>   Beside a pantry shelf
> Or counting pillow-case, soiled sheet.
>   They gave her purgatives.
> Soul-less, she tottered to the toilet.
>   Only her body lived.

Martha's excruciating demise is told in powerful understatement. Normality succumbs to the surrealism of a fairground outside her window. Bare statement figured with grisly detail (departing from the objective only once in a rich metaphor that contrasts Martha's suffering with the ignorant merriment and fund-raising outside) conveys the agony and confusion of her death in a most horrifying manner:

> Unpitied, wasting with diarrhea
> And the constant strain,
> Poor child of Mary with one idea,
> She ruptured a small vein,
> Bled inwardly to jazz. No priest
> Came. She had been annointed
> Two days before, yet knew no peace:
> Her last breath, disappointed.

The skill with which Clarke has moved the reader by means of implication and revelation of seemingly insignificant detail to this final vision of silent torment is the true measure of his altered poetic voice. Controlled rage gives the reader, no longer overwhelmed by the savagery of the poet himself, insight into the poem's realities, and a genuine sympathy for its character. 'Martha Blake' is one of Clarke's great poems.

Poems like 'A Simple Tale', 'Living on Sin', 'Unmarried Mothers', 'The Pill' and 'The Redemptorist' are in the same vein. They are as contentious as any of the earlier satires but, because they are less directly vehement, they are more credible and ultimately more profound. The case against what Clarke calls the modern 'Ill-fare State' and its uncaring, materialistic bureaucracy grows with almost every poem.

'A Simple Tale' (*Poems*, 257), about a 'casual labourer, Pat Rourke' who comes home to Ireland and to unemployment is (in its attention to particular facts and details) typical of these poems. The family, forced to live in squalor, are separated rather than supported by the State — had they stayed abroad, at least the State might have been more benign:

> Brought
> To Court, the little screaming boy
> And girl were quickly, for the public good,
> Committed to Industrial School.
> The cost — three pounds a week for each:
> Both safely held beyond the reach
> Of mother, father. We destroy

Families, bereave the unemployed.
Pity and love are beyond our buoys.

'Living on Sin' (*Poems*, 271) covers ground similar to
that of 'Mother and Child' without, however, the blasphemous conceits and with a repeated demand for social assist-
ance for a mother and her illegitimate child. The cold hypocrisy of the charity meted out by religious institutions is
once again the subject in 'Unmarried Mothers' (*Poems*, 272).
There are two poems in this new manner about the Church's
attitude to contraception, both of which enlarge the arguments already propounded in 'Marriage' and 'In the New
Statesman Office'. 'Precautions' is an extremely skillful
exercise in logic similar to Clarke's earlier challenges to the
Church's inconsistent rulings. The poem was occasioned by
a ruling that nuns in Africa would be allowed the pill in case
of savage rape, a decision that made the Vatican's previous
arguments appear ludicrous (*Poems*, 255). 'The Pill', however,
and 'The Redemptorist' are movingly personal poems. The
first is a sad elegy for a cousin who died in childbirth:

> Must delicate women die in vain
> While age confabulates? Not long
> Ago, I knew and wept such wrong.
> My favourite cousin, Ethelind,
> Bewildered, shaking a head of curls,
> Was gone at twenty-two, her babe
> Unmothered — she had so little breath.
> Now prelates in the Vatican
> Are whispering from pillar to pillar
> Examining in Latin the Pill,
> Pessary, letter, cap. What can
> We do until they have decreed
> Their will, changing the ancient creed,
> But lie awake on separate pillow?
> (Poems, 377)

The tragedy is handled without rhetorical flourishes. Instead,
the power of the Church is negated by a powerful metaphysical conceit which laments the dead cousin and underlines
the doom of women under Church dominion. The sacrifice
of Ethelind to celibate controversy is evoked in this final,

dark metaphor:

> Now in a sky-tormented world,
> These mighty watchers of the womb,
> May bind archangels by the pinion,
> As though they had dragged them down to marble
> And bronze, dire figures of the past
> That veil a young girl in her tomb.

Morality in Ireland, as Clarke has convincingly argued, is not a matter of human compassion and individual conscience but of public dictate and righteous incomprehension of specific cases. 'The Redemptorist' (*Poems*, 378) argues the case for changing this attitude:

> 'How many children have you?' asked
> The Big Redemptorist.
>   'Six, Father.'
>   'The last,
> When was it born?'
>   'Ten months ago.'
> 'I cannot absolve your mortal sin
> Until you conceive again. Go home,
> Obey your husband.'
>   She whimpered:
>   'But
> The doctor warned me . . . '
>   Shutter became
> Her coffin lid. She twisted her thin hands
> And left the box.

The doctor can only advise, the priest's task is to prescribe. It is the priest who is obeyed:

> 'No pregnancy. You'll die the next time,'
> The Doctor had said.
>   Her tiredness obeyed
> That Saturday night: Her husband's weight
> Digging her grave. So, in nine months, she
> Sank in great agony on a Monday.
> Her children wept in the Orphanage,
> Huddled together in the annexe,

> While, proud of the Black Cross on his badge,
> The Liguorian, at Adam and Eve's,
> Ascended the pulpit, sulphuring his sleeves
> And setting fire to the holy text.

Again, the imagery is spare, becoming more complex at the
end to force a recognition of the destructive, evil guidance
of Ireland's ignorant moralists. The truth revealed here is a
harrowing glimpse of hell.

The poems we have just discussed are typical of Clarke's
work during his most prolific period. The argument with
blind materialism and smug callousness continues in every
poem. The diction, however, is muted compared to the
earlier satires and the compassion almost explicit.

(iii)

Extending the range of his satiric verse, Clarke's poetry in
the period under consideration continues the debate on the
religious and political superstitions and the cultural myths
that blind his fellow-citizens to truly humane ideals. With
characteristic verve and a new urbanity, he offers 'A Reply'
(1968), a short poem defending his conscientious criticism of
the world as he sees it:

> Don Quixote, if I
> Remember rightly,
> After he rode from
> The dust of roads
> Along the plain,
> Ignored the millers
> Unbagging grain,
> But attacked the mills
> That had become
> Their feudal lords
> Confounding all comers
> With horde'd blows.
> (*Poems*, 437)

Clarke is no longer concerned with direct challenges to
belief or doctrine. Instead, he chronicles the more vulgar
abuses of piety and examines the smugness of religiosity.

'Flight to Africa' (1963), for example, examines the uncomfortable truth hidden under a particular piece of zealous cant. 'A bishop, one of our twenty-eight/Or so', ponders the plight of provincial youngsters:

> Too many are professed —
> He argued — boys, girls, all in black,
> Brown, white. The Church unbeds the State:
> Charity taught to emigrate.
> Farmyard and scythe gone. Grain unsacked or
> Let down by rain for lack of hand.
> Old times are off again. Great land
> Is measured by a man on tractor . . .
> . . . Munster seems a crypt.
>
> (*Poems*, 252)

The bishop in Cork may lament such emigration but the Vatican official who visits Ireland acclaims the devotion of the Irish:

> At a reception given to him in Cork during Patrician week, the Papal Legate said that emigration from Ireland was an act of Divine Providence and went on to say that the Church in Britain, the U.S.A., and indeed the entire English-speaking world, would be in a sorry plight but for emigration from this country.
>
> (*Poems*, 553)

There are practical advantages, Clarke asserts, to having missionaries in Africa. Visiting the various missions in Africa before returning home by way of Rome, the Taoiseach opens trade possibilities and ensures that the people, impressed by his religious activities, will re-elect him. The ironies culminate in Clarke's final images of former Republican heroes, now pious businessmen who are unaware of the conflict between their bourgeois vocations and their sanctimonious pretensions. These 'Knights who of old salaamed/ Mahoun' will not do much to free Ireland. 'Salaamed Mahoun' suggests the Gaelic 'póg mo thóin' and the vulgar 'arse lickers', descriptive of those who are subservient. 'Flight to Africa' is a bemused observation on misfired zeal.

There are other poems, like 'The New Tolerance' (*Poems*,

431 — 1968), that also show Clarke's fundamental scept-
icism. This poem is a mock-heroic catalogue of the many
claimant sects now struggling to assert their righteousness
in the ecumenical stakes: 'The Bible in a public frenzy'.
Clarke explains his own experience at a Quaker meeting.
He is struck by objectivity of the Quaker service and ends
the poem with this description:

> Shyly
> I heard the words of Holy Writ,
> Sat on a plain bench, void in spirit.

Similarly, 'At Middle Abbey Street Corner' (*Poems*,
376 — 1967) betrays by its primitive repetition and by the
echoing rhyme of its final lines, the hollow evangelism of

> Street preachers who have a boiling pitch
> Here, do not need to shout or pitch
> Their voices higher. Microphone
> Can burn or save Pat, Tom, Mike.
> With hymning hand, they sing to us.
>
> Harmonium wheezes: 'Jesus! Jesus!'

It is a piece of reportage both humorous and rhetorically
cruel. Clarke's punned rhymes on 'pitch', his half-rhymed
puns on 'microphone' and 'mike', and the appropriately
flat reiterations of 'wheezes' and 'Jesus' adroitly indicate his
appreciation of the ridiculous, while condemning the base
attempt to collect souls.

'Another Protestant Insult' (*Poems*, 467 — 1968), subtitled 'An Extravangaza', is an anarchic satire worthy of
Anier MacConglinne. In this poem Clarke uses his full weaponry of rhetoric, dramatic incident and fantastic surrealism
to sting the provincial pietism of Cork. It is a throwback
of sorts, reminding the reader of Clarke's vengeful, earlier
poems and making clear how far his controlled withdrawal
has taken him in other poems of the same period. Though
not akin to the Martha Blake poems, 'Another Protestant
Insult' (which is even set in another era, the 1920s) nevertheless illustrates the in-gathering of Clarke's powers. The
poem relates the indignation of a Christian Brother who

discovers sacrilege in the 'Cherry Tree Carol', a medieval
song in which Mary asks Joseph to pick her some cherries
to eat. Joseph's reply, 'Let him pluck thee/A cherry who
brought thee with child', is the insult. The shock of such
irreverence, indeed blasphemy, is too much for the devout
man. Cork itself is in an uproar. That night, the school-
teaching cleric has a marvellous vision of his order's founding and inspired vocation:

> The relics of
> The Waterford merchant, who piously sold the
>   provision shop
> His uncle had left him twenty-eight years before
>   our religion
> Was fully emancipated, Edmund Ignatius Rice,
> Called, night and noon, by his vocation from the
>   taking of orders,
> The weighing scales, the bags of tea, sugar, currants,
>   flour, rice,
> Had obtained permission from Rome to found a
>   a new teaching Order
> Of big strapping fellows to guide, to instruct,
>   young boys at thruppence
> A week, shone in the dark as if they were beatified.

In the next seventeen lines, Clarke uses synecdoche and
exact geography rather than the deliberate puns and sexual
innuendo of this vision to render particular details of pet-
tiness and atrophied squalor in provincial life:

> The River Lee was rumouring
> Down by the Mardyke. Up Military Hill, up
>   Montenotte,
> Gossip came back from the shops to villa, front
>   garden, guest-room,
> (Half-hid as a bit of dirt in the umbilical knot.)
> From Morrison's Island to Turner's Cross, the
>   North and South Malls,
> By Grand Parade, Maylor Street, Merchant Street,
>   the news was busy
> The very day that Mickie O'Mahoney quarrelled
>   with Molly Maguire. In bank, ship-office, it

> interrupted business.
> 'Be Jases!' swore burly dockers from the Coal
>   Quay spitting
> Beamish through smutty moustaches, while from
>   the cobbles
> Of Union Quay, French's Quay, Pope's Quay,
>   respectable
> Echoes replied with 'Be Japers!' 'We said so, the
>   very spit
> Of his father,' murmured the sons of Crispin, the
>   free-drinking cobblers,
> True to the last. That evening, in street or snug,
>   cardplayers
> Sniggered and asked for the Joker. Jealousy stared
> From a broken mirror on Saturday night, as
>   drunkards
> Beat up their wives.

The 'news of the hullaballoo had been hurried to Dublin' where Clarke's mentor, AE, had cleared the controversy and life resumed its normal pace. Almost casually (with incidental mention of the economics of Marian devotion and a final surrealistic image of smouldering piety echoing that of 'The Redemptorist') Clarke concludes his scrutiny of life in Ireland's second city:

> Cork was silent.
>   The Angelus rang devoutly:
> Noddles were bowed. The Council withdrew its
>   protestations.
> Strikers went back to work, the housewives to their
>   bus queues,
> Magistrates leaned from the Bench frowning at
>   those accused
> Of obscene language and brawling in the slums.
>   Cellophane
> Was reverently unwrapped from Madonnas. Book-
>   sellers
> Smiled. Ignorance was on retreat in its smoky
>   cell.

Several less gleeful poems cast aspersions on larger public

shows of devotion. 'A Statue for Dublin Bay' (*Poems*, 433 — 1968) treats the same theme as the earlier 'Local Complainer' in *Too Great A Vine*, but less vehemently. It attacks not so much those who seek to erect the monument in Dublin as it does 'Our hyperdulia', excessive devotion to Mary. Clarke sarcastically congratulates Galway in two poems for its architecturally grotesque cathedral, once in *A Sermon On Swift* but more ironically in the poem 'The New Cathedral in Galway'. Once again, all the epigrammatic concision of harder, earlier satire is employed:

> Here is the very spirit
> Of hard-drinking, sea-mouldering Galway:
> A building ugly as sin
> To prove the Boys sincere
> And still a decent crowd:
> Another thorn for the Crown
> Of Thorns, a large gall
> In the Sponge on Spear.
>   (*Poems*, 437 — 1968)

This poem shows how Clarke can sometimes undercut his new urbanity with a display of malicious rhetoric and humour. The compressed wit of this poem and of 'Another Protestant Insult' add depth to the other less vicious poetry which is more characteristic of this period. Poems like 'On the Mountain Tops' (*Poems*, 287 — 1963), for example, decry the equally tasteless campaign to fill the countryside with plaster-cast religious statuary.

Some poems, however, attempt to penetrate the impoverished realities glossed over by edifying speeches and concealed by plaster monuments. 'Street Game' (*Poems*, 256 — 1963) is such a poem. It records a minor incident Clarke observed while walking through that forgotten Dublin with which his writings are obsessed:

> Unholy bits, ring, neck, of porter and Bass bottle
> From the six public-houses at those four corners,
> Nicholas St, Clanbrassil St, the Coombe
> And Kevin St, shrine on high wall — fierce spot —
> Protecting the Sisters of the Holy Faith, warning
> By sun and moon the ruffians in top-back room

Or cellar. Last week I saw a marching band,
Small Protestants in grey clothes, well-fed pairs
Led by a Bible teacher, heard the noise
Of boot-heel metal by bread-shop, sweet-shop,
    dairy,
Scrap, turf, wood, coal-blocks.

Bigotry saddens the poet as much as poverty:

                           Suddenly Catholic joylets
Darted from alleys, raggedy cherubs that dared
    them:
'Luk, feckin' bastards, swaddlers, feckin' bastards!'
Too well they knew the words their mothers,
    fathers,
Used. Silent, the foundlings marched along the
    street-path
With clink of boot-heel metal. We have cast
Them out. Devotion, come to the man-hole at last,
Bawls: 'Feckin'   bastards,   swaddlers,   feckin'
    bastards!'

Religion is not only repressive but also socially divisive.

'Burial of an Irish President' (*Poems*, 250 – 1963) is an
important poem in Clarke's work because of the anger it
expresses at sectarian divisiveness and also because of the
personal injury Clarke reveals in it. Douglas Hyde, Clarke's
friend and former teacher (the academic and poet largely
responsible for the revival of interest in Gaelic literature)
was the Protestant head of the Irish state. His funeral in
St Patrick's Cathedral, 'Beyond the savage tomb of Swift',
was an embarrassment to the conspicuously absent Catholic
parliamentarians. Citizens of Dublin too stayed away from
the service itself:

Two Catholics, the French
Ambassador and I, knelt down.
The vergers waited. Outside.
The hush of Dublin town,
Costello, his Cabinet,
In Government cars, hiding
Around the corner, ready

Tall hat in hand, dreading
Our Father in English, Better
Not hear that 'which' for 'who'
And risk eternal doom.

In 'Above Party' (*Poems*, 420 — 1968) Clarke comments on
another Irish President, Éamonn de Valera and in doing so
confronts many of the incongruities and hypocrisies that
beset Irish politics in this century:

'I am a stayer,' declared
Our Chief, in drolling aside
That bonfired the hills of Clare.
Stalls cheered. History signed.
But Gallery had won:
'You're not the only one!'
How often he has stayed
Where every soul is staid,
Talking with Bishop, Head
Of Missionary Order:
High up with lowered head,
Pleasantly peering down
At Mother Superior.
He was our Liberator
Once, sternly disobeyed
What Hierarchy bade.

Clarke recounts the intrigue, dishonesty and recriminations
that underlay the alliance of Church and State in Ireland
and he questions de Valera's morality and integrity. Despite
the accusations of volte-face levelled at his party, the final
section of the poem praises de Valera and characteristically
it finishes in an equivocal punning rhyme:

When European
Cities were scattered to blazes
And skies gave blow for blow
As hate of the Great Powers
Changed banknotes into gunpowder,
He kept our country at peace,
Despite the lies and blame.
In age he bowed to the Church —

Not to the threats of Churchill.

'The Subjection of Women' (*Poems*, 433 – 1968) evokes
the days when already legendary Irish women (the like of
Maud Gonne, Countess Markievicz, Eva Gore-Booth, Mrs
Sheehy-Skeffington and Dr Kathleen Lynn) fought for
freedom and social equality for all. The poem is an elegy
for the ideals of these women. He laments that, with their
passing

> Still discontented, our country prays
> To private enterprise.

The poem ends with a terse envoy which illuminates the
contemporary loss of faith in such idealists:

> Women, who cast off all we want,
> Are now despised, their names unwanted,
> For patriots in party statement
> And act make worse our Ill-fare State.
> The soul is profit. Money claims us.
> Heroes are valuable clay.

Thus, Clarke's ageing but tireless tongue reminds his
country's leaders and citizens once again how Ireland's
modern condition belies the ideals of her supposed heroines.
Having begun his life in an era of high optimism and idealistic plans for a free Ireland, Clarke feels justified in writing
as he does in 'The Eighth Wonder of Ireland':

> To the seven wonders of Ireland, add an eighth.
> Thrones and Dominions have changed our copy-
>   books
> Crooked is straight, upside is down, pothooks
> Are hangers, good is bad now, pity, cruel,
> Free medicine, school-milk, contrary to Faith;
> The old, the sick, cannot have soup or fuel,
> Parents, who anguish vainly to support
> Their infants, are robbed of them, unhomed
>   in Court.
> Pelfing is grace, substance of self, a wraith.
>   (*Poems*, 288 – 1963)

In a few, powerfully rhetorical poems, he turns his eye to the modern world outside and its way of life towards which Ireland, its ideals cast aside, has striven. 'The Common Market', for example, concedes the wish to join Europe in a trading alliance:

> Why do you bog-trot from the wind
> And damp, hee-hawing into Europe,
> The latest cross upon your back,
> To join that unholy family,
> Forgetting all the patience, your rope
> And straw? To every star you see,
> Add stripe. The lion has been skinned:
> War has a new whip for tradelets. Come back,
> Poor Twenty-Sixer. Live on lack.
> *(Poems*, 247 — 1963)

This is a good example of straight-forward political poetry, indeed of poetry as political journalism, where the craft is directed to summing up a public question in a manner that is tight, pithy and, to a large extent, comprehensive. 'To every star you see,/Add stripe' is typical of the ease of compression that Clarke has developed, suggesting both the ideal of a European United States and the process of verifying pros and cons that entry into the EEC involved. The final 'Live on lack' is, of course, paradoxical.

'Ex Trivio' maintains this line of debate strengthened by a dazzling show of poetic wit:

> Our final act
> Will be an Act
> Of Union. Freedom
> Waits, feeble, dumb, for
> The gallows rope,
> When we are europed
> From nape to toe-nail,
> Scheduled, natoed.
>
> Why should we atone for
> Molyneux, Swift, Tone,
> Emmet, Lord Edward
> Fitzgerald?

                              Pearse
                          Ward
             Politicians, who trade
             When all's betrayed,
             Salute the Rising
             At Easter, rise to
             High Office, carpet,
             Government car.
                     (*Poems*, 471 — 1968)

The assonantal structure is remarkable and ties the sections
together. The sentences beginning with 'Freedom waits'
and ending with the first question mark are linked by a rhyming pattern that runs from 'rope' to 'toe-' and from 'nape'
to 'Nail'. 'Toe-nail' is anagrammatically repeated in 'natoed',
which turns on itself to form 'atone', which in turn begins a
similar rhyme and visual punning scheme. He argues that to
move into economic alliances with larger, impersonally
capitalistic countries is to betray the founders of the Irish
Republic. Leaders and spokesmen who fought for the rights
of impoverished Irish men and women are the 'valuable
clay' with which the new leaders and business chiefs have
paved their way to greater personal wealth and status. The
country has been cheated. With a bitter pun on 'Lynch',
the surname of Ireland's Taoiseach when the poem was
written, Clarke demands:

                          why not
             Relearn old manners,
             Call Englishman,
             West German, Belgian,
             When the doorbell
             Is answered: 'Your Honour',
             Forget that honour
             Has been lynched?

   The closing images of 'Ex Trivio' depict a violent, powerful American world, as an example to Europe. The United
States is an important emblem in Clarke's poetry. In the next
section of this study his travels through the eastern seaboard
and New England will be discussed. Now, we turn to poems
like 'Napalm', 'Black, White and Yellow' and 'The New

World', the last of which extends the images of a menacing power out of control that occur at the end of 'Ex Trivio'. Not content to make platitudes about the assasinated Kennedys, Clarke looks behind the popular images that adorn many Irish pubs and grimly comments on Jack Kennedy's role in world politics:

> There would have been no jack
> To lower with him, no cloud
> Of mounted skymen, crews shoving
> Half-drunken submarines
> Around the new Cape Krushev
> In Cuba, if he had dumped
> The bomb, no marshalling
> Of sympathisers, only
> A world that God disowned:
> And the sun, the moon, in a dump.
>   (*Poems*, 476-7 — 1968)

The second section of this poem achieves a sparse and elegiac dignity by linking reported detail with its final macabre image:

> And now his brother
> As bloodily slain
> In a corridor.
>
> Murderous America,
> Mourning with gun
> In pocket, moves on.

'Black, White and Yellow' (*Poems*, 421 — 1968) is a rhetorical exploration of the inequalities that riddle America at home while the country wages war in the name of peace and democracy abroad. But it is in 'Napalm' that Clarke has written his most haunting condemnation of American politics and American involvement in southeast Asia. Its power is derived from Clarke's reshaping of nouns into verbs, thus creating an impressively active confrontation between his reader and the unnatural, bestial atrocities he describes:

> Cloud-coming-down, American air-pilots

Tumble to risks. Trickle and rill
Are rivered again as, flying low,
Foresting propaganda, they pile
Revolt where ground-leaves are guerillas,
Branding the water-buffalo,
Unjungling tiger and elephant
With toss of napalm bombs that peel off
The shrieking skin of mother, infant,
While Bishop of Koutum appeals
For funds, though conscripts pray that soon
The big dropper, the dark one, the monsoon,
Will tent them. United Nations are mum
And Johnson lariats with the dollar.
Our clergy, faceless as mummers
Of darkness, have dressed up a rag doll
That must be nourished on paper money,
On public smother of their late victims,
Saffron to soot of Buddhist monks
Still petrol-stained. See the brown face,
Those slanting lids, the tin eye-brows:
Ambiguous Madonna of Victories.

(*Poems*, 363 — 1967)

This poem, with its awesome final image, is the equal of any of those written by American poets in disillusion and protest. One could compare Denise Levertov's sustained meditation on America's betrayed ideals in *Relearning the Alphabet* with this short poem, or Robert Lowell's sequence, *Notebook*, in which many themes are concentrated into a passionate sense of moral outrage at events in Viet Nam. Neither, however, are so concisely vehement or rhetorically condensed as Clarke's poem. Allen Ginsberg's *The Fall of America* is largely (and emotionally) concerned with the same topic, but the power of Ginsberg's individual poems depends on the poet's presence and performance during the recitation. In this poem, Clarke shows himself thoroughly in control of a non-Irish theme and capable of taking a firm grasp of an issue that has deeply troubled a younger generation. Injustices, at home or abroad, can be equally concerns of his art.

(iv)

Because of this commitment his poem 'Ezra Pound' (*Poems*, 364) takes on a wider meaning. Clarke admitted an early mistrust, even contempt, for Pound, who struggled independently to refashion 'classical' literature:

> His imagery is that of the catalogue, of the seedsman, the auctioneer, the bibliophile ... We can enjoy the same element of surprise and variety in any random page ... in glancing through a catalogue of flowers ... Mr Pound is giving us, in fact a gigantic poetic notebook in which he has jotted down, with a minimum of rearrangement and simple parallelism, everything that strikes his fancy in the midst of his extensive reading. But reading, as a Chinese poet has said, is not enough.[5]

In his poetry, according to an early review by Clarke, Pound exhibits

> the trans-Atlantic mania for collecting all the treasures of the past. He has remained the ubiquitous American tourist, indefatigable in his curiosity. . . . With the zeal of a maiden aunt, he has been making from the rag-bag of the centuries a gigantic patch-work quilt to keep young poets warm.[6]

The poem, however, ultimately accepts the American's brashness:

> Too often I pooh-poohed his poems
> Surveying the inkiness of the globe,
> Missouri, London, Paris, Po.
> Why should my pen, I thought, dip pity
> In praise for another American poking
> At European curios
> In the backroom of our Serendipity
> Shop, gawky stranger from Idaho,
> Rough rider with stetson, jaunty pose,
> Browning in holster, nudging the elbow
> Of Yeats and T.S. Eliot:
> Then, slipshod, pushing a Chinese cart

> Loot-laden with Oriental art;
> Discovering in Provence that Ver
> Had shown her greenness to young trouvere
> And troubadour?

Now, Clarke writes, he has admiration for a poet who continued to write and rage at the world 'Behind barbed wire and in asylum':

> Age has not diminished the remarkable energy and zeal of Ezra Pound. His long quarrel with his own country and the years of his imprisonment did not interrupt his work or cause him to modify his forcible opinions. Even his lifelong delight in the more intricate forms of European and Oriental art has not prevented him from using poetical forms so ample in their freedom that they seem to be devoid of technical 'controls'. [7]

Having enumerated the things he had found disagreeable, Clarke changes the mood of the poem to recall Pound's courageous and untiring example to other poets, standing alone, braving convention to write his own style of poetry:

> He counselled poets: 'Use your errors
> Wisely, forget the democratic
> Let down, the academic tie.
> Safety of the world go bare,
> While Spender wrestles with his fire-hose,
> In vain, Auden becomes a choir-boy.

It is not a kind of poetry which Clarke himself would spend a lifetime on, perhaps, but Pound's dedication to his mission earns Clarke's respect. The poem has to this point reverberated with the consonants and vowel sounds of its opening three lines. In the final section, summing up his view, Clarke achieves what visually resembles a crossword puzzle of sound. Its sound, however, is a composite of rhythmically shifting puns on Pound's name. It is a stylish, appreciative tribute to the 'language he compounded' which Clarke eventually singles out for praise:

> Rhyme, echo the name of Ezra Pound

Whom the war capitalists impounded.
For miserable years he pounded
The wall of modern verse, expounded
The madness of dollar, franc and pound.
Forget the theories he prepounded,
But praise the language he compounded.
The centuries are in that pound.

Visual and aural puns are but part of the larger conceit here, the 'rime riche' fulfilling the invocation's dictate.

As a volume, *Old-Fashioned Pilgrimage* marks the beginning of this kind of poem in Clarke's work, poems through which he pays tribute to poets whose work and lives interested him or influenced his own life. In their journal-like record of his impressions, these poems add new chapters to Clarke's autobiography. As poetry, however, these jottings about his travels and encounters with poetry and poets cannot stand beside Clarke's other work. Diaries and records are valuable in that a reader learns more about the writer than he might otherwise. The poems we will now consider fulfill this function. Clarke is, however, a better writer when his immediate and personal attitudes are directed away from other writers and other writings. Many of the poems in *Old-Fashioned Pilgrimage* and, later, in *The Echo at Coole* are of minor poetic interest. They reveal Clarke the man and, at times, betray his very conscious craftsmanship. In several places his imagery, assonance and use of identical rhymes are almost gratuitous. Parts of certain poems (for example the section in 'Old-Fashioned Pilgrimage' wherein Clarke examines the Irish who emigrated to America) are memorable, but much in these poems is unmemorable dross.

In 'More Extracts from a Diary of Dreams', Clarke explains the reason for his journey to New York:

Those voices again.
                       'Why do you want to go to
New York?'
                'If you were living long ago,
Wouldn't you like to visit Babylon?'
                            (*Poems*, 386)

'Old-Fashioned Pilgrimage' (*Poems*, 355) is the record of
this visit when, met by Padraic Colum, Clarke and his wife
marvelled at the city of New York which 'dollared the sky'.
Behind the dazzle and glare of Broadway and the busy
commercialism of the metropolis, Clarke's eye sees another
reality. The analogy with past empires and splendour is
strenghtened by his observations of the contemporary scene:

> Death-shriek of a police-car wakened me up at two
>   o'clock
> That morning. Cautious as pigeon or criminal, from
>   fourteenth
> Storey, I watched the silent bulleting below, the
>   police-car
> Still shrieking in the vacant light. Wealth — as
> In ancient Rome — at war, nightly, with black,
>   poor white.

Clarke's diary of the stay in New York and the journeys
into its suburbs is interesting because his wonder at this
affluent, modern empire never overcomes his sense of the
ironic or socially ludicrous. Searching for Edgar Allan Poe's
residence, for example, Clarke discovers the way beset by
modern effects:

>   A policeman knew the locality:
> 'You mean Poe Park. Turn left. You'll see it there
>   before you.'
> We came to the Poe Tavern, Poe Café, Poe Launder-
>   ette,
> Poe Park, the bandstand, benches — neatly inset
> Against the bushes, park trees, I saw, still legendary,
> Small, white, one-storied, the cottage of eighteen-
>   thirty-seven.

The joy of discovery which Clarke felt on first reading
Poe's works, remains 'still legendary' and is increased by the
immediacy of Poe's own surroundings and Clarke's own
knowledge of the doomed poet's life. The poetry remains
beautifully moving for Clarke. The crassness of Poe's one-
time neighbourhood, commercialised and trivialised for the

benefit of tourists like himself, cannot tarnish it.

A similar idea permeates, but with less poetic success, Clarke's discovery of Whitman's home. Another friend from Ireland, Vivian Mercier, drives the Clarkes along the speedway where they

> came at last
> To country shout of advertisements, the Whitman
>   Tavern,
> The Whitman Café, Whitman Launderette, turned
>   to the left,
> Into a tree-topped lane. There in an open field,
>   the farmhouse
> Where the poet had been born: the English, red-
>   hooded
> Well. Beside the door, good thought had planted
>   a lilac:
> But we saw no elegiac bloom upon it.

Searching Whitman's house for signs of the poet's person-ality, Clarke claims to have discerned the poetic worth be-hind its modern paraphernalia:

> I saw his leather-worn armchair, and his
>   round table,
> His grey sombrero hat, stout walking-stick, up-
>   stairs,
> The bed and hipbath. We added to the dusty stares
> Our mote and beam. In reverence, I touched the
>   bedpost,
> Then lingered awhile among the picture postcards
> And dallied with the janitress, a black girl, tall
>   and handsome;
> We talked of Whitman, Wordsworth, while in
>   secret my hand
> Pilgrimed among his manuscripts. Too soon we left
> The house, clothed again with afternoon, turned
>   left.

And yet after his claim is made, Clarke remains uncom-mitted, creating an imbalance and ignoring a paradox. If there is worth in Whitman's poetry or beliefs, that ludi-

crous final 'rime riche' ('Why should you care a whit, man?')
destroys any credibility in Clarke's discussion of it. The pun
is effortless and, finally, pointless. Despite his poetic record
of the visit, Clarke is as guilty as other tourists at the 'shrine'.
His argument is obscured by his own carelessness. He admits
this partially in that confession of irrelevancy, the 'mote and
beam' in his eye. Whatever Whitman's value, Clarke has
missed an opportunity. Here, the attempt at literary criticism fails and Whitman's importance remains to be settled
elsewhere.

In a review of Whitman's poetry published in *The Irish
Times*, Clarke explained his own reticence towards Whitman's
nineteenth century idealism.[8] Clarke recalls in this poem
Pound's rejection of Whitman's America but avers that the
optimism and idealism (to which he himself objects) are
justified and perhaps necessary in an increasingly commercialised world. This last assertion, about the necessity for idealism and the power of art to overcome the materially vulgar,
remains, unfortunately, unproved.

The poem is rich in extra-literary details. For example,
the section in which Clarke's sympathy with the Irish who
came to America to escape famine and hard times at home is
interrupted by his reflections on the consequences:

> At noon, we drove
> For a hundred miles along a great speedway,
>   past the
> Cashing of supermarkets, cafés, restaurants,
> Motels, garages and small factories. Here, there,
> On gateway, notice-board, roll-call of Irish names,
> O'Sullivan, MacNamara, Cassidy, Malone,
> Molloy, Lavelle, O'Herlihy, O'Driscoll, Carroll,
> Our emigrants, uncoffined on a huge shore, their
>   ragged
> Holes, empty pockets, the size of dollars. A hundred
>   miles
> To Washington. We drove, of a sudden, into the
>   future:
> A poster with large letters: NO PEDESTRIANS.

This exchange of past hopes for modern achievements is a
major concern of the poem. Clarke visited America in search

of Babylon and, finding it, sought those writers who shaped American literature during its high period of Romantic idealism: Poe, Whitman, Emerson, Thoreau, Longfellow and Hawthorne. His encounters with the extravaganza that changed their optimistic visions into launderettes and garages led Clarke to consider Irish writers: Mangan, Moore, Yeats, AE, Higgins and the Abbey touring company. Clarke had watched, and chronicled in his poetry, his own country's fall from idealism and its turn towards the materialism epitomised by modern America. His own writing had shifted from the idyllic to the bitterly polemical. Some Irishmen and some of the Americans whom he had seen still live in poverty, fed on illusions of national glamour and sharing an irrelevant, idealistic cultural heritage.

'Old-Fashioned Pilgrimage' is significant for the portrait it gives us of Clarke, momentarily uncontentious, finding solace in the Muse and admiring a fount of poetry now debased by the vulgarities of the new Rome (a debasement which none of the poets had foreseen). The final image of the poem is a justification and defence of this earlier literature and a definition of the poet's value in present times:

> We passed the battlefields
> Again, the city park where roses have their roots
> in cars.

Poetry is the force which connects significant images in memorable language. A poem which can find roses even in rushing traffic will survive to preserve beauty and meaning in human activities. Clarke tried to show in his discussion of Whitman, Poe and others that their heritage survives untarnished. The attempt at mixing genres fails; explicit literary criticism in poetry is not Clarke's forte.

'Fiesta in Spain' (*Poems*, 365) is the record of another visit as is 'The Paper Curtain' (*Poems*, 369) in which Clarke recalls the writers' conference he attended in Yugoslavia, 'seen as the kind of Utopia Ireland might have become — a political error of the poetic kind, alas'. [9] Clarke, however, admitted this mistake in his notes: 'I was not aware that a Yugoslav writer had been held for years in captivity' (*Poems*, 545). The poem's argument against the unnecessary poverty of many

Irish people, exploited under a free enterprise system is not, however, disproved by Tito's wrongdoings. The portrait of Yugoslavia presents Clarke as a poet in a mood we have not heard before — happy, excited, contented. Again, it is the final image which most fully conveys the poet's summing up of his experience:

> Often I think of that Utopia
> For so it seemed: but I remember most
> The lovely children of Yugoslavia
> At play in public park with sun-gold limbs.

The qualification in the second line is important, but surely the moral intended is drawn in the picture of children with sun-gold limbs at play. Clarke's poems about Irish children offer no such images of contentment, but if he had been a Yugoslavian, we wonder if he would have painted such images of contentment.

'Garcia Lorca' and 'Pablo Neruda' appear in 'Fiesta in Spain' and 'The Paper Curtain' (both also appear in *Poems*, 368). The first defends Lorca against the expedient defamation of his character by the Spanish establishment, which had a vested interest in the neglect of his poetry. The second captures Clarke's excitement at meeting the great Chilean socialist and poet at the P.E.N. conference. Here, the autobiographical impulse has unfortunately once more overcome the poetic impulse. The poem is not so much about Pablo Neruda and his poetry of commitment as it is about Clarke himself being 'all in a doo-da'. The name 'Neruda' is merely an excuse, the punning motivation for a very minor work, questionably poetic.

Meeting Robert Frost in Dublin was, as the poem about him relates, a disappointment for Clarke, (*Poems*, 363). Clarke's discomfort at seeing the frail and touchy older poet overrides any other sensation. The incident, however, gave Clarke a chance to explain his own methods of writing:

A couple of years ago, Robert Frost was given an Honorary Degree at Oxford University and, on his way back to the United States, stopped in Dublin to receive a similar honour from the National University of Ireland. After the Conferring, I had the pleasure of being introduced to him and, as we sat together on a comfortable sofa in Newman House, he asked me what kind of verse I wrote. Having been rarely asked such a question, I was confused and then, suddenly thinking of the 'strong man' whom I had often seen on his 'pitch' near St Martin's in the Fields, replied: 'I load myself with chains and try to get out of them.' 'Good Lord!' exclaimed the wise octogenarian poet, 'you can't have many readers.'

(Poems, 545)

Behind the self-effacement, Clarke here defends his practice of assonance and his adherence to a technical discipline which has been called 'classical'. A highly complex diction and an involuted rhyme are the chains that bind Clarke's poetry. The poems that succeed do so not in spite of but because of their technical virtuosities and linguistic revelations. The reader, to borrow Clarke's metaphor, like a spectator at a circus, admires the poet's statements while marvelling at his intricate performance.

'Letter to a Friend' supports this explanation of Clarke's particular craft in a manner which is at once whimsical and yet socially aware:

Local affairs are much the same.
Swallows are railing and our robin
Thinks we'll have snow. Hotels still rob
Our visitors. Grave-diggers are
On strike. Death loses dignity:
Priest mumbles, relatives must scab,
Pass picket, shovel in their dead
With tears, pass picket again. Headstone
In yard is waiting to be scabbled
And lettered for all time. Printers
Are out, this time on principle:
Newspaper offices closed down.
The Government is pulling down
Georgian houses before the strike
Is over lest the lightning strike
Them. Many advertising agents
Shopkeepers, vanmen, newsboys, deprived
Of work, have retired into private life.

I am consoled despite old age
And pen in need of book-reviews,
While you are changing all your views,
For something has happened to this eye,
Since it discovered homonyms.
All things shine now, all have nimbus,
Nature displays nimiety;
Though dampness lodge the grain,
Vague shadows move around in greyness,
A cloudy lid hide Ireland's Eye.

(*Poems*, 373)

The deflation of all things by comic equation shows Clarke
in a lighter humour than might be expected. Identical rhyme
is explained by his delight in homonyms and puns, and
defended by nature's example of 'nimiety' (repeating similar
patterns). Interest in birds is found elsewhere in Clarke's
poetry. The poem's ending is an allusive echo of his various
experiments with the aisling-form.

   The most historically significant group of poems, however,
are those of the first section of *The Echo at Coole* where
Clarke recalls with careful praise those Irish writers whom he
met, or knew, who are now dead. The interest, however, is
primarily historical. Again, Clarke's poems in memory,
praise or blame of other poets never achieve the level of
artistic statement of his other poems. In 'More Extracts
from a Diary of Dreams' (*Poems*, 386), he recounts his
fantastic adventures with the two novelists, Flann O'Brien,
'the bold Sir Myles na Gopaleen', and Mervyn Wall; he also
mentions his various adventures with radio and stage plays.

   The poem 'A.E.' was quoted earlier in this study. It is
ostensibly a portrait of Clarke's mentor but is paradoxically
more concerned with A.E.'s defence of Yeats' poetry:

               'If rhetoric can last,
   Then all that lonely, premeditated art must.

(*Poems*, 402)

This exchange between Clarke and Russell reveals that the
older poet understood Clarke's lack of sympathy with Yeats'
otherwordly poetry.

   In several poems, beginning in *Too Great a Vine* and

Flight to Africa and continued in *The Echo at Coole* with 'A Centenary Tribute', 'At the Saville Club', and 'The House-Breakers', Clarke writes cautiously about Yeats, under whose shadow he existed for so long. Two early poems deal with the fire that destroyed the Abbey Theatre's changing-rooms. 'Abbey Theatre Fire' in *Too Great a Vine* (*Poems*, 207) pays epigrammatic homage to Yeats' style and influence in founding the theatre. The second (confusingly similar in title), 'The Abbey Threatre Fire', is less bound to Yeats' rhetorical model and admits a kinship between the poets:

> So, I forgot
> His enmity.
> My own plays were seen there,
> Ambiguous in the blow of battens,
> Abbot, monk, sinner, black-out of Ireland.
> Finis.
> Stage, Auditorium, escaped
> That fire but not from policy,
> Planning new theatre, old mirth.
> Yeats had not dreamed an unstubbed butt,
> Ill match, would bring his curtain down.
>   (*Poems,* 248)

This tone governs all of Clarke's poems about Yeats. In 'A Centenary Tribute', Clarke admits his wariness before the unapproachable Yeats and humbly postulates that anything might happen in the future, even as Yeats predicted that:

> Some night, perhaps, the Great Mood
> Will change all in a dream: the house restored,
> Old mortar used again by it as in a story
> That Sato's sword may glitter at the moon.
>   (*Poems*, 398)

'In the Saville Club' (*Poems*, 398) is Clarke's confession that his lack of comprehension of *A Vision* and his need for exact facts proved insurmountable barriers to the book he was to have written about Yeats. It is in 'The House-Breakers' (*Poems*, 414) that Clarke defends Yeats, as he did in the Abbey Theatre fire poems, as an artist whose work is just-

ified by its intensely personal vision. Clarke's anger is directed
against the uncomprehending bureaucrats, the developers
and the philistines, who pull down theatres and national
monuments like Coole in order to build more 'lucrative'
memorials. Typically, Clarke leads into this defence with a
poem about the wildly poetic but inadequately housed and
fed 'Paupers' who still inhabit the Yeats country in Galway
(*Poems*, 411).

'James Stephens' is a delightful piece of imitation and
flattery of that poet's style and themes:

> Big, little, words,
> Were hopping on twigs,
> As though they were birds,
> But how could I twig them?
> With chirp and twitter,
> They teased and twitted me.
> Each cloud was white,
> Lark sang, the sun
> Was steady and bright,
> Grass, green, sky, blue,
> The breezes blew
> And were full of fun:
> Half abstract, essence,
> The songs of James Esse.
> And I joyed in his joy
> As if his enjoyment
> Had all been meant
> For me on young elbows,
> In the greenest of elms.
>   (*Poems*, 403)

Here, Clarke's homonymous rhymes and repetition of 'joy',
indeed the short, almost bouncing lines, echo poems by
Stephens like 'The Goat Paths'. Stephen's poem attempts to
convey the ramblings of a herd of goats on a sunny hillside
and is filled with such repetitions as 'Quiet sunniness',
'sunny quietness', 'quietly in the quietness', 'in the sunny
solitude' and 'in the deeper quietude'. Its effect is thus
imitatively indolent.[10]

'F.R. Higgins' (*Poems*, 405), the longest of these poems, is
an elegiac memoir of the times when, while living in London,

Clarke returned to the home of his friend in the west of Ireland, where both poets, with youthful enthusiasm, had studied and talked about the traditions, techniques and subject-matter of Gaelic poetry and had wandered together through Connemara.

In a poem called 'The Stump' Clarke once again refers by implication to that disparate entity now referred to as the Anglo-Irish tradition (*Poems*, 478). Indeed, the merit of all the poems under discussion is that in them Clarke is, as it were, drawing up his list of writers, defining his literary tradition. In 'The Stump', three poets, Brendan Kennelly, Eavan Boland and Clarke (himself the eldest, hesitantly, perhaps unwillingly, performing the very role Yeats had earlier filled) officiate at the unveiling of Henry Moore's monument to Yeats and 'give out' 'a tribute to what had been Beauty'. Clarke finds that the statue resembles the stump of Thomas Moore's tree in Avoca. His metaphor then, implies a line of continuity in Anglo-Irish literature. It is, I suppose, to be expected that so many writers, from such a small island, would be seen, in spite of their individual differences, to constitute a 'tradition'. There is a sort of coherence, and distinctiveness. Clarke's own part in this lineage has been to widen the field, enlarge the concerns with which Irish poetry may be involved. It can be argued that Clarke's contribution was on a par with that of Yeats; it is, perhaps, therefore not co-incidental that like Yeats he was recalcitrant, stubborn, cantankerously independent. An analysis of tradition is not, however, the main concern of the poem, which is more centrally concerned with an indictment of the crassness of a civilisation that sweeps away relics of its own heritage (the house at Coole has been demolished, Thomas Moore's tree is rotten) and is prepared to surrender its distinctiveness in joining Europe:

> But how could I refrain
> Hearing that western refrain
> And grieving with its notes,
> From speaking without notes
> About our ancient land,
> Soon to become part of
> The Continent, remote,
> Unfriended: the hated Act

Of Union re-enacted?

It is also, as always in Clarke's poetry, concerned with the relationship between the act of writing itself and the surrounding reality. The poem is 'stumped' by the noise of the street, the people crowding round at the ceremony, and the cameras of the press. The casual, 'thrown away' quality of the pun that ends the poem enforces its ambivalent statement: 'Poetry had been stumped.'

Although not a major poem, 'The Stump' records an event that draws Clarke's poems about Irish writers together with his other comments on public memorials in 'Old-Fashioned Pilgrimage'. The place of these in his work is at least an extension of his autobiographical memoirs and numerous literary reviews.

(v)

The loss of a richer, more elegant past is evoked not only in Clarke's poems about Dublin before its technological rape, nor only in those poems about neglected idealists and historic figures. This lost grandeur attains its finest metaphor in Clarke's conscious efforts to translate Gaelic culture and to re-fashion Irish verse-forms into English. His confrontations with modern civilisation in Ireland are immeasurably strengthened by the care with which Clarke imitates a lost tradition:

> Mr Clarke is a translator of genuis: If anyone deserves to be called Ireland's Ezra Pound it is he. He has never published a book of translations, rather are they to be found scattered throughout his various collections. For him a poem becomes a poem in the act of translation gaining new life and energy thereby, yet remaining faithful to the original ... This sustained act of translation, a salvaging from the wreck of Gaelic civilisation, is a dramatisation of the Irish artist's relationship with his tradition and a response to the tragedy of Irish history.[11]

The care and finish of poems like his 'Eighteenth century harp songs', which fill the second section of *Flight to Africa*, poems that exhibit an intricate artistry and an intellectual passion for the beauty of a way of life now irretrievably lost, offer an aesthetic and cultural challenge to the themes and styles of more contemporary poetry.

The hidden music of Clarke's earliest attempts at bardic style is extended and culminates in the precise craftsmanship of 'Mabel Kelly':

> Lucky the husband
> Who puts his hand beneath her head.
> They kiss without scandal
> Happiest two near feather-bed.
> He sees the tumble of brown hair
> Unplait, the breasts, pointed and bare
> When nightdress shows
> From dimple to toe-nail,
> All Mabel glowing in it, here, there, everywhere.
>
> (*Poems*, 295)

The assonated vowels and aspirated consonants blend, pulling together harmonious sounds, creating an appropriately musical form. The rhýming syllables of 'husband', 'hand', and 'scandal' are woven with rhythmical shifts into a larger unit rich with 'sunken' effects. The repeating vowels of 'head', 'happiest', 'feather-bed', 'hair', 'breasts', 'bare', 'nightdress' and the final 'there, everywhere' conceal a consonance linking 'happiest' with 'breasts' and 'nightdress'. Each stanza has a seemingly effortless melody enhanced by an imagery immediately sensual; as in the first stanza, underlined by the final alexandrine. The second stanza contains a lovely conceit:

> Music might listen
> To her least whisper,
> Learn every note, for all are true.
> While she is speaking,
> Her voice goes sweetly
> To charm the herons in their musing.

Here also is an assonance binding 'listen' to 'whisper', a consonance tying 'listen' to 'least', and another assonance joining 'least', 'she', 'speaking', and 'sweetly'. The echoes of 'Music' in 'true' and in the final half-rhyme, 'musing', further tie this stanza together.

The third stanza of 'Mabel Kelly' has a rhythmical structure different from the others, almost like a musical transition, enlarging the sweep of sounds and cadences.

This stanza is filled with an assonantal long *a* sound, echoing the very sound of Mabel's name:

> Gone now are many Irish ladies
> Who kissed and fondled, their very pet-names
> Forgotten, their tibia degraded.
> She takes their sky. Her smile is famed.
> Her praise is scored by quill and pencil.
>   Harp and spinet
>   Are in her debt
> And when she plays or sings, melody is content.

The metrical variations from the long to the short sixth and seventh lines demonstrates Clarke's deft manipulation of rhythm and his exact enunciation. The caesura of the last line slows the movement and separates the stanza's imagery with its epigrammatic conclusion.

In the final stanza, these rhythmic swings from line to line are tied once again to the aural patterns of assonance caught within an echoing consonance. The resulting poem has the cadence and complexity of an inspired fugue.

Clarke, by imitating the older traditions of Irish poetry, strengthens his own poetic line and encourages respect for the more astringent judgments and language of his more topical poetry. Were he less severe in his discipline, Clarke would be dismissed as another self-indulgent romantic with a nostalgic vision of the golden age. Here, a passionately accurate language is refined. This impersonal, exacting art rescues Clarke's poetry from being overwhelmed by private experience.

'Mabel Kelly' is unique in Clarke's poetry. The ornamental elegance of this eighteenth century imitation is very different from the rhetorical effects of his other poetry. His double rhymes and assonances in the satires and other poems about modern themes are often harsh and intentionally jarring. Martin Dodsworth notes this roughness and suggests that Clarke's poetry jangles on the ear because our modern age does not inspire him to elegance and musical grace.[12] 'Mabel

Kelly' is the one exception to this rule. It cannot be said, however, that his other late poems lack ornamentation or that they ignore Gaelic models:

> In his attention to the ornamental in verse, Clarke belongs to the mainstream of Gaelic poetic tradition. . . . Irish poetry frequently tends to ornament emotion in concrete terms and to dramatise it in human terms. Often the ornamental and dramatic strains run together, and when the concrete is eschewed, as in many of the eighteenth-century 'aislingi', the verse inclines to rhetoric. Only rarely does Clarke forsake the concrete; his ornamentation is so full of substance that he frequently has no space for the luxury of a relaxed syntax. His verse, bristling with verbs, strains to include as much actual fact, historical and contemporary, as possible. . . . In his later verse, especially, he ornaments emotion with strict fact and closely-observed detail, yoked together in a metrical texture astonishing in its discipline, swiftness and freedom.[13]

Clarke admits that 'Mabel Kelly' is more a free variation on the original than a translation. The history of the original is in his Notes along with an implied justification for his own free adaptation (*Poems*, 554). In 1929 and 1936 Clarke sought to achieve, through assonance and imitation, 'the very vox caelestis'.[14] In the 1960s and 1970s poems based on Gaelic originals this pious ambition is abandoned.

In various comments, Clarke constantly referred to the craft and technical skill of the Gaelic poets. He applied those disciplines of the lost heritage to English poetry. This 'classical' approach, in which the poet is a 'maker' rather than an inspired genius, has marked his entire work. *Poetry in Modern Ireland*, Clarke's essay on the development of a tradition, clearly defines his attitude to these earlier poets. Gaelic culture interested him because of its attempt to create from a random and sometimes hostile world an ordered and intricate beauty:

> The Celto-Romanesque era with its intricate patterns in verse, in stone, metal and illumination, its conventionalised impersonal forms, attracted us as objective

writers in an age of self-dramatisation and display. . . .
(The Irish were) makers of things, strugglers against
substance: they forge, dig, tan, knock carefully together. [15]

The loss of this culture affects Clarke in much the same way as
do the long passed charms of his Dublin youth. Gaelic poetry
is another victim of Ireland's struggle for the modern. The
conflict is described by Clarke as

the desire to conserve our tradition and develop the
Irish language again, and . . . the equally powerful
desire to industrialise ourselves, dam our rivers for
energy, burn up our bogs as fast as we can, and merge
ourselves with the twentieth century. During recent
years the struggle between separate culture and international standardisation, which has been carried
on elsewhere, can be seen here on a smaller scale.[16]

This is what M.L. Rosenthal calls 'the double presence in
Irish literature of a vividly exotic and meaningful past and
of the pressures of the modern'.[17] 'Mabel Kelly' is part of
Clarke's debate with progress, and it preserves in English
a lost elegance.

Classic modernism, George Steiner has written is 'an
artistic and spiritual impulse to put the museum in good
order before closing-time'.[18] It is impressive for its determination to preserve the classic heritage. This impulse informs
Clarke's diction and imagery in the imitations of traditional
Gaelic poetry and shapes the rhetoric and rigorous wit of
his more modern works. His concern with Gaelic heritage
has not hampered his participation in and sharp observation of life around him. The idea of a fast-approaching
'closing-time' is not, however, prominent in his work. Life,
however mean or debased, continues. Clarke's work scrut-
inises the losses inflicted by 'progress' and chronicles the
daily existence of modern humanity. There is a deep and
loving 'memory of the past in his work' but 'Clarke does lead
a parade of poets who find ways of being at once deeply
traditional, in his sense, and authoritatively modern.'[19]

The harp songs, 'Aisling', 'O'Rourke's Feast', 'The Song
of the Books' and other poems based on Gaelic themes or

models are surpassed by the excellence of 'Mabel Kelly'.
The vision poem 'Aisling' (*Poems*, 299), and another vision
in *The Echo at Coole* (*Poems*, 445) are once again exercises
in the elaborate conventions of allegorical poetry with which
Clarke first experimented in *Pilgrimage*. Neither has a traditional ending – the poet exalted by his visionary optimism.
In Clarke's poems, Ireland, still lavishly allegorised, no longer
inspires but disheartens the poet. In the first poem he senses
her betrayal and in the second he is aware that her promises
are unattainable. 'O'Rourke's Feast' (*Poems*, 300) is a brawl-
ing, dramatic poem, its rhythms changing from long, madly
swinging lines (which recount the licentious behaviour of
the revellers) to short, clipped exchanges (which capture
their snatches of conversation). The riotous occasion is
described in a high spirited and robust manner. The priest's
final censure of the events and people is well mocked. The
cleric's pretensions to culture and decorum are hilariously
deflated by the exposure of his basic uncouthness:

> Three Reverences tumbled
> Into the ashes; Father Superior bawling
> Until that congregation went deaf and dumb:
> 'While I was studying with His Holiness
> And taking Roman Orders by the score,
> Yiz set on a settle with an old story-book,
> All chawing roast potatoes at Sheemore.'

Other poems in the second section of *Flight to Africa* display
the same rowdiness found in Clarke's Irish models. Each
contains metric singularities and not always oblique references
to modern Ireland.

'Rustic Match-Making' (*Poems*, 303), for example, is yet
another instalment of Clarke's 'drama of racial conscience'.
A marriage is planned not by the couple themselves but by
their elders who squabble over a yellow pony. Discussing his
model for this poem – Hyde's translations from the oral
tradition of the West of Ireland – Clarke writes:

> Here, in the *Love Songs*, were the young in those far-
> off times as they saw themselves, struggling against an
> emotion which freed and bound them at the same
> time. They saw before them, in their own words, 'the

star of knowledge', but they were oppressed by custom
and their own bewilderment. They longed for early
marriage and for their own choice, but they were
frustrated by poverty and match-making. Fear of
scandal, betrayal, sorrow and shame — these were their
themes, and a traditional skill had given to their expression a simple, yet passionate directness.[20]

'Song of the Books' (*Poems*, 310) is a virtuoso display
of learning and literacy. In the form of an affectionate 'roll-
call', Clarke calls to mind Ireland's bardic poets and remembers and recognises the form in which they each pursued
beauty and knowledge. Juxtaposing images of a cosmopolitan
life with those of the countryside's endurable hardships, and
holding the poem's metre to a strict pattern, Clarke evokes a
credible past, updates it with a comment on modern Irish
education, and ends with an epigrammatic eulogy for a higher
culture now dead:

> Soon every snout
> Was gone. A century of gods
> And nymphs from Inch to Blacksod Bay:
> Old knowledge scattered from the noddle
> In whirlabout.

In 'How Covetousness Came into the Church' (*Poems*,
307), 'Cock and Hen' (*Poems*, 302) and 'The Adventures of
the Great Fool' (*Poems*, 304) Clarke plays with metre and
linear repetition in a manner very near to nursery-rhyme. The
last two poems display his fondness for bawdy innuendo.
Ribaldry is exuberantly explicit in 'The Adventures of the
Great Fool'. These poems present a sharp contrast to the
sophisticated elegance of 'Mabel Kelly'. In their coarseness
and simplicity they have the strength of the folk-tale or ballad.
Clarke's renderings of Gaelic originals in *The Echo at Coole*
share this coarseness, lewd imagery, harsher music. This is,
intentionally, a radically different Gaelic world from the
light-filled realm of 'Mabel Kelly'. Clarke's models are more
often the uncompromising satires of Ua Bruadair than the
elegant compositions of Carolan.

A middle-Irish tale provides a main theme for 'Lactuca
Prodigiosa' (the prodigious lettuce). The tone of this poem

is delightfully matter-of-fact (achieved to a large extent by its seeming to be prose rather than poetry); the effect is entirely comic. Clarke still wants to create satirical comments on his old pet subjects, in this case, once again, contraception. But vehemence has now been completely replaced by wit. Classical motifs from Greek and Latin are introduced slyly to create a sense of high tone in counterpoint to the lucid, prose-like rhetoric.

The plot of the poem centres on the middle-Irish tale which the 'scribe/Had kept in Latin because it was too ribald'. With an impish sense of humour (that reminds one of the fauns that seem to abound in the poem) Clarke also renders the climax of the tale in Latin: 'Dum masturbavit/Et, subito, ejecit. Seminis gutta/Cadit ad holum'. This was not to be a sterile act of masturbation, however, for, in fairytale fashion, the princess plucked the lettuce upon which the semen had fallen and bore in due time 'a red-haired lad'. The tale was the country's first account of artificial insemination 'but not by cattle officials'. Clarke's wit is everywhere, his skill with his materials consummate and yet apparently easy; it is as if the words and images have themselves become fauns and nymphs sporting in front of our eyes. As elsewhere in Clarke's work the middle-Irish tale is a tale within a tale having, of course, a moral for the main tale. A wise woman who has stolen a delf-egg (artificial nest egg) from a hen and put it in its proper place 'Between the tea-caddy and the box of Beecham's Pills' has told John's wife of a secret salad that, as his wife prepares it, reminds John of the middle-Irish tale. But the salad's effect for John and his wife is only temporary — 'till conjugal duty become a constant sally'. Clarke's evocation of their love-play is masterly but the transition to contraceptive 'precautions' is where the poem ends, but not without a most daring pun on 'lettuce' followed by a related one on 'let' in the next line:

> Gay from a spinney, a birded copse, the fauns
> Came in a merchant troop. Their shag was fawn.
> They chased the white rounds of the nymphs, their
>   hooves
> Clicking by privet hedge. They shook the brake
> With frisk and fisk. John heard the rascals break
> Into the open where the last trail of a Roman

Water-course glittered in grass nearby his home —
A nudist colony. They bandied with dryads
In scrub oak that none had entered for centuries.
The couple marvelled. Thessalian kisses were dry
Between their lips. They listened to the pad of cen-
    taurs
And sniffed at times ammoniacal scent,
Then laughed — Greek stable manners were so low
Behind the gate-post of the bungalow.
Cantharides are not more certain when July is out.
So John and Jane had to avoid such lettuce,
Take due precaution with pessary and let,
Pray — lest Priapus show his snout again.

                                              (*Poems*, 443)

In so far as this poem concerns itself with 'coarse' subjects —
masturbation, artificial insemination and so on, the concern
is incidental to the main purpose which is moral and humorous.

In two poems the subject is death. 'The House of Mercy'
is an intensely personal poem in which Clarke reflects on his
own old age and impending death. The first stanza evokes an
image of Mary that is unusual for Clarke and in some ways
reminiscent of Eliot. However, there are very un-Eliot-like
hints of irony and suggestions of parody, particularly in the
inclusion in the image of Mary's mother, Ann. Clarke's portrait of himself in the third verse is very revealing:

    And his ballad goes on and on
    But the balladmaker is happy at darkfall.

'The soul too, comes from a dark place', he observes before
enlarging the metaphor to encompass Ireland and her famine
and then asking somewhat bitterly:

    How many coffinships will bring
    Emigrants to God's own country?

The subdued, reflective mood of this poem is replaced by
one of passionate anger in 'Eire' where it is Ireland's death
that is considered. The poem is based on one by Ua Bruadair
and uses the Gaelic convention of summing up the poem's
'message' in a separate quatrain at the end. Clarke translates

the title of this quatrain as 'the binding' which itself suggests a burial winding cloth. In the poem Ireland is allegorised as a whore:

Intricate turns of your body
Have pleased the foreign churls

     *   *   *

You played the harlot with those you hated
And those who loved you dearly.

The rich history of Ireland is evoked by the catalogue of her heroes who have known Eire. The extended metaphor of the Norman conquest is particularly effective:

The Normans went under your mantle,
   Whenever a stronghold burned,
And you pushed back their basinets,
   Cathedral mail, spurning
The meadows inching with dew, the thickets
   At dawn, the river harbours,
Hill-bounding of the hunted prickets,
   For wanton snirt and farding.

THE BINDING

God will soon humble your pride, pucker your
   cheeks,
And bring the wife of Fintan and Diarmuid — flaxed
With hair-dye — to the church door, ragged, meekly,
Her placket no longer open to the Saxon.

                                    (*Poems*, 446)

In the binding quatrain the rhythm and metre change to a slow funeral march as the spent body is brought 'to the church door, ragged, meekly'.

In the poems just considered corporal and sometimes brutal imagery is used for powerful metaphoric effect. In 'The Happy Saint', Clarke seems to abandon any delicate touch. In the early stanzas the language is light and lyrical but the refrain, repeated after each stanza with apparently only minor changes, is threatening. The language soon becomes more torpid and then turns horribly brutal. The fish images become more clawing in each stanza. No explanation is offered beyond the repeated suggestion of 'jealous saints' for the monk's horrible death.

> Cholera Morbus yellowed his limbs,
> Clap burned his sperm with glair and glect,
>   Demons beset him, gleeing,
> Immodest. Skeleton was limned
> Beneath his skin, a brattle of terror.
>   Crabs laid in his pubic hair.
> *Then, jealous saints, the old, the sly ones,*
>   *Prayed louder for him to die.*
>
> Tongue out for drop, the stricken sighed
> That he was dead. His wits were crazed.
>   He clawed stone-bed like a cray-fish.
> The body turned upon its side,
> Dripped slowly, a corrupted mass
>   Of stench that stopped the Mass.
> *The jealous saints, the old, the sly ones,*
>   *Had known how Enda would die.*
>
>   (*Poems*, 450)

The imagery of 'Martha Blake at Fifty-One' retained a tone of sympathy. Here, physical details of disease are brought by harsh rhymes and assonances to an appalling intensity, where the dying monk is without dignity or sympathy. The tension in the poem exists between these brutal images and those jaunty images in the earlier stanzas such as 'Lightly noting, Enda sang'. The link between the two sets of images is the inscrutable refrain. In contrast to 'Eire', there is no *political* dimension to the metaphor of 'The Happy Saint'.

'Phallomeda' (*Poems*, 453) is concerned with images of grossness and sexual failure. It is a witty piece but lacking the power of many of the other poems. The Dagda, the Irish God, eats too much stirabout at the annual Feis of the gods and is quite unable to take advantage of the happy coincidence that a Greek goddess, naked and shameless, comes to share the same 'shake-down' with him. The poem is hilariously funny. In the end the poor Dagda has to be satisfied with enjoying her in his snores. The last stanza here too is a 'binding' with the expected pun that some might find atrocious:

So in the words of the Great Mahaffy,
Annalists frolicked with the pen and laughed
At what they saw in the Hereafter,
    Forgetting their horn-beads.
Anticipating Rabelais,
They wrote of the god who lay
With loveliness. I copy that lay,
Applaud their disobedience.

In these imitations of Gaelic poems, there is an emphasis on images of coarseness, grossness, physical decay and physical sexuality. Anyone who has read Brian Merriman's *Cuirt an Mhean Oiche*, or the poems of Ua Bruadair, will not be surprised to find Clarke concerning himself with the tradition of ribaldry in Gaelic poetry. It should be remembered, too, that it was only with the development of the Romantic Movement and the prurience of the Victorian era that ribaldry and bawdy became less common in English poetry. In turning to these expansive and vital impulses, Clarke is establishing himself in the tradition of Rabelais, Shakespeare and Swift. In old age Yeats too, especially in the Crazy Jane poems, had turned to human, physical sexuality for subject matter. Compared to Yeats, Clarke takes his pre-occupation with 'coarse' subjects much farther. Compared to Yeats his treatment is more witty and his humour broader. Like Yeats, however, Clarke's ultimate concern is with making profound statements about the human condition, physical or spiritual.

In 'The Council of Churches: A Serious Trifle', Clarke implies a reason for this pre-occupation with images of decay and the cruder aspects of sexuality. He is attempting to create a coarse humour in order to bring back to consciousness the fact that, as Yeats wrote, 'Love has pitched its mansion in the place of excrement' — or as Clarke put it himself:

Humour is coarse
Because the duct
Has a double use,
Yet joy at its source
Was never deuced.
        (*Poems*, 423)

Whereas sexuality is always associated with freedom and

dignity in Clarke's earlier and later poetry, here it is often
associated with misery and debasement. Sex is linked with
brutal images of the body and the human condition. Clarke
demands of his reader an acknowledgement of the physical
workings of the body, eschewing the myths associated with
it in love literature. Only when the animalistic, sometimes
brutal, side of life is understood can he begin to celebrate
sexuality in his last poems. To gloss over the reality would
be to romanticise human love. The full impact of this bleak
imagery is, however, limited to his Irish 'imitations' and to
parts of *Mnemosyne Lay in Dust*.

An easy, though hardly infallible, explanation for Clarke's
imagery of diseased and decaying human beings, is to be found
in the personal poem, 'Impotence', which closes the section.
It is a confession, frankly and vulnerably made, of sexual in-
capacity in old age. The pain of such discovery for a writer
whose earlier rage had been for sexual liberation is movingly
conveyed in an ironic rhyme and diction which transcend the
almost 'voyeuristic' tone of 'The Happy Saint':

> Now that I am almost impotent,
> Thought faltering four times out of ten,
> And only patience can be tender,
> Regular verb is in the past tense.
> Disarmed, I lie, a malcontent,
> Outside the white-and-crimson tent-flap
> Of idle love. I cannot tent
> That wound, for all is good intent
> And yet desire becomes more wanton
> With every failure. Must I want on?
> Well, I remember how sinew was tense
> And the nearer the kiss, the more intense . . .
> Knowing that love is but a pittance,
> Enwrinkled as the fig-leaf of Cupid,
> Booby can do no more than piddle.
> Off clothes: I'll pray to great Priapus,
> Although he turn delight to a pus.
>
> (*Poems*, 455-6)

The bitterness of that inevitable last rhyme is hardly checked
by the earlier cavalier imagery and wit. The poem has affin-
ities with Clarke's earlier poems in the same collection and

with the compact, wittily obscene verse of Rochester. 'Impotence' is an effective poem, moreover, because of the openness with which Clarke writes about powerful taboos, the sexual memory and desire of an ageing man.

'A Jingling Trifle', another poem 'after Ua Bruadair', repeats in its final stanzas the allegory of a destroyed Ireland in much the same manner as 'Eire'. The 'binding' of this poem dictates the poet's relationship to his art and the world:

> False hair in hood is eyeshade for a milch cow.
> Chignon for Madam suits her cauldron bottom.
> So let the worn-out, the useless, the frayed, the
>   bowed-in,
> Patch up the songs that no longer bother me.
>
> The pound is used to falling, the point to boiling.
> The rich pass by themselves, all pomp and pump,
> The poor still know themselves by blotch and
>   boils:
> And dirty water comes first from a new pump.
>
> Bandy-legged, crotchetty Sister of our Nine,
> Forgive my farrowing words. I've learned to muff,
> Yet need more delicacies in my decline.
> Young Maeve has something better in her muff.
>
> THE BINDING
> Now that no man respects the poetic word
> And experience cannot unblind an Irish stare,
> Now that the knowledgeable have grown tired,
> Jingle-go-jangle is all that I will care for.
>   (*Poems*, 448)

The lines of 'binding' have been taken as a statement of Clarke's own metrical and assonantal practice. Martin Dodsworth, in an essay with valuable criticisms of individual poems and some illuminating comments about the whole of Clarke's poetry, enlarges his thesis to state:

> The poet's singularity, it seems, is in the first place imposed on him, for 'no man respects the poetic word',

and is then intensified by the poet in defiance and reproach of the indifference with which he is received. What we encounter in his work is a deliberate and willed carelessness ... Most obviously, Clarke uses assonance to get back to something of a Gaelic style. It could be said, even, that he has 'revived' this assonance. But that would not be true, in my opinion, to the spirit in which he most often uses it ... the weariness of the knowledgeable has a double reference, to the present, and to the past in which disrespect also existed for the poetic word, damaging the Galiec poetic tradition if not destroying it. (Clarke's writing in English implies, of course, a measure of destruction.) Assonance in this poem is associated closely with the other qualities of defiance, reproach, and 'barbarous' intensity. It looks back to a past which was destructive and effectively was destroyed ... He does, of course, use assonance in tender and lyrical verse, as well as in poetry of satiric and aggressive intent. Here it seems to go with feelings of pathos, and even of tragedy. The point is that it is rarely associated with positive feelings. [21]

Though Dodsworth claims that Clarke uses assonance in 'tender and lyrical verse', he also contends that Clarke's primary motivation in employing assonance is to confront the less harsh aural conventions of rhyme in English. Dodsworth sees this intention as the formal analogy to Clarke's anger with tasteless modernism. If life is harsh, then verse must also be harsh. This argument, which accounts for such practice as 'willed carelessness', ignores too many instances of masterly control in Clarke's work.

Dodsworth's major error is his failure to grasp Ua Bruadair's poetic motivation and financial circumstances, suggested in the line 'Unmetrical verse is neither bed nor board'. Hyde helps to explain the meaning of the line. He says that Ua Bruadair wrote at a time which saw

the great breaking up and total disruption of the Irish prosody employed for a thousand years by thousands of poets in the bardic schools and colleges. The principles of this great change may be summed up in two sentences: first, the adoption of vowel rhyme in place

of consonantal rhyme; second, the adoption of a certain
number of accents in each line in place of a certain
number of syllables.[22]

Ua Bruadair's plaint is that of a poet who, caught between
two traditions, admits defeat. The elegant bardic past is
uprooted and bardic poetry unrewarded. Significantly, the
same period saw the advent of new and elaborate forms of
Irish verse, among them the 'aisling', all based on vowel-
rhyme.[23] Ua Bruadair's 'classical' discipline is no longer
financially practical (a fact which adds new meaning to the
'jingle-go-jangle' with which he wants to fill his pockets).
The poetry against which Ua Bruadair is raging – and this is
what Dodsworth has missed – is the kind Clarke has written
all along. The phrase, 'jingle-go-jangle', expresses contempt
for the kind of rhymes Dodsworth finds in Clarke's poetry.
Ua Bruadair would rather have written the fiercely rigorous
consonantal poetry of the disappearing bards:

> Of the poets . . . towards the end of the seventeenth
> century, the most noted was certainly David O'Bruadar,
> or Broder, whose extant poems would fill a volume.
> They are in the most various forms of the new metres,
> but their vocabulary and word-forms are rather those of
> the more ancient bards, which renders his poetry by no
> means easy of translation.[24]

Thus, it is a mistake to consider Clarke's poem to be a
personal statement. Through the persona of an earlier poet
who witnessed important historical changes, Clarke throws
light on his own sense of the contemporary scene and effectively uses the Irish tradition of bitter satire. Ua Bruadair's
outraged metaphors for social and political themes are
worlds away from Clarke's less elaborate allegories of progress. Clarke is more avowedly the public, social writer.
Ua Bruadair's contempt for the advent of a different poetry
and his regret for the loss of a richer past are a standard
against which Clarke's own satires must be carefully judged.

'A Jingling Trifle' is one of the last poems in which Clarke
carries on his argument against the modern world, its advanc-
ing technology and its bureaucratic indifference to individual dignity. Like Alexander Pope's *The Dunciad*, which it

resembles in tone, it makes great claims in seeming to refute the challenge. Clarke's own career, however, is that of a poet who, learning the skill and commanding the authority of the past, has striven to use and adapt that knowledge in a relevant, modern way.

(vi)

The major characteristic of contemporary poetry is that 'real passion and energy . . . are reserved for works not of buffoonery but of wildly realized madness and suffering'. [25] Maurice Devane, a victim of 'madness and suffering' first appears in Clarke's work during the 1960s in *Mnemosyne Lay in Dust* (or, as it was titled in America, *Loss of Memory*).[26] Long and autobiographical, this poem is rooted in the confessional mode not only of Clarke's Gaelic precedents but also the American poetry of Robert Lowell, Sylvia Plath, John Berryman, and Allen Ginsberg. *Mnemosyne Lay in Dust* has been hailed as 'one of the memorable long poems of the age'.[27]

According to 'Notes Toward a Biography', in 1919, 'Clarke has a mental breakdown . . . Enters St Patrick's Hospital for treatment'.[28] Motivation for the poem can be traced to this event in Clarke's life, but the bare historical fact does not explain the poem. Clarke alludes to the event in his memoirs. *Mnemosyne Lay in Dust* does not attempt to obscure the autobiographical background, and there are internal clues pointing to Maurice's possible identity. Clarke's poem 'Fragaria', published in the *Flight to Africa* collection, (*Poems*, 323) becomes Section XII of this longer poem with the significant substitution of 'him' for 'me'. Mnemosyne, the Greek goddess of memory, is the mother of the Muses, and Maurice, searching for her, is an artist. At several places it is obvious that Maurice is a contemporary poet. Fifty-seven years after the event, private experience has been fused into an artistic and psychological resolution that lends *Mnemosyne Lay in Dust* 'a greater intensity than any other recent poem in Ireland possesses'. [29]

In its treatment of madness and recovery, its compassionate yet stylistically disciplined analysis of a mind disintegrating and then struggling to piece the world together once more, in its grasp of the particulars of life in Dublin's streets and life in Dublin's institutions, *Mnemosyne Lay in Dust* is the fullest integration of Clarke's other poetry (as represented by 'The Loss of Strength' or *Forget Me Not*, and by his poems about victims like 'Martha Blake').

Mnemosyne Lay in Dust, in eighteen sections varied in rhyme and metre, recounts the entry of Maurice into the asylum, his sojourn and release. His malaise is sexual, as implied in various images, the most significant of which is that of the satyrs in the garden of the hospital whom Maurice wants to worship (V, 333). He is also ridden with an inexplicit guilt concerning the two women in his life, his mother and Margaret, 'his pale protectress'. Repression (of the kind that threatened Gormlai's health in *The Singing Men at Cashel*) has crushed Maurice who

> For six weeks . . . had not slept,
> Hours pillowed him from right to left side,
> Unconsciousness became the pit
> Of terror. Void would draw his spirit,
> Unself him. Sometimes he fancied that music,
> Soft lights in Surrey, Kent, could cure him,
> Hypnotic touch, until, one evening,
> The death-chill seemed to mount from feet
> To shin, to thigh. Life burning in groin
> And prostate ached for a distant joy.
> But nerves need solitary confinement.
> Terror repeals the mind.
>   (I, 327)

There is a harsh irony in Maurice's observation that Dublin is celebrating its national holiday as he approaches the hospital named for the same saint:

> Cabs ranked at Kingsbridge Station, Guinness
> Tugs moored at their wooden quay, glinting
> Of Liffey mudbank; hidden vats
> Brewing intoxication, potstill,
> Laddering of distilleries
> Ready to sell their jollities,
> Delirium tremens. Dublin swayed,
> Drenching, drowning the shamrock: unsaintly

> Mirth. The high departments were filed,
> Yard, store, unlit. Whiskey-all-round,
> Beyond the wealth of that square mile,
>   Was healthing every round.
>
> (I, 327-8)

The next stanza avoids the sardonic wit of this 'healthing'.
Its seemingly objective narration of history and the approach
to the asylum as seen through Maurice's eyes conveys the
Gothic dimensions of his terror. It is a sympton of his madness that he dwells morbidly on what is common knowledge,
exaggerating his horror:

> The eighteenth century hospital
> Established by the tears of Madam
> Steevens, who gave birth, people said, to
> A monster with pig's snout, pot-head.
> The Ford turned right, slowed down. Gates opened,
> Closed with a clang; acetylene glow
> Of headlights. How could Maurice Devane
> Suspect from the weeping-stone, porch, vane,
> The classical rustle of the harpies,
> Hopping in filth among the trees,
> The Mansion of Forgetfulness
>   Swift gave us for a jest?
>
> (I, 328)

Images of soiled and besotted neo-classicism, of a nightmarish Georgian architecture, recur throughout the poem.
Maurice's ultimate acceptance of this world signals his
ability to live outside the hospital in a world where he
cannot be brutalised because of his sensitive reactions.

The second section of the poem uses the same stanzaic
form and casual 'rime riche' to portray Maurice's gradual
adaptation to his new surroundings. He is roughly treated
and cannot understand what is happening to him:

> Straight-jacketing sprang to every lock
> And bolt, shadowy figures shocked,
> Wall, ceiling; hat, coat, trousers flung
> From him, vest, woollens, Maurice was plunged
> Into a steaming bath; half suffocated,

He sank, his assailants gesticulating,
A Keystone reel gone crazier;
The terror-peeling celluloid,
Whirling the figures into vapour,
    Dissolved them. All was void.

                                        (II, 328)

In drugged sleep Maurice has visions of accidents, death and
violence. A train crashes, a crowd riots and, in a clash with
brutal police, women fall to the sidewalks, giving birth in
shrieking torment. Awake, Maurice is numbed and introverted
(notice the change in the stanza above, for example, to
passive verbs), aware of being watched through the peephole
in his cell door. He is completely overwhelmed by fear of
death. Everywhere he looks, Maurice, who comprehends
so little, sees intimations of his own mortality:

One afternoon, he looked in dread
Into the ward outside. The beds
Were empty. Quiet sunshine glowed
On waxed floor and brass. He hurried
Across to the high window, stood
On the hot pipes to see the view.
Below there was a widespread garden,
With shrubberies, walks, summerhouses.
He stared in wonder from his bars,
    Saddened by the boughs.

                                        (II, 330)

The verse-form, like Maurice's traumatic perception, is
immediately broken.

Maurice watches other men in the garden, lost like himself outside the bounds of normality. The third section's
bare simplicity is controlled by a final rhyme in each stanza.
The pathos of the situation is illustrated by tragic understatement: 'As if they had lost something/They could not
find'. The inmates seem to be searching naively for a clue to
fit all else together. The final rhyme of each stanza breaks
the rhythm and interrupts an otherwise obvious pattern:

Men were looking up
    At the sky

As if they had lost something,
  They could not find.

Gesticulating by summerhouse,
  Shrubbery, side-path,
They wandered slowly, pallid dots,
  Faces gone blind.

Looking down from the bars
  With mournful eye
Maurice could see them beckoning,
  Some pointed, signed.

Waving their arms and hands,
  They wandered. Why
Should they pretend they did not see him,
  Lost to mind?

They walked to and fro
  By shrubbery, side-path,
Gesticulating like foreigners
  Or loitering behind.

But all were looking up
  At the sky
As if they had lost something,
  They could not find.

                                    (III, 330-1)

From this point, the poem records Maurice's retreat into his own disordered mind. Small victories are recounted in triumphant plainness, lending a stark dignity, for example, to Maurice's ploy with a soap-dish which he is sure has been used to trick him (IV, 331-2). The answer that can save him, the insight that might restore balance, is always just out of Maurice's reach: 'There, memory afoot, he listened' (IV, 332). His dreams blend curiously with visions in which he is displayed humiliatingly before crowds of visitors and with idylls in which he comprehends the sexuality of nature and imagines that the columns of the Georgian hospital were designed to suggest and harmonise with that natural power:

Once, wandering from a hollow of asphodel,
  Still flowering at mid-night, he saw the glint of

Gigantic row of columns beyond the dell,
  Templed, conical, unbedecked
And knew they were the holy ictyphalli
Curled hair for bushwood, bark or skin
Heavily veined. He worshipped, a tiny satyr,
  Mere prick beneath those vast erections.

(V, 333)

Immediately, the scene shifts from the physically erotic
to the spiritually ideal: children, playfully free and happy.
Eden is theirs; Maurice is moved to bless their delight and
vitality:

Joyously through a gateway, came a running
Of little Jewish boys, their faces pale
As ivory or jasmine, from Lebanon
  To Eden. Garlanded, caressing,
Little girls ran with skip and leap. They hurried,
Moon-pointing, beyond the gate. They passed a pale
Of sacred laurel, flowers of the future. Love
  Fathered him with their happiness.

(V, 334)

There is an imagistic link here between Clarke's earlier
The Fires of Baal and Joyce's story, 'Araby', in *Dubliners*.
In both, the exotic and alluringly sensual image of Jewish-
ness (in Joyce it is an 'Eastern enchantment') promises
escape from the ascetic puritanism of Irish Christianity.
One feels that the children, being Jewish, represent a sensual
innocence. For Maurice, these implications join his chaotic
impressions, which turn immediately from this picture of
uncorrupted love and beauty to one of awesome justice. His
sense of doom makes him fear recovery:

Always in terror of Olympic doom,
He climbed, despite his will, the spiral steps
Outside a building to a cobwebbed top-room.
  There bric-a-brac was in a jumble,
His forehead was distending, ears were drumming
As in the gastric fever of his childhood.
Despite his will, he climbed the steps, stumbling
  Where Mnemosyne lay in dust.

(V, 334)

Maurice escapes this tortuous quest in dreams of anarchy
and rebellion that offer temporary relief in fantasy. There is
always, however, a phantom inquisitor to unsettle his easy
escapism:

> . . . someone by his bed. A melancholy
> Man, sallow, with black moustache, sat there.
>   'Where am I?' Voice was hollow.
> The other brooded: 'Think.' His gaze
> Was so reproachful, what was his guilt?
> Could it be parricide? The stranger
>   Still murmured: 'Think . . . Think.'
>
> (V, 334)

The mention of parricide suggests the real source of Maurice's
sadness: his mother and sisters are dead and he is alone now.
Frantic with his imploding thoughts, Maurice is bundled off
into solitary confinement where, for a moment, he understands what is happening and what has upset him:

> He tumbled into half the truth:
> Burial alive. His breath was shouting:
> 'Let, let me out.' But words were puny.
> Fists hushed on a wall of inward-outness.
> Knees crept along a floor that stirred
> As softly. All was the same chill.
> He knew the wall was circular
> And air was catchcry in the stillness
> For reason had returned to tell him
> That he was in a padded cell.
>
> (VI, 335)

In terse sentences Clarke compresses a realm of perceptions,
using new compounds like 'catchcry' to full advantage.
Maurice is temporarily

>   shocked back
> To sanity. Lo! in memory yet,
> Margaret came in a frail night-dress,
> Feet bare, her heavy plaits let down
> Between her knees, his pale protectress.
> Nightly restraint, unwanted semen

Had ended their romantic dream.

(VI, 336)

The power of Clarke's poetry lies partly in the development of a language and diction with which he is now able to
describe honestly even the most difficult or potentially
embarrassing subjects. There is an inherent decorum in
Mnemosyne Lay in Dust, which is in no way compromised
when, in the next stanza, Clarke depicts the animal-like
degradation of Maurice:

> Early next morning, he awakened,
> Saw only greyness shining down
> From a skylight on the grey walls
> Of leather, knew, in anguish, his bowels
> Had opened. He turned, shivering, all shent.
> Wrapping himself in the filthied blankets,
> Fearful of dire punishment,
> He waited there until a blankness
> Enveloped him . . . When he raised his head up,
> Noon-light was gentle in the bedroom.

(VI, 336)

The imagery is only superficially shocking. Its intention is
not to shock — in the manner of 'The Happy Saint' — but to
arouse pity for Maurice's uncomprehending state. Later in
the poem, a similar control allows the poet to convey images
of defecation, urination and masturbation without being
overwhelmed by the crudeness of his imagery. The tone is
not one of outrage, but of corrosive pity. Bound to a disciplined form, Classical allusion, an impersonal objectivity
and an extended but tight narrative, Clarke's scrupulous
language strengthens the grim truths his poem investigates.
The repulsive image of baseness and squalor in this poetry is
not an end in itself but a condition of the madness under
investigation. It is necessary to help the reader, for example,
to understand Maurice's terror when he gags and vomits over
the doctor who is force-feeding him. The burning language
and abusive imagery record his mind's most violent, most
basic struggles. The fight is not against shame, 'but only
blankness' (VII, 337).

'Summer Lightning' which appeared in the collection,

Night and Morning, is a harrowing interlude offered as the
eighth section. This section extends our field of vision to the
ward that surrounds Maurice. He is only one of many desperate men driven by guilt and fear of lost faith into madness:

> When sleep has shot the bolt and bar,
> And reason fails at midnight,
> Dreading that every thought at last
> Must stand in our own light
> Forever, sinning without end:
> O pity in their pride
> And agony of wrong, the men
> In whom God's image died.
>   (VIII, 339)

It is these men, each trapped in his own hellish mind, whom
Maurice now observes. Listening to them ramble and rant,
Maurice learns a talismanic charm but cannot yet solve his
own dilemma:

> Often he heard them repeating a tale
> Of the Gate, the Garden and the Fountain:
> Three words that lulled him as he fell
> Asleep: Mesopotamian sound
> Of a claustral stream that stelled him.
>
> The words became mysterious
> With balsam, fragrance, banyan trees,
> Forgetting the ancient law of tears,
> He dreamed in the desert, a league from Eden.
> How could he pass the Gate, the sworded
> Seraphim, find the primal Garden,
> The Fountain? He had but three words
> And all the summer maze was guarded.
>   (IX, 340)

Maurice is at an impasse. The metre reinforces the air of
futility, imparting the dreary sense of a dead-end:

> They lie, in the dark,
> Watching the fire, on the edge
> Of a storybook jungle: they watch

The high boots of the colonists.

The scales are broken.
Justice cannot reach them:
All the uproar of the senses,
All the torment of conscience,
All that twists and breaks,
Without memory or insight,
The soul is out of sight
And all things out of sight
And being half gone they are happy.

They lie in bed, listening
To the sleet against the bars, train
That whistles from the country . . .

(X, 341)

In dreams, led by Mnemosyne, memory and mother-
figure, Maurice explores the city outside the hospital's gate.
This classical elevation from the gloom of the immediately
preceding stanzas leads directly to an allegorical representation
of onanism:

Often in a priestly robe on a
Night of full moon, out of the waste,
A solitary figure, self-wasted,
Stole from the encampments — Onan,
Consoler of the young, the timid,
The captive. Administering, he passed down,
The ward. Balsam was in his hand.
The self-sufficer, the anonym.

(X, 343)

The image of Onan combines gothic, ghostly qualities with
those of waste. This 'self-sufficer', 'consoler of the young', is a
ghoulish figure. The meaning of the stanza rests on and descends into the last image, ' the anonym', which suggests the
ultimate destruction of personality.

The two sections that follow (XI and XII) describe
Maurice's fast-breaking in direct and immediate terms. The
first conveys Maurice's distrust, then his awakening curiosity
and finally his rhapsodic delight in a dish of strawberries.

The sense of their actuality, not the least of poetic delights, is portrayed in a manner that the early imagists might have envied:

> Maurice lay quiet. A summer month
> Was at the window. He eyed the plateful
> Of tea-time cakes that Mr Prunty
> Was gobbling up, saw in dismay
> Pinking icing disappear in grunts,
>   Hearing below,
> Far-away voices of the May
>   Leaf-thin and low.
> In June, upon the little table
> Between the beds, he saw a dish
> Of strawberries. As they lay
> There, so ripe, ruddy, delicious,
> For an hour he played with his delay
>   Then in delight
> Put out two fingers towards the wished-for,
>   Ate for the first time.
>
> (XI, 343)

Clarke has dramatised Maurice's perceptions and lifted them to a new level. The concentrated imagery effectively depicts his joy, but it also conjures, by its rhythmic halt and careful selection of detail, almost real strawberries. This contrasts sharply with the lyrical, rhythmically swaying, surging hymn in thanksgiving to nature which follows. Maurice accepts the strawberries as a gift from 'the lovely hand of his despairing mother'. Nature is identified both as a sort of life-giving earth mother and ironically as Maurice's own dead mother. The same clay that holds his mother's remains — and which might also have become Maurice's grave — gives life to the strawberries and ultimately to Maurice himself:

> Nature
> Remembering a young believer
> And knowing his weakness
> Could never stand to reason
> Gave him from the lovely hand
> Of his despairing mother,
> A dish of strawberries

> To tempt
> And humble the fast
> That had laid him nearer than they were
> Along her clay.
>
> (XII, 344)

This incident is a turning-point in Maurice's recovery. He has
recognised, rejoiced at and begun to live with the objective
world around him. The meaning of things, like the dish of
strawberries, lies in their actuality, the 'thingness' that
Clarke has poetically conveyed. Perception of reality becomes
a gift, not a torture. With this release from terror of life
itself, Maurice might recover.

The adventures continue, however, inside the asylum.
Maurice's mind has not been fully healed. In stanzas describing the exercises in the yard, Clarke uses 'rime riche'
to underline the apparently inane routine. This technique
allows the inmates' actions and solipsistic clowning to speak
for itself:

> Round and round for exercise,
> The trio pranced upon the concrete,
> Each of them a different size,
> Madder than athletes trained in Crete
> Maurice forgot his ancient sighs,
>   Round and around
> Escaping out of the Asylum,
>   With leap and bound.
>
> They squawked and muttered. Maurice laughed
> To find he was an imbecile,
> The quickest of them and the daftest.
> Faster and faster the trio reeled
>   In loony-go-round
> John Ball snatched dirt and tried to eat it,
>   Stamping the ground.
>
> (XIV, 345-6)

The poem now catalogues the plight of the other men,
using incidental detail and allusion to imply a larger stage.
Ben, for example, had a childhood sweetheart who was
locked away in another asylum. Their romance had been

clandestine, disguised by pulling the lavatory chain. One
constructs a whole history from a few allusions. The victim's
reaction is simple and haunting: 'Ben laughed, sighed, played
lawn tennis' (XV, 349).

Maurice's journey back to sanity is cautiously made.
Reading is dangerous; his mind too ready to retreat when it
encounters a story in a book:

> One afternoon he opened the bookcase
> Found *The Black Monk and Other Stories*
> By Anton Chekov. Nothing could hold his
> Attention. The words had changed to pothooks,
> Hangers. Words hid their meaning from him.
> They turned to Russian again. His steps
> Faltered. Lear roamed across the Steppes.
> The jester disappeared in dimness.
> (XVI, 350)

Once more, however, the verse implies by its fulness (before
the lapse back into a punning, identical rhyme) a hesitant
confidence, a limited recovery.

A journey 'Into a Picture Postcard Of the Phoenix Park'
where other people 'Stopped at the gay kiosk/For real
Picture Postcards', has more effect (XVII, 350-1). Maurice
is even moved, while putting much into perspective, to joke
about the ridiculousness of being a poet. 'An engine whistle'
which he hears 'Piffle away in the distance' is 'Poetic Personification' (XVII, 351). This is very like Clarke's own self-
effacement.

Maurice's departure from the asylum is a reconciliation
of many disparate images and themes in the poem. The
gate, garden, and fountain are real, he discovers. Dublin is
living once again. Images that suggested death become
symbols of the familiar, comfortable pace of life in the city.
There is a calm acceptance, too, in Maurice's evocation of his
mother's past and continued presence:

> Rememorised, Maurice Devane
> Went out, his future in every vein,
> The Gate had opened. Down Steeven's Lane
> The high wall of the Garden, to right
> Of him, the Fountain with a horse-trough,

Illusions had become a story.
There was the departmental storey
Of Guinness's. God-given right
Of goodness in every barrel, tun,
They averaged. Upon that site
Of shares and dividends in sight
Of Watling Street and the Cornmarket,
At Number One in Thomas Street
Shone in the days of the ballad-sheet,
The house in which his mother was born.

(XVIII, 351-352)

The street is pieced together like a jigsaw puzzle. Carefully and yet with assurance Maurice passes the same places he watched on entering the asylum. Life goes on; the cliché gains new significance for Maurice with every step he takes on his way home.

Maurice is re-introduced by Clarke in a shorter poem, 'A Student in Paris' where

Maurice became an earnest student
Of venery, hieing to the stews
At darkfall, roaming about the red light
Quarter, impatient, always ready
In café, at kerb, to stop a likely
Girl.

(*Poems*, 383)

After many and varied escapades with the ladies of leisure told in language ripe with double entendres and classical allusions and full of ribald frankness, Maurice gradually earns his freedom and returns home: 'The law of natural pleasure saned him.' At the end of the poem, he is penniless but ardent:

He left the Hotel Jules
Caesar with only his return
Ticket, five francs, a Juvenal;
Too young to weigh the mediaeval
Degrading of Phallomeda,
Whose votaries take off fallals
To earn their living, pay their homage,

By night to what is called unholy:
The street a temple, bidet a throne.

This is the sort of pilgrimage Clarke has written about before; the pilgrimage, however, is now from madness (not Christian virtue) to sexuality and its joyous liberation. Maurice's madness is in part induced by Christian virtue. At the end of this poem Maurice is 'too young', Clarke writes, to be jaundiced by the coarsely physical, less romantic aspects of sexuality which so occupy some of Clarke's other poems during the same period. He worships and participates in the sublimities of sexual freedom. His adventures provide the fullest clue to the purpose of the crude, clinically observed facts of human sexuality in those last poems of *The Echo at Coole*.

A young man needs the freedom Paris offers him; the older poet, however, can live without the adventures of the street. Maurice sees goddesses but Clarke describes him 'hieing to the stews'. Clarke's description betrays the difference between the unrepressed experience of an older man, acknowledging the full reality and the sublimation that is the privilege of the young. For Maurice, the 'street is a temple, bidet a throne'. In these poems Clarke advances two views of sexuality that are not reconcilable and must represent therefore a duality of joy and decay deep in the human condition.

The route by which Maurice Devane's recovery proceeds offers significant pointers to Clarke's outlook. The plate of strawberries that occasion the beginning of the recovery has a certain quality of absolute existence. It is also of course an image for the sweet pleasures of life. Maurice comes to acknowledge physical things and, as he does, his mind begins to heal. He begins to come to terms with the world alive around him rather than to retreat into the 'anonymity' of the self. The last stage of the therapy, the conscious resorting to the brothels and their many variations of pleasure, has the effect of purging all vestiges of 'celibate training'. But it must be remembered that Maurice 'dreamed of pure romance' not 'piston' romance before he 'became amourous as Paris'. As Phallomeda discovered, the ambivalance, the duality can only be partially removed.

Clarke saves *Mnemosyne Lay in Dust* from the excesses of Sylvia Plath or Robert Lowell in their poems about madness by his meticulous use of language and his controlled imagery.[30] The poem is exhilarating because it avoids the banality of self-indulgence. Clarke has made the real identity of Maurice Devane unimportant. One can, unfortunately, too easily imagine Allen Ginsberg, for example, declaiming Clarke's succinct 'The law of natural pleasure saned him'. In these two poems about Maurice Devane Clarke has described instead his most intense pilgrimage: his aim is cure, not stridency. The language of the poem, not the torn emotions, conveys Maurice's breakdown and gradual return to a tenuous sanity.

In 'Lapis Lazuli' Yeats wrote that art is the performance and controlled grandeur of a Lear who, faced with catastrophe, continues to speak poetic lines rather than break into hysteric ranting. Clarke, in Section XVI of *Mnemosyne Lay in Dust*, alludes to Lear. In that image lies the distinction between Clarke's long poem and those other more virulent, self-absorbed and publicly acclaimed poems about mental breakdown.

Plath's hysteria and self-disgust are overcome by her images of Nazism and sadistic rites. The reader first reacts against the atrocities she catalogues and only then understands her message. A similar loss of concentration is apparent in Robert Lowell whose neo-Gothicism becomes introverted and mannered, his poems macabre and at times unclear. Ginsberg, in listing every possible expletive and crude neologism, performs rather than poeticises. It is effective, but the power resides only fleetingly in the printed word. The continued abusive language of Ginsberg's whining catalogues corrodes the reader's response to his poems. Rosenthal objects to Ginsberg's over-dependence on sexual slang and other vulgarisms. His criticism is powerful because his objection is linguistic; it is not based on spurious ideas of decorum: 'The final effect of their continued usage, in poetry as in everyday life, is at one and the same time to discharge them of their special power to shock or amuse and to devalue the more complex reverberations of language.'[31]

None of these American poets have captured and managed to contain the impersonal art of *Mnemosyne Lay in Dust*, the allusive concision of Clarke's rhythmical and imagistic understatement. The formal structures of the poems themselves reveal Maurice's breakdown. The words accumulate and the lines become dense, identical rhymes and assonances pulling the narrative inwards on itself until the magnificent release, when the narrative bursts lyrically outwards as Maurice recognises the strawberries, and reality.

Mnemosyne Lay in Dust is a moving, elegant poem. It justifies Clarke's long concern with the involuted intricacies and discipline of Gaelic prosody. It is a unique statement in contemporary English poetry of the worth of the individual.

Maurice regains the world at the end of the poem, something which does not happen in any other major contemporary poem about mental breakdown. *Mnemosyne Lay in Dust* pulls together many disparities in Clarke's work. It is his best poem, indeed, a masterpiece.

Old Myths · New Poems

The under-mind is our semi-private part:
Not senile lust but stirring of religion
Long since abused, below in the pit of us.
The goddess, striding naked, with prodigious
Limbs — worn-out image — thyrsis clad in ivy.
Satyrs in grove, back-gardening Priapus,
Pimp of the privet hedge, a watering-can spout,
Latin still blooms from our clay . . .
                    Loins are the ages
Unknown to us.
            — Austin Clarke, 'From a Diary of Dreams'
                                    (*Poems*, 259)

(i)

In his 'A Sermon on Swift', a 'lay sermon' (as he calls the
poem he delivered in St Patrick's Cathedral at the third
centennial celebrations in honour of the Dean), Clarke
decides to 'speak the truth' (*Poems*, 457). What intrigues
him is that Swift could lead a double life. He was able to
be a cleric and

              . . . the chuckling rhymster who went,
Bald-headed, into the night when modesty
Wantoned with beau and bell, his pen in hand.
Dull morning clapped his oldest wig on. He looked
    from
The Deanery window, spied the washerwomen
Bundling along, the hay carts swaying from
The Coombe, dropping their country smells, the
    hackney —
Clatter on cobbles — ready to share a quip

Or rebus with Sheridan and Tom Delaney,
Read an unfinished chapter to Vanessa
Or Stella, then rid his mind of plaguey curling —
Tongs, farthingales and fal-de-lals. A pox on
Night-hours when wainscot, walls, were dizziness,
Tympana, maddened by inner terror, celled
A man who did not know himself from Cain.

Clarke then recalls the first lesson he gleaned from an early
reading of the 'fables and scatological poems':

                humour, unlike the wit o' the Coffee
House, the Club, lengthens the features, smile hid by
A frown.

Sobered by this insight and aware of his audience, the church
congregation, Clarke pauses, is reassured, and praises Swift
for his honest appraisal of humanity:

The pure clear ray, that Swift had known, entered
   the
Shady church and touched my brow. So blessed
Again, I gathered 'em up, four-letter words,
Street-cries, from the Liberties.
                      Ascend,
Our Lady of Filth, Cloacina, soiled goddess
Of paven sewers. Let Roman fountains, a-spray
With themselves, scatter again the imperious gift
Of self-in-sight.

Clarke identifies himself with Swift, stylistically and thematically:

           In prose, plain as pike, pillory,
In octosyllabic verse turning the two-way
Corner of rhyme, Swift wrote of privy matters
That have to be my text

He praises also Swift's era:

Reasonable century of Bolingbroke,
Hume, hundred-quilled Voltaire. Satyr and nymph

Disported in the bosk, prim avenues
Let in the classical sky. The ancient temples
Had been restored. Sculptures replaced the painted
Images of the saints. Altars were fuming,
And every capital was amaranthed.
Abstraction ruled the decumana of verse,
Careful caesura kept the middle silence
No syllable dared to cross.

Clarke enlarges the tradition he seeks to define; his own elegant style and diction, refined from his study of Gaelic poetry, becomes by implication an extension of Swift's Augustan English. Irish culture is thus defined as part of a larger European tradition.

Clarke recalls Swift's other works, his quiet but passionate defence and aid of the Dublin poor or the bequest to the nation of a 'mansion of forgetfulness' where Clarke himself was a patient. He is impressed, he writes, by a man who gave so much time to his work and who could still be politically aware and active. Yet Swift could also while away his leisure time by reading to Vanessa. The remarkable man Clarke writes about and celebrates lived by a rigorous morality. And so, before his modern congregation, Clarke summarises the legacy of Swift, a message of truth and freedom:

In his sudden poem *The Day of Judgment*
Swift borrowed the allegoric bolt of Jove,
Damned and forgave the human race, dismissed
The jest of life. Here is his secret belief
For sure: the doctrine of Erigena,
Scribing his way from West to East, from bang
Of monastery door, click o' the latch,
His sandals worn out, unsoled, a voice proclaiming
The World's mad business — Eternal Absolution.

In Clarke's view Swift vindicates human, wordly concerns; eternity and guilt are irrelevant. Clarke's 'Sermon' is his testament to Swift's intelligence, his sense of morality, and his humane compassion. His final tribute is a declaration of ultimate liberation. By following natural insticts, Clarke asserts, we find health and fulfilment.

The last books of poetry (*Orphide and Other Poems*

and *Tiresias*), the play that Clarke published before his death (*The Impuritans*) and the two plays which have since been published (*The Third Kiss* and *Liberty Lane*) exuberantly proclaim this doctrine. They are visionary and rich in their display of Clarke's intellect and imagination:

> These poems have ushered in his last poetic theme . . .
> a cheerful sensuality gathered up from the novels and plays and set glittering wickedly before us in the limpid, classic narratives in *Orphide* and *Tiresias*, poetry as pure entertainment, serene and full of life.[1]

Two of the poems, 'Orphide' and 'The Quarry', and the play, *The Impuritans*, are Clarke's farewell to the religious controversies that influenced his work for so long.

The influence of Irish events on Clarke's ideas is evident throughout these works. During the last years of his life, Clarke witnessed the resurgence of bigotry and violence in Northern Ireland. But neither the Northern question nor the many social and political issues of the day in the South stirred the 'savage satirist' of the fifties to write about them. The righteous, angry poetry of the fifties and the subtler satires of the sixties are succeeded by the sly, witty, good-humoured, artistically self-conscious, consummately skillful, even transcendent, poetry and plays of the early seventies. It can be argued that Clarke's last work does not entirely abandon political and social questions but rather transcends them.

Every character in Clarke's last works is carefully defined. No one is stereotyped or dismissed. He writes about characters whose actions transcend religious or social conditioning, and he describes their hopes and desires. He offers a vision of regained innocence and a challenge to ignorance, repression and violence.

In the poem, 'The Quarry' (*Poems*, 496), we are on familiar Irish ground:

> The people wanted
> To believe in this or that, forget
> Seaweed on soil, their want.

The poem, set in Donegal in the north-west of Ireland, creates a sense of curiosity in the reader by giving an account of

an alleged apparition of the Blessed Virgin. Father O'Donnell
is unsure how to tell his parishioners about other hoaxes:

> And what of the bleeding statues
>   In a kitchen at Templemore?
> Was it the I.R.A. who bartered
>   Red ooze for rifles? No more
>
> Had been heard of that. Ocean was hazing
>   The forelands of Donegal.
> He went to the side-board, hesitated,
>   Drink was bad for his gall-stone.

The reader, however, is being set up for a surprise as hinted
in 'Shy words would shuffle uncapped/Or shawled into the
Presbytery'. Clarke's rhyme-scheme is quietly effective and
unlaboured. It contains casual identical rhymes (e.g. 'Temple-
more' — 'more') and rhymes in which homonymous puns
occur in separate syllables, like 'Irish Press' — 'suppressed'.
It also contains an assonance that holds various stanzas
together unobtrusively, as in 'hazing' — 'hesitated' and in
the same section the links between 'Ocean' — 'side-board' —
'gall-stone'. Syntactical units (sentences or clauses) that cross
the gap between stanzas cement the poem. The overall
impression is of ease in the writing and joy in camouflaging
the rhyme so that it is less apparent to the eye, but still
discernible to the ear. In the last lines quoted above, the
alliterative *sh* is equally discreet. Clarke has seldom been so
comfortable with his technique. He exercises his skills in a
language that is natural and fluent.

This 'farewell' to Christianity is relaxed and cunning.
Like the other 'characters' in the poem, the priest with his
doubts and his glass of whiskey is credible. All this credibility brings the reader with Father O'Donnell to the quarry
anticipating something worthwhile. They are not disappointed. Those who nightly viewed Mrs Gallagher lift up her
nightdress must indeed have 'shared a rapture': 'Hail Queen
of Heaven, Mistress of Earth!' The reader is not offered an
explanation as to why it was Deputy Michael Gallagher
himself who asked the priest to quell the lies that were
'spreading about this wonder'. There is still bite in this
satire.

We might add that for those who wish to see it there
is a pun in the title. It may be that the poem relates a cleverly
hatched plot to capture as quarry an uncertain and fumbling
cleric. Knowing Clarke the pun is likely, if not entirely
successful.

'The Quarry' concerns an apparition in Donegal where:

> Among forgotten hills the Gaeltacht
> Held stories out of mind.

One of Clarke's finest poems 'Orphide' also concerns an
apparition and is set in the wintry Pyrenees. The tone,
language and structure of 'Orphide' are entirely different:

> Clouds held every pass of the Pyrenees
> On that February day:
> The Pic du Midi, Mount Perdu
> Were overshadowed, vapour hid
> Cirque, coll, down-drift of snowage glimmered
> From massifs, to the unwethered slopes
> Of pasturage. Far on the plain
> The apparition waited. Cave would
>   Bring millions to their knees.
>
> Escaping from boulders to moraine
> And gorge, the Gave du Pau, hurtling
> With cataract foam through gap, defile —
> Faster than superstition — turned
> Noisily to the plain, a widening
> Tributory of the sky,
> Aldering to the little hill-town
> Of Lourdes. Waves charged the Roman bridge.
>   Some were thrown back. More ran.
>
> On that February day, three children
> Came from the Rue des Petits Fossés
> Under the Château up a side-street
> Of Lourdes, sabots a-clatter on the frosted
> Cobbles, then down Rue Basse by sleety
> Shop-corners. No washerwoman beetled
> Blankets below the river-arches,
> Antoine, the swineherd, had left the commonage.
>   Eagerness stopped there, chilled.

At Massabieille, the unfamiliar
Gloom of forest about them — youngsters
In a folk tale — Toinette Soubirous
And Jeanne, a neighbour's little girl, stirred
In the undergrowth gathering firewood,
Darting as near as breath to ivied
Oak-tree, fearful of seeing a fay,
Nymph beckoning from a damp cave,
    Dwarf, witch with her familiar.

                  (Poems, 485-6)

The identical and half-rhymes that bind each stanza, the shorter lines that close each section and the elusive assonantal patterns that pull the rhymes inward and move the cadence away from the end of each line present a technical complex more impressive than similar effects in several earlier poems by Clarke which were equally rich in puns, homonymous 'throw away' lines and echoing aural patterns. None of these effects are laboured here. Notice the rhymes and puns of 'Pyrenees' — 'their knees', 'moraine' — 'More ran', 'children' — 'chilled', 'unfamiliar' — 'familiar'. The seven-line gap between each pair obscures the 'rime riche' (the less than subtle use of which may be noted in 'The Hippophagi', for example, and in Clarke's attempted homage to Whitman). The rhyming of 'unfamiliar' and 'familiar' is a particularly apt example of true 'rime riche', suddenly waking the reader to that other connotation of 'familiar'. Here, the techniques so luxuriantly employed impose an impressively disciplined form on this poem about Bernadette's vision at Lourdes.

The first few stanzas set the scene and establish the mood for the story of these 'youngsters in a folk tale', vividly evoking the Pyrennean terrain, the 'unwethered slopes' (this pun definitely requires an etymological dictionary) and the plunging river. The transition from the descriptions of the terrain to the social life in the village is made by the repetition of a phrase, 'On that February day', in much the same way that a story-teller might catch his breath and pause to recall the next episodes before relating them to his audience. This also emphasizes the importance of what is to be related. The incidental description of a river 'faster than superstition', the deadpan yet unexplained statement that the 'Cave would bring millions to their knees', the image of a river fighting a bridge, and the implication in the third stanza that the village is strangely still, as if awaiting some momentous event: all these create an atmosphere of suspense and subtly win the reader's attention. The fourth stanza with its gloomy forest, ivy and oak-tree, fays, nymphs, caves and the 'Dwarf, witch with her familiar', is inspired neo-Gothic.

Bernadette, her friends and then the vision are described tenderly:

> Drawing the white capouche around
> Her shoulders, Bernadette Soubirous, the third girl,
> Coughed, shivered, waiting by the shelterless
> Gave du Pau, unable to work
> Like Toinette and Jeanne, although the eldest,
> So often her asthma came back by stealth.
> She heard, as she stooped to tie her garter,
> Sound of a runnel, saw in the far clouds
>   The sun, a sleet-grey round.

> Along the cliffs a breeze wintled.
> The last gleam of evening had reached
> A small cave, made it so fine
> With summer hues that it seemed unreal,
> Bowering with blossom the eglantine
> Above it. Standing there, all shining,
> She saw a fair girl who was robed in
> White with a blue sash. Yellow roses
>   Half hid her bare toes, unwintered.

> Envisioned there, the girl of fourteen
> Trembled. Was it a river nymph
> Or shiny flower-girl from the forest,
> About her own age? She wore a simple
> Necklace of pure white beads, a chaplet,
> Smiled for a moment at Bernadette
> And, then, as if she would speak, raised
> One hand and faded away. The cave
>   Was darker than before.

The simplicity and ingenuous belief of this 'envisioned' peasant girl are never called into question. It is her manipulators that Clarke castigates. The mother's self-aggrandising dreams, for example, portend Bernadette's fate:

                             Enraptured,
She lay awake that night. Banners
Swayed with high blessings from the Cathedral
As thousands moved with Ave Marias
Towards the Grotto. She had conceived
And borne a saint for France. Her beads
Ivoried.

Bernadette dreams of tending sheep, unconcerned with the hullaballoo that soon surrounds her. Here, as in 'The Quarry', children are uninhibited and irreverent; they throw stones at the cave. The nun and priest-confessor who watch over Bernadette are more cautious. Lourdes itself 'was bespelled'. Public hysteria overcomes the local population:

                        Day had been nightmared.
Smoke-demons peered from a fire-balloon
Above the roof-tops. In a white capulet,
Black shirt and blouse, a lassie swooned
Before the Grotto, like Bernadette, then
Unfastened her flannel drawers and let
Them down. At Mass in the Cathedral
Urchins, surprised by a natural need,
    Bolted out, bawling: 'Merde! Merde!'

The hierarchy and the aristocracy intervene; the grotto is barricaded. Lourdes is riot-torn and has suddenly become the centre of the world. Bernadette, meanwhile, is quietly removed from the scene.

The Church is seen as an over-cautious, life-draining force. The casually related, undeveloped incident in the Dean's garden, where a thrush tears the life out of a snail indicates what will happen to the humble shepherdess. Her father is exhilarated by sudden celebrity, loses his job through drink, and, in a neologism coined by Clarke, discovers his vocation:

Poverty zola'd him into truth.
His child of fourteen was the future
Of Lourdes. To her new hospices,

Convents, shops, cafés, banks, offices,
   Hotels were all beholden.

No miracle would ever cure
Arthritis, leucaemia, cancer,
And pox — as he called it — grim diseases.
So many rosaries unanswered,
So many throttled by hope, fatigue,
Anguish, urged on by the cry of steam.
Dear Lourdes, our spiritual resort,
Chips from the saint's door, plaster all-sorts:
   Beads, crosses, curios.

From this point in the poem, Clarke gradually intensifies his weaponry of wit and rhetoric. The Vatican and the merchants who ruin Bernadette's life and spoil the country-side are condemned. In the convent Bernadette has another vision. She saw herself, leading her sheep

                              by the Romanesque
Arches, then, turning, saw a speck,
Far off, upon a brink. Rosin
Thickened in rufous stems. It was
   The demon-goat, Orphide.

Feverish dreams gave her no rest.
That local legend fled up mist
With her into the alpine passes.
Gigantic rocks were bared. Mistral
Blew. Beard divided, horns rafale'd it:
Orphide pursued her along the trackless.
Fallen on hands and knees in cave-slime,
At Massabieille, she was limed in
   The obliterating forest.

Orphide is the 'Centaur at a house of prayer', the folktale demon that Bernadette cannot understand or explain. She is led astray by a dogmatic Christian interpretation of events. Orphide's domain is the countryside, the rivers and the woods which are so wonderfully evoked in the poem. The girl's mother is the first to seize on the opportunity for personal aggrandisement that Bernadette presents. The village and the world soon follow. The Church then takes note and decides that she 'must be sheltered'.

Society and the Church alienate Bernadette from her rustic existence by forcing their ideals on her and subjecting her experience to the need for sensationalism and commerical exploitation.

A most significant feature of Clarke's poem is his concern to present a 'realistic' account of Lourdes. It is always clear that Clarke is not in sympathy with the Christian miraculous. Nevertheless he does not attempt to explain away the apparition in any polemical way. He rather concentrates on what effect it had on Bernadette's life, on Lourdes and on society at large. The thematic power of the poem resides in this concentration and in the tension that it creates between Clarke's version of the Lourdes story and the conventional Catholic one. It is, however, Clarke's technical virtuosity that makes 'Orphide' great poetry. This virtuosity is evident at many levels: the richness, power and discipline of the language, the allusions to symbols of folk-tale, mythology and so on, that enlarge the metaphoric reference, the disciplined use of rhythmical and metrical technique.

The last section of the poem concentrates completely on Bernadette, conveying a powerful sense of the breakdown of her health and mind. The account is always realistic: for example, thurible incense was not calculated to improve Bernadette's asthma, no more than confinement in a convent met her ambitions to be a servant or to marry. Bernadette's dream of minding her sheep 'In bluebell weather/Beyond the chestnuts' is gone: 'At noon, my sheep will be weary of feeding'. The demon-goat Orphide comes to haunt her sleep. And then:

> Pain, fearful of losing her too soon, held
> Body down in that last illness
> Of strange deliria. Lourdes water
> Given in galling sponge, in sipple,
> Special novenas, had not brought
> Relief. By day, by night, shriek followed
> Moan for the scarlet-black corolla
> Of morphine, dismayed the Ursulines.
> How could they know Orphide had sullied
>   All that she once beheld?

Bernadette's end is tragic. Clarke uses the full power of his satire to convey the tension between her fate and what Lourdes represents. Even his organic, rhythmically moving lines, his classically bound poetic form are altered. With halting rhythms Clarke utters his final denunciation:

> Bernadette died of caries
> At twenty-nine, irrelicable.
> No statue or memorial can
> Be seen at Lourdes, no visitors tell
> Her grave at Nevers. The candle-grease
> Around the miraculous Grotto increases,
> While the sick, dipped sorely in sourceful pipe-
>   drawn
> Germ-killing-earth-chilled holy water,
>   Murmur their Ave Marias.

At the end of 'Orphide' the reader is left remembering the sylvan language of the opening. Compare the lines 'Cirque, coll, down-drift of snowage glimmered' . . . 'the Gave du Pau, hurtling with cataract foam' . . . 'Aldering to the little hill-town/ Of Lourdes' with 'While the sick, dipped sorely in sourceful pipe-drawn/Germ-killing-earth-chilled holy water,/ Murmur their Ave Marias.' If language itself is the measure of reality as well as of poetry, Clarke's view is clear.

(ii)

In America 'the burden of Europe' is less constraining. This is the implication of *The Impuritans*. This new land, unlike Connemara or Provence, is not full of 'hidden', ancient stories. The play is mainly entertainment and resembles in structure, style and linguistic pattern the *Two Interludes* which, five years earlier, Clarke adapted from Cervantes.

In Nathaniel Hawthorne's story, 'Young Goodman Brown', the main character encounters a Black Mass and a group of witches devoted to devil worship, recognising among the coven his spiritual mentors and his wife, Faith. The story portrays his horror and thorough disillusionment with Puritan New England, and Brown is ultimately exiled from the community he might have loved. It is difficult to discern in Hawthorne's original whether Brown's vision is real or fanciful. He is damned by what he feels is a glimpse of the truth, harrowed by doubts at the close of the story.

Clarke's freely adapted version of the story is a parody. The relationship between Goodman and Faith in Clarke's play, with early suggestions of connubial sexuality, is hardly puritannical:

```
GOODMAN:            I have to go, sweet love,
  I'm late already and the Man from Boston
  Has lengthier legs than I have.
FAITH:                   What can he want
  With thee? Thou did'st not tell thy little wife
  Last night even in bed when she was warming
  Thy cold toes.
GOODMAN:         He is a merchant, a corn-factor,
  And when I have done a secret business for him,
  All that we wish for will tumble into our laps, like,
  Like . . . buckets of blueberries, huge water-melons,
  Oranges, nectarines.
FAITH:                Our cot, the bit,
  The sup, what more do we want?
GOODMAN:                   Delay will empty
  The poke. I dare not disappoint him. Just say
  A prayer for me before thou takest thy skirt off,
  My Saint, for it has kept me close to Heaven.
```
                                                    (7)

This is the coy, sexually suggestive language of Pierrot, Columbine and Pierrette, from Clarke's earlier, masque-like plays. Faith and Goodman, however, are involved in much larger issues. All the citizens in New England, it seems, are walking through the forest tonight, and so are the Indians.

Clarke indulges in his fondness for the sound of words, enjoying the winning earnestness of these early American names:

```
FAITH:                         O God above,
  The Wampanoias are padding towards the village
  Again.
GOODMAN:  No.
              People are coming from it, two
  By two. Look, there's old Ebenezer Muggins,
```

With Hookham, the tanner, Thomas Maul, Deliverance
Parker from Poison Lane.

FAITH: And Alice, his third wife,
Ann Pudento, Mary Easty of Topsfield,
Her grannie, Good Easty, hobbling on
A stick.
                    What can it mean?

GOODMAN: Keep in the shade of
The butternut tree.

FAITH: There's Bethial Carter, Dorcas
Hoare, Abigail Hobbs, Bartholomew Gender, Martha
Gunne, Jonathan Ruck and Mary Ripper from Main
Street.

GOODMAN: Who'd believe it, Faith?
                          Matthias Pilgrim, ·
The anchor-smith, with David Hodge, the boatman
From Cat Cove, closer than a pair of smugglers
Running a cargo from Nantucket.

FAITH: Goodman,
I saw your mother and mine go by, hiding
Their faces as they passed, but I would know
Those Sunday bonnets of theirs from the whipping-
    post
Of Salem to Sateschewan.

GOODMAN: Your father and mine
Are with them. All's well. It must be a midnight
Revival. Yes, there ride the Reverend Ezekiel
Burroughs and Deacon Gookin with three Select
Men. One of them is holding up a heavy
Bible.
          It must be from our Village Hall.

FAITH:
But tell me, Goodman, why is Titibu,
The Indian, among them in his war-dress,
Head-feathers aflaunt, when he has twice renounced
The Devil and all his pomps, saved by the Holy
Spirit that drew him from the bench to testify?
And look at her — Mistress Bibby with her broom-
    stick.
They say she is —
                    a witch —
                          although she has taken

A tight little corner, safe from draughts, at our Sunday
Services.
GOODMAN: What's to fear?
                                        They share the Holy
Spirit with us and come to offer up
Their follies to-night. If all were wickedness
Below, how could we cherish our fellow-beings,
Disperse the Gospel?
FAITH: Husband, thou must be right
And speakest as well as any preacher. The Saints
Of Salem are going into the wilderness
To find their true selves.
                              Others to come will hymn,
Hack, fell, a westward trail, drive out the evils,
The strange superstitions, that dumble out of
The forest a night-come, making our very
Scalps shiver, the mask-men, cruel as the black bears
That snuffle around our middens.
GOODMAN: Spirit has moved thee,
Thou speakest so well. Remember these words and
Rise from the bench, next Sunday.

                          (8-10)

Notice the ironic deflation of the religious meeting. Faith,
in a state of fright, is moved by the spirit of revelation. The
catalogue of names continues for two more pages, and
includes such gems as 'Goliath Muggeridge, the 'quill-man'
(a topical allusion to Malcolm Muggeridge, a leading moralist
in Britain's Festival of Light Campaign).

Goodman meets the Man from Boston who seems to know
a lot about genealogies, past temptations and present sins.
Goodman does not recognise him as the Devil until the Man
from Boston aids Goody Cloyes (a disarming name for a
witch). The discussion between the two, which Goodman
overhears, is part herbal lore, part reminiscence and a great
deal of fun-poking at traditional superstitions concerning
devil-worship (16-17). Goody Cloyes meets Goody Bibby and
the two witches quarrel, then fight:

GOODY CLOYES: What are you doing here
    In the forest, Goody Bibby?
GOODY BIBBY: The same as you,

Good Mistress Cloyes.

                                        Old women want it still
When their man's bedridden.
GOODY CLOYES: Then go to the Devil for it.
GOODY BIBBY:
  I'm going, duckie.
GOODY CLOYES: Yestr'een, you pinched my broom-
    stick
  And smeared your filthy hide with my fine ointment,
  Slabbered your you-know-what three times to please
  His Lordship.
GOODY BIBBY: He is most particular.
GOODY CLOYES:
  Now, give me back broom-handle, grease-pot.
GOODY BIBBY: I can't.
GOODY CLOYES:
  Why not?
GOODY BIBBY: I haven't got them.
GOODY CLOYES: You hag, you're using
  My broom to sweep the thrash under your bed
  And you frothed the philtre-pot I charmed
  For Mary Titch, last Hallowe'en.
                                        Bid your
  Familiar fetch them from Salem or by the giblets
  Of Thoth and Set, I'll embalm your shabby remains,
  Pyramidise them by old Nilus.
GOODY BIBBY: I'll strip
  Your smicket off, sockdolger your tail
  By Azrael and Ahriman, the doers i'
  The dark.
GOODY CLOYES: Let go my diddies.
GOODY BIBBY: Let go my mousie.
GOODY CLOYES:
  Come all ye, Spirits of salt, from Sprinkledom,
  Help Goody Cloyes.
                                        (18-19)

Goodman, watching and listening to this burlesque display
of witchcraft, is discomfited.

  The Devil's explanation of history and false virtue further
confuses him. In this play, Clarke 'deflowers the holy language of Teresa' with his own 'mad vocabulary' and jesting

ridicule of piety.[2] The Black Mass (22) in this play is more
than a travesty of normal church services. It is a new version
of Anier MacConglinne's exorcism in *The Son of Learning*,
written thirty-six years earlier. All is turned upside-down.

The next morning Faith relates a bad dream to Goodman.
She describes an illicit union with the Devil with quotes from
the Song of Solomon, using 'holy' scripture to blaspheme:

FAITH: Goodman, thank heaven thou
    Art back for I have had an evil dream in
    The night. I thought that I was slowly drawn
    Will-sleeping, out of the bed, then, inch by inch,
    Across the matting to ewer. O then
    My hand was on the doorknob and, Goodman, it
    Was hot and sticky — with an odour of almonds. And
    I remembered the words of the Scripture, heard my Black
    Beloved, behind the golden tasselled curtains
    Of Solomon, heard my own words: 'Lo! my hands are
    Under thy belly, sweet as calomel, aloes or
    The hill-waters of Siloah. Thy twin fruit
    Are rounder than pomegranates.' 'But thine are two
    Rose, knee-deep among lilies. Vine-curlets that cluster
    Thy virtue,' he sang, 'hide not the honeycomb
    That yields as thy scarlet lips yield.' Inch by inch
    He drew me into his blackness and I knew
    Too late, O Heaven, too late, that he was unclean.
    Moonrays were fingering my nightdress. Inch
    By inch, I was pulled into the forest, ran
    Back, our cottage was gone, our butternut tree
    A crackle of flame, a shower of sparks that midged me
    Back into the forest. Then I was hurried past rows
    Of measurement; yard by yard; they aimed at me
    And I saw that they were fusils. Blasphemy
    Spittled me. Foulness lipped my breath.
                                I stumbled
    Along a clearing, fell and the Nubian
    Possessed me under a totem pole, graven
    With dreadful grimace of idols while the half-clad
    Women and men from Salem danced around us
    With whoops of Red Indians . . .
                        (24-5)

Clarke 'unasterisks' the Song of Solomon.[3] Goodman realises
that Faith is describing a real incident, not a dream. His response is surprising. Though we expect the cuckolded husband
to respond with righteous anger, he treats the affair as a lesson
in sensuality and shows himself as eager to exploit the ambiguity of holy scripture as his wife:

GOODMAN: It was no dream for
   I saw your haunches mooning two letchers into
   A forest ride: I hid, watching my wife
   Take both together, spend them, then go beneath
   Her Nubian, white legs, black legs, bandying it
   Out.
   Why dost thou start like that, so goo-goo-eyed?
   I see them at it still, the saints of Salem,
   There in the forest around the accursed Maypole
   Naked as flowers, patriarchs who Chattled
   The women of Chaldea, casting lots in
   The Land of Moab for the pectoral,
   The square of gold or dicing for the royal
   Ones, concubines of Siloah double-shotten
   At midnight, when the moving Pillar of Fire
   Glows under the sky-pegs of their tents, taking
   Their promises from the Old Testament.
                               So by
   My Faith, I'll give and take as they do, borrow
   Their amulets, lie down to it
   And never trust thy dainty placket-hole
   Till Doomsday.
FAITH: Thou thouest me again.
GOODMAN:
   Thou are my wife, my whore.
FAITH: Thy wife, thy whore for better
   Or worse.
GOODMAN: Come, let us try the worst.
   Do all that we saw in dream or earnest. We
   Are Bible-mad. Prophetic words possess us. God stays
   The pilgrim ships that carry salvation ever
   Westward and on their homeward voyage, bring
   The pox that rages in Europe, uncovering monarchs,
   Their nobles, rutting 'em, rotting 'em, in and out,
   Bedevilling the brainpans of their subjects.
                             (26-7)

Goodman then has a vision of the future and asks, rhetorically, how any Christian, bound to a doctrine based on repression of natural instinct and bodily appetite, can hope to create a peaceful kingdom in this world. Goodman asserts that liberation from Christian dogma is the only solution and he boldly supports his new belief with quotes from the Bible. European Christianity is purposefully misinterpreted (otherwise it is a lie, Goodman asserts, destructive of human trust and co-operation).

The peace-pipe of the Indians suggests another bawdy joke:

GOODMAN: But I've a text
  From the Epistles of St Paul.

                                      Thou knowest it!
      Marry or burn.
              I burn for it.
FAITH: And I
  For thee.
GOODMAN: Let frolics missrule our known
        behaviour.
  We'll randy it out together, cuckold ourselves
  And watch each other sporting in the handglass
  Of a dream played out in Genesis.
                                  So, off with
  Puritan costume and cap, petticoat, shift,
  Thick drawers. Let immodesty fill our chamber.
                                      White chief
  Feel bad, want favourite squaw in her red skin
  To pow-pow with him, squat in the wigwam, share
  Big pipe of peace until the last puff is gone.
                                      (28-9)

What Clarke offers in *The Impuritans* is an entertainment based on the oldest joke in the world, with variations delightfully discovered in the double-edged meanings of seemingly innocent words and images. The play's chief insight is that any definition of reality which denigrates the human body and sexuality is less than profound. Goodman and Faith are, at the final curtain, exuberantly guilty, free and happy in the knowledge and mutual awareness of their natural instincts.

(iii)

Guilt and suppression of natural instinct are also the themes
of *The Third Kiss*, a play which, like *Liberty Lane*, has been
published since Clarke's death. In *The Third Kiss* we meet
Pierrot and Pierrette again with a new character, Harlequin.
It is a more intricate piece of stage writing than either *The
First Kiss* or *The Second Kiss* and displays both Clarke's
delight in and command of language and his theatrical
control.

Pierrot and Pierrette are first seen backstage in the changing
rooms at the Abbey Threatre. It is 1913 and they are to play
real human beings for once. Pierrot is attracted by a glimpse
of Pierrette's real flesh. She is worried for chastity and
decency's sake that he might forget himself in front of the
audience. Their self-conscious banter is humorous, with
revealing   comments on literary fashions thrown in for
good measure:

PIERROT: Too many underclothes for petting.
    Corset
          — or stays —
                    camisole,
                              petticoat
(pulling up her skirt)
Big drawers.
PIERRETTE: Pierrot, you should not misbehave.
    Have you forgotten we are human beings
    Tonight?
PIERROT: New, pretty ancle . . .
                              another peep,
    Pierrette,
PIERRETTE: Not now. We are respectable people
    According to the play —
PIERROT: Unhappy,
PIERRETTE: Tormented
    By conscience,
PIERROT: Fear of sin.
PIERRETTE: The Author meant
    The play, perhaps, to be satiric.
PIERROT: They call
    It — 'Realism'.
                                        (9-10)

Harlequin has confronted Pierrette, threatening to ravish her, and she confides her fears to Pierrot, who tells her not to worry: 'The human mind is obscene.' The strangeness of this advice is passed over as the two characters wait in the wings for their cues to go on stage. Their excitement, caused by stage fright and sexual tension, moves them to rebellion. The Prologue ends with their vowing to give the play a happy ending in defiance of the author's intentions. The play itself has not yet begun. This declaration of independence from the characters is borrowed equally from Clarke's earlier plays and from the surrealistic games-playing of Flann O'Brien's novels. (Clarke has already written of his debts to O'Brien in the poem 'More Extracts From A Diary of Dreams'.)

The four acts of the play within *The Third Kiss* are pure Clarke, however, and relate closely in style to *The Viscount of Blarney* and *As The Crow Flies*. Scenes change instantaneously, and Pierrot and Pierrette (who are now Peter Blake and Pauline Quinn) inhabit a Dublin that is realistic but which veers into fantasy and back again. Waiting at a bus stop, Pauline obsessively relates the story of an exhibitionist, an old man who springs out from behind a lamppost or hedge and scares young women. Clarke is poking fun at the taboo against looking at the male organs. Peter struggles to allay her fears but Pauline is confused. Frightened of sexual knowledge, even of knowledge about her own body, she is unaware that this inhibition is the real source of what she proudly calls her 'vocation'. Peter, who is more worldly, distracts her from her preoccupation with convents and the celibate life by recalling childhood memories and idyllic fantasies.

The scenes change rapidly from bus stop to unlit streets (where young girls run in fear from hedge to lamppost) to a seaside resort where children play in the sand and then to the Black Church in Dublin (which gave Clarke's first autobiographical memoir its title). There Peter and Pauline remember childhood rhymes and a game:

> Run, run around
The Black Church in St Mary's Place.
Three times at night.
— and see the Devil, face to face.

(19)

Peter omnisciently explains how authorities, especially religious teachers, frighten and repress children: 'They fit the conscience on when boot and shoe are smaller' (20). Scene one ends with the pair re-enacting the chase around the Black Church. Pauline bumps into a man in an opera cloak, screams and disappears. With every attempt by Peter to dispel Pauline's fears, some ogre or memory has pushed her farther away from him. Now they are separated and lost.

Scenes two and three tell one story with a minimum of setting or character manipulation. The two principals are on a walk in the country, as is a priest. The priest has come to the country in an attempt to scourge his own sexual desires. Father Doyle resorts to a medieval monastic cure for proud flesh. Stripping off, the priest rolls through stinging nettles, causing himself great agony, which he attempts to feel as spiritual grace. Clarke expresses no antagonism towards the priest; the facts speak for themselves. He even pities the priest's misguided actions. Pauline, looking for shelter from a sudden downpour, finds the sore, naked, blistered priest and thinks she is seeing some demon. She screams again and begs Peter to take her home. Later, during confession, she recognises the priest and her faith is altered.

The final scene is a continuation of the first. Pauline foreswears her vocation at the bus stop, and they both go in to change back into Pierrot and Pierrette. Harlequin now comes on stage, in front of the closed curtains, and delivers his only speech. Through voyeurism and coarse innuendo the audience is offered a sophisticated and philosophical explanation of life and instinct and a short, witty digression on literary technique:

> HARLEQUIN: (to audience)
>   She's in the dressing-room again.
>   (Peeps through curtain)   There go her stays,
>   Camisole, lace-trimmed petticoat, and now . . .
>   What stays me?
>   (hesitates)
>   I will, I must.
>   (Peeps again)
>   Pierrot is laughing — she's in her drawers.
>   One moment, please,
>   The modest author.
>   I must not draw

Undue attention to them . . .
He knows that voyeurism is my vice.
(Chuckling)
He thinks his couplets experimental but *rime
     riche* is
Double-entendre in English. In Irish, plain *aris*
Or, as they say, the same again . . .
          We laugh, love, sigh, quarrel, bedevil to
                    earn our
Existence, parody your worst thoughts . . .
          In sleep, your world is willy-nilly
And virtuous. 'I won't' quickly becomes 'I will'.
Pleasure is in the affirmative.

                                        (32-4)

Pierrot and Pierrette have been acting human roles in the
realistic manner of the Abbey Theatre. In the epilogue they
again appear as themselves. They plan their evening: a quiet
meal — and then to bed. As they leave the stage for the final
time, Pierrette leaves her music box playing, and the play
ends as elegantly as it began.

The Third Kiss is an Irish version of *The Impuritans*, admittedly less audacious, but an indication of how far Clarke
has come from the heavier satire and sermonic tone of some
earlier works. The audience responds to and interprets what
the characters say and do without authorial intrusion. *The
Third Kiss* is, above all else, imaginative and entertaining
theatre by a writer fully in command of his language and with
a well developed sense of the dramatic — powers that had continued to develop throughout the fifty years during which
Clarke wrote.

As if to assert his true strength, imaginative vitality and
technical skill even in his last hour, Clarke's last published
work, *Liberty Lane*, is a theatrical extravaganza. Using traditional ballads as part of the dramatic framework and set in
the Liberties of Dublin (one of the older parts of the inner
city near St Patrick's Cathedral), *Liberty Lane* is a pageant.
It is also Clarke's tribute to the people of Dublin, rich in
accented dialogue and local characters. There is a Prologue
and two 'acts', but in reality there is little division and the
action is merely an excuse to move history, legend, gossip,
song and colourful incident before the audience's eyes. The

main action is a re-enactment of the wake for Zozimus, a ballad-singer of the nineteenth century. Clarke had already mentioned this character in the notes to this collection of satires, *Too Great A Vine* (*Poems*, 549).

Liberty Lane is also something of a collaboration. In his notes to the play, Clarke explains that it is really a revision of another play by F.R. Higgins, called 'Deuce of Jacks'. Clarke had altered the last scene in 1938 for dramatic purposes, hoping that the Lyric Theatre Company, which he founded, would give Sunday performances of the play. These never happened, and the play lay almost forgotten. 'Eventually,' Clarke explains in his note, 'I could not resist adding to the new ending my own version of the traditional story.'

This new version is like a mummers' play. There are over thirty characters, including Jonathan Swift, the ballad-singer Zozimus (and the street trader who is impersonating him for the 'play'), Edward Carson (the lawyer who prosecuted Oscar Wilde and later organised Protestant armies in Ulster in the early years of this century), Terence O'Neill (head of state in Northern Ireland during the 1960s), fruit sellers, families of tenement dwellers, priests and prostitutes. The time scale is irrelevant and no single character dominates. *Liberty Lane* celebrates Dublin as if all history and all incident were happening simultaneously.

Into the general framework of a wake, Clarke incorporates ballads of the early 1800s, street slang and jokes, a poem by Swift ('Epilogue to a Play for the Benefit of the Weavers in Ireland, 1721') and his own 'O'Rourke's Feast' (*Poems*, 300).

Conflict (between the priest, for example, who cannot allow the wake to occur and its celebrants, or between the married women and the prostitutes) is jovially resolved or jokingly ignored. In fact, *Liberty Lane* is a festival, a mirth-filled, hugely enjoyable pageant of Dublin life. The history and politics of the nation are largely irrelevant in this play to the citizens of this, the economically poorest but culturally richest, part of Dublin. The presence of Edward Carson and Terence O'Neill should raise the question of Northern Ireland. But drinking and story-telling are the burning issues of this play. If Clarke's interludes were designed as an elegant entertainment to be played between the courses of a meal, then surely *Liberty Lane*, in all its exuberant high-spirited fun, belongs in some equally sophisticated setting, perhaps in a club, close to a public bar.

(iii)

We turn now to an aspect of Austin Clarke's poetry not sufficiently emphasised. After the hard satires of the fifties, it is
easy to fall into the trap of seeing Clarke's development as
being exclusively by route of increasingly subtle and more
technically skilled satire. However, a glance at the poetry
reveals that side by side with the finest satires are many
poems that, while containing satirical elements, are celebrations of the natural beauty of Ireland, that earn Clarke the
right to be regarded as one of the great nature poets of the
twentieth century. This is perhaps surprising for a poet who
was born, reared and lived in a city and whose best work is
commonly thought of as witty, satirical, urbane and Augustan.

Clarke's great gift as a poet of nature is his power of observation and evocation. This has already been alluded to in discussing his romances as well as poems as different as 'Pilgrimage'
(1929) and 'Orphide' (1970). We have frequently remarked
on Clarke's appeal to nature as the true source of religion and
insight. We discuss now two poems that draw together his
vision of nature as the curative context of insight. Both are
imitations (either specifically or generically) of medieval
Gaelic poetry, where the music of nature is everpresent. The
Fianiacht poetry is full of melodious evocations of the forests,
the mountaintops and the beautiful places of Ireland. Because
this poetry is written in accordance with highly disciplined
metrical conventions, it has a hard, clean edge that allows
little scope for swooning sentimentality. Clarke, more than
any other attempter of renderings, had mastered the metre
and diction of the originals. Largely as a result, his 'nature'
poetry is powerfully original.

The splendid poem 'Beyond the Pale' is described by Clarke
as an 'old-fashioned descriptive poem . . . suggested by the
"Walks" and "Gig Drives" of Victorian parson-poets' (*Poems*,
554). Published with a number of other 'nature' poems in
Flight to Africa (1963), it is an updated version of his much
earlier poem, 'The Itinerary of Ua Clerigh' (*Poems*, 120).
Clarke says that 'itinerary poems were favourite forms among
the later Gaelic poets' (*Poems*, 546). 'Beyond the Pale' is
also an elaborate poem of appreciation and love for his wife

Nora whom he continually addresses:

> Pleasant, my Nora, on a May morning to drive
> Along the roads of Ireland, going south,
> See Wicklow hilling from car window, down
> And pinewood, buttercupping grass, field-wire,
> The shelves of hawthorn, konker bud on chestnut
> Bulging with sun-shadowings, brook-lime,
> The yellow iris-curl, flower o' the cress
> And Slaney gliding around a sandy nook
> Through flaggeries into the narrower falls,
> Beyond the mills with the rusty flange, cogwheel
> And moss of the sluice, hear the jackdawing,
> Yet sad to speed from the inn, along the bogland
> Where State machines are cutting turf for miles
> That furnaces may stop the centuries
> Of turbary, put out an ancient fire.
> Hardly a living soul upon these roads:
> Both young and old hasten to quit the dung,
> The chicken-run, lean-to, sty, thistle blow
> Of fields once measured by buckshot, midnight bung.
> Foreign factories in towns employ
> Chattering girls: few levers for a boy.
>
> (*Poems*, 289)

The poem continues with their rambles south and then west across Ireland. Clarke describes the shape of wildflowers and sounds of birds, displaying his 'direct sensual interest in things',[4] while always maintaining an awareness of the new, spreading industrialisation of Ireland. The poem, as illustrated in the quotation above, effortlessly makes the transition from natural descriptions to social comment. Clarke's knowledge of local history and legend overlays this basic form; for example, when visiting Kilkenny, he recalls the story of Alice Kyttler:

> . . . stripping to the pelt,
> Leftwise, she wrote the Tetragrammaton.
> The Devil came, volumed in smoke from a gorge
> Beyond the Caucasus, breakneck upon
> Foul wind. She wanted topsy-turvy orgy
> And, taking her by the loblongs, Fiery dawdled,

Unpadlocked her with ice-cold key. Melled, twisting
In exquisite pain, she lay with open wards
While her companion, Petronella, was kissed
Introrsely by Black Fitzjames, knighted in hell.
He picked her keyhole with his skeleton,
Fire-freezing through her pelvis, but she missed
The bliss, though he was cap-à-pie as Guelf.
Soon afterwards, they say, that demon sired
The black cats of Kilkenny. They fought for scales
Of market fish, left nothing but their own tails
And their descendants never sit by the fire-side.
Disedifying Latin, clerical tales
Corrupt us.

The parallel with the play *The Impuritans* is unmistakable.
Clarke also considers in this poem the poetry of the Victorian
Coventry Patmore:

who wived three times, has written of love
In matrimony, pulled the curtain back, showed
From post to post, the hush of featherbed,
Lace counterpane, mahogany commode:
And here from hoop and bustle, petticoats, pleating,
Long drawers, to eiderdown, our Fanny glowed;
Too cushiony, too gross, in such an abode
For Psyche.
Our convert, right or wrong,
believed
That in the midnight transport, every spouse
Knew Heaven, like us, by the oriental spice.
So Virtue, blushing at a little vice,
Turned down the incandescent mantle, unbloused
The globes of sin.

It is odd that Clarke should pay such beautiful and frank
tribute to his wife by referring to Patmore's prim and cloying
poem 'The Angel in the House'. Clarke is, of course, aware
of Patmore's shortcomings (having described his poetry elsewhere as 'bathetic'), but he nevertheless praises the man 'who
dared to allow marriage a spiritual place'.[5] These themes
foreshadow the lines of 'A Sermon on Swift' where Erigena
(whose books were burned because he saw the ultimate joy

and pardon of all human creatures in sexuality[6]) is said to have taught the same moral Clarke found in Swift: 'the jest of life . . . Eternal Absolution'. And in this central section of 'Beyond the Pale', Clarke decorously describes what in *The Impuritans* he flaunts: the idea that 'divine' understanding and transcendence can be attained through full response to sexuality — 'the midnight transport'.

The poem ends in a harsh, epigrammatic identification of Ireland with a crone:

> Now, after a century of rags, young girl
> With skin the insolent have fondled, Earl
> And settler in his turn, the Hag of Dingle
> Is stretching. Eire, clamant with piety,
> Remembering the old mythology.

This image links 'Beyond the Pale' with the entire body of Clarke's work, fusing heretical doctrine and ideas of sexuality, with social comment, and exacting natural descriptions. 'The Hag of Dingle' is Sweeney's hag, an alternative to Cathleen ni Houlihan, a symbolic embodiment of Ireland. Sweeney's myth is enlarged to represent Clarke's entire literary output. In Clarke's last poems the idea of holy madness is explored in a poem explicitly concerned with Sweeney, 'The Trees of the Forest' (*Poems*, 507).

'The Trees of the Forest' is another instance in his last poems of a gathering of materials, a summary of the major themes and devices of his works. In his autobiography, *A Penny in the Clouds*, Clarke recalls a conversation he had with George Moore about the legendary mad king:

> '*The Frenzy of Sweeney* is one of the great stories of the world, and yet how many know of its existence? There is no more local colour in it than in Theocritus — yet was Nature ever so near, so wild and so tender? A King of Ireland cursed by a saint because he refused to give him land to build another church. He wanders witlessly through the woods, living on cress, herbs, berries and spring water. He hears the stag, "the little bleating one, the melodious little clamourer". He shelters by the sharp holly, "a door against the wind". He dreads the ash tree because it is used for making "weapons of war".'

'And when his senses are returning to him,' I exclaimed, 'he is looked after by the Hag of the Mill.'
'The crazy conversation of the old crone brings back
his madness. The tattered couple rush out and race
together, playing hopscotch over the hills. And centuries
before Shakespeare confronted Lear and Gloucester,
that unknown storyteller brought the madman of Ireland
across the sea to meet the madman of Britain, and the
two old men wandered together in torment through
those other woods.'

(*Penny*, 210)

Thirty-five years before the publication of 'The Trees of
the Forest' (a hymn to Nature, a sensual description of
Ireland's flora) Clarke published 'The Frenzy of Suibhne' in
The Cattledrive in Connaught and Other Poems (*Poems*, 131).
In this 'glimpse of *Buile Suibhne*',[7] Sweeney, as his angli-
cised name is rendered, rambles and rants about his furious
journeyings across Ireland and back again. He hides from all
mankind: crazed, exiled by the Church, finding comfort in
a 'nest in the drenching ivy'. The poem has thematic affini-
ties with 'The Music Healers' of the same period and with
the episode in Glen Bolcan, valley of the mad, in *The Bright
Temptation*. It could also be argued that *Mnemosyne Lay in
Dust* is Clarke's personal version of the legend. In *The Singing Men at Cashel*, too, it will be remembered, Gormlai
dreamed of Sweeney and found solace in his story when she
was alone among the trees and wild creatures.

The legend of Sweeney looms behind Clarke's work and
links his themes of madness, freedom, exile and rebellion
against authority. Loftus' interpretation of the legend assumes
a political connection as well.[8] The truth hidden from most
men, but discovered by Sweeney, is that one may be pro-
tected from the condemnation of society, or from victimisation, by coming closer to nature. This reconciliation with
the natural world is the theme of 'The Trees of the Forest',
a hymn to Nature and an evocative tribute to the land of
Ireland itself:

Stag on the westward ridge, melodious
One, clamourer with your high nodes
Of point and tine. Below, the roe-bucks

Are grazing in a dappled row.

Oak, mighty one, my shelterer,
I lie beneath you, acorn in shell.
Crush of your bark will cure a mastoid,
Swine root among the years of mast.

The water-willow is never hostile.
I pull down sweetness, cross green stile,
Frail blossom of the catkin. Baskets
Are woven, supple as your sap.

The wicked blackthorn, claws sharp as Pangur
Baun's. Each prickle is a pang,
Appetite has been well sustained by
Those berries, juicy, darksome, stainful.

(Poems, 507-8)

The intricate 'rime riche' and incidental details in the description of the blackthorn and the rowan are, to the best of my
knowledge, found in none of the other English versions.
Describing a tree with 'claws sharp as Pangur Baun's', Clarke
enriches his imitation with an allusion to another poem in
Gaelic about a scholar and his cat.[9] The ash 'that brings con-
tention, Quarrel on chessboard' is, according to George Moore
in his previously quoted discussion of the Sweeney legend, a
negative image in all the versions. Yet the chessboard is an
image of Clarke's fond invention and alludes to that episode
in the pursuit of Diarmuid and Grainne when they hid in an
ash-tree that was in full berry. Fionn and Oisin sat under the
same tree and played chess, unaware of the lovers above them
because Grainne's enfolding cape was scarlet like the berries.
Diarmuid helped his friend Oisin to win the game by dropping
a berry onto each square where a move had to be made.
There was an ensuing quarrel.[10] Clarke thus buries an allusion
to his first poem, The Vengeance of Fionn, within this complex lyric. The overlapping, intertwining rhymes and echoing
assonances tie this poem together. Here, in his last explicit
reference to Sweeney, Clarke conveys in particular and concrete details, full of praise and wonder at the natural beauty
of Ireland, the message that the Blackbird of Derrycairn tried
to give Patrick: 'Knowledge is found among the branches'.
The inclusion of 'The Trees of the Forest' in a book of poems

about apparitions and sexual myths is most appropriate.
Like Clarke's other uses of the Sweeney legend, 'The Trees of
the Forest' contains suggestions of the profound serenity to
be achieved by an awareness of nature and the acceptance of
one's instinctual feelings. This is Clarke's most concerted
effort to find a diction and imagery adequate for the description of the natural world in all its particularity. Nature's
'nimiety' is mankind's unheeded blessing.

(iv)

We turn now to consider Austin Clarke's last great poems:
'The Healing of Mis' (1970), 'The Dilemma of Iphis' (1970)
and *Tiresias* (1971) — another shorter poem, 'The Wooing of
Becfola', was published after the poet's death in 1974. In
1970 Clarke was 74. He had a writing career of more than
half a century behind him but he had not won great critical
acclaim and certainly not international fame. At home in
Ireland, he was regarded as something of an enigma, an old
man with a wry smile who had read poetry on the radio, an
agnostic — though that was now almost forgotten; not by
any means a popular figure — he did not encourage vulgarity;
a sombrely dressed gentleman passing quietly and perhaps, for
all his fellow citizens knew, wringing his ageing hands in
prayer in the shadows of the Pro-Cathedral. Among the
litterati Clarke's poetry was at least acknowledged; there was
the tribute published for his seventieth birthday, and in 1974
an issue of the *Irish University Review* was devoted to his
work. There were the occasional civic honours bestowed on
an elder poet, but not many. In-depth critical appraisal was
almost completely lacking. However, Clarke's work was the
subject of a few doctoral dissertations and there was a somewhat vague awareness of his importance. But for the most
part the critics, and indeed the younger poets, were less than
wholehearted in their praise. There were accusations of
obscurity and fragmentation, suggestions that the poetic output was uneven with much indifferent verse, that Clarke had
been preoccupied with anti-Catholicism to the exclusion of
almost everything else. Significantly also, the three romances
were unavailable and almost unknown.

It might have been expected that the spurned and ageing
poet would have become embittered or given up. One of the
most remarkable things about Clarke, however — and this he

shares with Joyce — was that his urge to write even greater poetry was not stifled by critical vacillation. The last 'truly great' poems, written in his seventies, testify to a creative imagination developing and expanding its horizons even more forcefully than before.

'The Healing of Mis', 'The Dilemma of Iphis' and 'Tiresias' are all based on sexual myths. 'The Wooing of Becfola', which appeared in print for the first time at the end of the 1974 *Collected Poems*, is a tautly constructed and beautiful piece in which we learn towards the end of the poem that Becfola's night of bliss and fantasy with a young, god-like man had all happened 'in less than/A minute'. In this case the dream directly affects the waking world as Becfola becomes 'All May and murmur' in her husband's arms. These poems, although carefully structured, are wonderfully relaxed narratives. 'The Healing of Mis', like 'Orphide' and 'The Quarry', has characteristics of the folktale and is a rendering of an Irish story, 'reminding one both of Swift's Yahoos and of Mad Sweeney'.[11] The others are jubilant elaborations of Ovid. (Clarke contested the banning of Ovid's works in 1938 with his poem, 'Penal Law'.) In all three of these major poems, Clarke has gradually distanced himself from his work. The achievement of this impersonal power, that of the teller of myths, the bearer of traditional wisdom, is Clarke's most astonishing accomplishment.

Mis, principal character in 'The Healing of Mis' is a long-lived but mad princess who inhabits the mountain named for her, Slieve Mish, in Kerry. She is wild and terrifying to the local people:

> In winter when turf was raked under the household
>   cauldron,
> Stories were told of a Geilt that flew over forest
>   top and
> Cliff to pray from the sky. Sometimes a shepherd,
>   hatted
> By crack of twig, had a glimpse of hairiness
> Crawling from filth and hurried back to safe
>   pasturage.
> Those cloudy cantreds were dreaded and accursed
> For a legend endured from the Paps of Dana to
>   Mount Brandon
> Of a lonely sorrow time could not cure.
>
> (Poems, 509)

A harper, Duv Ruis, who claims the ability to cure, is given three months to do so or face death. The mood has overtones of the traditional ballad. Duv Ruis's methods are unusual to say the least. Exposing himself and:

> Holding his harp, the consolation of his bosom,
> He played a suantree with grace-notes that enspelled
> Traditional tunes and, smiling quietly at his ruse,
> Waited. Soon his senses knew that loneliness
> Stood by, a bareness modestly draped in tangle-
>   black hair,
> With timeless hands, listening to the special
> Melling that drew and soothed her mind as she stared
> In surmise at his rising flesh.

As with Maurice Devane, 'the law of natural pleasure' will 'sane' her, together with music, cooked food and quiet, soothing talk. The harper will interpret and calm her night-mares too. First he will wash and cleanse the wild woman:

> He coiled up
> Each sweeping tress from her filthy body, saw
> Her nipples harden into blackberries. 'Bogholes
>   have spoiled them
> But soon that pair will be redder than haws . . .
> He soaped her body, washed it down,
> Drawing the wad of deer-skin to-and-fro
> Softly between her glossing thighs, turned her
>   around
> And frizzled her neglected faddle . . .

The inclusion of such frank description, followed immediately by an evocation of gentle love-making, creates an earthy yet lyrically tender atmosphere. After two months, the cure succeeds: her nightmares are assuaged, her manners changed and her lover's life saved. Mis and Duv Ruis ride forth, brightly apparelled and happy. Bardic romance and Freudian dream-analysis might have seemed an odd mixture but Clarke has combined them to exquisite effect. His imitations have developed greatly since he first tried in 'Pilgrimage' to achieve 'the vox caelestis'. 'The Healing of Mis' is rather 'the vox naturae'.

In 'The Dilemma of Iphis' Clarke borrows an idea from Ovid and creates a completely pagan, Mediterranean world in which the Gods intercede in human affairs. Iphis' mother brings her up as a boy in order to protect her from being put to death as a useless female infant. (Is there a vestige of savage indignation here?) Iphis is to be married to her beloved companion but finds it all rather upsetting:

>   'Why am I afflicted,
> Alas, with so wicked, so unnatural a passion
> As this? Can cow inflame cow? Mare burn for mare?
> The ram in season
> Tups, raddles the ewes. Far in the forest glades the
> roe-deer
> Follow the buck. All creatures mate rightly, in the
> paddock,
> Thicket, air, water. Ruffling their feathers up, the
> fowl are roostered
> At daybreak in turn. No female covers another
> female . . .
>   . . . Europa
> Wanted the bull that carried her across the wave-
> tops.
> So to avoid unnatural forcing, the pang of rupture,
> Jupiter changed her into a cow before he mounted
> her.
>   (*Poems*, 500-4)

The details of Europa's, Danae's and Leda's couplings with Jupiter are among Clarke's additions to the story from the *Metamorphoses*. As Welch said of Clarke's Gaelic imitations, he is 'impatient of reproduction'; he goes beyond Ovid, fleshing out the themes and details, lending to his re-tellings of the legends the licentious cynicism of Ovid's other great text of pagan lore, *The Art of Love*.[12] Where Ovid merely mentions that Daedalus would be of no help, Clarke explains what he might try to do:

>   Hail storms
> Hid mountainous Crete, when our Daedalus flashed
> on those artificial
> Wings of the future. Yet had his invention succeeded,

> For all his knowledge and skill, juggling with coggle,
>   wire, main-springs,
> He could not have made for my pelvis from any
>   material private
> Parts that would work . . .

The passion and disappointed ardour belong to the original; the actual sensations, conveyed in graphic details and lyrical imagery, are new in Clarke's poem.

The goddess Isis, approached in a prayer clearly modelled on the litany of the Blessed Virgin, intervenes miraculously. The imaginative power of Clarke's language is such that the miracle seems inevitable. There are, nevertheless, mundane details to retain our sense of realism: 'In twenty-five/Minutes they reached their home'. The vision of a phallic procession, also Clarke's addition, provides us with a further example of this parody on the Christian mysteries: the 'precious wood' of 'the sanctified image' is clearly a reference to the cross of Christ's crucifixion:

> High in front of the chanting priests, newly painted,
>   carven
> From the most precious wood, the sanctified image
>   was slowly
> Approaching.

The parody reaches its climax in the lines:

> 'O look, dear Iphis, at the delicate ivory-tinting,
> The great bluish vein, the little violet ones, the
>   crimson
> Ring of flesh-fold and above all the adorable ruby-
>   like
> Heart-shaped sex-cap. How proudly it tilts above
>   the masses
> Of people'.

The humorous finale, with its Freudian touches, imparts again a dimension of realism to the fantastic. The poem ends with a Latin inscription that reaffirms the satirical linking of modern-day shrines with those of the classical world.

Tiresias is a similar myth of the human comedy, but

emphasising a feminine point of view. It demonstrates the
fullness of Clarke's poetic powers and extends his vision of
human freedom and liberation of the instincts. It is reward-
ing to notice the assurance with which Clarke approaches
this final testament. Borrowing only an idea from Ovid,
Clarke (in his note to the poem) casually criticises Tennyson
and Eliot for their inability to do the story justice: 'Tennyson
has depicted the seer in gloomy terms . . . Eliot . . . expresses
his own Puritanism' (Poems, 557). It is a pleasure to be able
to confirm Clarke's confidence. The style and language,
mirroring the rich classical landscape, are rounded and
mellow. Miltonic cadences, Shakespearian echoes, Ovidian
airs, even the occasional hint of Hopkins or of a grandstand
finish at the Curragh follow each other with easy grace as
the development of the theme dictates.

Once again, the natural setting is evoked. Tiresias wanders
up the hillside of Mount Ida:

> Stopping his wonder to look down
> On the groves of lemoning trees, orangeous orchards,
>   Bacchanalian
> Vine-stock, Greek fire of the labyrinthine blossom
> Seiging with steady rounds of scarlet the hundred
>   cities of Crete . . .
> . . . He noticed how mountain flowers had lessened
>   in size, stepped
> Into a glory of broom that unsentried his sight,
>   heard far off
> Thunderclap. Sky questioning earth. Straightway
>   half-blind from
> Preternatural bloom, he became aware of Presences
> Aloof yet near. All-powerful Jove had been harang-
>   ing
> Juno.
>
>   (Poems, 517)

According to Clarke, Tiresias is not yet blind although he has
already been changed from a man into a woman and then
back again. Jove explains his argument with Juno and asks
Tiresias to settle the question of who, male or female, more
enjoys the pleasure of love-making. The God demands an
answer even though the mortal hesitates. (It is a less than

omniscient pantheon who are obliged to seek the answer to
this question from mere mortals.)

Tiresias begins a rambling discourse, full of associations
and pleasant memories of what it was like to be a woman and
mother. The octametric lines, rich in cadence and shot
through with buried rhyme and alliterative harmonies, continue for twenty-three pages. The poem is enriched and the
narrative controlled by the resulting tumble of rhythm and
imagery.

Clarke reaches the heart of the poem on the second page.
Tiresias is transformed into a woman and, overcoming the
initial masculine shame at his disfigurement, begins to learn
new truths and pleasures. Tiresias, however, is prevented from
realising the full pleasures of being a woman by the intrusive
social definitions of a woman's role typical of our culture.
The description of the transition is both powerful and comic:

> 'Strolling one day, beyond the Kalends, on Mount
>   Cyllene,
> What should I spy near the dusty track but a
>   couple of sun-spotted
> Snakes — writhen together — flashen as they copu-
>   lated,
> Dreamily! Curious about the origin of species, I
>   touched them.
> Tunic shrank. I felt in alarm two ugly tumours
> Swell from my chest. Juno, our universal mother,
>   you
> Know how easily a child wets the bed at night.
>   Pardon
> Frankness in saying that my enlarged bladder let
>   go. "Gods," it
> Lamented, "has he become an unfortunate woman,
>   humbled by
> Fate, yes, forced twice a day, to crouch down on
>   her hunkers?
> Leaf-cutting bee affrights me, Ariadne within her
>   web-round."
> Timidly hidden as hamadryad against her oak-bark,
> I dared to pull up resisting tunic, expose my new
>   breasts —
> Saw they were beautiful. Lightly I fingered the

nipples
And as they cherried, I felt below the burning
   answer;
Still drenched, I glanced down, but only a modesty
   of auburn
Curlets was there. If a man whose limb has been
   amputated
Still feels the throb of cut arteries, could I forget now
Prickle of pintel? Hour-long I grieved until full
   moonlight,
Entering the forestry, silvered my breasts. They rose
   up so calmly,
So proud, that peace — taking my hand in gladness —
   led me
Home . . .
                                    My mother wept loudly . . .
                                               Next morning
Gaily she said:
                       "I must instruct you in domestic
Economy, show you, dear daughter, how to make
   your own bed, lay
Table, wash up, tidy the house, cook every sort of
Meal, sew, darn, mend, do your hair, then find a
   well-off
Husband for you. As a young man you have spent
   too many
Hours in the study of history and science, never
   frequented
Dance-hall, bull-ring, hurried, I fear, too often to
   the stews."
Laughter-in-sigh, she handed me a duster.'
                                               (*Poems*, 518-19)

In the lavish, baroque world of his last major poem, Clarke
explains things that were only hinted at in his two novels,
The Singing Men at Cashel and *The Sun Dances at Easter*.
He satirises preconceptions about the role of women, exposing the rationalisations used to enforce inequality. Even the
mother, who becomes the perfect pander eventually, is
initially distraught at discovering that her son has lost his.
position as a man and must now learn to be submissvely,
industriously female. She explains female biology to Tiresias,

who is now Pyrrha, and hustles to find her daughter a suitable husband. The daughter, however, is more independent,
perhaps because of those years spent as a man.

The story continues, rich in allusions to and associations
with Clarke's other work. Pyrrha, for example, is deflowered
by a student who believes she is a goddess (clearly reminiscent
of Anier MacConglinne!). It describes in detail the act of love-
making and how Pyrrha unused to her new body, must work
to achieve sexual satisfaction.

> Faster, yet faster, we sped, determined down-thrust
>   rivalling
> Up-thrust — succus glissading us — exquisite spasm
> Contracting, dilating, changed into minute pre-
>   paratory
> Orgasms, a pleasure unknown to man, that cul-
>   minated
> Within their narrowing circles into the great
>   orgasmos.
>
>   (522)

Clarke follows the conventional solution to the argument
between Jove and Juno: sexually, a woman far outstrips a
man in her capacity for enjoyment and in the endurance of
her fulfilment. However, at this stage in the poem Clarke is
more concerned with his lyrical description of sexual encounter on the one hand and his satire on social conventions
on the other — the portrait of Demetrius as the suitable
husband is a good example of the latter.

For those who wish to read it as such, *Tiresias* must be
the bawdiest of all Clarke's poems. There is indeed no reticence
in the language, but coarseness is not the end. In this poetry
lyricism and satire are combined inextricably:

> Silent-tongued, all that afternoon, we swived, swal-
>   ing together.
> Silent, too, the woods, as we listened, cheek on
>   pillow.
> Only the chirr of cicala, grump of tree-frog. In a
>   frenzy
> Chelos leaped from our Colchian fleece, darted
>   whitely —

Arrow-red-kiss-marks all over his body — shouting.
                                              'Hoof off!'
At the doorway.
              'Rascally pimp, self-abuser.'
                                        'Who was it?'
'A dirty old satyr. I saw him trotting into the
    shadowed
Forest reserves.'

                                              (*Poems*, 526)

In his comic elaboration of his reply to Jove's question, Tiresias gives us a version of the Prometheus myth as an explanation of the allegedly slow sexual response of women:

'"Theologians assert that Prometheus, a flinty
    firebrand,
Riled against the gods, declared they were mythical
    figures.
Men, abandoning the true faith, became his fuming
    disciples.
Women have always been temple-goers, so priestesses
Wore the white, purple-hemmed vestment that had
    been discarded.
All the human race was punished by the offended
Deities. Life-giving scrotum, whose simultaneous
    seed-flow
Doubled by both ducts, as they spurted, and so
    enabling
Women to share without difficulty the bliss, was
    altered.
Now they must hurry, Pyrrha."
                          I smiled, but kept the secret
No man has suspected, as we turned again to each
    other.'

The ambiguity and irony inherent in the use of the words and phrases 'Theologians', 'mythical', 'Men abandoning true faith' are as we shall see relevant to an understanding of Clarke's use of myth. The last lines are of course a reference to the line 'Yet joy at its source/Was never deuced' (*Poems*, 423) to which we have alluded earlier.

As Tiresias moves on to discuss his lovemaking with

Demetrius, there are subtle changes in the language and rhythms which betray the more business-like approach of these encounters. Notice, for example, the hint of disgust in 'I assume, as they say, the matrimonial position'. The legal and commercial words 'duty', 'obedient', 'wager', 'deposit' are found fitting to describe the lovemaking of the 'wealthy merchant of Cydonia'.

One of the themes of Clarke's poem is of course sexual differentiation, the subject of the Tiresias myth itself. There are many points in the poem where Clarke alludes to relations between the same sexes, among them the statement of Chelos' grief at Tiresias becoming a man again:

> 'Tear-dazed, I mourned for Pyrrha under that blue
> mantle,
> Within reach, yet unpossessible except by perverted
> Desire'.
>
> (*Poems*, 530)

When, thought-tormented and led by fate to Mount Parnassus, Tiresias sees a 'sky-woman' bathing, he imagines her to be Pyrrha, his female self, and: 'Body/Wanted its other self'. Tiresias is blinded by the goddess Pallas Athene for 'having looked on what is forbidden' and at the same time given the gift of prophecy for having 'shown to a goddess such stout admiration'. No moral explanation is offered for this double-edged decision of Justitia. Tiresias' prophecy of 'future happenings, half legendary' commences. The prophecy ranges with apparent confusion over classical history, literature and mythology with much of the power of a frenzied dream.

The opening of the last section of the poem is in complete contrast:

> Over the wine-pug, the ageing pair still talked of
> wonders,
> What were their purpose?
>
> (*Poems*, 535)

Soon, however, Tiresias' mind wanders back again to his years as a woman, and at last he unfolds 'the secret' learned as a woman and alluded to several times in the poem. This is the answer to Jove's question:

> Keep the secret, Chelos, I attended once the
> Eleusinian Mysteries. Fragrant myrtling in forest
> Groves, kettling, lightly-fingered flute, danced pro-
>   cession
> Flaring from temple-steps, women undoing calyptra.
> I, too, leaped among the hairpin-scatterers, divesting
> Themselves for the limb-gleaming whirlabout of
>   maenadic
> Love-embrace. Broached, lined, by the vine-men. I
>   sank through the last
> Shudder of bliss into the Divine.
>
>   (*Poems*, 535)

The secret is out, though at the very end of the poem doubt is cast upon it again when it is suggested that Tiresias has, perhaps, been deceived by Jove, simply to win his wager — the gods care little for anything except their own little games.

There follows a deflation of the gift of prophecy, but soon the powers from the 'oblivion/Below us' take over again and Tiresias returns to a prophecy that encompasses all history and then the future. Clarke has created an immense poetic scope. His final statement about the great question of life is, however, something of a guffaw: 'No wife has/Ever blabbed about her bliss, even on the bolster.' The final image of the poem is serene and peaceful. Life, like this poetic extravaganza, is over. Tiresias, like Clarke and Swift, has reached a point where 'savage indignation can lacerate his heart no more':

>   Come in, dear
> Friend, for the purple-robed hours pass by. Luna
>   has led her
> Star-flocks home — and your cup of hot milk waits
>   on the table.

In his Notes, Clarke writes with tongue in cheek: '. . . in our new permissive age, I have tried to present a cheerful account of the experience of Tiresias as wife and mother' (*Poems*, 557). This he has certainly done. The true measure of his unconquered spirit is that *Tiresias* should be his last poem.

In that rather unequal volume of poems, *Old-Fashioned Pilgrimage*, Clarke finished 'More Extracts from a Diary of Dreams' with the challenging demand:

> Why should the aged be unhappy,
> Mope in the dark, when the unhappenable
> Is theirs and they can glide between the shades
> Of meaning in a dream, talk to the shades,
> Unchaperoned, watch every jog of nature
> That proves the midnight merriment innate —
> Fire in the great vein — and when desire has
>   chased
> After high boot and bulging stays, be chaste?
>
> (*Poems*, 394)

It is the most impressive stanza in that collection and adds the final footnote to Clarke's last highly polished, lavishly embellished poetic myths. *Orphide and Other Poems*, *The Impuritans* and *Tiresias* all ask the same question and prove that Clarke would once again refuse to act or write in the socially approved manner. They are the poems of a man grown old but filled with imaginative zest. Sweeney meets the centaur at the house of prayer in these last poems, and the result is a vital, wicked, resonating, full-bodied laugh. *Tiresias* ends, not with the chronical which it seemingly promises; historical considerations, political and cultural insights are interrupted and abandoned as the two old men chuckle and begin to reconsider human sexuality. It is a pleasing prospect and fitting close to the work of a writer who, throughout the fifty-seven years of his literary career, refused polite silence, rejected social pretension and demanded honesty.

Austin Clarke's writings, chronicling the emergence of Ireland as a modern state, remain the most impressive and thoroughly under-rated (indeed unacknowledged) body of work by any twentieth century Irish writer. *Tiresias* marks the real end of a career in which Clarke, as novelist, playwright and poet, challenged the parochial loyalties, patriotic orthodoxy and the complacent prejudice of what many of his intended public would still regard as holy, Mother Ireland.

(v)

It is one of the theses of this book that Austin Clarke's work could not have been properly appreciated within the critical parameters applied to the literature of the Celtic revival in Ireland or indeed those applied to twentieth century

poetry generally. Clarke had already begun to move away
from romantic poetry by the time he published *Pilgrimage
and Other Poems* in 1929. By the time his satires of the 1950s
appeared, he was writing poetry that was centred on the
society around him rather than on a poetic persona alone in
an alien world, suffering from all the rueful effects of the
'dissociation of sensibility'. Clarke's world view was different.
He sought to place the blame for the ills of the world firmly
where it belonged, on the heads of the churchmen and politicians, who took it upon themselves to organise the world,
and on their systems of dogma and prejudice. Clarke was self-
consciously adopting the role of the Irish bardic poets or of
the Augustans in England. He was in a sense practising poetry
as journalism. Contrary to the expectations arising from a
narrow, romantic definition of poetry, his poetic power was
not diminished but rather strengthened and developed. It
has taken time for the poetry-reading public to become
fully aware of what Clarke was doing. Many readers, while
appreciating individual poems, find others difficult and the
language not 'poetic'. Clarke's great satires of the Fifties will
not be forgotten, however. Even in the most angry of them
there is a poetic genius at work. 'Those children charred in
Cavan' have gained poetic eternity — poetic justice.

Another problem for readers of Clarke in the fifties and
sixties was the sheer volume of the poetic output. When
readers had become accustomed to the cathartic pain of
'Martha Blake at Fifty-one', Clarke was already writing with
new techniques, with new images and new metres, about new
themes. Apart from the lapses in some of the poems of
Old-Fashioned Pilgrimage and *The Echo at Coole*, the poetry
is of a consistently high quality. Even when he writes, as it
were, 'trial pieces', we are aware of his skill with words.

It has been said of Clarke that he became almost completely preoccupied in his writing with his attack on the
Church and with Rabelaisian wit and humour. It is of course
true that Clarke saw the suppression of the natural order as
unnatural and immoral. It is also true that the Church's
'supernatural' teachings, with their emphasis on the transcendent and the after-life, are a principal excuse for this
suppression. It is scarcely helpful, however, to conclude that
in poems like 'Martha Blake at Fifty-one', 'Precautions',
'Ancient Lights' or 'Mnemosyne Lay in Dust' Clarke is

obsessed with his alleged 'pet' themes.

Clarke was profoundly opposed to the suppression of the natural order for the sake of the, at most, uncertain 'miraculous' order. Again and again his satires expose the results of this suppression and attack its propagators, the Church and the State. Clarke saw the suppression of sexuality as being a deep-seated manifestation of the effects of 'supernaturalism' — deep-seated in the human psyche and deep-seated also in its social implications. He chose to investigate this suppression with all the vehemence (and later subtlety) that his poetic powers could bring to bear on it. Throughout his work, suppressed sexuality is a symbol for suppressed nature. Clarke was of course aware that sexual and other bodily functions can be associated with the sordid. In many of his poems, however, disease of the body and disease of the mind (including the immorality of social neglect) are seen as the real sources of the sordid. In Clarke's investigation of sexuality as in all his work the poetry is at its best when it is determined by what the creative imagination can conceive and language convey. Satire, humour and wit are always present, but the underlying motive is moral — moral, that is, in a sense that redefines morality. It is at this point that Clarke and Swift are most closely related. Clarke's last poems are restatements of his central tenets through 'versions' of ancient myths. In 'The Healing of Mis' the myth is Gaelic, the imagery, language and metres recognisably Irish: 'Stories were told of a Geilt that flew over forest top and/Cliff'. But there are echoes that expand the myth's geographical and psychological provenance ('Invaders who had sailed out of Greece', 'Her fingers adrip with her father's blood').

In *Tiresias*, the myth is from the ancient Classical world, and the language and imagery imitate classical models, thus creating a sense of universality in time and place. In 'The Dilemma of Iphis' Clarke had already entered the world of classical myth. The purpose was partly satiric: to compare the miracles wrought at the shrine of the ancient goddess Isis with those claimed for the modern shrines of the Blessed Virgin. What impresses itself on the reader of this poetry more than anything else, however, is the grace, serenity and beauty of the language. Clarke is taking myths and stories now, as it were, from wherever he chooses; he is creating modern versions of them in superb poetry varied in style and diction to suit his purpose. In his seventies, not understood by his reading public, he has perfected his art to the point where he is, like the old, blind Tiresias, an eternal seer.

Thomas Kinsella wrote that by the time he wrote *Tiresias*, Clarke was telling stories in 'poetry as pure entertainment, serene and full of life'. It is, however, incorrect to suggest that Clarke ever abandoned satire: *Tiresias* abounds with gentle and humorous satire. In these last poems, however, the principal concern is with language, imagery and other poetic devices. The secret of this poetry resides ultimately in the language.

Mention must be made of Clarke's attitude to and use of myth. In the first place, as a classicist Clarke was concerned to rework classical material, to write 'versions'. The fact that his originals were in other languages gave added incentive to the creative process of rendering them in English. Even a cursory glance at the language and stylistic differences between 'The Healing of Mis' and *Tiresias* will show with what skill Clarke was able to 'imitate' the language and style of the originals, thereby allowing English poetry to nourish itself from two very different sources.

Yeats regarded mythology as having 'supernatural', numinous qualities that made it the fitting raw material of poetry. Generally speaking myth is associated with questions of deep human significance: the source of fire (physical and metaphorical), sexual duality and so on. Many myths are rooted in ancient religious ritual. This does not mean that they offer realistically acceptable explanations, but it does mean that because of the importance attached by society to religion, they will be handed on. It also means that their form is likely to be ritualistic and therefore memorable. As myths ceased to have a religious context as such, they were taken up by writers, presumably because of their dramatic and poetic qualities rather than their credibility. Such writers added to the metaphoric reference of the myths thereby making them potentially more useful for later writers. Meanwhile, later religions, particularly Christianity, in offering their own explanations — 'myths' — dismissed existing explanations, making the word 'myth' take on the meaning *false explanation* or *falsehood*. To make matters even more complicated, stories that did not have a religious origin but did have the ritualistic and poetic qualities associated with myth came to be regarded as mythological.

Clarke's use of myths clearly implies that he did not regard them as offering special supernatural or magical explanations: *Tiresias*, for example, is to a considerable extent a humorous satire on the myth itself. Clarke clearly regarded the function of the myths he used as commanding his audience's attention and offering him a theme rich in imaginative associations. His *poetic treatment* of the myth is his statement. The greater power of Isis compared to Mary in the final analysis resides in the power of Clarke's poetry and not in Isis being a more supernatural goddess than Mary.

It has been suggested also that in Clarke's poetry the miraculous or supernatural is transferred into the natural order, and that, in particular, sexuality takes over the preternatural healing and curative powers of the miracle. Undoubtedly, Clarke saw sexuality as being deeply regenerative — he also saw it as being at times hilariously funny. It seems more correct to say that Clarke's 'miraculous' was the dream-world, which is at once real and imaginary, where the ordinary rules of the real world do not apply and where miraculous (and curative) events do take place. Reference has been made earlier to Clarke's powerful use of dream sequences in *The Sun Dances at Easter*. There are many, many other examples of the phantasmagoric in his work. Myth and magic are introduced into the natural order by means of dream. The dream-world, like fantasy, indeed like myth and poetry themselves, offers a 'miraculous' domain beyond the 'faed fiad' but within the natural order. Such ideas are necessary in order to understand Clarke's writing, but always providing that we appreciate that Clarke never allows himself to be carried away into the false myths of romantic or religious Faith. The prophylactic against this is satire, and it is always present.

Notes

Introduction

1. Richard Loftus, *Nationalism in Modern Anglo-Irish Poetry*. University of Wisconsin Press, Madison and Milwaukee, 1964, pp. 3-4.

Chapter 1

1. Louis MacNeice, *The Poetry of W.B. Yeats*. Faber and Faber, London, 1967 (first publ. 1941), p. 46.

2. Frank Kermode, *The Romantic Image*. Collins/Fontana, London, 1971, p. 158.

3. Rachel Bromwich, *Matthew Arnold and Celtic Literature*. Oxford University Press, London, 1965, p. 6.

4. Austin Clarke, *Later Poems*, Dolmen, Dublin, p. 90. This was not included in the *Collected Poems* (1974).

5. Lilian Furst, *Romanticism*. Methuen, London, 1969, p. 64.

6. T.E. Hulme, 'Romanticism and Classicism', in *Speculations*. Routledge and Kegan Paul, London, 1960 (first publ. 1924), p. 118.

7. ibid., p. 127.

8. Austin Clarke, 'Gaelic Ireland Rediscovered: The Early Period', in *Irish Poets in English: The Thomas Davis Lectures*, ed. Sean Lucy. Mercier Press, Cork and Dublin, 1973, p. 37.

9. Donald Davie, *Articulate Energy: An Enquiry into the Syntax of Modern Poetry*. Routledge and Kegan Paul, London, 1965, p. 148.

10. K.K. Ruthven, *The Conceit*. Methuen, London, 1969, p. 5.

11. See Frank Kermode, *The Romantic Image*, and C.K. Stend, *The New Poetic: Yeats to Eliot* (Hutchinson, London, 1964).

12. F.W. Bateson, *A Guide to English Literature*, 2nd edition. Longmans, London, 1967, p. 104.

13. G. Sigerson, *Bards of the Gael and Gall*. 3rd edition, Talbot Press, Dublin, 1925 (first publ. 1897), pp. 2-3.

14. ibid., p. 23.

15. William Larminie, 'The Development of English Metres', *Contemporary Review*, vol. LXVI, Dublin, November 1894.

16. Brian Earls, reviewing *The Penguin Book of Irish Verse* in *St Stephen's: Literature and Opinions*, series II, no. 19 (Hilary Term 1971) pp. 44-5.

17. T.S. Eliot, 'Euripides and Professor Murray', in *The Sacred Wood*. Methuen, London, 1960, p. 73.

18. J. Carney, *Early Irish Literature*. Routledge and Kegan Paul, London, 1966, p. 819. Cf. J. Carney, *The Irish Bardic Poet* (Dolmen, Dublin, 1967) and

J. Carney, *Medieval Irish Lyrics* (Dolmen, Dublin, 1967).

19. Myles Dillon, *Early Irish Literature*. Univ. of Chicago Press, Chicago and London, 1969 (first publ. 1948), pp. 153-4.

20. Eleanor Knott, a booklet titled 'Irish Classical Poetry', rptd in *Early Irish Literature*, ed. J. Carney, p. 62.

21. John Montague, in *A Tribute to Austin Clarke on his Seventieth Birthday*, eds. J. Montague and L. Miller. Dolmen, Dublin, 1966, pp. 9-10. Contributions to this anthology are untitled.

Chapter 2

1. Monk Gibbon, in the foreword to *Letters from AE*, ed. Alan Denson. Abelard-Schumann, London, 1961, p. ix.

2. Eavan Boland, 'Austin Clarke: The Artist in Old Age', *Hibernia* review of books, Dublin, 27 April 1973, p. 13.

3. Thomas Kinsella's note to *The Tain*, the Irish epic *Táin Bó Cuailnge*. Oxford University Press, London, 1970, p. vii.

4. Austin Clarke, 'Poetry and Contemporary Facts: Donagh MacDonagh's First Book of Poems'. *The Irish Times*, 19 April 1941, p. 3.

5. Brendan Kennelly, *Modern Irish Poets and the Irish Epic*. Unpublished thesis, Trinity College Dublin, 1967, p. 323.

6. Padraig Colum in the introduction to Clarke's *Collected Poems* of 1936, pp. 14-15.

7. G.T. Stokes, *Ireland and the Celtic Church*. Hodder and Stoughton, London, 1886.

8. Padraic Colum, introducing *Collected Poems* of 1936, p. 16.

9. Karl Beckson and Arthur Ganz, *A Reader's Guide to Literary Terms*. Thames and Hudson, London, 1970, pp. 184-6, and p. 115. Cf. Robert Welch, 'Austin Clarke and Gaelic Poetic Tradition', *Irish University Review: Austin Clarke Special Issue*, vol. 4, no. 1 (Spring 1974) for a discussion of Clarke's verse forms and rhyme schemes.

10. C. Ricks, *A Tribute*, p. 19.

11. J. Montague, *A Tribute*, p. 8.

12. Montague, *A Tribute*, p. 9.

13. Frank O'Connor, from the anthology, *Kings, Lords, and Commons*, 2nd edition. Gill and Macmillan, Dublin, 1970, p. 72.

14. Robert Welch, *IUR: Austin Clarke Special Issue*, p. 41.

15. D. Corkery, *The Hidden Ireland*, 2nd edition. Gill, Dublin, 1967, pp. 126-30.

16. Jessie Weston, *From Ritual to Romance*. Cambridge University Press, London, 1920, p. 118.

17. See especially Hyde's chapter on Brigid, in *A Literary History of Ireland*, pp. 156-65.

18. ibid., 160-2.

19. Thomas Kinsella, 'Austin Clarke', in *Contemporary Poets of the English Language*, ed. Rosalie Murphy. St James Press, Chicago and London, 1970, p. 200.

Chapter 3

1. F.N. Robinson, 'Satirists and Enchanters in Early Irish Literature', from *Studies in the History of Religion*, eds. D.G. Lyon and G.F. Moore. New York, 1912, p. 123.

2. Vivian Mercier, *The Irish Comic Tradition*. Oxford University Press, London, 1962, p. 18.

3. Helen Waddell, *The Wandering Scholars*, rptd by Collins/Fontana, London, 1968 (1st edition, 1927).

4. ibid., p. 129.

5. ibid., p. 50.

6. ibid., p. 114.

7. ibid., pp. 134-5.

8. ibid., p. 192.

9. ibid., p. 82.

10. ibid., p. 187.

11. ibid., p. 175.

12. ibid., p. 199.

13. ibid., p. 165.

14. Wilhelm Wollner, introduction to *Aislinge Meic Conglinne/The Vision of MacConglinne: A Middle-Irish Wonder Tale*, ed. and transl., Kuno Meyer. David Nutt, London, 1892, p. xiii. ff.

15. Kuno Meyer, *The Vision of MacConglinne*, p. 86.

16. *Playwrights on Playwriting*, edited by Toby Cole, has a valuable essay by Christopher Fry, 'Why Verse?' (MacGibbon and Kee, London, 1960, pages 125-30). Raymond Williams details the history of contemporary theatre and mentions Yeats' and Eliot's ventures with poetry in his *Drama from Ibsen to Eliot* (Penguin Books, Harmondsworth, 1964). But Denis Donoghue offers the most complex analysis of contemporary poetic drama in his *The Third Voice: Modern British and American Verse Drama* (Princeton University Press, New Jersey, 1959).

17. G. Wilson Knight, 'On the Principles of Shakespeare Interpretation', in *The Wheel of Fire*. Methuen, London, 1968 (first publ. 1930), p. 11.

18. See Tina Hunt Mahony, 'The Dublin Verse-Speaking Society and the Lyric Theatre Company', *IUR: Austin Clarke Special Issue*, pp. 65-73, for a comprehensive listing of the productions.

19. Kennelly, *Modern Irish Poets and the Irish Epic*, p. 307.

20. W.H. Auden in the foreword to Louis MacNeice's *Persons from Porlock*. Faber, London, 1969, p. 8.

21. L. MacNeice in the introduction to *Christopher Columbus*. Faber, London, 1944, p. 11. MacNeice's notes to *The Dark Tower and Other Radio Scripts* are a good starting point to any study of this modern genre (Faber, London, 1947, pp. 9-17).

22. Auden, op. cit., p. 9.

23. Quotations from this 1968 publication are referred to with page numbers in brackets.

24. Peter Happé, in his introduction to *Tudor Interludes*. Penguin, Harmondsworth, 1972, pp. 8-9.

25. ibid., pp. 12-13.

26. Michael Jamieson, introduction to *Ben Jonson: Three Comedies*. Penguin, Harmondsworth, 1970, pp. 11-15.

Chapter 4

1. D. Donoghue, *A Tribute*, p. 21.

2. *The Bright Temptation*, pp. 248-9. Quotations from this novel are taken from the 1965 hardback edition. Quotations from the other novels refer to the editions as listed in the bibliography of Clarke's works.

3. Thomas Kilroy, 'Tellers of Tales', *Times Literary Supplement*, 17 March 1972, pp. 301-2.

4. Eva Figes, *Patriarchal Attitudes*. Panther Books, London, 1972, pp. 13-17.

5. ibid., pp. 41-2.

6. See Kuno Meyer, 'The Triads of Ireland', the *Royal Irish Academy Todd Lecture Series*, vols. xiii-xvi, Dublin and London, 1906.

7. James Stephens, *The Crock of Gold*. Pan Books, London, 1953 (first publ. 1912), pp. 84-5.

8. ibid., p. 168.

9. Dillon, *Early Irish Literature*, pp. 67-73.

10. Mercier, *The Irish Comic Tradition*, p. 44.

11. Gillian Beer, *The Romance*. Methuen, London, 1970, p. 79.

12. Mercier, *The Irish Comic Tradition*, p. 44.

Chapter 5

1. A listing of Clarke's published articles and reviews can be found in the Appendix.

2. Maurice Harmon, 'Notes Towards a Biography', *IUR: Austin Clarke Special Issue*, p. 19.

3. ibid., p. 22.

4. A. Alvarez, 'Poet in a Cage', *The Observer Review*, 5 November 1972, p. 27. For Clarke's reaction to Pound, see Chapter Six, (iv), below.

5. Robin Skelton, in the introduction to *Six Irish Poets*. Oxford University Press, London, 1962, pp. xi-xii.

6. Kinsella, *Contemporary Poets of the English Language*, pp. 199-200.

7. MacNeice, *The Poetry of W.B. Yeats*, pp. 30-1.

8. Clarke reviewed Williams' *Paterson* in an article called 'City of Man', *The Irish Times*, 16 May 1953, p. 6.

9. M.L. Rosenthal, *The New Poets: American and British Poetry Since World War II*. Oxford University Press, New York, 1967, p. 15.

10. ibid., p. 26.

11. W.Y. Tindall, *James Joyce, His Way of Interpreting the Modern World*. Scribner's Sons, New York, 1950, p. 10.

12. Richard Ellman, *James Joyce*. Oxford University Press, London, 1968, p. 67.

13. W.J. Roscelli, 'The Private Pilgrimage of Austin Clarke', *The Celtic Cross*. Purdue University Studies, 1964, p. 64.

14. Sean O'Casey, 'Inishfallen, Fare Thee Well', *Autobiographies II*, Macmillan, London, 1963, p. 3.

15. Loftus, *Nationalism in Modern Anglo-Irish Poetry*, p. 271. Unfortunately Loftus confuses the Protestant 'Black Church' of Clarke's childhood with the Roman Catholic church in contemporary Ireland. (See discussion immediately below).

16. ibid., p. 275.

17. See J.H. Whyte, *The Church and State in Modern Ireland: 1923-1970*, for a full discussion of the intrusion into state affairs by the Church (Gill and Macmillan, Dublin, 1971).

18. This poem, 'Marriage', is enriched by Clarke's reading of it on *Beyond the Pale*, Austin Clarke reads his own poetry. Claddagh Records (CCT2) recorded in Dublin, 1964.

19. Letter to the Editor of *The Irish Times*, headed 'Mother-And-Child Scheme', 9 November 1979, p. 11. See also J.H. Whyte's *The Church and State in Modern Ireland: 1923-1970*, especially Chapters VII and VIII which discuss this proposed legislation and Dr Noel Browne's clashes with the hierarchy (pp. 196-272).

Chapter 6

1. Thomas Kinsella, 'The Poetic Career of Austin Clarke', *IUR: Austin Clarke Special Issue*, p. 134.

2. ibid., p. 136.

3. Robert F. Garratt, 'Austin Clarke in Transition', *IUR: Austin Clarke Special Issue*, pp. 108-9.

4. Kinsella, *IUR: Austin Clarke Special Issue*, p. 129.

5. From a review by Clarke of Ezra Pound's *Cantos*, 'Gigantic Poetic Notebook: *More Cantos*', *The Irish Times*, 30 March 1940, p. 5.

6. Another review of the *Cantos* by Clarke, 'Patchwork Poet', *The Irish Times*, 28 January 1950, p. 6.

7. Another review of the *Cantos* by Clarke, 'A Pound Sterling', *The Irish Times*, 7 May 1960, p. 8.

8. Austin Clarke, 'The Poet of Democracy', *The Irish Times*, 11 March 1961, p. 8.

9. Martin Dodsworth, ' "Jingle-go-Jangle": Feeling and Expression in Austin Clarke's Later Poetry', *IUR: Austin Clarke Special Issue*, p. 125.

10. See James Stephens, *The Collected Poems*. Macmillan, London, 1965, p. 3.

11. Earls, reviewing *The Penguin Book of Irish Verse*, op. cit., pp. 44-5.

12. Dodsworth, *IUR: Austin Clarke Special Issue*, pp. 117-19.

13. Welch, *IUR: Austin Clarke Special Issue*, p. 44.

14. Notes to *Collected Poems* of 1936, p. 309.

15. Austin Clarke, *Poetry in Modern Ireland*. Mercier Press, Cork, 1962, pp. 45 and 62.

16. Clarke, *Poetry in Modern Ireland*, p. 54.

17. Rosenthal, *The New Poets*, p. 265.

18. George Steiner, '1973', *The Listener*, vol. 91, no. 2336 (3 January 1974) p. 14.

19. Rosenthal, *The New Poets*, pp. 266-8.

20. Clarke, *Poetry in Modern Ireland*, p. 26.

21. Dodsworth, *IUR: Austin Clarke Special Issue*, p. 117-18.

22. Hyde, *A Literary History of Ireland*, p. 541.

23. ibid., pp. 596-7.

24. ibid., p. 592.

25. Rosenthal, *The New Poets*, p. 19.

26. References to *Mnemosyne Lay in Dust* in the following discussion are by section and page number as it was published in the 1974 *Collected Poems*, i.e., (I, 327) refers to a quotation from the first section, on p. 327 of the *Poems*.

27. Rosenthal, *The New Poets*, p. 4.

28. Harmon, *IUR: Austin Clarke Special Issue*, p. 18.

29. Rosenthal, *The New Poets*, pp. 269-72.

30. I refer to Plath's *Ariel* and Lowell's *Life Studies*, and later to Ginsberg's *Howl*. Rosenthal discusses these in *The New Poets* as seminal 'confessional' poets and works.

31. Rosenthal, *The New Poets*, pp. 90-1.

Chapter 7

1.   Kinsella, *IUR: Austin Clarke Special Issue*, p. 136. Quotations from these uncollected plays (*The Impuritans, The Third Kiss* and *Liberty Lane*) are followed by page number in parentheses, referring to editions listed in my bibliography of Clarke's published works.

2.   From Clarke's adaptations of Cervantes, discussed in Chapter Three.

3.   Clarke coined this usage in the earlier poem, 'The Hippophagi'.

4.   Kinsella, *IUR: Austin Clarke Special Issue*, p. 129.

5.   From a review by Clarke of Coventry Patmore, 'Victorian Poets', *The Irish Times*, 17 November 1956, p. 6.

6.   From a review by Clarke, 'The Hidden Poetry of Wales', in which he discusses a few heretical Irishmen as well as the Mabinogi cycle of legends, *The Irish Times*, 6 February 1943, p. 2.

7.   Notes to *Collected Poems*, page 547. Cf. Myles Dillon, *Early Irish Literature*, pp. 94-100. Gerard Murphy, in *Early Irish Lyrics* (Oxford University Press, London, 1962) prints a bilingual text of the poems about and attributed to Sweeney, pp. 112-41. Robert Graves, in *The White Goddess*, also considers Sweeney (Faber, London, 1961) pp. 450-5.

8.   Loftus, op. cit., pp. 3-4.

9.   Frank O'Connor's translation of 'The Scholar and the Cat' begins, 'I and Pangur Baun my cat, Happy with the chores we're at'. *Kings, Lords & Commons*, rptd by Gill and Macmillan, Dublin, 1970, p. 14.

10.   This story is recounted by Myles Dillon in *Early Irish Literature*, p. 47.

11.   Vivian Mercier discusses the original, 'The Romance of Mis and Dubh Ruis', in *The Irish Comic Tradition* on pp. 41-2.

12.   Robert Welch's comment on 'Mabel Kelly' is also true for these three versions of Classical story-telling. (op. cit., p. 47). See *The Metamorphoses of Ovid*, translated by Mary M. Innes, for the legend of Iphis' transformation (Penguin, Harmondsworth, 1971), pp. 221-4.

APPENDIX: A listing of some of Clarke's journalistic writings

Gerard Lyne, in the *Irish University Review: Austin Clarke Special Issue*, has assembled the preliminary outline of the Clarke Bibliography. Relying, as he says, on the standard bibliographical controls, Lyne lists the published works of Clarke and the shorter prose works which appeared in various journals like *The Bell* or *The Dublin Magazine*. [1] This was completed before Clarke's death in March, 1974, and Lyne himself demurs from the compilation of a full-length bibliography of a living writer: 'a considerable quantity of material which Mr Clarke published in newspapers . . . has, perforce, been omitted.' [2]

Using Lyne's work as a starting-point, and checking against the encyclopedic *Sources for the History of Irish Civilization: Articles in Irish Periodicals, Volume 1: Persons A-C*, I am able to offer the following list of Clarke's work in at least three newspapers as definitive. There are advantages to be gained from such a listing: not the least being the light that certain of Clarke's reviews and reminiscences in these newspapers throw on his more important writings. His comment about A.E.'s criticism of his early poetic style (quoted in Chapter Two, footnote 4) or Clarke's review of Pound, which I have also used in my discussion of his poetry are both good examples.

There are first, two isolated articles, one signed and one anonymous which Clarke seems to have claimed. In *A Penny in the Clouds* (p. 200), Clarke explains that once, while Yeats was ill, he wrote a leading article for the *TLS* which was some years later used as the obituary for Yeats. This must be: 'Yeats' Inner Drama: A poet of Two Reputations', *TLS*, 4 February 1939, pp. 72-4. Certain inner, textual clues (the hesitation to praise Yeats where others do and the determination to find value in the plays and later, harder-

edged poetry) might lead one to suspect Clarke's hand in
this essay, even had he not claimed it. Another article appears
on its own as well: 'Dunsany: Diehard of the Celtic Twilight',
Hibernia, 9 June 1972, p. 10. This, however, is signed.

What follows is a compilation of previously unlisted and
signed articles by Clarke from what are basically three
publications: *The Daily News and Leader* (London), which
became *The News Chronicle* and in both of which signed
reviews appear, *The Spectator*, and *The Irish Times*. Articles
are listed chronologically and by page number as they appeared in these three papers respectively.

The Daily News and Leader, London (date, page and title):

3.10.23	7	'An Imp in Yorkshire: A Woman Journalist's Problems'
7.11.23	9	a review of Padraic Colum's novel, *Castle Conquer*
29.11.23	9	'A Warning to Readers: Four Kinds of Novelists'
4.12.23	8	'Notable Novels'
10.1.24	7	'Ladies and Dishes: Love in Fiction'

The News Chronicle, London (formerly the above, in same
manner)

22.12.30	4	'The Epic of Science'
13.1.32	4	'Censor and Dramatist', a review of Lennox Robinson's *Bryan Cooper*
9.2.32	4	'The Age of "Sally in our Alley" ', a review of an anthology of Augustan poetry
23.8.32	4	'A Poet Used to Slang', a review of a life of John Clare

The Spectator (volume-page, date and title)

140:236	18.2.28	'Lyrics and Eclogues'
140:572	14.4.28	'Satire and Song'
141:535	20.10.28	'Recent Poetry'
141:783	24.11.28	'The Sphere of Poetry', includes a review of Noyes mentioned in *A Penny* (p. 189)
142:377	9.3.29	'Unconstitutional Poetry', reviews Pound and Sitwell

183:704 18.11.49 'Mr. Blunden and Others', reviews some
                    minor poets
185:708 15.12.50 'Things of the Spirit'
186:52   12.1.51   'A Nature Poet', reviews Andrew Young
187:714 23.11.51 'Literature in Verse?', discusses Marianne
                    Moore
189:168 1.8.52   'Irish Authoresses', discusses Somerville
                    and Ross
190:160 6.2.53   'Metaphors and Language'
190:643 15.5.53   'On the Nursery Floor', children's toys
192:26   1.1.54   'The Riddle of Emily Dickinson'
196:27   6.1.56   'Christina Rosetti'
196:58   13.1.56   'Mirth-Maker', discusses a life of Grimaldi,
                    king of clowns

The Irish Times (from the Saturday 'Books of the Week'
page, listed by date, page and title)

30.3.40   5   'Gigantic Poetic Notebook: More Cantos',
               reviews Pound
9.11.40   5   'Seumus O'Sullivan, Poet of Dublin'
15.3.41   5   'The Poetry of W.B. Yeats', reviews
               MacNeice's 'extremely irascible guide'
19.4.41   3   'Poetry and Contemporary Facts', reviews
               some poems by Donagh MacDonagh
24.5.41   5   'The Contemporary Scene in Poetry'
21.6.41   5   'Old-Fashioned Hymns of Hate', reviews
               war poems by Lord Dunsany
9.8.41   5   'No Time to Stand and Stare', reviews
               poems by W.H. Davies and T.S. Eliot
4.10.41   5   'The Poetry of Ulster', W.R. Rodgers and
               Robert Greacen
15.11.41 5   'A Return to Light Verse'
6.12.41   7   'The Age of Anthologies'
17.1.42   5   'Some Recent Poetry'
28.2.42   5   'New Verse'
9.5.42   5   'Three New Anthologies'
27.6.42   3   'Timeless Verse', Walter de la Mare
5.8.42   2   'Recent Poetry'
31.10.42 2   'New Verse'
7.11.42   2   'The Poet in Debt', an essay on poetic
               plagiarism in Yeats, T. Sturge Moore,
               Hopkins, and Emerson

14.11.42	2	'Herbert Trench', an essay
9.1.43	2	'Go and Catch a Falling Star', an essay on the Gaelic poetic tradition
23.1.43	2	'New Poetry and New Poets', Eliot, de la Mare, and others
6.2.43	2	'The Hidden Poetry of Wales', on the Mabinogi and Erigena, 'whose books were burned because he saw the ultimate joy and pardon of all human creatures'
20.2.43	2	'Two Women Poets'
13.3.43	2	'Conversation at Ebury Street', on George Moore and as in *A Penny*
27.3.43	2	'The Yeats Tradition', on cadences
10.4.43	2	'On Learning Irish', on Hyde, Sigerson, and as in *Black Church*
24.4.43	2	'Nature Poetry in England', a humorous essay of his own attempts to write
8.5.43	2	'Popular Poetry', essay on radio programme of verse
22.5.43	2	'An Irish Poet in India', James Cousins
12.6.43	2	'Poetry and the Weather', an essay on modern Irish poetry
19.6.43	2	'Poetry and Clothes', fashion in literature
10.7.43	2	'A Penny in the Clouds', about climbing Croagh Patrick
24.7.43	2	'Anthology Overseas', on Padraic Colum
7.8.43	2	'Repentant Puritan', essay on the censure of D.G. Rosetti
21.8.43	2	'Some American Poets', Melville and Frost
4.9.43	2	'The Poetry of Connacht', on translations from the Irish
18.9.43	2	'Books Beyond Reach', on censorship and general unavailability of some books
9.10.43	2	'Recent Poetry'
23.10.43	2	'Poet in the Shetlands', MacDiarmid
20.11.43	2	'Sir Richard Wittington'
11.12.43	2	'Recent Poetry'
8.1.44	2	'In the Shadow of Folklore', on Yeats' Countess Cathleen and Fitzmaurice

29.1.44	2	'Ulster Anthology'
19.2.44	2	'First Visit to the Abbey'
11.3.44	2	'Scottish Verse', anthologies
8.4.44	2	'The Romance of Ruins', on art collectors
15.4.44	2	'A New Irish Epic', reviews Farren's *The First Exile*
13.5.44	2	'Wanted: A Tradition', on new anthologies of Irish Verse
27.5.44	2	'The Countess Cathleen's, commemorates opening (7.6.44) of new Lyric Theatre with this play
1.7.44	2	'Poets, American and English'
22.7.44	2	'Scotland and Wales'
12.8.44	2	'The Chesterton Legend'
9.9.44	2	'English Pilgrim's Progress', anti-censorship essay
16.9.44	2	'Detective Stories'
30.9.44	2	'Early Anglo-Irish Poetry'
14.10.44	2	'New Verse'
4.11.44	2	'A Fallen Giant', the Birr telescope
25.11.44	2	'New Verse', dismisses Eliot's *Four Quartets* because 'poverty of language and thought, in these curious poems, becomes a kind of paradoxical Christian virtue'
13.1.45	2	'The Art of Translation'
3.2.45	2	'The Poetry of Blunden'
24.2.45	2	'Two Irish Books of Verse'
17.3.45	2	'Modern Poets', Auden, MacNeice, and others
5.5.45	2	'An Epic of Christ'
26.5.45	2	'Across the Atlantic', on the dearth of available Irish literature
18.8.45	2	'Poems of our Times'
29.9.45	2	'The World's End', an essay about London
20.10.45	2	'The Spirit of the Shillelagh', essay on Irish standards of literary criticism
17.11.45	2	'Genuflection', an essay on his conversion at the Black Church
8.12.45	4	'New Poetry'
12.1.46	4	'Lady Gregory and Folk Fantasy', an essay on the Abbey tradition

19.1.46	4	'Recent Verse'
9.2.46	4	'Potted Biography'
23.2.46	4	'The Commerce of Poetry', links Rilke with Yeats
16.3.46	4	'Pilgrims to Parnassus', reviews Graves and others
30.3.46	4	'Appointment for Tuesday', recalls first journalistic experiences
20.4.46	4	'A Vision of Glendalough', a memoir of Higgins, Campbell
18.5.46	4	'Private Lives and Public Men', on Blunden's life of Shelley
1.6.46	4	'Recent Verse'
13.7.46	4	'Recent Verse'
17.8.46	4	'Local Talent'
14.9.46	4	'Private File', letters of Shaw and Yeats to Florence Farr
5.10.46	6	'Three Poets'
12.10.46	6	'Perspectives'
9.11.46	6	'The True Background', rural craftmanship
21.12.46	6	'Strange Enchantment', Mervyn Wall's *The Unfortunate Fursey*
4.1.47	6	'Lady Gregory's Journals'
18.1.47	6	'Singers and their Songs', de la Mare and others
15.2.47	6	'Three Translations' of Villon, Leopardi, Baudelaire
22.2.47	6	'Home Ground', recent Irish poetry
15.3.47	6	'Church Parade for Poets', the Irish schools' anthology
29.3.47	6	'The Bitter Word', on Caradoc Evans
19.4.47	6	'A Bundle of Poets'
17.5.47	6	'Prospects'
21.6.47	6	'The Affairs of Verse'
16.8.47	6	'Matters of Choice' on anthologies
20.9.47	6	'A Sheaf of Poets'
25.10.47	6	'The Crowded Hours' reviews Mary Colum's *Life and the Dream*
8.11.47	6	'The Private Heart', Alice Meynell
20.12.47	6	'Garlands of Poets'
10.1.48	6	'Along the Trail'

21.2.48	6	'The Artist and the World', William Morris
28.2.48	4	'Poet and Priest', G.M. Hopkins
20.3.48	4	'Gentlemen of Letters', Henry James and Ford Madox Ford
3.4.48	4	'The Doctor's Dilemma' on Ernest Jones's biography of Freud
29.5.48	6	'A Handful of Verses'
12.6.48	6	'Critics' Circle'
26.6.48	6	'The American Muse', anthologies
17.7.48	6	'Poet of the English Twilight', de la Mare
14.8.48	4	'Born of Fire'
4.9.48	4	'The Poet's Stage'
18.9.48	6	'Scotland's Own'
9.10.48	6	'Auden and Others' MacNeice, Durrell
23.10.48	6	'From the Russian' anthologies
6.11.48	6	'The Eggman Cometh'
4.12.48	9	'For Art's Sake', anthology of '90s verse
11.12.48	6	'Mr. Eliot's Notebook', *Definition of a Culture*
18.12.48	6	'A New Poet?'
8.1.49	6	'Art and State', on individual liberty in the modern welfare state
29.1.49	6	'Och, Johnny, I Hardly Knew Ye!', on O'Casey's autobiography
5.2.49	6	'The Burning Tiger', on Blake
12.2.49	6	'Nature and Art'
19.2.49	6	'Period and Place' on Betjeman
12.3.49	6	'The Magical Art' on Graves' *The White Goddess*
19.3.49	6	'On the Stage' on Eric Bentley
26.3.49	6	'Critical Approach' on Cléanth Brooks
2.4.49	6	'The Roaring Boy' on Robert Service
16.4.49	6	'The Riotous are Bold' on O'Casey's *Cock a Doodle Dandy*
23.4.49	6	'Lives and Times'
30.4.49	6	'The Good-Humoured Man', George Farquhar
14.5.49	6	'A Poet's Progress', Jeffares on Yeats
28.5.49	6	'Poets' Gallery'
11.6.49	6	'As Others See Us'

2.7.49	6	'Scholarly Pursuits'
23.7.49	4	'The Devil in the House' on Coventry Patmore, author of the only 'epic dedicated entirely to the theme of domestic bliss, . . . its concealed connubiality'
27.8.49	4	'A Company of Poets'
17.9.49	6	'London Lights'
24.9.49	6	'Personal and Public'
1.10.49	6	'The Defeat of Don Juan'
29.10.49	6	'Three Victorians', Henley, Tennyson and Rosetti
12.11.49	6	'The Last Ditch' on Hough's *The Last Romantics*
19.11.49	6	'Ladies' Day'
10.12.49	6	'Oedipus and Philomel' memories of Yeats and A.E.
17.12.49	6	'Sense and Satire' on Irish mythologies and the censor
24.12.49	6	'Apollo's Men', on critics
14.1.50	6	'Vade Retro' on Swift
21.1.50	6	'After 50 Years' on Wilde
28.1.50	6	'Patchwork Poet' on Pound
11.2.50	6	'Verse in Action' on Christopher Fry
4.3.50	6	'Critics' Circle'
25.3.50	6	'The Muse as Mistress' on Pope
22.4.50	6	'The Crystal Screen' on Chinese poetry
6.5.50	6	'Beyond the Mulberries' on anthologies
27.5.50	6	'Muscae Volitantes' on Victorian and Edwardian poetry
17.6.50	6	'High Jinks' on Eliot's *Cocktail Party*
1.7.50	6	'The Star Gazers'
22.7.50	6	'Ex Machina' on Georgian literature
5.8.50	6	'The Return of the Native' on Gogarty
16.9.50	6	'The Age of Anxiety' on Auden, MacLeish and MacNeice
30.9.50	6	'Scalping the Muse', Lowell and Pound
14.10.50	6	'Deirdre and Her Rival' on Grainne and Myles Dillon
18.11.50	6	'Letting off Steam' on Day-Lewis, Blunden and Edward Thomas
9.12.50	6	'The Achievement of T.S. Eliot'

30.12.50	6	'Travelling Man' on R.L. Stevenson
13.1.51	6	'A Clutch of Critics'
27.1.51	6	'The Mind's Eye' on Henn's *Lonely Tower*
10.2.51	6	'Lyrical Allsorts'
17.2.51	6	'The Melting Pot' on American verse
24.2.51	6	'Green Helicon' Irish 19th century poetry
3.3.51	6	'Religion and Poetry'
10.3.51	6	'Down the Ages'
24.3.51	6	'Bandwagon from Babel' anthology of American poetry
31.3.51	6	'Greek in Modern Dress'
7.4.51	6	'Footlights for Poetry'
14.4.51	6	'Every Man his own Crusoe', Auden and Pound
21.4.51	6	'Treasure Trove'
28.4.51	6	'Torchlight for Processions'
5.5.51	6	'Poet and Peasant' on John Clare
12.5.51	6	'The Fire-born Moods' on Yeats' last poems
19.5.51	6	'Haste to the Heavens'
26.5.51	6	'The Votive Flame' on Gide and Valéry
2.6.51	6	'The Ailing Muse'
16.6.51	6	'A Western Parnassus'
23.6.51	6	'Seasonal Change'
30.6.51	6	'Miltonic Mysteries'
7.7.51	6	'A Poet Come to Judgment' on Donne
21.7.51	6	'The Riddle of the Sands' de la Mare's continued popularity
11.8.51	6	'Greek Fire' on Cavafy
1.9.51	6	'A Knight Errant Rides Out'
8.9.51	6	'The Leaning Tower' on Pound
15.9.51	6	'Tinkers Galore' on anthologies
6.10.51	6	'The White Blackbird', on Rilke
13.10.51	6	'Displaced Poet', reviews Auden
20.10.51	6	'Mr. Eliot on Mr. Eliot'
27.10.51	6	'Tramping to Heaven', W.H. Davies
3.11.51	6	'Shelley and His Critics'
10.11.51	6	'The Zenith and the Rainbow'
17.11.51	6	'The Future Tense'
8.12.51	6	'The Laurels of Yesterday'

22.12.51	6	'The Wooden Horse'
29.12.51	6	'Victorian Eminence', on Clough
5.1.52	6	'Shadowing Skies'
19.1.52	6	'Pieces of Eight'
2.2.52	6	'North and South'
9.2.52	6	'The great Unread', on Dryden
23.2.52	6	'Leander II', on Gogarty
1.3.52	6	'Before the Ides'
15.3.52	6	'Fire-New Words', on Elizabethan poetry
29.3.52	6	'The Stuff of Youth', on Masefield
12.4.52	8	'A Sop to Cerberus'
19.4.52	8	'Beauty and the Beast', on W.R. Rodgers' *Europa and the Bull*
10.5.52	8	'Little lights'
17.5.52	8	'March of a Nation'
24.5.52	8	'Museum Pieces', on Pound
8.10.52	8	'Plays in Search of a Theatre', on Yeats
1.11.52	6	'Poetry in the Parlour', on Emily Dickinson
8.11.52	6	'Spiritual Affairs'
13.12.52	6	'The Unacknowledged Master', Browning
20.12.52	6	'The Arrows of Apollo', on Davie's *Purity of Diction*
27.12.52	4	'The Spring Tide', on Rimbaud
17.1.53	6	'Without Pride or Prejudice', on critics
24.1.53	6	'Ancient and Modern', anthologies
31.1.53	6	'Public Papers', on critics and Pound
7.2.53	6	'Flight from Fog', on E.B. Browning
14.2.53	6	'Sky Shades and Lamp Shades', on Wallace Stevens
21.2.53	6	'Towards a Verse Theatre'
28.2.53	6	'Ourselves and Others'
7.3.53	6	'The Cuckoo's Church', on Welsh poetry
21.3.53	6	'The Colloquial Muse'
28.3.53	6	'Critic at Ease', Desmond McCarthy
4.4.53	6	'The Higher Gossip'
11.4.53	6	'The Pierian Spring', on Blake and Yeats
18.4.53	6	'Willow Pattern'
25.4.53	6	'Another Opinion'
2.5.53	6	'Critic in the Cathedral', on Eliot
9.5.53	6	'The Poet's Wife', on Mary Shelley
16.5.53	6	'City of Man' on W.C. Williams' *Paterson*

23.5.53	6	'The Eyes of Youth'
30.5.53	6	'The Woman Who Did', on George Sand
6.6.63	6	'Pastoral Poet', on William Barnes
13.6.53	6	'Tremors and Thrills', on Dylan Thomas
27.6.53	6	'Spirit of Laughter', on *Midnight Court*
11.7.53	6	'Between Friends', letters of Yeats to Katherine Tynan
25.7.53	6	'No Signature', on de la Mare
8.8.53	6	'You Never Can Tell'
15.8.53	6	'The River and its Sources', on Pound
22.8.53	6	'No Pudding for Poets', on Hopkins
29.8.53	6	'The Middle of the Road'
12.9.53	6	'What you Will', on Shakespeare critics
19.9.53	6	'World Beyond Words'
26.9.53	6	'Sing a Song O' Suburbs'
3.10.53	6	'Give and Take', letters of Yeats and T. Sturge Moore
17.10.53	6	'The Happy Warrior', on Chesterton
24.10.53	6	'A Long Look Back'
31.10.53	10	'The American Way', on Sandburg
7.11.53	6	'Enigma at Amherst', on Emily Dickinson
14.11.53	6	'Recapitulation', histories of English Literature
21.11.53	6	'Age and Youth', poetry for children
12.12.53	6	'Poetry and Pomps', on E. Sitwell
19.12.53	6	'Family Album'
2.1.54	6	'Dreams Lie Deep'
9.1.54	6	'Remembered Fields', on Colum
16.1.54	6	'The Case of Mr. Keats'
23.1.54	6	'Venus and Her Prey', on Zola's *Nana*
30.1.54	6	'Man and Superwoman', on Emily Brontë and George Eliot
6.2.54	6	'Faith and Works', on Wordsworth
13.2.54	6	'For Smaller Shelves'
20.2.54	6	'Rabbie and Robert', on Burns
27.2.54	6	'Surprise Attacks', on Pound's criticisms
6.3.54	6	'Two on Tower', on Valéry and Gide
13.3.54	6	'The New Collegians', on American poetry
20.3.54	6	'Family Disunion', on Eliot's *Con-*

fidential Clerk

27.3.54	6	'Sporting the Leek', on Dylan Thomas
3.4.54	6	'Out of Office Hours', on Huysmans
10.4.54	6	'The Third Woman', on Swift, 'an Irishman who could hold his temper'
17.4.54	6	'The Fall of Icarus', on Marlowe, Shakespeare, and subversion in literature
24.4.54	6	'The Hill of Vision', on James Stephens
1.5.54	6	'Wolf! Wolf!'
8.5.54	8	'The Gentleman's Not for Burning'
15.5.54	6	'Band of Hope'
22.5.54	6	'No Silver Lining', on R.P. Warren
29.5.54	6	'The Man from Stratford', Shakespeare's poetry
12.6.54	8	'Put Aside the Lute', on Geo. Herbert
19.6.54	6	'Ancient Enemies', Russia, Poland, and The West
26.6.54	8	'The Great Anon', on Swift
3.7.54	6	'As in a Glass Darkly', on C. Fry's plays
10.7.54	6	'In their moods'
24.7.54	6	'Themes and Theses', on Milton
31.7.54	6	'Wind from the North'
7.8.54	6	'Behind Lace Curtains'
14.8.54	6	'Around the Gates'
21.8.54	6	'Bright Intervals'
28.8.54	6	'Magic of Europe'
4.9.54	8	'Second Thoughts', on Ellmann on Yeats
11.9.54	8	'Out of Breath', on Rilke
18.9.54	6	'Reforming Zeal'
2.10.54	6	'The Mighty Puzzle', on Shakespeare
9.10.54	8	'Gay Days', on Gogarty's calling Joyce a lunatic
16.10.54	6	'Father and Sons', on Vyvyan Holland
23.10.54	8	'The Poet as Playboy, on Apollinaire
30.10.54	6	'Catching the Post', on Yeats' Letters
6.11.54	6	'Cock-A-Doodle Dandy', on O'Casey's autobiographies
13.11.54	6	'Some Elizabethans'
20.11.54	6	'The Incomplete Egotist', on Wordsworth
11.12.54	6	'The Wearers of the Bays', on poet laureates
18.12.54	6	'Down to Earth', on Shelley

15.1.55	6	'The Burns Dilemma'
22.1.55	6	'The Cost of Freedom', on exiled writers
29.1.55	6	'What You Will', on Shakespeare
5.2.55	6	'From the Country: An Anthology of Irish Writing'
12.2.55	6	'A Gathering of Poets'
19.2.55	6	'In Modern Dress', on Aristophanes
26.2.55	6	'Poet of Peace: a New Study of Alexander Pope'
5.3.55	6	'The Master Builder: An Interpretation and Study', on Ibsen
12.3.55	6	'Carriages at Nine: Theatre in Stuart Ireland'
19.3.55	8	'Confucius Worse Confounded', on Pound
26.3.55	6	'The Amoralist', on Lawrence
2.4.55	8	'Cast a Cold Eye', on Yeats' Autobiographies
9.4.55	8	'Poems of Ireland'
16.4.55	8	'The Dark Worlds'
23.4.55	8	'Comrades-in-Arts'
30.4.55	8	'Around Parnassus'
7.5.55	8	'La Fontaine Revisited', on Marianne Moore
14.5.55	8	'The Voice of the Swami', on Tagore
28.5.55	8	'A Tribute to A.E.', who 'brought into our literary movement the spirit of co-operation . . . (Yeats) preferred private enterprise'
4.6.55	8	'Wise Man from the West'
11.6.55	8	'Don Screwtape'
18.6.55	8	'Once Upon a Time', on the Grimms
25.6.55	8	'The Narrow Screen'
2.7.55	6	'Pierian Spring', on M. Bowra
9.7.55	8	'The Storytellers'
16.7.55	8	'Looking Backwards'
23.7.55	6	'The Lowland Muse', on Scottish verse
30.7.55	6	'The Prince of Darkness'
6.8.55	6	'The Lost Hours'
13.8.55	6	'Fallen Woman'
20.8.55	6	'For Jamie Joyce', on a poem by MacDiarmid
27.8.55	6	'Stager in Sack-Cloth'

3.9.55	6	'Poet of Meath', on Ledwidge
10.9.55	6	'The New Discipline', on Donald Davie
17.9.55	6	'Indian Summer'
24.9.55	6	'Poetry and Prejudice', on Graves
1.10.55	6	'Style and the Man'
8.10.55	6	'Women of Destiny'
15.10.55	8	'The Higher Criticism', on Davie's *Articulate Energy*
22.10.55	6	'A Major Poet?', on Wallace Stevens
29.10.55	8	'All for Hecuba', on Treece
5.11.55	6	'The Cryptic Key', on Empson's poetry
12.11.55	8	'Three Poets'
19.11.55	6	'Gownsmen All', on John Wain's *Interpretations*
10.12.55	8	'Poems of To-day and Yesterday'
24.12.55	6	'Salve', a critical re-appraisal of George Moore
7.1.56	6	'The Age of Conformity'
14.1.56	6	'Blake and Yeats'
21.1.56	6	'Robert Wilson'
28.1.56	8	'The Dunce's Epic', on Pope's wit, clarity, and elegance
4.2.56	6	'The Cheerful Critic'
11.2.56	6	'Poems of Happiness'
18.2.56	6	'Bards in the Wood'
25.2.56	6	'From the Imagined Corners'
3.3.56	8	'A Citizen of the World', on Gibbon
10.3.56	8	'Dead Men's Tales'
17.3.56	6	'Eminent Victorians'
24.3.56	8	'A Poet of Faith', on Edwin Muir
31.3.56	8	'The Cactus has its Prickles', on Aldous Huxley
7.4.56	8	'Critic's Choice'
14.4.56	8	'Mask and Motley'
21.4.56	8	'Fine Books'
28.4.56	8	'Mirth for Millions'
5.5.56	6	'The Land of Memory'
12.5.56	6	'Welsh Concert'
19.5.56	8	'Walter de la Mare
26.5.56	6	'Three Poets'
2.6.56	6	'The Lost Disciple'
9.6.56	6	'Divers Hands'

16.6.56	8	'No Prospect Pleases'
23.6.56	6	'The Novelist's Eye'
30.6.56	6	'Voices in the Fog'
7.7.56	6	'American Witch-Hunt', on Miller's *The Crucible*
14.7.56	6	'Modern Poetry' anthologies
21.7.56	6	'The Last Aesthete', on Cocteau
4.8.56	6	'East and West'
11.8.56	6	'The Fallen Soldier', on Edward Thomas
29.9.56	6	'The Wicked Lord', on Byron
6.10.56	6	'Memories of Moore'
13.10.56	6	'American Poetry', on anthologies
20.10.56	6	'Out of School', on anthologies
27.10.56	6	'Ten Years Old', on the BBC
3.11.56	6	'Ariel Observed', on Shelley
10.11.56	6	'The Spirit and The Word', on 17th century poetry
17.11.56	6	'Victorian Poet', Coventry Patmore who is 'bathetic, but dared to allow marriage a spiritual place'
8.12.56	6	'Poems from Wales'
15.12.56	6	'Hopkins' Letters'
22.12.56	6	'An Irish Poet', on Aubrey de Vere
29.12.56	6	'Travelling Men'
5.1.57	6	'The Bloomsbury Set'
12.1.57	6	'Lawrence'
19.1.57	6	'Péguy as Poet'
26.1.57	6	'Poets Cannot Err', on Margaret Schlauch
9.2.57	6	'Poet of Auld Reikie', predecessors of Burns
16.2.57	6	'New Poems', Pound did not read Clarke's *Fionn*: and asked instead, 'Why do people still insist on writing long poems?'
23.2.57	6	'Dear Edward' (Martyn)
2.3.57	6	'Man Uncertain'
9.3.57	6	'On Translation'
16.3.57	6	'A Writer Born', on A.E. Coppard
23.3.57	6	'Synge and the Irish'
30.3.57	6	'Down Fleet Street', on Priestley
6.4.57	6	'Here Be Dragons'
13.4.57	6	'New Poetry'

20.4.57	6	'Tiddly-Winks and Toss-Pots', on Rabelais
27.4.57	6	'Enter Iago'
4.5.57	6	'Poems by L.A.G. Strong'
11.5.57	6	'The Late Romantic', on Lawrence's poems
18.5.57	6	'The Common Muse', on ballads
25.5.57	6	'Signposts to Stratford'
1.6.57	6	'Storm and Stress', on Hopkins, Eliot and Crashaw
8.6.57	6	'Thirty Years Back'
15.6.57	6	'Ars Poetica', on Shakespeare
22.6.57	6	'The Poets Pass By'
29.6.57	6	'Eternity Observed', on Dante
13.7.57	6	'The Yea-Sayers'
20.7.57	6	'Irish Classical Poems', on Eleanor Knott
27.7.57	6	'The Open Mind', on Lord David Cecil
10.8.57	6	'Anatomy of Melancholy', on John Ford's drama
17.8.57	6	'The Modern Sitwells'
24.8.57	6	'Three Voices'
31.8.57	6	'Fog and Sunday'
7.9.57	8	'Why the 12:30 Was Late', on Beckett's *All That Fall*
14.9.57	6	'The Western Word'
21.9.57	6	'A Murmuring of Moderns', anthologies
28.9.57	6	'Tea-Time in Twickenham', on de la Mare
5.10.57	8	'Behind the Scenes', on Gordon Craig
12.10.57	6	'The Senior Revolutionary', T.S. Eliot as critic
19.10.57	6	'In Quest of Shakespeare'
26.10.57	6	'A Dreamer's Child'
2.11.57	8	'Love and Magic', on Betjeman's anthology of love poetry'
9.11.57	8	'Whence the Green Man?'
16.11.57	8	'Oscar in Earnest', on Wilde
23.11.57	6	'Poet Without His Legend' on Dylan Thomas
14.12.57	6	'A Poet of Dissent', on Donald Davie
21.12.57	6	'Forbidden Fruit', on Ouida
28.12.57	4	'Poets of Silence', on Colum and Thomas Merton
4.1.58	6	'Virtue Triumphant', on popular fiction

11.1.58	6	'The Study of Blake'
18.1.58	6	'The Poems of Rilke'
25.1.58	6	'On the Track of W.B.' (Yeats)
1.2.58	6	'The Storm and the Calm', on Priestley
8.2.58	6	'Studies in Evaluation', on critics
15.2.58	6	'A Guide to Bardolatry', on Shakespeare
22.2.58	6	'The Age of Reason', on Johnson, Boswell, and Goldsmith
1.3.58	6	'Neglected Poets'
8.3.58	6	'Sing a Song of Silly Sooth', light verse
15.3.58	8	'Andromeda Unrescued', on criticism
22.3.58	6	'The Perfectionist', on Yeats' poetry
29.3.58	8	'Poor Noll', on Goldsmith
5.4.58	6	'The Scholar Poet', on Housman
12.4.58	8	'East and West', on Noh drama
19.4.58	8	'Family Reunion', on Djuna Barnes
26.4.58	6	'The Struldbrugs'
3.5.58	6	'Situation Vacant', on Genet's *Maids*
10.5.58	8	'All Hail, Great Master', on Joyce
17.5.58	8	'Fellow of Infinite Jest', on Sterne
24.5.58	8	'The Poet of Reform', on Swift
7.6.58	8	' "Dear, Dirty Dublin" ', on the dramatisation of *Finnegan's Wake*
14.6.58	6	'Prophet on the Warpath'
21.6.58	8	'A Discreet Victorian', on Thackeray
28.6.58	8	'Sweeney on the Rack', on poetic lampoons
5.7.58	6	'The Last Hellenist', on W.S. Landor
19.7.58	6	'Poets Young and Old'
26.7.58	6	'Opinion and Reality'
2.8.58	6	'Virginia Woolf the Critic'
9.8.58	6	'Mon Cher Ami'
16.8.58	6	'Heroes of History'
23.8.58	6	'A New View of Swift'
30.8.58	6	'Question and Answer'
6.9.68	6	'Night Thoughts', on Melville, Poe, and Hawthorne
13.9.58	6	'Poor Theo' (Gautier)
20.9.58	6	'The Songs of Steam', on industrial ballads
27.9.58	6	'A Quartet of Poets'
4.10.58	6	'A Colloquy of Critics'

11.10.58	6	'New England Century'
18.10.58	8	'Tragic Interlude', on Edward Thomas
25.10.58	6	'Daring Young Woman'
1.11.58	6	'Straight Elizabethan', on Middleton
8.11.58	6	'Under Two Flags', Continental poetry anthologies
15.11.58	6	'Portrait of Mr. W.H.', on Wilde and Shakespeare
22.11.58	6	'Kings and Chronicles', on Charles Williams and Shakespeare
6.12.58	4	'Writers at Ease', on Graves and Maugham
13.12.58	6	'Signals of Distress', on USSR underground writing
20.12.58	6	'On Boswell on Johnson'
27.12.58	4	'Two Modern Poets'
3.1.59	6	'Turgenev and Others'
10.1.59	6	'Pedagogue on Parnassus'
17.1.59	6	'Ben in His Humour' (Jonson)
24.1.59	6	'Soothsayers All'
31.1.59	6	'The Regent's Gadfly'
7.2.59	6	'For A' That', on Burns
14.2.59	6	'A "Makar" of the Scots Revival', on Soutar
21.2.59	6	'Hither and Thither'
7.3.59	6	'Poets Three'
14.3.59	6	'The Bard on One Wing', on Shakespeare
28.3.59	6	'Mood of Disillusion', on John Montague and Yeats
18.4.59	6	'A Fading Art', on letter-writing
25.4.59	8	'A New-Old Tristan'
2.5.59	6	'Shelley's Wife'
9.5.59	6	'The Muse and the Critics'
16.5.59	10	'On the Brink', on Eliot
23.5.59	6	'Poets of Today'
30.5.59	6	'The Real Anne' (Brontë)
6.6.59	6	'Seumus Beg', James Stephens
13.6.59	6	'New Light on Synge'
20.6.59	6	'Ring and Blasted Heath', on the faeries in Shakespeare
27.6.59	6	'Rifles and Roses', on various poets
4.7.59	6	'Critic and Artist'
11.7.59	6	'Three Translations'

18.7.59	6	'Job Uncomforted'
25.7.59	6	'Wales in Verse'
1.8.59	8	'A Matter of Symbols', on Coleridge
8.8.59	6	'Three Women Poets'
15.8.59	6	'Prince of Letter-Writers', on Walpole
22.15.59	6	'Poets with Honour'
29.8.59	6	'Irish Poems from Rome'
5.9.59	6	'The Actor's Masks'
12.9.59	6	'Laureate of Canada', on E.J. Pratt
19.9.59	8	'The Innocents Abroad'
26.9.59	6	'H.P.B. and the Colonel', on Mme. Blavatsky
3.10.59	10	'A Publisher's Memoirs'
10.10.59	6	'The Tenth Muse', on Berryman's *Homage to Mistress Bradstreet*
17.10.59	6	'A Wicked Trade', on Molière
24.10.59	6	'The Augustan Age', on Pope
31.10.59	6	'A Scholar in Elfland', on the readers' guide to Yeats
7.11.59	6	'The Common Touch'
14.11.59	6	'A Neglected Poet'
21.11.59	6	'Testament of Beauty', on an anthology by Edith Sitwell
28.11.59	4	'The Augustan Muse'
5.12.59	6	'Mask for a Modern', poems by Davie, Updike, and Fry
12.12.59	8	'Legion of the Lost', on J.C. Squire
19.12.59	8	'Poetry Off Stage', on Donoghue's *Third Voice*
2.1.60	8	'Whack-Fol-the-Riddle-O', on critics on *Finnegan's Wake*
9.1.60	6	'Decent Ornaments'
16.1.60	8	'The Last of the Georgians'
23.1.60	8	'The Amorous Gael', on Kennelly
30.1.60	8	'Nothing to Declare', on Anouilh and Henry Miller
6.2.60	6	'Cues as Clues', on critics of Shakespeare
13.2.60	6	'Busy and Brisk', on literary criticism
20.2.60	6	'Technique and Poetry', on P.J. Kavanagh
27.2.60	8	'Exhilarating Optimism', on Priestley
5.3.60	6	'Business as Usual', on Wallace Stevens
12.3.60	8	'Grave and Gay', on Herbert, Herrick

19.3.60	8	'Blithe Spirit', on Shelley
26.3.60	8	'Greek to Gothic', on Aristophanes in translation
2.4.60	8	'Two Ulster Poets', Shane Leslie, Padraic Gregory
9.4.60	8	'Another Round', the Guinness book of poetry
16.4.60	6	'Published and Be Damned'
23.4.60	8	'Wyndham Lewis'
30.4.60	8	'Form and Informality', on Kinsella
7.5.60	8	'A Pound Sterling', on Pound
14.5.60	8	'Playing 'Possum', on Eliot
21.5.60	8	'Poets Collective', on Muir, Durrell, and Plomer
28.5.60	8	'Never Wrote a Book', on T.E. Hulme
4.6.60	6	'The Lonely Child', on C. Day-Lewis
11.6.60	8	'Life is Real'
18.6.60	8	'The Buzz of Criticism'
25.6.60	6	'Poems Pleasant and Unpleasant'
2.7.60	6	'Cosmopolitan Interlude', on the bookshop called Shakespeare and Co.
9.7.60	8	'Books and the Man', on Gide and Berenson
23.7.60	6	'Hither and Thither', on Yeats' iconography
30.7.60	6	'A Silenced Poet'
6.8.60	6	'College Interlude', on Auden's *Homage to Clio*
13.8.60	6	'The Hidden Hand', on Shakespeare
20.8.60	6	'Odd Man Out', on Edward Fitzgerald
27.8.60	6	'A Restoration Poet', on Oldham
3.9.60	6	'A Life of Poetry', on Colum
10.9.60	6	'The Poet's Pilgrimage'
17.9.60	6	'A Goddess Not So White', on Rider Haggard
24.9.60	6	'Weighty Words' on Daiches' history of English literature
1.10.60	6	'Victorian Rebel', on Swinburne
8.10.60	6	'The Lessening Temptation'
5.11.60	8	'What They Saw', on Irish faeryland
12.11.60	6	'Poet of War', on Wilfred Owen
19.11.60	8	'Desk and Stage', on critics of Shake-

speare

26.11.60	6	'Without his Cloak'
10.12.60	6	'Mint and Roses', on the poems of Pasternak
17.12.60	6	'Mistakes of Milton', on critics
24.12.60	6	'Swan Songs', on Melchiori on Yeats
31.12.60	6	'All Irish', on a life of Branwell Brontë
7.1.61	6	'Three Poets', including Sylvia Plath
14.1.61	6	'Poetry of Poland'
21.1.61	6	'Through the Paper Hoop', on Wilde and Dylan Thomas
28.1.61	6	'The Lion's Share'
4.2.61	8	'Barque and Bight', anthologies of sea-verse
11.2.61	8	'Augusta', on Lady Gregory
18.2.61	8	'Family Likeness'
25.2.61	8	'The Prose of Yeats'
4.3.61	6	'The Turn of the Screw', underground Russian poetry
11.3.61	8	'The Poet of Democracy', on Whitman
18.3.61	10	'Poet's Pie', on e.e. cummings
25.3.61	8	'London Calling'
8.4.61	8	'Modern Greek Poetry', on Seferis
15.4.61	10	'At Home and Abroad', poetry by MacNeice and Nabokov
22.4.61	8	'Lake and Fell', on Wordsworth
6.5.61	6	'The Romantic Books'
13.5.61	8	'Master of Arts', the poems of Michelangelo
20.5.61	8	'The Prodigal Father', on Shakespeare's sonnets
27.5.61	8	'Sensitive Satirist', on Sassoon
3.6.61	8	'A Francophilic Critic'
10.6.61	8	'Beyond the Lyre', on Sewell's *Orphic Voice*
17.6.61	10	'Amaryllis and Amanda', on Milton and Pope
24.6.61	8	'The Poet Laureate and Oisin', Masefield
1.7.61	8	'Poet of Loneliness', on Yeats
15.7.61	6	'The Last Gleeman', on James Stephens
22.7.61	8	'Beyond their Ken'
29.7.61	6	'Here and There'

5.8.61	6	'A Man of Property', on Shakespeare
12.8.61	6	'Poet of India', on Tagore
19.8.61	6	'Dublin Days'
26.8.61	6	'The Brother', on Branwell Brontë
2.9.61	8	'Stage Lovers'
16.9.61	10	'Resurrection.
23.9.61	8	'Edward Martyn'
30.9.61	8	'The Round Table'
7.10.61	8	'The Quality of Thought'
14.10.61	8	'The Way of Words'
21.10.61	10	'The Leopard and the Ring', Christopher Fry
28.10.61	8	'Frolic and Fan', on Horace Walpole
4.11.61	10	'The Sad Critics'
11.11.61	8	'Gloom and Glow'
18.11.61	8	'Among the Essayists'
25.11.61	6	'Among the Lassies', on Burns
2.12.61	8	'Voice of the Rebel', on Rimbaud
9.12.61	8	'Flight of the Furies'
16.12.61	10	'The Irish Liberal', on Yeats as senator
23.12.61	6	'Cauliflower and Toothpaste'
30.12.61	6	'Chinese Crackers', on official Maoist poetry anthologies
6.1.62	6	'Quip and Crank', on wit in 17th century poetry
13.1.62	8	'Solanum Tuberosum'
27.1.62	8	'Synge and Style'
3.2.62	8	'Three Irish Poets', on Beckett, Payne and J.B. Keane
10.2.62	8	'Players and Painted Stage', on a history of the theatre
17.2.62	8	'The Spoken Word'
24.2.62	6	'Ad Parnassum', on prosody and metre as disciplines
3.3.62	8	'Dr. Faustus', on Thomas Mann
10.3.62	8	'Things That Go Bump in the Night'
17.3.62	8	'Arctic Night', on Eskimos and their poetry
24.3.62	8	'Rock of Ages'
31.3.62	6	'Poems and Prizes', on McGinley, Wain, and Jennings
7.4.62	6	'At the Play', on Henry James

12.5.62	8	'In Memory of the Dead', on Colum's elegies
26.5.62	7	'The Land of Snows', on Tibet
2.6.62	8	'Past and Present', on methods of critics
9.6.62	8	'In Green Recesses'
16.6.62	8	'A Forgotten City', on Marco Polo
30.6.62	8	'The Sage of Ferney', on Voltaire
7.7.62	6	'In Memoriam', various poets
14.7.62	6	'The Man From Stratford', on Shakespeare
21.7.62	6	'The Cave of Mammon', on Ben Jonson and commercial theatre
28.7.62	8	'Cap and Bells', on a history of the fool in which Clarke mentions Harlequin and Pierrot, Commedia dell'Arte
11.8.62	6	'On Losing One's Head', a history of the guillotine
25.8.62	8	'Sun Worshippers'
1.9.62	8	'The Terrible Years', on Strindberg and Cocteau
		(nothing for 5 years, 3 months)
27.1.68	10	'Real and Absurd', on Chekhov and Günther Grass
10.2.68	8	'American Pioneers', on Sherwood Anderson and Gertrude Stein
24.2.68	10	'Chuch Militant', on a history of Jesuits
9.3.68	10	'Lover of all Humanity', on Whitman
23.3.68	10	'More on Ariel', on Shelley
6.4.68	8	'The Higher Gossip', on lives of Byron and Shelley
20.4.68	10	'A Victorian Diary'
4.5.68	10	'Ruler of the Waves'
18.5.68	8	'Modern Irish Playwrights'
8.6.68	10	'Jail Journal', on *The Enormous Room* by e.e. cummings
15.6.68	8	'Self-Portrait of the Artist', on Wm. Carleton
6.7.68	10	'The Lay Bible of Agnostics'
20.7.68	10	'Guilty or Not Guilty', on a life of Byron's sister.
3.8.68	10	'The Artist as Hermit', on Flaubert,

		Turgenev
17.8.68	10	'Happy Larry and Sad Sam., on Sterne, Beckett
14.9.68	8	'Yeats late and early'
21.9.68	8	'The Art of Quotation', on Eliot's *The Waste Land*
5.10.68	8	'Ruskin on Tour'
12.10.68	8	'The Three Fathers', on Frank O'Connor
26.10.68	8	'"Goddess Excellently Bright"', on Grub Street
9.11.68	10	'Adopty Duncle', on Edward Lear
23.11.68	10	'The Dismal Nineties'
30.11.68	8	'Hidden Land', on Welsh Literature
14.12.68	10	'Ave Atque Vale', on George Moore
28.12.68	8	'Gloom Galore'
11.1.69	8	'Mangan to Joyce', on Boyd's *Renaissance*
25.1.69	10	'The Picturesque mode', on Pre-Raphaelite poetry
8.2.69	10	'Saving the Sonnet'
22.2.69	10	'Outside the Garden Gate', on Edwardians
8.3.69	8	'The Last Essayist', on Priestley
22.3.69	8	'The Return of the Native', on Henry James
19.4.69	10	'Destined Victims.
3.5.69	8	'On Being Sponged'
17.5.69	8	'Ancient Springs', on primitive and tribal poetry
31.5.69	8	'O Rare Amanda'
14.6.69	10	'Meeting the Neighbours'
28.6.69	10	'Travellers' Tales'
12.7.69	8	'Joyce and O'Casey'
26.7.69	8	'Heretics All', on Blake, Racine, and Pasternak
9.8.69	8	'Ez and Old Billyum', on Pound and Yeats
23.8.69	10	'Modern Welsh Poetry'
6.9.69	8	'The Fear of Literature', on censorship
27.9.69	8	'Darwin and his Voyage'
4.10.69	8	'Letters and Tales'
18.10.69	8	'Man and Superman', on da Vinci, Donne, and Casanova

1.11.69	10	'John Synge Comes Next', on *Riders to the Sea*
15.11.69	8	'Magician without Wand', on Crowley
6.12.69	8	'The Ruling Class'
20.12.69	8	'Victorian Rebels', on the Pre-Raphaelites
10.1.70	8	'The Blossom Time', on H.E. Bates
17.1.70	8	'The Courts of Poetry', on medieval poetry
31.1.70	10	'Count Your Syllables'
14.2.70	8	'A Voice from Beyond', on Somerville and Ross
28.2.70	8	'Decadence and Uplift', on Firbank and George Eliot
14.3.70	10	'Patchwork Poets', on Eliot and Pound
28.3.70	10	'The Monkey's Paw', on Herbert Read
11.4.70	8	'In English and Scots'
25.4.70	8	'Thomas Love Peacock'
9.5.70	10	'Defending the Faith', on Chesterton
23.5.70	8	'The Hollow Men', on various biographies of politicians
6.6.70	8	'Nineties' Period Pieces'
20.6.70	8	'Words to Avoid', on Shaw's *Pygmalion*
4.7.70	10	'The Good Apprentice', on Gissing
18.7.70	10	'Changing Times', on the TLS
1.8.70	10	'Kisses Galore', on William Gerhardie
15.8.70	10	'Reviews Past and Present'
29.8.70	8	'Unsolved Mysteries'
12.9.70	8	'Every Man in His Humour'
26.9.70	10	'The Higher Gossip'
10.10.70	10	'Short-Cuts to Success'
24.10.70	10	'Call Me Circe', on E. Sitwell and Roethke
7.11.70	10	'Turkish Delight', on Lady M.W. Montagu
21.11.70	11	'The Path to Rome', on the Oxford Movement
5.12.70	9	'When Rome Burned', on Nero
19.12.70	10	'The Great Refusal', on Fielding's *Joseph Andrews* and *Shamela*
2.1.71	8	'The Bad Fairy of Abbey Street', on Yeats and the literary Journals
16.1.71	10	'Devotia Moderna', on Erasmus and Shakespeare
30.1.71	10	'Read On', on Johnson and Wordsworth

13.2.71	8	'Genius Loci'
27.2.71	10	'Eminent Georgians', on Strachey, Carpenter and Lawrence
20.3.71	10	'The Rector of Diss', on poetry of John Skelton
27.3.71	8	'Fetch and Carry', on Thackeray and Rupert Brooke
17.4.71	10	'A Case of Red Tape', on Solzhenitsyn and Gurdjieff
8.5.71	10	'Death in Trieste'
29.5.71	10	'The Great Tradition', on Nathanael West
12.6.71	10	'Gentlemen as Poets', on Fulke Greville, Sir Walter Scott
26.6.71	10	'Plain Poetry', on Dryden
10.7.71	10	'A Rake's Progress' on Smollet
24.7.71	8	'A Priestess of Venus', on Ninon de L'Enclos
7.8.71	10	'The Prussian Eagle'
21.8.71	10	'Parisian Kisses'
4.9.71	8	'Trials of a Convert', on Frederick Rolfe
25.9.71	8	'Life with Father', on the letters of Maria Edgeworth
9.10.71	10	'The Wreck of the Three-Decker', on the decline of circulating libraries and large novels
23.10.71	10	'Sentimental Journey', on Cecil Beaton
30.10.71	10	'Would-Be Celibate', on the last days of Tolstoy
6.11.71	8	'Soup and Sex', on Isherwood's *Kathleen and Frank*
20.11.71	10	'Turn of the Screw', on Alvarez's *Savage God* and Plath's last poems
4.12.71	10	'The Last Puritan', on Shaw
18.12.71	10	'Burying the Hatchet', on Mary Wollstonecraft
8.1.72	10	'The Wicked Magician', on Crowley
22.1.72	10	'Veteran Bookman', on Howard Spring
12.2.72	8	'Literary Revivalists., on Yeats, Joyce
19.2.72	10	'Why Browne Was Nolan', on Ellmann's *Ulysses on the Liffey*
4.3.72	8	'Synge's Fiancée'

18.3.72	10	'Welfare Statist'
1.4.72	10	'French Views on Eng. lit'. (sic)
15.4.72	10	'A Spiritual Anthology'
29.4.72	10	'Syngespiel'
13.5.72	10	'The Absurd', on Ionesco
27.5.72	10	'Deep Waters', on a study of Yeats and his 'Druid craft'
15.7.72	10	'Ruskin and e.e. cummings'
12.8.72	10	'Tories Galore'
4.11.72	10	'Looking Back', on biographies
2.12.72	13	'An Indoor Man', on Proust and the CBEL
16.12.72	10	'Musical Affairs', on Elizabeth Lutyens
27.1.73	10	'Husband and Wife', the wit and works of Seumus O'Sullivan and Estella F. Solomons
24.2.73	12	'Cross and Crescent', on histories of the Crusades
25.8.73	10	'Some Talk of Alexander' (the Great)
3.11.73	12	'End of a Big House', on Somerville and Ross

BIBLIOGRAPHY OF SOURCES

In this bibliography, critical anthologies or casebooks will be listed by the title of the book and not by the name(s) of the editor(s). All other books are listed alphabetically by the last name of the author. Journals are listed alphabetically by title in a separate section at the end.

Beckett, J.C. *The Making of Modern Ireland 1603-1923*. London, 1969.

Bergin, Osborn. *Irish Bardic Poetry*, Texts and Translations, compiled and edited by David Greene and Fergus Kelly. Dublin, 1970. 'Poems attributed to Gormlaith', in Miscellany Presented to Kuno Meyer. Halle a.s., 1912.

Bromwich, Rachel. *Matthew Arnold and Celtic Literature, The O'Donnell Lecture*. London, 1965.

Carney, James. *The Irish Bardic Poet*. Dublin, 1967. *Medieval Irish Lyrics*. Dublin, 1967.

The Celtic Cross: Studies in Irish Culture and Folklore, edited by Ray B. Brown, William J. Roscelli, and Richard J. Loftus. Purdue University Studies, 1964.

Corkery, Daniel. *The Hidden Ireland: A Study of Gaelic Munster in the Eighteenth Century*, first paperback edition. Dublin, 1967.

Davie, Donald. *Articulate Energy: An Enquiry into the Syntax of English Poetry*. London, 1955.

Dillon, Myles. *Early Irish Literature*. Chicago and London, 1965.

Donoghue, Denis. *The Third Voice: Modern British and American Verse Drama*. New Jersey, 1959.

Early Irish Literature, edited by James Carney. London, 1967.

Early Irish Poetry, edited by James Carney. Cork, 1965.

Farren, Robert. *The Course of Irish Verse in English*. London, 1948.

Ferguson, Samuel. *Poems*, edited by Padraic Colum. Dublin, 1963.

Figes, Eva. *Patriarchal Attitudes*. London, 1970.

Fischer, Ernst. *The Necessity of Art: A Marxist Approach*. Harmondsworth, 1971.

Flower, Robin. *The Irish Tradition*. London, 1966.

Freud, Sigmund. *The Interpretation of Dreams*, translated and edited by James Strachey. London, 1967.

Furst, Lilian R. *Romanticism in Perspective: A Comparative Study of Aspects of the Romantic Movements in England, France and Germany*. London, 1969.

Graves, Robert. *The White Goddess: A Historical Grammar of Poetic Myth*. London, 1961.

Henry, Francoise. *Irish Art*, in three volumes. London, 1965-70.

Hewitt, John and Montague, John. *The Planter and the Gael*. Belfast, 1970.

Hogan, Robert. *After The Irish Renaissance: A Critical History of the Irish Drama, since 'The Plough And The Stars'*. London, 1968.

Hyde, Douglas. *A Literary History of Ireland*, 3rd impression. London, 1967.

Irish Literary Portraits: W.R. Rodgers's broadcast conversations with those who knew them. London, 1972.

Irish Poets in English: The Thomas Davis Lectures on Anglo-Irish Poetry, edited by Sean Lucy. Dublin and Cork, 1973.

Joyce, P.W. *Old Celtic Romances*, reprint. Dublin, 1966.

Kermode, Frank. *The Romantic Image*. London, 1971.

Kinsella, Thomas. *The Tain*, translated from the Irish Epic Táin Bó Cuailnge. London, 1970.

Literary Ideals in Ireland: Essays by John Eglinton, William Larminie, George Russell (AE), and W.B. Yeats. Dublin, 1899.

Loftus, Richard J. *Nationalism in Modern Anglo-Irish Poetry*. Madison and Milwaukee, 1964.

MacDonagh, Thomas. *Literature in Ireland*, reprint. New York, 1970.

MacNeice, Louis. *The Dark Tower and Other Radio Scripts*. London, 1947.

The Poetry of W.B. Yeats, reprint. London, 1967.

Mercier, Vivian. *The Irish Comic Tradition*. London, 1962.

Meyer, Kuno. *Aislinge Meic Conglinne*. London, 1892.

A Primer of Irish Metrics. Dublin, 1909.

Selections from Ancient Irish Poetry, 2nd edition. London, 1913.

'The Triads of Ireland'. *Royal Irish Academy-Todd Lecture Series*, vol. xiii. Dublin and London, 1906.

Murphy, Gerard. *Early Irish Lyrics*. London, 1962.

O'Casey, Sean. *Autobiographies I and II*. London, 1963.

O'Duffy, Richard J. *Diarmuid: The Pursuit of Diarmuid and Grainne* in two parts with translation. Dublin, 1881-4.

O'Grady, Standish Hayes. *Silva Gadelica*, a collection of tales in Irish with translation, volume 2. London and Edinburgh, 1892.

Pollard, Arthur. *Satire*. London, 1970.

Pope, Alexander. *Selected Poetry and Prose*, edited by William K. Wimsatt. New York, 1966.

Pound, Ezra. *The Spirit of Romance*, reprint. New York, 1968.

Quiggin, E.C. *Prolegomena to the Study of the Later Irish Bards 1200-1500*, reprint. Chicago, 1970.

Robinson, F.N. 'Satirists and Enchanters in Early Irish Literature', from *Studies in the History of Religion*, edited by D.G. Lyon and G.F. Moore. New York, 1912.

Rosenthal, M.L. *The New Poets: American and British Poetry Since World War II*. New York, 1970.

Russell, George William (A.E.). *Collected Poems*. London, 1920.

Letters from A.E., edited by Alan Denson. London, 1961.

Schlauch, Margaret. *Modern English and American Poetry: Techniques and Ideologies*. London, 1956.

Seven Centuries of Irish Learning, edited by Brian Ó Cuiv. Cork, 1971.

Sigerson, George. *Bards of the Gael and Gall*, 3rd edition. Dublin, 1925.

Stokes, G.T. *Ireland and the Celtic Church*. London, 1886.

A Tribute to Austin Clarke on his Seventieth Birthday, compiled and edited by John Montague and Liam Miller. Dublin, 1966.

Waddell, Helen. *The Wandering Scholars*, reprint. London, 1968.

Whyte, J.H. *The Church and State in Modern Ireland 1923-1970*. Dublin, 1971.

Wimsatt, W.K. *The Verbal Icon: Studies in the Meaning of Poetry*. London, 1970.

Wimsatt, W.K. and Brooks, Cleanth. *Modern Criticism*, volume 4 of *Literary Criticism: A Short History*. London, 1970.
    Neo-Classical Criticism, volume 2 of *Literary Criticism: A Short History*. London, 1970.
Yeats, W.B. and Kinsella, Thomas. *Davis, Mangan, Ferguson? Tradition and the Irish Writer*. Dublin, 1970.

Journals
Boland, Eavan. 'Austin Clarke: The Artist in Old Age'. *Hibernia*, 27 April 1973, p. 13.
'The Irelands of Austin Clarke'. Unsigned. *TLS*, 1 December 1972, p. 1459.
Irish University Review: Austin Clarke Special Issue. Edited by Maurice Harmon, vol. 4, no. 1, (Spring 1974).
Mercier, Vivian. 'The Verse Plays of Austin Clarke'. *Dublin Magazine*, vol. xix, no. 2 (April-June 1944), pp. 39-47.
Montague, John. 'Order in Donnybrook Fair'. *TLS*, 17 March 1972, p. 313.

INDEX